T0355183

The Exorcist Effect

The Exorcist Effect

Horror, Religion, and Demonic Belief

JOSEPH P. LAYCOCK AND ERIC HARRELSON

OXFORD
UNIVERSITY PRESS

OXFORD
UNIVERSITY PRESS

Oxford University Press is a department of the University of Oxford. It furthers
the University's objective of excellence in research, scholarship, and education
by publishing worldwide. Oxford is a registered trade mark of Oxford University
Press in the UK and certain other countries.

Published in the United States of America by Oxford University Press
198 Madison Avenue, New York, NY 10016, United States of America.

Library of Congress Cataloging-in-Publication Data
Names: Laycock, Joseph P., 1980- author. | Harrelson, Eric, author.
Title: The Exorcist effect : horror, religion, and demonic belief /
Joseph P. Laycock and Eric Harrelson.
Description: New York, NY : Oxford University Press, 2024. |
Includes bibliographical references and index.
Identifiers: LCCN 2023032612 (print) | LCCN 2023032613 (ebook) |
ISBN 9780197635391 (hardback) | ISBN 9780197635421 | ISBN 9780197635407 |
ISBN 9780197635414 (epub)
Subjects: LCSH: Horror films—History and criticism. |
Motion pictures—Religious aspects.
Classification: LCC PN1995.9.H6 L378 2024 (print) | LCC PN1995.9.H6
(ebook) | DDC 791.43/6164—dc23/eng/20230713
LC record available at https://lccn.loc.gov/2023032612
LC ebook record available at https://lccn.loc.gov/2023032613

DOI: 10.1093/oso/9780197635391.001.0001

Printed by Sheridan Books, Inc., United States of America

Contents

Acknowledgments

We would like to thank many people who made this book possible, especially the artists and writers who granted us research interviews. Diana Pasulka, Grady Hendrix, Ray Garton, Matt Baxter, Sarah Colwell, and Jerry Solfvin were all incredibly gracious in helping us to assemble and contextualize the details that went into this book. Chad and Carey Hayes were especially generous with their time, even volunteering to speak to an undergraduate demonology class over Zoom. We are immensely grateful to Frank Dennis of St. Bonaventure University without whose help we would know far less about Ed and Lorraine Warren. We also thank Texas State University librarian Tricia Boucher and Megan Bryant of the Sixth Floor Museum at Dealey Plaza for helping us track down rare tabloid issues. Finally, we would like to express gratitude to our editor Cynthia Read for seeing the value of this project when other publishers failed to understand it.

1

The Exorcist Effect

"It is thanks to movies that we find a renewed interest in exorcisms."
—Father Gabriele Amorth, founder of the International
Association of Exorcists.[1]

"Religion, for better or worse, is vastly more like a film than an intellectual proposition."

—S. Brent Plate[2]

On March 4, 1990, Cardinal John O'Connor made headlines when he told reporters that two exorcisms had been approved in the last year in the archdiocese of New York. The announcement followed a Sunday sermon given in St. Patrick's Cathedral on Matthew 4:1–25, wherein Satan tempts Jesus in the wilderness. During the sermon, O'Connor read passages from William Peter Blatty's 1971 novel *The Exorcist*, which he described as "gruesomely realistic." While acknowledging that *The Exorcist* is fiction, he pointed out that the story is a distillation of accounts of actual demonic possession. O'Connor went on to warn that Satanic worship was increasing, including black masses and "cults" such as the Manson family. "Diabolically instigated violence," such as abortion and divorce, were also on the rise. Furthermore, a key factor driving this trend was heavy metal music, which he denounced as "pornography in sound." This music was not only distasteful but could lead to suicide and demonic possession, especially the song "Suicide Solution" by Ozzy Osbourne. Osbourne's song had been the subject of a 1986 lawsuit in which parents alleged the song's gloomy lyrics drove their nineteen-year-old son to suicide. Osbourne retaliated in a statement addressed to O'Connor, telling him, "You have also insulted the intelligence of rock fans all over the world, and I recommend you do a little more research before making your opinions public in the future."[3] The sermon and its aftermath were covered

The Exorcist Effect. Joseph P. Laycock and Eric Harrelson, Oxford University Press. © Oxford University Press 2024.
DOI: 10.1093/oso/9780197635391.003.0001

by *Time* magazine, *The Washington Post*, and United Press International, and it sparked a wave of media interest in Catholic exorcism.

Journalists seeking commentary reached out to James LeBar, a Catholic chaplain at the Hudson Valley Psychiatric Center in Poughkeepsie, New York. In addition to being an advocate for exorcism, LeBar was active in the counter-cult movement, an area traditionally dominated by evangelicals. In 1988, he appeared on Geraldo Rivera's notorious "investigative report," *Devil Worship: Exposing Satan's Underground*. Moving to capitalize on the sermon, ABC's *20/20* (and then *Nightline*) tapped LeBar for a show idea in which an authentic Catholic exorcism would be shown on national television. With LeBar's help, they located a sixteen-year-old girl in Palm Beach, Florida, who was approved for an exorcism and whose parents agreed to have it filmed.[4] The show aired April 5, 1991, and featured LeBar prominently. Footage of the ritual was accompanied by Carmina Burana's "O Fortuna." This is a secular piece of music but viewers almost certainly associated the Latin singing with Jerry Goldsmith's "Ave Satani," which was composed for the film *The Omen* (1976). (*The Omen* won an Oscar for best original score.) LeBar went on to appear on numerous talk shows and paranormal programs about exorcism.

What can we make of this interweaving of Catholic demonology and media entertainment? In his work *American Exorcism: Expelling Demons in the Land of Plenty* (2001), Michael Cuneo argues that Blatty's novel, and especially its 1973 film adaptation, triggered a resurgence of exorcism not only in Catholicism but in evangelical culture as well. Examining an incident when a Catholic cardinal read from a horror novel alongside the Gospel of Matthew, Cuneo asks, "Is there anything more that needs to be said regarding the symbiotic connection between religion and popular culture in contemporary America?"[5] This book begins with the assumption that, yes, there is more that needs to be said.

The Exorcist polarized Catholic leaders, with some praising it for reminding the public about the reality of the devil and others condemning it as pornography and a study in embarrassing superstition. And both conservative and liberal Catholics expressed embarrassment over the depiction of exorcism on ABC. But while some might prefer to live in a world where Church authorities are above the trends of Hollywood, chaplains in psychiatric centers do not spread rumors of Satanic cults on *Geraldo*, and cardinals do not debate song lyrics with Ozzy Osbourne—this is not the way religious cultures actually work. The line between "ecclesiastical" and "popular" expressions of religion has always been an ideal rather than a reality.[6]

Historian of American religion David Hall noted that the "lived religion" approach to religious history is about "breaking with the distinction between high and low that seems inevitably to recur in studies of popular religion."[7] What might the religious landscape look like if we examined the relationship between horror films and actual religious beliefs and practices not as an embarrassment or an example of "religion gone wrong," but as part of the ordinary lived experience of religious people? Viewed from this approach, new questions present themselves about the relationship between religion and supernatural horror films. Why would a cardinal like John O'Connor deploy the gruesome imagery of *The Exorcist* in a Sunday sermon? Why do films have this power to shape the religious imagination? And why do the best horror films so often claim to be based on "a true story"?

The Exorcist Effect

In *The Exorcist*, when Chris MacNeil approaches Father Damien Karras about performing an exorcism, Father Karras responds, "Well, the first thing, I'd have to get them into a time machine and get them back to the sixteenth century. Well, it just doesn't happen anymore, Mrs. MacNeil, since we learned about mental illness, paranoia, schizophrenia." This was a typical North American perspective of exorcism in 1973. But exorcism never truly died in Western culture, it only waxed and waned. And in the years since 1973, belief in demonic possession and the practice of exorcism have risen steadily. In 1964, a national poll conducted by the University of California at Berkeley found that thirty-seven percent of Americans believed in Satan as a literal entity. By 1973 that number had risen to fifty percent.[8] Subsequent studies indicate this trend has only continued. Gallup polls show that the percentage of people who believe in the devil has increased from fifty-five percent in 1990 to seventy percent in 2004. In a 1998 Southern Focus Poll, fifty-nine percent of respondents answered "yes" to the question, "Do you believe that people on this Earth are sometimes possessed by the Devil?" The 2007 Baylor Religion Survey found that 53.3 percent of respondents "agreed or strongly agreed" that it is possible to be possessed. In a 2013 YouGov poll, fifty-one percent responded that they believe in demonic possession.

Churches have warmed to exorcism as well. In 1990, Father Gabriele Amorth, exorcist of the diocese of Rome—who once stated that *The Exorcist* was his favorite film—founded the International Association of Exorcists for the purpose of training more exorcists. In 2009, the Association of Catholic Psychiatrists and Psychologists reported that, in Italy, half a million people a year undergo exorcisms.[9] The International Association of Exorcists received formal recognition from the Curia in 2014. It is now fairly common to see stories of conservative Catholic authorities performing public exorcisms to frame social issues, such as gay marriage or the toppling of monuments by leftist protestors, as demonic.[10]

The demonic has also become mainstream through "Third Wave" theology associated with the writings of C. Peter Wagner and the New Apostolic Reformation movement that has infiltrated the conservative political sphere for over a decade. As Sean McCloud observes, "Demons play *the* crucial role in the Third Wave imaginary."[11] Perhaps the starkest index of the demonic's arrival into mainstream culture was a prayer given in January 2020 by Paula White, a figure in the New Apostolic Reformation movement and chair of President Donald Trump's evangelical advisory board. In a video, White invokes a highly specific lexicon of evangelical spiritual warfare with statements such as, "We cancel every surprise from the witchcraft in the marine kingdom—any hex, any spell, any witchcraft, any spirit of control, any jezebel, anything that the enemy desires." She then went on, "In the name of Jesus, we command all Satanic pregnancies to miscarry, right now. We declare that anything that's been conceived in Satanic wombs, that it'll miscarry." It was this second statement—in which an evangelical pastor tied to the Trump administration appeared to call for abortion—that drew criticism. But most media outlets no longer found it newsworthy that someone described as the president's personal pastor claimed to be actively battling witchcraft, "jezebel" demons, and demons of "the marine kingdom."[12] Certainly this situation would have been unimaginable when Blatty wrote *The Exorcist*.

Demographic research notes that the belief in the demonic correlates with regular church attendance, low levels of income, and low levels of education. Most sociological models of contemporary demonic belief regard it as a kind of coping mechanism that explains failure and misfortune.[13] While the explosive growth of exorcism and evangelical "deliverance ministry" since 1973 was fueled by multiple social and political changes, many scholars have cited *The Exorcist* as an important catalyst in this shift, along with *Rosemary's Baby* (1968), *The Omen* (1976), and the slew of demonic horror films that appeared in the wake of this "unholy trinity."[14] So while other sociological factors may influence belief in demonic forces, horror movies play an important role in imagining what those forces might look like.

It is difficult to understate what a phenomenon William Friedkin's adaptation of *The Exorcist* was after it was released on December 26, 1973. A *Time* article from 1974 described 8:00 a.m. screenings and lines five thousand people long. Harry Francis, manager of a theater in Los Angeles, told reporters, "I've been in this business 47 years, and I've never seen anything like it." He estimated each showing produced an average of four blackouts, six cases of vomiting, and numerous people fleeing the theater.[15] He was quoted, "My janitors are going bananas wiping up the vomit."[16] A report that appeared in the *Journal of Nervous and Mental Disease* in 1975 claimed that the film had induced in some viewers "cases of traumatic neurosis and even psychosis."[17]

Cuneo was among the first to write about the connection between *The Exorcist* phenomenon and an increased demand for exorcisms. He managed to interview two Jesuit priests who appeared in the film. As many people know, Blatty based his novel on the 1949 exorcism of a boy from Maryland. In the acknowledgements of *The Exorcist*, Blatty states, "I would also like to thank the Rev. Thomas V. Bermingham, S. J., Vice-Provincial for Formation of the New York Province of the Society of Jesus, for suggesting the subject matter of this novel."[18] Father Bermingham had been Blatty's Latin teacher in Brooklyn and later taught at Georgetown University while Blatty was a student there. In the 1960s, Blatty reached out to Bermingham for advice in writing his novel. In the film adaptation, Bermingham played the president of Georgetown University. Another Jesuit, William O'Malley, played Father Dyer who discovers Damien Karras's body at the end of the film. Both priests also received screen credits as technical advisors. In an interview with Cuneo, Bermingham, then in semi-retirement, recalled:

> Making the movie was strange enough, but the aftermath was completely bizarre .... I knew very little about exorcism and demonic possession prior to helping Blatty do research for his book and working on the movie, but when the movie came out, I found myself on the hot seat. People saw my face and my name on the screen, and they assumed I was the answer to their problems. For quite a while dozens of people were trying to contact me every week. And they weren't all Catholics. Some were Jewish, some Protestant, some agnostic, and they all believed that they themselves or someone close to them might be demonically possessed. These were truly desperate people, and I did my best to meet with as many of them as possible and discuss their problems. Of course, I approached these discussions

with a great deal of skepticism . . . . I arranged psychological counseling for some people, but this was sometimes a big disappointment for them. They assumed, because of my association with the movie, that I'd be able to resolve their various difficulties with an exorcism. The funny thing is, I wouldn't have been able to do this even if they were possessed. I've never even participated in a genuine exorcism, and I certainly don't regard myself as qualified to perform one.

Father O'Malley's story was much the same:

I was teaching at a Jesuit high school in Rochester at the time, and for a while the phone wouldn't stop ringing . . . . They called looking for an instant fix—pleading with me to expel their own demons, their kids' demons, even their cats' demons. It's not that I rule out the possibility of demonic possession. As the saying goes, "There are more things in heaven and earth, Horatio, than are dreamt of in your philosophy." But this movie seems to have set off some really strange vibrations.[19]

Churches and popular culture both scrambled to respond to this new demand for exorcisms. In 1976, Malachi Martin, a laicized Jesuit priest, published *Hostage to the Devil: A Documentary Report on the Possession and Exorcism of Five Living Americans.* This book was presented as a true account of actual exorcisms, even though nothing from Martin's book was ever corroborated and Blatty immediately denounced it as a fraudulent imitation of his novel. Where Blatty's novel presented exorcism as incredibly rare, Martin—who still identified as a priest—insisted it was actually quite common. Martin's work has been cited as an important factor in the revival of Catholic exorcism.[20]

In 1977, Jay Anson published *The Amityville Horror*, based on the allegedly true story of the Lutz family's attempt to live in a demon-infested house in Long Island, New York. The book sold over six million copies and the house became a pilgrimage site for those fascinated by the paranormal.[21] In 1979, Anson's book was adapted into the second-highest grossing film of the year. Father Thomas Bermingham was once again tapped as a religious consultant. The film spawned numerous sequels and remakes. Contributing to the mystique of the Amityville case were lay Catholic demonologists, Ed and Lorraine Warren, who "investigated" the house in 1976. The Warrens had been researching haunted houses since the 1950s, but in the 1970s they rebranded themselves as demon hunters and became celebrities. When Catholic authorities turned away people seeking exorcisms, the Warrens stepped in and connected them with an exorcist. Often these exorcisms were performed by people who either were not Roman Catholic priests or were operating without the permission of their bishop.[22] Because the Warrens essentially created a backdoor to exorcism, Catholic authorities were left with less incentive to deny exorcisms: If they didn't do them, someone else would.

Journalists scrambled to speak with the Warrens following Cardinal O'Connor's 1990 exorcism sermon.[23] The Warrens claimed they had been present during the two exorcisms described by O'Connor—and that both cases had featured impressive levitation and projectile vomiting![24] The following year, the Fox Network aired a made-for-TV movie, *The Haunted*, based on demonic hauntings experienced by the Smurl family between 1974 and 1989. The Warrens not only helped the Smurls by investigating their haunting, but they also connected them with journalist Robert Curran, who adapted their story into a book and then a screen adaptation (Curran, the Smurls, and the Warrens all shared writing credits). Beginning with *The Conjuring* (2013), the Warrens' adventures have subsequently been adapted into an entire series of horror films all based on "true events."

This explosion of demonic media beginning in the 1970s coincided with the rise of the New Christian Right.[25] In 1975, Billy Graham published *Angels: God's Secret Agents*, which sold one million copies in the first ninety days.[26] In that book, Graham cited *The Exorcist* as the key example of the culture's "current cult of the demonic." Graham's interest in *The Exorcist* bordered on obsession and he was widely rumored to have stated that evil was embedded in the very celluloid of the film.[27] Paradoxically, in *Angels* he condemns films like *The Exorcist* while also calling for more people to recognize the reality of the devil and praising poll numbers showing that more people *do* believe in the devil. There is a sense that Graham was secretly pleased with the film's effect on religious culture even as he professed his contempt for it. He also related the following story:

> Some years ago I had dinner with several senators and congressmen in a dining room in the Capitol building. We began discussing the rising interest in the occult with special reference to *The Exorcist*. One of the senators, who had recently passed through a deep religious experience, said that due to his past experience with the occult, whenever he knew of a theater that was

showing *The Exorcist* he would drive a block around it. He was afraid even to go near it. He said, "I know that both angels and demons are for real."[28]

Here the film itself—even without watching it—is a manifestation of spiritual evil and therefore evidence for Graham's moral cosmology. The fact that senators were discussing the occult dangers of this film in the capitol building shows this cosmology is as much a political reality as a religious one.

In some cases, the authors behind these films expressed remorse over the effect their work had on American culture. In 2002, Ira Levin, author of *Rosemary's Baby* (1967) (on which the 1968 film was based) told *The Los Angeles Times*, "I feel guilty that 'Rosemary's Baby' led to 'The Exorcist,' [and] 'The Omen.' A whole generation has been exposed, has more belief in Satan. I don't believe in Satan. And I feel that the strong fundamentalism we have would not be as strong if there hadn't been so many of these books . . . Of course, I didn't send back any of the royalty checks."[29] David Seltzer, who wrote the novel *The Omen* and the screenplay for the film (both were released in 1976) confessed, "I did it strictly for the money . . . I just wish I'd had this kind of success with something I personally found more meaningful. . . . I do find it horrifying to find how many people actually believe all this silliness."[30]

So, are novelists like Levin and Seltzer actually responsible for people's religious beliefs? Do movies like *The Exorcist* cause people to believe in demons? We are aware of only one experiment that sought to measure empirically whether *The Exorcist* caused people to believe in the demonic. In 1973, Gerald Heisler of the University of Missouri school of medicine set up an experiment to test the psychological effects of watching the film. Heisler put an ad in the paper that read, "Already interested in seeing *The Exorcist*? See it or another first run movie for free and earn $2.00/hour for completing anonymous questionnaires." Fifty-nine subjects between the ages of fifteen and sixty-three volunteered for Heisler's experiment. They were all given a series of standard tests to see how they scored on indexes of mental illness, including the Minnesota Multiphasic Personality Inventory (MMPI) and the Spielberger State-Trait Anxiety Inventory. Heisler also designed his own seventeen-question test that he called the "Mysticism Scale." The Mysticism Scale asked questions about such topics as belief in sin and the devil. After getting this baseline data, the subjects were divided into three groups. Group 1 watched *The Exorcist*, Group 2 watched *Cinderella Liberty* (another R-rated film that came out in 1973), and Group 3 agreed to watch no films until the study was completed. Then all subjects were re-tested immediately after watching the film, a week after watching the film, and one month after watching the film.

Group 1 actually scored slightly lower on the MMPI after watching *The Exorcist*, showing less tendency toward mental illness. However, they scored higher on the Mysticism Scale. Specifically, subjects were more likely to answer "yes" to the following questions: "I believe bad times fall on those who sin"; "I think there are some events in the world which man cannot understand"; "I feel unable to change any events in my life"; "I believe the devil actually exists"; "Black masses or other rites can often cure sufferers when physicians cannot"; and "If I have difficulty controlling my thoughts I would first want to go to a professional counselor." Significantly, Group 1's score on the mysticism scale *continued* to increase a week and then a month after watching the film, rising from an average score of 21 before watching *The Exorcist* to 26.3 to 36.5, and finally to 37.21. This effect did not occur with the other two groups. Heisler found that no one in the group increased or decreased religious service or prayer, but he concluded, "Viewing *The Exorcist* did change the audience's attitudes and beliefs."[31] He also speculated that this may have had less to do with the intrinsic properties of the film and more with the larger social phenomenon and media campaign surrounding it. Heisler was working with a small sample and some participants quit the experiment. Because of this, Group 1 shrunk from twenty-four people to eighteen to fourteen by the time the study ended. Still, Heisler's findings lend further evidence to what many historians already concluded—that *The Exorcist* affected beliefs and attitudes about the supernatural.

It should be noted that audiences do not passively absorb ideas suggested in supernatural horror novels and films. An outmoded theory of mass culture held that cinema acts like a hypodermic needle that "injects" audiences with the ideology of the filmmakers. Today there is greater recognition that movie-viewers take an active role in constructing whatever meaning they take away from a film.[32] When one author assigned undergraduates to watch *The Exorcist* their reactions ranged from stark terror, to puzzlement, to dismissive mockery. Only some of the ways audiences use these films to construct meaning inform religious beliefs and practices. We outline four such ways below.

First, horror movies can be "good to think with." They can function as what sociologist Peter Berger called a "plausibility structure" or a sociocultural context that makes ideas seem believable and imaginable.[33] As religion scholar Christopher Partridge notes, popular culture can help people to think through theological and metaphysical issues and provide resources for constructing religious and paranormal worldviews.[34] Cardinal O'Connor's deployment of *The Exorcist* is a good example of using a horror text in this way. O'Connor did not claim the story was true, only that it was "gruesomely realistic." Here the text functions as a model for imagining actual cases of demonic possession.

Second, in some cases horror films come to be interpreted as historical events rather than fiction. This can occur in a number of ways. Audiences may simply take claims that a film is "based on a true story" at face value. Fact and fiction can also become blurred through confabulation, a type of memory error in which fictional images and narratives come to "fill in gaps" in memory, thus confusing fact and fiction. Cognitive scientists such as Jeffrey Zacks, who has written on this problem as it relates to movies, have noted that the brain is better at retaining information than the source of that information, especially over time.[35] During the Satanic Panic of the 1980s many people described "recovered memories" of Satanic ritual abuse, often while under the influence of hypnotic therapy sessions. Narratives produced through these methods, such as *Michelle Remembers* (1980), often resemble a pastiche of images borrowed from horror films.[36] Finally, conspiracy theorists may engage in what Michael Barkun called "fact-fiction reversal," claiming that fictional films are in fact a disguised truth.[37] For example, Michael York, the founder of the Nuwabian nation, claimed that the Antichrist had been born in New York in 1966 and that the film *Rosemary's Baby* was an attempt to "camouflage" actual events.[38]

Third, as we saw with Billy Graham, in some cases horror films are incorporated into a demonological worldview not as texts but as material objects. Their mere physical presence has supernatural significance. Rebecca Greenwood, a deliverance minister and a faculty member at an institute founded by C. Peter Wagner, describes the following anecdote about investigating a house where a nine-year-old girl was allegedly suffering from demonic attacks:

> I inquired if there were horror movies in the home. The mom answered, "Yes, my husband has a bookshelf of them. He watches them all the time, but Lisa [their daughter] is not allowed to." We explained that it does not matter if she is not allowed to watch them, having the movies in the home was an open door to the demonic harassment. After learning the names

of the movies, we prayed and broke the demonic assignment of death and witchcraft off of Lisa.[39]

Here the movies serve as a kind of material anchor for Greenwood's narrative about demonic attacks. The movies do not have to be watched to invite demons and yet the *names* of the movies are needed to banish demonic influences. In a sense, the movies *are* demons and must be exorcized as such.

Finally, the narratives of horror films have a strange way of coming to life. In October 2014, Pazuzu Algarad (né John Lawson) of Clemmons, North Carolina, and his girlfriend were arrested for murdering two people and burying them in their backyard. Algarad had legally changed his name in an apparent homage to the Mesopotamian wind demon Blatty chose as the antagonist for his novel. He had also heavily tattooed his face and the walls of his home were covered in swastikas, pentagrams, and Halloween decorations. David Frankfurter describes this sort of behavior as the "mimetic performance of evil."[40] More often though, people choose to imitate the protagonists of these films. Take Bob Larson, an evangelical pastor who performs exorcisms (usually in exchange for a fixed donation to his ministry). In photographs, Larson often brandishes a large, ornate crucifix. Sometimes he also wears a black suit with a clerical collar. These are strange choices for an evangelical pastor, but they make sense if Larson is trying to resemble Max van Sydow's performance as Father Lankester Merrin in *The Exorcist*. We suggest that Algarard and Larson were both living out *The Exorcist* in a process that folklorists call ostension. Ostension, in essence, is the transmission of a legend by performing it rather than communicating it through words. As folklorist Bill Ellis puts it, "Events provoke stories, but it is far more likely that stories provoke events."[41]

This brings us to our theory of the relationship between supernatural horror and religious cultures. If events provoke stories and vice versa, then supernatural horror films are actually part of a feedback loop wherein: (1) actual events become the basis of films; (2) those films shape the way audiences interpret the world, giving rise to new beliefs and experiences; and (3) these beliefs and experiences lead to new events that become the basis of new horror films, and the cycle begins again. We call this feedback loop "*The Exorcist* effect." This is not an entirely new insight. Partridge has already referred to this relationship between popular culture and alternative spiritualities as "a hermeneutic circle."[42] However, this book uses this theoretical framework to perform a historical survey, mapping out the intricate webs of connections between demonological beliefs and practices and their cinematic counterparts. By doing so we arrive at a new perspective on Western religious culture at the turn of the century. Furthermore, as Cardinal O'Connor's sermon demonstrates, *The Exorcist* effect is not limited to alternative or marginalized religious practices. Increasingly, it is part of mainstream culture.

Rethinking Religion and Horror

A detailed examination of the historical connections between supernatural horror and contemporary demonology can help to inform and enrich three larger conversations: (1) "horror studies," or the critical study of the horror genre in literature and film; (2) the sociology of religion; and (3) the sociology of moral panic. For the study of horror films, attention to religious history presents a new direction that moves beyond interpreting horror either as a metaphorical discourse about social issues or through the lens of Freudian psychoanalysis. For religious studies, examining the influence of supernatural horror films raises challenges for theories of secularization and can lead to a more accurate and complete picture of the religious landscape. Most importantly, though, this feedback loop should be studied because the real-world beliefs and practices associated with horror—exorcism and Satanic conspiracy theories—have real world consequences as evidenced by the Satanic Panic of the 1980s and 1990s.

In 1985, English professor James Twitchell gave the following summary of the state of horror studies: "The attraction of horror can be understood in essentially three ways: (1) as counterphobia or the satisfaction of overcoming objects of fear; (2) as 'the return of the repressed' or the compulsive projection of objects of sublimated desire; and (3) as part of a more complicated rite of passage from onanism to reproductive sexuality."[43] Since then, the repertoire of horror studies has expanded surprisingly little. While these approaches have their merits, a growing number of voices in religious studies have expressed frustration with the idea that these are the *only* ways horror films may be interpreted—especially when so many of these films deal directly with religious texts, beliefs, and practices.

One of the most common moves in horror studies is to claim that the success of a horror text indicates its function as a metaphorical reflection for some social issue. Critical responses to *Jaws* (1975) are a classic example of how facile this sort of argument can be. Some critics claimed the shark was a metaphor for communism while Fidel Castro claimed it represented the threat of capitalism.[44] The suggestion that audiences were reacting to their fear of *literal sharks* was too quotidian to be taken seriously. Stephen King offers a stronger example of this approach when he argues that *The Exorcist* is a "social horror film" in which a possessed child reflects anxieties about delinquent youth in the aftermath of the 1960s. King points out that audiences in West Germany had a tepid response to the film and concludes that something specific to American culture must have caused the massive reaction to the film.[45]

The other common interpretation of *The Exorcist*—and horror films in general—is that the monster reflects some repressed psychosexual desire. The scene in which the possessed Regan seizes her mother's head, holds it to her bleeding vagina, and growls "Lick me!" certainly begs for a Freudian reading. Barbara Creed offers the following take of this scene: "Regan's transformation into devil is clearly a sexual one; it suggests that the family home, bastion of all the right virtues and laudable moral values, is built on a foundation of repressed sexual desires, including those which flow between mother and daughter."[46]

The problem with these kinds of approaches is that they all seek, as sociologist of religion Douglas Cowan puts it, "to explain eggs in terms of bacon."[47] More than half of Americans believe in the reality of the devil and demonic possession. The argument from parsimony suggests that strong audience reactions are due more to their fear of demonic possession than anxiety over their repressed sexual desires. Friedkin himself opined, "I don't think the mood of the times had anything whatsoever to do with the success of *The Exorcist*. In fact, I'm not aware of any far-reaching social problems that *The Exorcist* dealt with. That usually comes later—when people have run out of things to say about the film, they start describing the social implications of it."[48] It may be that psychoanalytical interpretations of horror were adopted early on to justify the study of horror films—a famously "ghettoized" genre—as academically rigorous and that "explaining eggs in terms of eggs" seemed unsophisticated. But to ignore the religious cultures on which these films are based impoverishes horror studies. As film historian Carlos Clarens noted, "Horror is nourished by myth, tradition and legend—all of which require centuries of rich elaboration."[49] Bible scholar Brandon Grafius argues that returning to these original narratives can revitalize the study of horror and expand it beyond its foundations in "the triumvirate of [Noel] Carroll, [Carol] Clover, and [Barbara] Creed."[50]

Religious studies could also benefit from taking horror films seriously as a manifestation of religious culture. In 1976, Mircea Eliade pointed out the connection between popular film and occultism and queried, "But who will interpret for us the amazing success of *Rosemary's Baby?* . . . I am merely asking the question."[51] In the 1970s, movies could only be seen in theaters. With the advent of smartphones and digital streaming many modern people now live in a sea of media. Alarmingly, literary critic N. Katherine Hayles has suggested that we now think with, through, and alongside media such that media changes us just as we change it in a condition she calls "technogenesis."[52] Religious cultures are naturally affected by this media environment as well, and understanding film is increasingly important for understanding the religious landscape. Films such as Mel Gibson's *The Passion of the Christ* (2004) have become religious rituals with some churches screening them every Easter. Chad and Carey Hayes, the writers behind *The Conjuring* franchise, hoped that their movies would be similarly adopted for annual viewings by religious communities. This is one reason why they described their films as "religious supernatural" rather than "horror" films.[53] There has, of course, been a great deal of scholarship on how religious traditions are reflected in film, as well as how film resembles religion. John C. Lyden has argued persuasively that all genres of film share *functions* in common with religion, such as myths, morals, and rituals.[54] But supernatural horror films like *Rosemary's Baby* overlap with religion in a *substantive* way because the narratives of these films explicitly revolve around supernatural forces and the question of who believes in them.

Supernatural horror is uniquely concerned with propositions about that which William James called "an unseen order." In *Rosemary's Baby*, a woman must decide whether her kindly neighbors are witches. In *The Exorcist*, a priest-psychiatrist must decide whether a girl is demonically possessed or mentally ill. And in *The Omen* a diplomat must decide whether or not to ritually murder his son, who may be the Antichrist. Supernatural horror is really about epistemology—determining what is real and questioning what we thought was real. For this reason, supernatural horror can be read as a public conversation about the secularization narrative—the theory that as societies modernize and advance in technology, they will become less religious and faith-based institutions will have less influence. In fact, the emergence of horror as a serious genre in 1968 with the two films *Rosemary's Baby* and

Night of the Living Dead seemed to coincide with the heightened popularity of the secularization narrative.

One explanation of this connection is that films like *Rosemary's Baby* represented a "last gasp" of supernaturalism as these ideas were relegated to mere entertainment. This was the perspective of sociologist Marcello Truzzi writing in 1972 who opined, "As long as these mass phenomena represent a playful and non-serious confrontation with the supernatural elements, they then represent a possible cleansing or purging of the old fears and myths still present in our society. The more we eliminate these old fears and myths, the more we develop a naturalistic rationalism, a scientific view of the universe."[55] Truzzi's thesis became difficult to sustain one year later when audiences were fainting while watching *The Exorcist* and Catholic priests were being inundated with requests for exorcisms. Writing in 1974, Peter Berger interpreted people waiting in line to see *The Exorcist* as an act of rebellion against the banality of secularism. In Berger's view, the overbearing cultural apparatus of secularism gave the idea of supernatural evil a forbidden, titillating quality, akin to pornography: "Modern man doing magic is akin to a Puritan in a whorehouse."[56]

Sociologists now recognize that religion was not really dying in the 1970s. A more likely explanation is that modern horror took hold during a period of collective speculation about the future of supernatural belief. As Douglas Cowan writes, "Indeed, the issue is not one of *secularization*—that cinema horror discloses to us the abandonment or minimization of religious belief in late modern society—but an overwhelming *ambivalence* toward the religious traditions, beliefs, practices, and mythistories by which we are confronted, in which we are often still deeply invested, which we are distinctly unwilling to relinquish, and which we just as often only minimally understand."[57] In this sense, these movies are a public conversation about the supernatural. This makes horror films an important data point in assessing claims about secularization and should be taken seriously by scholars studying contemporary religion.

Finally, *The Exorcist* effect must be studied because many of the films examined here act as plausibility structures that support dangerous conspiracy theories. Ira Levin and David Seltzer expressed feeling "guilty" and "horrified" over cultural changes associated with their stories. While they did not state explicitly what they felt guilty about, it seems they saw a connection between demonological beliefs and demonstrable harm. Cardinal O'Connor's sermon on the combined dangers of demonic possession,

Satanic cults, and heavy metal music represented a high-water mark for a moral panic over Satanic cults. This was a period in which numerous people were wrongly accused and imprisoned for involvement in Satanic conspiracies. What then was the connection between these films and the panic?

David Frankfurter has written on how *Rosemary's Baby* helped set the stage for the panic over ritualized daycare abuse that manifested twenty years after the film. By showing how Rosemary's kindly neighbors, as well as obstetricians and other experts from the helping professions, could actually be Satanists plotting to bring about the Antichrist, Polanski's film helped audiences to imagine *what it would look like* if seemingly ordinary people were in fact part of a Satanic conspiracy. By the 1980s this became a model through which to think about conspiratorial accusations. Frankfurter writes, "What makes the process of Rosemary's awareness of Satanic conspiracy so frightening, in fact, is that the neighbors do *not* change personalities or characteristics or clothes . . . . I am reminded how, during various investigations of ritualized daycare abuse over the 1980s, the solid reputations and sociable personalities of the accused women and men altogether did nothing to exonerate them or mitigate popular condemnation: they remained *monsters*."[58]

Drew Beard, who has also written on the role of horror movies in shaping the panic, notes that throughout the 1980s these films were widely available as VHS tapes and featured in heavy rotation on both cable and network television.[59] In fact, by the 1980s, self-declared experts on "occult crime" were holding seminars for law enforcement where horror films were being *explicitly* presented as models of actual Satanic crime. Robert Hicks, a criminal justice analyst for the Virginia Department of Criminal Justice Services, became a whistle-blower on these seminars. At a seminar on ritual crime in 1988, he watched detective Bill Lightfoot describe *Rosemary's Baby* as "an accurate depiction of Satanism of the clandestine sort." Lightfoot also cited *The Believers*, a horror film about Santeria practitioners who perform human sacrifices, as a realistic depiction of "Santeria-inspired crime."[60]

So, while horror movies did not *cause* the panic it seems that claims that might otherwise seem ludicrous were rendered more plausible to juries and law enforcement because of exposure to the tropes and narratives in these films. Jeffrey Zacks suggests that films influence the way we see the world not because we think they are real but because they become part of the apparatus our brain uses to construct models:

It's not the case that you have one bucket into which you drop all the real-life events, another for movie events, and a third for events in novels. Remember, there is one model-building mechanism in there that grabs information from lots of different sources. The same machinery can combine what you see with what someone tells you to build a model of an event. That machinery is perfectly happy to operate on stuff from your life, from a movie, or from a book. I think that is a big part of the appeal of narrative films and books—they appeal to our model-building propensities.[61]

It is not the films themselves that lead to innocent people being convicted of Satanic crimes but rather a failure to question where our ideas about things like Satanic cults come from. Nevertheless, the harm that arises from these models is real. Frankfurter concludes his analysis:

Motivated by a spectacle of transgression from which we cannot turn away, that is totally spellbinding in its obscenity and cruelty, we move systematically and brutally to destroy the cultists utterly, to purify the landscape of them. Lynching, burning, dismemberment, gassing, torture, drowning, exposure, cremation—these are the methods that follow when we conjure evil cults. These are the acts, I would argue, that have historically followed when a community "awakened" to some evil conspiracy.[62]

The Plot of the Book

This book is a history of the intersection of supernatural horror films with beliefs and practices related to the supernatural. Chapter 2 explores the prevailing theories through which films influence belief, including the insights of cognitive science, the theory of ostension, and theories of "veracity mechanisms" that make fictional narratives more amenable to being repurposed into religious beliefs and practices. Chapter 3 considers the legacy of the "Unholy Trinity" of films: *Rosemary's Baby*, *The Exorcist*, and *The Omen*, and examines their cultural context in the 1970s.

The next two chapters outline specific cycles in which events have inspired films that have, in turn, inspired events. Chapter 4 looks at the careers of Ed and Lorraine Warren, who rode the popular reaction to *The Exorcist*. The Warrens lent their authority to a number of alleged hauntings, inspiring several books and films about these cases. Numerous tropes of contemporary demonology can be traced to the Warrens and, with the success of *The Conjuring* franchise, the hermeneutic cycle surrounding their legacy continues to grow and develop.

Chapter 5 looks at the strange career of Malachi Martin, author of *Hostage to the Devil*. Although the cases in this book appear to have sprung from Martin's imagination, Martin created vocabulary and models of demonic possession that are still taken seriously today. One of Martin's key disciples was New York police Sergeant Ralph Sarchie, whose book, *Beware the Night*, about the intersection of law enforcement and demonic possession became the basis of the film *Deliver Us From Evil* (2014). Sarchie's career shows that the intersection of popular culture and law enforcement is not a relic of the 1980s. Martin is currently in vogue again with a 2016 documentary about his life and a film currently in production about an exorcism he allegedly performed at an Army base.

The next three chapters consider how supernatural horror films helped to create models of the three dangers Cardinal O'Connor warned of in his 1990 sermon: demonic possession, Satanic cults, and heavy metal music. Chapter 6 considers the depiction of Satanic cults in film going back to the 1930s to show how these films influenced actual beliefs about Satanic cults as well as self-identified Satanists, such as Anton LaVey, founder of the Church of Satan. Chapter 7 examines films relating to possession, which perhaps more than any other genre, claim to be based on "true events." Chapter 8 considers a niche genre of supernatural horror films related to heavy metal. These films are significant in that they reinforce the claims of the moral panics but also satirize them. This chapter also considers the trial of the West Memphis Three in 1993, which became a public conversation about media and moral panic. The final chapter considers the role of film in the current resurgence of the Satanic Panic, particularly the QAnon conspiracy, and offers some suggestions about how the more harmful aspects of *The Exorcist* effect can be mitigated.

2

How Horror Movies Become Real

"It's as if our imaginations have become exterior to ourselves, existing out there in our media, and our media then determines what is in our heads."

—Diana Pasulka[1]

"You can raise issues in the horror genre that you can't raise so easily in other types of films. Characters can talk about the existence of God in a horror movie, whereas in other films that would be incredibly pretentious."

—Screenwriter Nicholas Kazan[2]

Oscar Wilde famously wrote that, "Life imitates Art far more than Art imitates Life."[3] *The Exorcist* effect is a möbius strip in which actual beliefs and events shape, and are in turn shaped by, horror films. One direction of this möbius strip—in which art imitates life—is undeniable. It has become *de rigueur* to advertise supernatural horror films as "based on a true story." The opposite direction—in which life imitates art—leaves more room for skepticism. Can fictional movies (sometimes with poor writing and laughable special effects) actually affect real world beliefs and practices? And if so, how is this possible?

One of the first public screenings of a film was Auguste and Louis Lumiére's *L'arrivée d'un train en gare de La Ciotat*, which was projected onto a sheet in a Paris café in 1896. It was a fifty-second reel of a train pulling into a station. Early filmmaker Georges Méliès reflected on the screening: "We were open-mouthed, dumbfounded, astonished beyond words in the face of this spectacle."[4] Newspapers reported that audiences jumped out of their chairs and fled to escape the oncoming train. But reports of a panic were almost certainly false. If you watch the Lumiére brothers' film, the camera is located on the platform, not on the tracks. So even if one *did* believe the black and white

The Exorcist Effect. Joseph P. Laycock and Eric Harrelson, Oxford University Press. © Oxford University Press 2024. DOI: 10.1093/oso/9780197635391.003.0002 image were an actual train, there would be no reason to flee. Furthermore, the Lumiére brothers had begun screening films in Paris cafés in 1895, so this technology would not have been entirely unknown. The story of an audience fleeing a film of a train is a myth. The function of this myth appears to be self-congratulatory: Our naive ancestors were fooled by movies, whereas we are technologically sophisticated.

While we underestimate our ancestors' ability to discern film from reality, we overestimate our own. Modern people often assume that our ability to separate film from reality is so complete that we can become engrossed in films only if we make what Samuel Taylor Coleridge called "a suspension of disbelief." Religion scholar Diana Pasulka concludes that this is just the opposite of how people actually respond to movies: "When we experience a story, our default is to accept what it tells us as true. We have to do extra work to override that default and question what we are reading. Rather than needing will to *suspend* disbelief, we have to engage in a willing *construction* of disbelief in order to keep the story world from infecting our real-world beliefs and attitudes."[5]

Anyone who has difficulty watching horror films knows what Pasulka is talking about. Wes Craven's *The Last House on the Left* (1972)—an influential shock horror film inspired by Ingmar Bergman's *The Virgin Spring* (1960)—invoked the audience's need to construct disbelief with its movie poster that instructed, "To avoid fainting, keep repeating: 'It's only a movie, only a movie, only a movie . . . .'" Religion scholar Robert Orsi cites the experience of cartoonist R. Crumb, who was raised in a Catholic household in Philadelphia and described his frustration at being unable to suspend his disbelief while watching *The Exorcist*: "Remember the movie *The Exorcist*, that came out in 1973? I was completely terrified by that movie. I felt really stupid but it got to me in such a deep way that I realized that I'm not past all that Catholic crap at all. Even though I think it's stupid, it's still there." Orsi, also shaped by his Catholic upbringing, confessed he has never been able to bring himself to see the film.[6]

The train myth suggests that films "seem real" only when their technological sophistication outpaces the savvy of the audience. But technology and special effects seem to be a distraction from what is really going on when we watch films. A key example of this comes from the final scene of *Rosemary's Baby*. In Ira Levin's novel, Rosemary meets her baby for the first time and discovers it has golden eyes with vertical slits like those of a cat. Producer William Castle pondered over how they could portray this on film and suggested ordering a live cat that they could somehow make look like a baby. But director Roman Polanski explained it was not necessary to show the baby at all, telling Castle, "If I do my job right, people will actually believe they've seen the 'baby.'" According to Castle, Polanski's trick worked, and the audience's minds simply filled in the demonic baby. Many people left the theater believing they had seen it. When the film aired on television, people trusted their memories more than their eyes and columnists reported that "due to censorship, ABC had cut scenes where the 'baby' was shown."[7]

As Michel Koven notes, "Cinema is an analogue to reality, not its replacement. And when audiences react to fantasy cinema (e.g., horror movies), they react not to a confusion of the presented image with reality but to the presentation of images as cultural discourse."[8] All audiences understand that a film of a train cannot run them over. While some horror films have been misinterpreted as "snuff films" or actual found footage of supernatural events, generally audiences know that what they are seeing is an illusion created using actors and special effects and enhanced with scary music. Koven's point is that none of this matters. As an analogue to reality, horror films still shape our ideas of *what is possible*.

A striking example of horror films changing ideas of what is possible comes from Peter Laws, a Baptist minister and host of a podcast on horror movies called "The Flicks the Church Forgot." A former atheist, Laws attributes his conversion to Christianity to watching a VHS tape of *The Exorcist*: "This film, and the thousands I watched after it, forced me to consider an utterly subversive notion: that God might be real and the church might sometimes be filed under 'solution,' not 'problem.' As a dedicated Christian-basher, this was revelatory."[9] While Laws's experience may not be typical, it raises important questions about how these films shape religious attitudes.

This chapter approaches the question of how horror films shape beliefs and attitudes from four angles. First, the genre of horror is uniquely concerned with epistemology. Perhaps more than any other genre, horror is preoccupied with challenging and playing with our conceptions of what we believe to be possible. Second, religious studies has long known that narrative has a potent ability to shape the way we understand the world. Markus Altena Davidsen has researched "fiction-based religions" such as "Jediism"— a small religious movement based on the *Star Wars* franchise. He notes that some supernatural fiction narratives possess certain qualities called "veracity mechanisms" that make them more amenable to being repurposed into religious beliefs and practices. Many of the films explored in this book contain veracity mechanisms that give the stories significance beyond the frame of the film. Third, while audiences can easily distinguish movies from real life, there is evidence that film as a medium possesses certain qualities that facilitate confabulation, or the production of false memories, thus further blurring the story world of the film with the real world. Finally, folklorists have long noted that stories have a way of coming to life through a process known as "ostension." Ostension provides a way of thinking about situations in which horror movies provide a "script" that informs people's actions and interpretations of events in the real world.

Genre: Horror and the Revolving Door of Skepticism and Belief

When Warner Brothers studios approached screen-writers Chad and Carey Hayes about writing a ghost story, they responded that they were only interested if the film could be based on "a true story." In an interview with Diana Pasulka, Chad Hayes explained, "We purposely look for stories that are based on true events. We do that for this very reason: because people can relate. They can Google the story and see that maybe it's folklore, or it's real, but it is out there and is an experience for other people. So that contributes, no doubt, to the scare factor."[10] The ghost story the Hayes brothers wrote was *The Conjuring*, based on the adventures of Ed and Lorraine Warren. Significantly, Chad Hayes did not envision his audience passively absorbing a ghost story but rather doing active investigation—presumably either before or after viewing the film—and that this participation would enhance the scariness and, ultimately, the entertainment value of his narrative. The Hayes brothers were right. There is a lot to unpack here about the nature of the horror genre and its relationship to what we believe to be true.

As research for this book, we interviewed Grady Hendrix, who is a successful horror novelist as well as an authority on the history of the genre. Hendrix commented, "Horror is the only genre that says it's true" and cited some of the earliest examples of horror fiction. Horace Walpole's *The Castle of Ortranto* (1764) is widely considered to be the first gothic novel. The first edition presented itself as a manuscript printed in Naples in 1529, translated by one "William Marshal." Henry James's novella *The Turn of the Screw* (1898) employed a similar framing device. In a move that anticipated "live-record horror films" such as *The Blair Witch Project* (1999), an unnamed narrator reads a manuscript written by a governess who has died. Similarly, when folklorist Bill Ellis interviewed camp counselors about the ghost stories their teenage campers liked to hear, one counselor responded, "If you tell 'em it's not true that ruins the whole thing. You have to leave that fact that it might actually be true in there."[11]

When we explained our project of examining the connection between horror films and figures such as Ed and Lorraine Warren, Hendrix made a rather blunt observation that he and the Warrens were essentially in the same business of telling persuasive lies: "You speak with authority and you use first person and people are like, 'Why would somebody make this up?' You know?' And the reason I made it up is the same reason the Lutz's made up Amityville, it's the reason the Warrens made up all their cases, it's the reason Michelle Smith made up her cases: Money." Although the adventures of the Warrens, along with books like *The Amityville Horror* and *Michelle Remembers* are sold as non-fiction, Hendrix suggests these works are essentially horror novels that have taken the premise of "saying it's true" a bit further by perpetrating full-fledged hoaxes—the techniques of telling a horror story remain the same, the only difference is how honest the authors are. But why are these techniques (speaking with authority, using the first person, etc.) necessary at all? Why is horror alone more enjoyable (and more profitable) if it seems true? Other genres (Westerns, romantic comedies, etc.) do not benefit substantially from these kinds of complex framing devices. This is part of the larger question of why the horror genre exists at all.

David Hume's essay "Of Tragedy" (1757) was one of the first inquiries into why it is pleasurable to watch performances of tragic stories. Philosopher Noel Carroll sees Hume's question as a precursor to what he calls "the paradox of horror": Why would a normal person enjoy being frightened and watching terrible things happen to people? First, Carroll argues that horror thrives as a *narrative* form and not, as some critics would have it, a parade of *images* seeking to outdo each other in special effects or gruesomeness. Second, what drives these narratives are curiosity and discovery. Carroll writes:

These stories, with great frequency, revolve around proving, disclosing, discovering, and confirming the existence of something that is impossible, something that defies standing conceptual schemes. It is part of such stories—contrary to our everyday beliefs about the nature of things— that such monsters exist. And as a result, audiences' expectations revolve around whether this existence will be confirmed in the story . . . . Applied to the paradox of horror, these observations suggest that the pleasure derived from horror fiction and the source of our interest in it resides, first and foremost, in the processes of discovery, proof, and confirmation that horror fictions often employ.[12]

So, horror (at least for Carroll) is not about sadism, but epistemology: The pleasure of horror is the pleasure of questioning our assumptions and determining what is real. A horror narrative is a kind of game in which the given model of reality is destabilized, and we vicariously follow the characters in their attempt to discover a new, stable model of reality. William Peter Blatty's *The Exorcist* is a prime example of this as the reader follows a skeptical priest attempting to make sense of seemingly impossible events.

This destabilization of reality is both what makes horror disturbing and what makes it pleasurable. In *The Uncanny*, Sigmund Freud described a feeling of the *unheimlich* or "eeriness." Freud notes that fairy tales cannot inspire a feeling of the uncanny because, although cannibalistic witches and ogres might be frightening, the existence of these beings is accepted as fact within the frame of the story world. However, the idea of such creatures in *our world*—or a storyworld similar to ours—does arouse a sense of the uncanny. The uncanny comes from a "conflict of judgment" about what is real. As Freud puts it, "An uncanny effect often arises when the boundary between fantasy and reality is blurred, when we are faced with the reality of something that we have until now considered imaginary."[13] We often feel the uncanny most acutely not while watching a horror movie, but afterward when we are trying to fall asleep and reminding ourselves that monsters are not real.

Yet this blurring of reality and imagination is also fun. Horror "says it's true" because part of the pleasure involves the vertigo of determining whether this story could be real. Letting the audience "figure it out for themselves" is key to the success of "live-record" horror films. Even films that are honestly presented as fiction present a storyworld where things that should not happen do happen, and audiences must work to construct their disbelief, producing both a sense of the uncanny and an epistemological game to be mastered.

Psychologist Alison Gopnik has even suggested that we possess a "theory drive" that rewards us with pleasure when we create an explanation for something. As she puts it, "Explanation is to cognition as orgasm is to reproduction."[14] Furthermore, just as there are many ways to reach orgasm that do not result in reproduction, devising explanations can be pleasurable even when they are wrong or nonsensical. From this perspective, supernatural horror films, where inexplicable events occur and no explanation is off limits, are a veritable orgy for the theory drive.

Significantly, media scholar Annette Hill suggests nominally true media about the paranormal holds a similar appeal. Writing in 2011, Hill described a "paranormal turn" in popular media, marked by a spike in reality television shows in which people hunt for ghosts and other supernatural beings. Echoing Hendrix, Hill suggests the paranormal turn was largely a calculated response to a market. For example, the British show *Most Haunted* was created after a producer purchased a copy of every magazine marketed to women, laid them on the floor, and noticed that each one contained an article on the paranormal.[15] Hill conducted an ethnography of the consumers of this media using focus groups and research interviews. She found that, for these audiences, the shows were not about the putative existence of ghosts at all. Instead, the shows were really about *them* and where they as viewers located themselves on the continuum between belief and skepticism. It was important to the interviewees that they be understood as neither gullible nor overly skeptical, but rather as holding a nuanced position. Watching reality television where people speculate about the source of strange noises and other possible evidence of a haunting provided an "ambiguous cultural experience" where assumptions and attitudes could be tried on and experimented with.

Furthermore, in constructing their identities regarding media claims about the supernatural, the purpose seemed to be not to reach a conclusion but to remain in a suspended state of play. Hill writes:

> The best way of describing the multimodal responses of audiences to ghost hunting TV is to picture them going through a revolving door of scepticism and belief . . . . To describe audiences as going through a revolving door of scepticism and belief may imply they are caught up in circumstances beyond their control. But this is not the case. People know which way round they are going through the revolving door. Audiences provide the momentum themselves. In this way, they help to produce beliefs and disbeliefs in paranormal matters.[16]

To return to Hendrix's point that both horror novelists and hoaxers are "making up" stories for money, it seems that good horror stories and good hoaxes function equally well as "culturally ambiguous experiences."

Consumers find this material pleasurable, at least in part, because they are drawn to the ambiguity over "what really happened." They create spaces where new possibilities can be explored. And, if the story is presented as possibly true, it provides opportunities for identity construction as the audience locates themselves on the revolving door of skepticism and belief.

Additionally, the questions people enjoy exploring when they watch supernatural horror movies or paranormal reality shows cannot be separated from religious questions. In her ethnography of how teenagers consume supernatural media, religious studies scholar Lynn Schofield Clark found that horror media competes and coexists with stories from religious traditions and that audiences may regard both genres "as equally possible and plausible or equally fictional."[17] Hollywood has begun to lean into this connection, seeing religious communities as built-in audiences. *The Conjuring* partnered with a marketing firm that specializes in reaching Christian audiences. Grace Hill Media was founded by evangelical Christian Jonathan Brock, a former publicist for Warner Brothers. Carey Hayes even coined the term "religious supernatural" to describe films like *The Conjuring*, emphasizing that they are harmonious with a religious worldview.[18]

Narrative: Veracity Mechanisms

This chapter began by challenging the assumption that special effects and other physical technology are the factors that cause people to interpret movies as "real." Everyone knows that films are "not real" because they are an analog to reality, not reality itself. However, some films exert a greater influence over what we imagine to be possible than others. What gives certain horror films this ability is not special effects technology but *social technology*. As Grady Hendrix pointed out, both writers and hoaxers have a repertoire of tactics they can use to give their stories more verisimilitude. H. P. Lovecraft was very explicit about these tactics when he wrote, "My own rule is that no weird story can truly produce terror unless it is devised with all the care & verisimilitude of an actual *hoax* . . . . My own attitude in writing is always that of the hoax-weaver."[19] Lovecraft, of course, was a bit too effective at this and many people assumed features of his stories, such as the Necronomicon, actually existed. Lovecraft's secret was not his writing style but his ability to confound the reader by weaving actual history as well as other stories into his fiction. The best horror films often rely on similar tactics.

Markus Altena Davidsen has studied what he calls "religious affordances" in supernatural fiction. Certain novels and films seem to lend themselves to belief in actual supernatural forces. Davidsen has attempted to isolate the features of these narratives to create a catalog of "veracity mechanisms." Davidsen's findings parallel Diana Pasulka's research on the ways supernatural films shape beliefs. This body of research identifies the social technologies horror films use to "seem real" and to influence religious beliefs and practices.

Davidsen's first three veracity mechanisms are "evidence mechanisms" that affirm the supernatural forces as real within the story world. (After all, if demons do not seem real within the context of the story, they are unlikely to seem so outside of the story.) The first and simplest of these is called the "matter-of-fact effect," meaning that the supernatural forces in the story are, ultimately, real. Significantly, Davidsen notes that when characters doubt the existence of these forces this only enhances the veracity effect when these doubts are inevitably proven wrong. Doubt is a major theme of *The Exorcist* and the trope of the skeptical character insisting that "there's a rational explanation for everything" has become a cliché in supernatural horror films. The second mechanism is "teacher discourse justification" in which authoritative characters instruct less knowledgeable characters about the supernatural. Father Lankester Merrin in *The Exorcist* is a classic example of such a character. So are Ed and Lorraine Warren as portrayed in *The Conjuring* franchise. The third mechanism is "justification of the tale" in which the narrator relates their sources of information. In the horror genre, this mechanism goes all the way back to *The Castle of Otranto*. The claim of being "based on a true story" is now a widely used trope in supernatural horror. There is also an entire genre of "live-record horror" pioneered by such films as *Cannibal Holocaust* (1980), *The Last Broadcast* (1998), and *The Blair Witch Project* (1999) that presents the film as "found footage" recovered from an actual event. Some people were confused as to whether these films depicted real or fictional events. In fact, Ruggero Deodato, the director of *Cannibal Holocaust*, was arrested on obscenity charges amid allegations that his movie was a "snuff" film depicting actual murder.[20]

A second category of veracity mechanisms is "anchoring mechanisms" that link the story world to the real world. Anchoring destabilizes the story's status as fiction by making it hard to tell where fact ends and fiction begins. One such mechanism is "onomastic anchoring" or placing real people, places, and events in the film. All the films discussed in this book use this technique to some degree. One striking example is "*The Exorcist* steps" in Washington, DC. Not only is this a real place, but on Halloween weekend 2015, the mayor officially honored the steps as a landmark in a ceremony attended by William Friedkin and William Peter Blatty. At the peak of *The Exorcist* phenomenon, faculty at Georgetown University were inundated with so many demands for interviews that the school ordered all such requests cleared with the public information office first.[21]

Anchoring can also be achieved through what Pasulka calls the "realist montage" technique in which scenes and images from the real world are spliced into the story. The end of *The Conjuring* juxtaposes photos of the Perron family (who are real people) alongside pictures of the actors portraying them. Visually, this serves to anchor the story and destabilize its status as fiction.[22]

There are also "transtextual" anchoring techniques that create a sense of veracity by linking the narrative to other texts. Some novels contain "paratexts" such as prefaces that explain to the reader what the genre of the main text is. *The Conjuring* ends with an actual quote from Ed Warren: "Diabolical forces are formidable. These forces are eternal, and they exist today. The fairy tale is true."[23] This is a paratext suggesting that the film has been a true story, not fiction, and that audience members may encounter demonic forces in real life.

Another transtextual anchoring technique is to allude to existing texts, sometimes borrowing their authority. The most referenced text in supernatural horror movies is, of course, the Bible. In *The Last Exorcism* (2010) (another live-record horror film), pastor Cotton Marcus looks at the camera and tells the audience, "The Bible is filled with demons. If you believe in God, you have to believe in the devil. Jesus himself was an exorcist. Therefore, if you are Christian and you believe in the Bible and you believe in Jesus Christ, you have to believe in demons." Significantly, horror films such as *The Omen* (1976) and *Lost Souls* (2000) have simply invented verses that do not actually appear in the Bible, and there is little evidence audiences noticed or cared. Bible scholar Steve A. Wiggins notes that while American culture has a high rate of Biblical awareness, its rate of Biblical literacy is low, leaving popular culture to fill in the gap.[24] The *authority* of the Bible remains useful to horror films, even if the audience has never read it.

Finally, texts may use "metatextual reflection"; that is, generating stories about the story. This can include things like interviews with writers or directors. However, it can also include the strategic deployment of expert "consultants." There is a long history of this strategy in horror films, especially those that claim to depict alternative religious practices such as Paganism or Satanism. Margaret Murray, the archaeologist who wrote *The Witch-Cult in Modern Europe* (1921), was invited to an event promoting the film *Night of the Demon* (1957).[25] *Eye of the Devil* (1966) hired Wiccan leader Alex Sanders as a consultant. *The Craft* (1997) employed Gardnerian Wiccan priestess Pat Devin. The director of *Book of Shadows: Blair Witch 2* (2001) consulted with Pagan scholar Peg Aloi. That film also flew Peter H. Gilmore, the head of the Church of Satan, to Los Angeles to perform a Satanic ritual that could be streamed on the internet as a promotional stunt.[26] The 2007 remake of *The Wicker Man* consulted Pagan author Fiona Horne. Promotional agents for *The Witch* (2016) reached out to the Church of Satan, and eventually struck a deal with performance artist Jex Blackmore, who was then a leader for the Detroit chapter of The Satanic Temple. Some observers noted that consulting with scholars and practitioners did not seem to make the portrayal of alternative religions in these films any more authentic.[27] This is because the function of these consultants was never really to make the story more "accurate" but rather to make it seem more "true" using transtextual anchoring. This was Pasulka's conclusion after she was hired as a consultant for *The Conjuring*. Although she was nominally hired to help get the Latin right for exorcisms, she was referred to as a "demonologist" and director James Wan began tweeting about her expertise. Pasulka argues that hiring cultural authorities is a strategy used to generate publicity for films. But beyond this, it is another way of destabilizing the fictional status of the story. She writes, "Advertisements, extra discourse surrounding the productions in social media, and urban legends all contribute to the fascination with and the questioning of the truth claims and possible reality of the production's content."[28]

Another metatextual strategy is to suggest that literal demonic forces surround the film. William Friedkin pioneered this technique after a fire and several injuries occurred on the set of *The Exorcist*. Although Friedkin has been described as a secular Jew, he asked Jesuit Thomas V. Bermingham to exorcize the set. It is reasonable to assume that Friedkin's real interest in having the set exorcized was to spread the rumor that the film was cursed, essentially as a form of viral marketing. *The Conjuring* franchise has further refined Friedkin's strategy. A short film called *Faith and Fear* (2020) created to chronicle and promote *The Conjuring* series, features Bryan D. Ouelette— an "autocephalous eastern Orthodox/western Catholic bishop"—blessing the set of *The Conjuring 3: The Devil Made Me Do It* (2021) before filming began in 2019. Ouellette tells the crew, "The cosmos doesn't know the difference between fiction and non-fiction" and warns that even depicting "dark archetypes" can cause actual demons to manifest. Taken at face value, Ouelette's warning makes no sense. Why is a bishop creating content for a horror franchise if he believes depicting demons in movies causes literal demonic possession? However, as a strategy of transtextual anchoring, the featurette does a lot of heavy lifting. As a paratext, it primes the viewer to believe they are (or possibly could be) meddling with literal demonic forces just by watching a film (After all, if the cosmos itself cannot distinguish fiction from non-fiction, why should we be able to?) At the same time, it functions as a metatextual reflection (and advertisement) for another *Conjuring* film by showing the audience that the set had to be blessed because making the film was spiritually dangerous. Like the larger promotional campaign for *The Conjuring* franchise, the featurette demonstrates sophisticated social technology designed to disorient audiences about the difference between fiction on the one hand, and history and authentic religious traditions on the other, by presenting a web of interconnected narratives. These veracity mechanisms are sophisticated, and they seem to have a greater influence on audience beliefs than flashy special effects ever could.

Medium: Film and Confabulation

While genre and narrative are important for explaining how horror films "become real," there are also some elements of film as a medium that warrant examination. One of the first film theorists felt there was something almost ineffable about film. In his 1916 book, *The Photoplay*, Harvard psychologist Hugo Munsterberg suggested that the pleasure of watching film comes from its ability to experience consciousness directly, without the constraints of physical reality. He wrote, "The massive outer world has lost its weight, it has been freed from space, time, and causality, and it has been clothed in the forms of our own consciousness. The mind has triumphed over matter and the pictures roll on with the ease of musical tones. It is a superb enjoyment which no other art can furnish us. No wonder that temples for the new goddess are built in every little hamlet."[29] Munsterberg's theory of film hints at transcendence, that film enables us to access a Platonic reality of mind and spirit, beyond "the outer world" of matter, space, and time. It is not surprising that in the horror genre, film and television are often a vector through which spirit entities invade our world, as seen in such films as *Poltergeist* (1982), *Ringu* (1998), and *White Noise* (2004).

More recently, philosopher Colin McGinn has written on what he calls "the mind-movie problem" or theorizing "how it is that the two-dimensional moving image as we experience it in a typical feature film, manages to hook our consciousness in the way it does."[30] Echoing Munsterberg, he suggests that the blank screen on which any conceivable image can be projected acts as an analogy to the human mind. He also notes that the stream of images in film simulates the dream state, possibly creating heightened suggestibility. Certainly, films have demonstrable effects on the body and memory that are significant for understanding how they shape beliefs and practices.

Approaches to film that emphasize the mind may overlook the fact that watching a film is an embodied experience. This is especially true of horror movies, which can cause viewers to experience spikes in adrenaline, nausea, or other somatic symptoms. Cognitive scientist Jeffrey Zacks notes that film triggers a human reaction he calls "the mirror rule" in which humans naturally begin imitating the movements and mannerisms of people they are watching or speaking to. Children, especially, may demonstrate the mirror rule while watching a film, for example by waving their arms around during an action sequence. Zacks suggests that humans are an extremely social species, and the mirror rule has likely helped us to survive by making it easier to learn skills and coordinate action.[31] However, when watching horror movies, the mirror effect may cause us to vicariously experience the anxiety of characters on screen or even wince in sympathetic pain. In 1974, Ted Reggelin, the manager of the Gateway theater in Chicago, tried to explain what was happening to audiences when they watched *The Exorcist*: "People are getting fully involved in what they're seeing on the screen. Some of them actually feel they were exorcized themselves."[32] Religion scholar S. Brent Plate suggests that these experiences have consequences for what we believe:

> The horror film spectator can attempt to sit back, detached, and logically say this is all fake (the green vomit is pea soup, the head spinning is just a doll), but the sensing body reacts on another level, the level "somewhere in oneself" that says it might be true . . . . The body's reactions to a horror film trigger intellectual questions; the sensed sounds and visions of the film, in a real sense, haunt the mind, revealing a split between logic and the aesthetic. To say that one is real and the other not is to miss the deeper operations of

human life. By stirring the body through sensational sounds and images, horror film makes us doubt, eradicating the certainty of a logical self.[33]

In other words, these embodied experiences are "a way of knowing" independent of our intellectual assessment of the story. For Plate, these experiences are key for understanding how *The Exorcist* shaped American religious culture in the 1970s. Douglas Cowan gives some insight into this embodied knowledge in his own account of viewing this film, "I saw *The Exorcist* when it was released in 1973, and it affected me deeply enough that parts of the experience still haunt me whenever I screen it for a class today."[34]

In addition to our bodies, films also affect our memories. There is evidence that over time depictions of events in film trump other sources of information in shaping what viewers believe to be true. Zacks performed a research study in which subjects were presented with accurate essays about several historical events. The subjects were then shown movies that depicted the same events they had just read about, but clearly distorted the information in the essays. When subjects were asked to recall accurate information about the events, they accepted about forty percent of the film distortions as true. It did not matter whether the subjects watched the movies before or after they read the essays: the movie version was consistently remembered as the "true" version. Zacks suggests the full effect of bad information in historical movies was probably not captured in the experiment because people do not normally read an accurate essay immediately after watching a history movie.[35]

Zacks notes that human memory is adapted to be good at recalling information but not necessarily the source of that information. He explains, "I think we are optimized to build representations of events that allow us to function effectively, and most of the time there is no particular need to sort out the source of our memories."[36] Furthermore, film as a medium is likely more suited than books for creating false memories. If you are trying to remember something and you recall verbal content, you may also recall that this is information you read somewhere. But if you recall images or a feeling of emotional intensity, you may conclude that you are remembering something you personally experienced. Finally, in a phenomenon called "the sleeper effect," there is evidence that the influence of films increases over time as audiences remember the information but forget where they were exposed to it. This is consistent with Gerald Heisler's experiment, discussed in Chapter 1, which found subjects were more likely to report belief in the devil a month after watching *The Exorcist* than immediately after viewing.

In 2000, a group of psychologists actually set out to see if they could instill false memories of having witnessed someone in a state of possession.[37] In the wake of the Satanic Panic of the 1980s, some argued that while witnesses might have false memories of mundane events, they could not have false memories of things that were implausible. Possession was chosen as an example of something that was implausible, but not impossible. Additionally, several therapy patients had expressed belief in demonic possession. The experiment was conducted in Italy where, at the time, belief in possession was more common than in the United States.

The experiment proceeded in four phases. First, sixty-five students from the University of Florence were given a list of thirty events and asked to rate how plausible they were on a scale of 1 to 8. Then they were asked how likely it was that they had witnessed each of these events before the age of three. This was also scored on a scale of 1 to 8, with 8 indicating certainty the event happened, and 1 indicating certainty it did not happen. The subjects were then secretly divided into three groups: one group was manipulated to see if they came to believe they had seen a possessed person as a child, a second was manipulated toward thinking they had nearly choked as a child (a plausible event), and a third was not manipulated at all.

Phase two began one month later when all subjects were given a series of twelve articles on various topics and asked to judge them for writing style. In fact, this phase was an attempt at "plausibility manipulation" to see if the subjects could be biased toward thinking certain events are plausible. The articles given to the "possession group" included three articles about possession. One explained that possession is common in Italian culture. Another falsely stated that demoniacs sometimes show signs of possession in front of children, assuming there will be no consequences because children are too young to understand what they are seeing. The choking group was given articles about choking and the control group was not subjected to any deliberate manipulation.

Phase three occurred a week later. All subjects were given a survey about their fears. Then—individually—researchers told each subject in the possession group (falsely) that their survey responses indicated that they likely witnessed a possession before the age of three. Similar claims about choking were made to the choking group. The final phase began a week after this when subjects were again asked to score events as plausible or implausible on a scale of 1 to 8 and whether these events happened to them as children on a scale of 1 to 8. For those in the possession group, the average "plausibility" score that they had witnessed a possessed person as a child increased significantly. This does not mean that anyone came to believe they had witnessed such an event, only that it seemed more plausible. By comparison, the choking group already found it plausible that they nearly choked on something as children and there was little increase.

The (seemingly obvious) conclusion of this study was that it is possible to have a false memory of an "implausible" event, provided someone no longer considers such an event to be implausible. Obviously, no movie can subject someone to the sort of targeted and deliberate manipulation used in this experiment (although some therapists did plant suggestions like this during the Satanic Panic and still do today). This experiment also looked at college students whose ideas about what is plausible may be more flexible compared with older people. However, this study does have implications for how horror movies can affect plausibility, as well as memory and other types of experience—especially when these movies are accompanied by experts explaining that such things really happen. Elizabeth Loftus, a memory researcher who participated in this experiment, predicted that a 2000 documentary called *Possessed*, about the 1949 case that inspired *The Exorcist*, would lead to a jump in alleged possessions.[38] There is no precise data to measure whether her prediction was correct.

False memories aside, the larger phenomenon in which films shape our ideas of what is plausible—often without our realizing it—has serious implications for how horror films might affect belief in demons and other supernatural forces. When people are asked whether they believe in demons—possibly in their church or other religious setting—their brain may well begin to conjure images, sounds, and embodied feelings related to demons while failing to recall that these experiences came from watching a film. If this effect is combined with the veracity mechanisms discussed in the previous section, it is easy to imagine films shaping religious beliefs and practices.

Ostension: Performing the Script

On April 15, 1989, *The Washington Post* ran the headline, "Movie Linked to Alleged Cult Slayers." It described a series of murders committed by a drug cartel in Matamoros, Mexico, culminating in the abduction and slaying of Mark Kilroy, an American college student who was visiting the border town on spring break. The cartel had retained the services of Cuban-born Adolfo de Jesus Constanzo, who claimed that through the Afro-Cuban practice of Santeria and other magical traditions he could perform human sacrifices that would render cartel members invisible to authorities and bestow other forms of supernatural protection. At the cartel's ranch, law enforcement found thirteen bodies, most of which had been ritually mutilated, in a shed. (The other murders appear to have been committed out of more mundane criminal motives, whereas Kilroy was targeted exclusively for one of Constanzo's rituals.) As *The Washington Post* correctly observed, "Santeria sometimes calls for the sacrifice of animals, but never humans." So where did Constanzo get his ideas about this practice? Apparently from the 1986 film *The Believers* directed by John Schlesinger. *The Believers* depicts a Santeria cult that practices human sacrifice, possesses literal supernatural powers, and has infiltrated elite levels of society. After interviewing two of the suspects, Cameron County Sheriff's Lt. George Gavito reported, "They keep bringing the movie up . . . . They talk about it like that had something to do with changing them." Constanzo had taken on a college student named Sara Maria Aldrete as his apprentice. Aldrete was recruiting new members and urging the entire cartel to watch *The Believers*.

How to explain this connection? While some scenes in *The Believers* seem sympathetic to practitioners of Santeria, Paul Thomas has compellingly argued that this is just a set up for the film's climax when all the audience's worst fears about this religion are proven true.[39] Santeria is ultimately depicted as an evil and violent religion, closely linked to colonialist ideas of "primitive Africa." Significantly, a review of the film *Variety* stated, "It isn't difficult to accept that the things that happen in *The Believers* could happen in real life, which is why the picture is so riveting. Consider the weird goings-on of other cults that have flourished in the United States recently, notably attempted murders by the followers of Synanon and the Bagwan Shree Rajneesh, to name just two . . . If nothing else, Schlesinger knows how to produce a film where pain and horror are beautiful to watch, a sick thought, but one that has its believers."[40] Obviously Constanzo and Aldrete understood *The Believers* was not a documentary, yet it clearly informed their ideas of what it would look like for a cartel to obtain wealth and power using sinister, magical means. Because they used this film as a sort of "how-to" manual, Constanzo and Aldrete brought a racist depiction of a minority religion from a horror movie to life, resulting in an actual human sacrifice. In folklore studies, this phenomenon of stories manifesting into action is known as ostension. While rare, horror films sometimes do become subject to ostension. When horror films become "scripts" for how to think about the world or how we should act, they can contribute to actual crimes as well as moral panic.

Folklorist Bill Ellis broke the concept of ostension into four subtypes. Ostension proper involves the literal acting out of a narrative. This is rare and Ellis counts the murder of Mark Kilroy as an example. Pseudo-ostension is more common and refers to a hoax in which participants produce evidence of a narrative without actually acting it out. The promotional campaign for the re-make of Stephen King's *It* (2017), launched in August 2016, included a "viral marketing" component that did things like leave red helium balloons floating above storm drains. The campaign even organized a fake rally of people claiming to be professional clowns whose careers had been ruined by the film. Thanks to these efforts, *It* broke all pre-sales records for a horror movie. But the excitement also inspired others to "get into the act." In September, law enforcement all over the country were receiving reports of menacing clowns. Some of these were false reports while others seem to have resulted from adolescent pranksters attempting to frighten people. Sales of clown masks tripled from the previous year. In October 2016, a *Bloomberg* reporter at a White House press conference asked whether President Barack Obama was aware of the clown reports and associated arrests. The press secretary referred him to the FBI.[41] No one actually murdered anyone like Stephen King's Pennywise, but both the viral campaign and the adolescent clowns were engaged in pseudo-ostension by creating "evidence" of killer clown attacks.

Quasi-ostension involves misinterpreting events in terms of an existing legend. In some cases, horror films become the framework through which the world is interpreted. A stark example of this was the "occult crime" seminars offered to police during the Satanic Panic, where *Rosemary's Baby* and *The Believers* were presented as accurate depictions of criminal cults. The officers who attended these seminars were essentially asked to investigate crimes with the assumption that situations they would encounter in the real world would be similar to the fictional cults from these films.

Finally, proto-ostension occurs when people take a story alleged to have happened to someone else and claim it as a personal experience. Grady Hendrix described the Warrens, the Lutzes, and Michelle Proby (who wrote as Michelle Smith) as lying about their experiences. A folklorist might interpret these narratives as proto-ostension in which these individuals drew on existing stories of demons, haunted houses, and Satanic cults, many of which they like encountered through film.

To summarize, it is not the assumption of this book that people are unable to distinguish between film and real life or that horror movies possess some nefarious power to program people with certain beliefs. As an analog to reality, film does not so much suggest "what is" as "what could be." The ability of horror movies to shape beliefs and experiences is enhanced by the fact the horror genre is uniquely preoccupied with questioning assumptions and exploring possibilities, certain "veracity mechanisms" in the narratives of these films that allow them to serve as plausibility structures for certain beliefs, and aspects of film as a medium that lend themselves to confabulation. In these ways, not only do horror films have the capacity to influence ideas about the supernatural, but they can become scripts performed in real life through processes of ostension.

3

The Unholy Trinity

"The story of *Rosemary's Baby* was happening in real life. Witches, all of them, were casting their spell, and I was becoming one of the principal players."

—Producer William Castle[1]

"I'm very conscious of making a movie that will enter the minds of those who see it, and that will grow in their minds and alter and affect them."

—Director William Friedkin[2]

Horror scholars frequently cite 1968 as the year that horror came to be taken seriously as a genre.[3] Two films marked this date. The first was George A. Romero's *Night of the Living Dead*. This film was originally called *Night of the Flesh Eaters*, and when the title was revised the change was not entered into copyright, which immediately entered the film into public domain. The result was that theaters all over America screened it, and its vision of a global apocalypse resonated with audiences living through the Cold War and the urban riots of the 1960s.[4] The second film was Roman Polanski's *Rosemary's Baby*, which was a critical success and was nominated for numerous awards. Ruth Gordon, who played the nosey neighbor/Satanic conspirator won both a Golden Globe and an Academy Award for best supporting actress. These films proved that horror—even when it featured fantastic elements like zombies and demon babies—could be more than drive-in schlock.

Rosemary's Baby was followed by two more films, *The Exorcist* (1973) and *The Omen* (1976), that also dealt with themes of demons and Satanic conspiracies. These films were instantly regarded as a trilogy. A *New York Times* review published the day after *The Omen* premiered was titled " 'Omen' is Nobody's Baby," in reference to *Rosemary's Baby,* and declared *The Omen* "a member of *The Exorcist* family."[5] Ever since, these three films have been

The Exorcist Effect. Joseph P. Laycock and Eric Harrelson, Oxford University Press. © Oxford University Press 2024.
DOI: 10.1093/oso/9780197635391.003.0003

called "an evil triad," a "Satanic cycle," and "the unholy trinity." The unholy trinity reflected popular ideas about such topics as Satanic conspiracy
theories, demonic possession, and the Antichrist, but they also shaped how
Americans imagined and talked about these topics: *Rosemary's Baby* set the
stage for the Satanic Panic of the 1980s, *The Exorcist* caused the public to
diagnose themselves and others with demonic possession, and *The Omen*
influenced ideas about end-times prophecy. These films also inspired countless imitators that further saturated American culture with images of the demonic, especially after cable television and home videos began piping these
films into American homes. This chapter examines the cultural moment that
gave rise to the unholy trinity, the veracity mechanisms incorporated into
each film, and their influence regarding supernatural beliefs and practices.

It Came from the Seventies

Rosemary's Baby and *The Exorcist* are sometimes associated with "the death
of the sixties."[6] This connection is owed largely to the fact that just over a
year after the premiere of *Rosemary's Baby*, actress Sharon Tate, the pregnant
wife of director Roman Polanski, was murdered in her home by followers
of Charles Manson. The "Manson family murders" of 1969 became a preoccupation for the anti-cult movement and Satanic conspiracy theorists.
They were also regarded as a sign that the utopian hopes associated with the
hippie movement had degenerated into madness and violence. The 1970s
was a decade remembered for cynicism and paranoia. It was also a formative
era for horror in which the genre grew more popular, even as films became
more gruesome. It saw the emergence of the "slasher" genre with such films
as *The Texas Chainsaw Massacre* (1974), loosely inspired by the crimes of Ed
Gein, and *The Town that Dreaded Sundown* (1976), which depicted a series
of murders that occurred in Texarkana in 1946. Today, it has become almost
a cliché to claim that horror films of this era are a reflection of America's national trauma. In 1974, William Friedkin told an interviewer, "I think a large
part of our entertainment today is a result of our national nervous breakdown
since the three assassinations and the Vietnam war. I think we are coming out
of another kind of seizure with the Nixon administration."[7] In *The Christian
Century*, theologian Carl Raschke opined, "The madcap rush of middle
Americans last year to see the demons rage in Panavision and technicolor,
together with proliferating clergy reports soon thereafter of parishioners

convinced of their own possession, became a living allegory of our collective trauma . . . . Both Watergate and *The Exorcist* have been psychodramas of the American soul."[8] And Ralph R. Greenson, a professor of psychiatry at UCLA, declared, "In the days when we all had more trust in our government, our friends, and ourselves, *The Exorcist* would have been a bad joke. Today it is a danger."[9]

As historians know, it is difficult to prove causation between historical events and an audience's reaction to a film. In a reply to Dr. Greenson, film critic Hollis Alpert noted, "I doubt that anyone is responding to *The Exorcist* because of the Watergate affair."[10] While it seems a stretch to claim the social upheaval of the era *caused* the unholy trinity, it also seems unlikely that the books and films discussed in this chapter would have had the same reception in a different decade. In an interview with the authors, horror novelist Grady Hendrix offered his perspective on this connection:

> This is something that I only say as someone who writes books—because I sort of thought it was bullshit before I did—I feel like there's an argument to be made that times get the books they need. You know what I mean? If Ira Levin hadn't written *Rosemary's Baby* then maybe Fred Mustard Stewart's *The Mephisto Waltz* would have been the big book. That stuff's floating around out there and I think sometimes you write the book and sometimes the book writes you and I think in an optimal situation it's 50/50: You are the right person writing the book that at that moment people want to read because of something that's out there in the culture.[11]

With this perspective in mind, there are some specific historical developments that contributed to the success of these films and their influence on religious culture: (1) a move toward realism in the horror genre, (2) a relationship between films and the literary market that paved the way for more horror films and provided ready-made transtextual anchoring devices, (3) a peak in the secularization narrative accompanied by anxieties about the loss of traditional religion—especially in the wake of Vatican II (1962–1965), and (4) a supernatural turn in horror movies. These last two features worked in tandem and caused some to view these films as a sign of a societal crisis.

Peg Aloi notes that beginning in the 1960s there was a new emphasis on authenticity in film. For horror, this meant "stories that were subtle, psychological and, thus, plausible."[12] At the forefront of this trend was Alfred Hitchcock, who specialized in macabre stories that felt like they could happen to anyone. In a 1948 interview, Hitchcock reflected on his thrillers, "In none of these was the house filled with shadows, the weather dull and stormy throughout, the moor windswept, and the doors creaky."[13] Before the novel *Rosemary's Baby* was published, literary agent Martin Birdt sent galley proofs to Hitchcock hoping he would be interested in a film adaptation. But Hitchcock, who was raised Catholic, was reportedly appalled by a story of a woman being impregnated by the devil.[14] Instead, Birdt sold the film rights to William Castle. Paramount agreed to make Castle's film but only if Roman Polanski directed. Like Hitchcock, Polanski wanted his film to seem not only realistic, but ordinary. It was even supposed to replicate a first-person perspective of events. Polanski later recalled, "Ideally the lens should be at the same distance from the subject as the eye of the notional observer."[15]

William Peter Blatty wanted William Friedkin to direct *The Exorcist* after he watched *The French Connection* (1971). That film won Friedkin an Oscar for best director, but what Blatty really admired about *The French Connection* was "the look of documentary realism."[16] Friedkin's style has been called "hyperrealism."[17] He liked to cast non-actors, and several actual Jesuits appear in *The Exorcist*. He also literally tormented the actors by keeping sets at sub-zero temperatures, firing a gun on stage to make actors anxious, and using wire stunts that caused actual injuries. For all of this, Blatty wanted an even more realistic film. He objected to the famous "head-spinning scene," commenting, "Supernatural doesn't mean impossible."[18] David Seltzer's original script for *The Omen* involved the protagonists being chased through a cemetery by cloaked figures that left hoof prints in the dirt. But a friend convinced him that the film needed to seem plausible. The demons were replaced with wild rottweilers, and the Satanic forces always manifested as accidents and outrageous coincidences.[19] The realism of these films was key to their success and demonstrated that horror could contain supernatural elements and still seem plausible. However, seeing realistic depictions of Satanic conspiracies and demonic possession also functioned as a plausibility structure by presenting a model of how these events could unfold in real life.

Another important trend was the close relationship between horror and the literary market. *Rosemary's Baby* and *The Exorcist* were novels before they were films, and *The Omen* was hastily adapted into a novel that was published just ahead of the film premiere. The transformation of the horror film genre was preceded by an explosion of horror novels that came in the wake of *Rosemary's Baby* and lasted for two decades. *Rosemary's Baby* (1967), Thomas Tryon's *The Other* (1971), and *The Exorcist* (1971) were the first horror novels to appear in *Publisher's Weekly* annual bestseller list since World War II. These three books made horror a genre fit for adult readers. Grady Hendrix notes, "Every paperback needed Satan on the cover and a blurb comparing it to *The Exorcist, Rosemary's Baby,* or *The Other.*"[20] (One truly terrible imitator was *Exorcism* (1974) written by "Est Natas" (Latin for "is" followed by "Satan" backwards).) The back cover stated, "*Rosemary's Baby* opened the door to the occult. You are now invited to witness: exorcism." There are unsubstantiated rumors that Est Natas was actually Stephen King, whose first published novel, *Carrie,* came out the same year.)[21]

Peter Hutchins argues that the transformation of horror literature at the end of the 1960s precipitated a new wave of horror films because studios liked to make films that had "pre-sold" elements.[22] Novels were seen as an index that a film would do well and so numerous horror films of the era were adapted from books including *The Mephisto Waltz* (1971), *Jaws* (1975), *Burnt Offerings* (1976), *Carrie* (1976), *The Sentinel* (1977), and many others. Significantly, an attempt to ban screenings of *The Exorcist* in Grosse Pointe Woods, Michigan, failed when city attorney George D. Catlin ruled the film was immune to state obscenity laws because it was based on a book and therefore had "serious literary value."[23]

This arrangement worked both ways, as movies often increased sales of the related novels. In 1974, Richard Woods, a Dominican priest teaching at Loyola University in Chicago described the enormous black and purple cardboard display promoting *The Exorcist*. Woods opined, "Satan is back. That is unmistakably clear considering only recent paperback titles in bookstores everywhere. Besides the ordinary feeling of finitude that oppresses the browser in the midst of those thousands of volumes, the emphatic presence of *The Exorcist* and its proliferating imitators gives many contemporary Catholics a slightly suffocating feeling of nostalgia mixed with nausea."[24] Woods argued that these novels were not just entertainment but had become "a major part of current theology of the devil."[25]

Unlike films, the literary market was not limited to fiction and there was an explosion of books on the occult in the wake of *The Exorcist*. So much so that, in 1974, William Peter Blatty complained to *Time* magazine, "I'm sick of hearing that the movie is a success because of a rediscovery of the occult. A thousand or more books have been written on the occult in the last ten years—they've each sold about ten copies."[26] The occult book market also included nominally "true" stories such as *The Amityville Horror* that provided the same pre-sold appeal for film adaptations as novels.

The synergy between horror novels and films during this period functioned as a transtextual veracity mechanism. When one narrative simultaneously manifested as a film, a book, and reportage speculating on the "true story" behind the narrative, it created an "echo chamber" effect that lent itself to the impression that the sort of things described in this narrative really happened. In 1974, two sociologists administered a survey to high school and college students in Montana in which thirty percent answered that the novel *The Exorcist* was a true story.[27] Probably these students understood the *film* was imaginary, but assumed the book it was based on was nonfiction. Some people had not seen the film nor read the novel, but assumed these narratives were true because of the sheer volume of discourse surrounding them. In his memoir, *Running from the Devil* (2018), Steve Kenning describes experiencing symptoms of epilepsy for the first time in 1975 when he was in the fifth grade and believing that he was experiencing demonic possession. As he explained it, "My hallucinations began about a year after 'The Exorcist' was released in theaters. While I was too young to see the movie, I had heard all about it, and I mistakenly understood it to be a highly accurate documentary. Though my head wasn't spinning and I wasn't spewing green bile, the things I was experiencing were unbelievably vivid and defied logic. I had every reason to believe that I might soon start exhibiting the same disgusting and frightening behavior as the girl in 'The Exorcist.'"[28] Kenning's self-diagnosis of possession was a case of quasi-ostension in which a narrative became the framework through which events were interpreted. One wonders how many people had experiences similar to Kenning's that were never made public.

A third factor is the secularization narrative or the prediction that science would inevitably destroy the influence of religion. Today, few social scientists still subscribe to the secularization narrative, but in the 1960s and 1970s many Americans assumed it to be true. A Gallup poll begun in 1957 asked whether religion is gaining or losing influence. In 1970, seventy-five percent of respondents answered that religion was losing influence. This was the highest percentage that figure reached during the twentieth century and it would not be surpassed until 2010.[29] Modern surveys indicate that many Americans feel the country might be better off without religion, but in the 1960s, the anticipated death of religion was a source of great anxiety. Many people assumed traditional religion was necessary for people to be moral.

On April 8, 1966, *Time* magazine ran its famous cover asking, "Is God Dead?" in red font on a black background. The cover—referencing an article about the "death of God" theology of Thomas J. J. Altizer—served as metonymy for the secularization narrative. In the novel *Rosemary's Baby*, one character explicitly discusses Altizer and the *Time* cover. (Rosemary herself is a lapsed Catholic, the product of a secularized society.) In Polanski's adaptation, the cover can be spotted when Rosemary sits in the waiting room of Dr. Sapirstein, her obstetrician (and also a Satanist). And, of course, at the denouement of the film the warlock Roman Castevet shouts triumphantly, "God is dead! Satan lives!" The opening card of *The Exorcist* also invokes the "Is God Dead?" cover by using red font over a black background. This same font and color combination appeared again in the first printing of Malachi Martin's *Hostage to the Devil* (1976) and in the marquee for *The Omen*. Through this signaling, these films represented a public conversation about the secularization narrative. What would happen if traditional religion was lost? What would replace it? What if there was no one left to protect us from the devil?

This anxiety was felt especially by traditionalist Catholics, disoriented by the reforms of Vatican II that sought to modernize the Catholic Church. In a 1974 interview, Thomas J. Dove, a Paulist priest, commented on the irony that *The Exorcist* signaled a supernatural resurgence just as the Church was attempting to modernize: "First we dropped the rosary and now the hippies are wearing beads. Then we get rid of the exorcism of Satan in the baptism ceremony now people are rushing to see this film."[30] Religion scholar Bernard Doherty has argued that during this period Catholic horror became a resource for defending a pre-Councilor worldview.[31] William Peter Blatty was supported by several priests who wanted to make a response to *Rosemary's Baby* and its death of God message. Ed and Lorraine Warren and Malachi Martin were all traditionalists Catholics who claimed the church reforms had left the public vulnerable to demonic attack.

Significantly, similar anxieties about the loss of traditional religion were also being posed by those participating in the occult revival. Ed Fitch was an electronics engineer from San Bernardino and high priest of a Gardnerian Wiccan coven. In an interview with a tabloid about the possible dangers of viewing *The Exorcist*, he stated, "The state of psychic health in the 20th century is at about the same stage as sanitation was in the walled towns of the Middle Ages . . . . Modern man is dangerously vulnerable to bad psychic influences. He doesn't have much, if any, religion to help him out."[32]

If supernaturalism had become an embarrassment to churches, it had ceased to be one for horror. By the 1970s, horror films were increasingly using themes of religion and the supernatural as opposed to political commentary like *Invasion of the Body Snatchers* (1956) or psychological thrillers like Hitchcock's *Psycho* (1960). This move was simultaneously catering to a demand and fueling the occult revival of the 1960s. Sociologist Peter Berger, in his 1974 essay on *The Exorcist*, suggested that all this anxiety about modernity was the very thing fueling interest in the occult: "Let me, then, state a simple hypothesis: *The current occult wave (including its devil component) is to be understood as resulting from the repression of transcendence in modern consciousness.*"[33]

Others offered less plausible interpretations, viewing the occult revival, and the films that reflected it, in pathological terms as a social problem. For some, the success of horror in the 1970s seemed to upset basic assumptions about civilization. The secularization narrative was preceded by the nineteenth-century anthropologist James G. Frazer, who theorized that civilizations progress from magic to religion to science. In fact, Frazer's teleology is referenced in the tagline for *The Exorcist*: "Somewhere between science and superstition." In the wake of *The Exorcist*, both psychiatrists and religious leaders suggested that the natural course of civilization had been reversed: society was retreating from science and religion and experiencing an atavistic regression to magic. Billy Graham, who never saw *The Exorcist* but claimed he read the novel before tearing it up and flushing the pieces down the toilet, claimed it was "pandering to man's innate superstition and fascination with the supernatural."[34] In an article entitled, "A Psychoanalyst's Indictment of The Exorcist," Greenson declared, "Mysticism, supernaturalism, occultism, are flourishing today because many people are disillusioned by the deterioration of our moral standards, the social and economic inequities, the excessive permissiveness and punishments, the hypocrisy and the corruption of people in high places."[35]

Over and over, *The Exorcist* phenomenon was described in Freudian terms of "the return of the repressed." The reaction to the film was described as the irrational "breaking" and "thrusting" through the surface of a secularized, modern society. *Newsweek* opined, "The Exorcist . . . brought into frenzied focus the underground anxieties, fantasies and fears that have lately broken through the surface of contemporary American society."[36] Dr. Thayer Greene, a United Church of Christ minister and Jungian analyst suggested that, "Modern consciousness has become so rationalized that the reaction to this kind of movie is a compensatory upthrust of irrational forces—not necessarily evil."[37] Experimental psychologist Lawrence Leshan added, "The materialist ethic born in the seventeenth century is finally breaking down. So where else can we look for meaning now that the value system we inherited is disintegrating? We can't look outward, so we turn inward—to sexual sensation, mysticism, or just plain shock."[38]

Both religious leaders and the therapists noted that it was lapsed Catholics—people like Rosemary—who seemed most likely to suffer psychological problems after viewing *The Exorcist*. Richard Woods told *The New York Times*, "I've received dozens of calls from people who are horribly frightened or so confused that they have begun to lose their grip on reality. I also know of two kids who came out of the movie thinking they were possessed, and they have now been hospitalized." He noted that many of the people who contacted him were raised Catholic, adding "[*The Exorcist*] stirs up memories of all those descriptions of hell that you got from nuns."[39] Similarly, Greenson described treating a woman who was experiencing crippling agoraphobia after watching the film: "It was easy for me to show her that the movie had remobilized her fears of God's punishment carried out by the Devil, with which her parents had threatened her in her early childhood."[40] Both these comments associate belief in demons with childhood fears and imply that guiding institutions (either secular medicine or the right kind of church) are needed to keep these fears from resurfacing.

The irony of this discourse is that an atavistic return of demons directly contradicted the secularization narrative, which predicted an inexorable march toward scientific skepticism and what sociologist Max Weber called "the disenchantment of the world" (*entzauberung der welt*). An epidemic of possession was not supposed to be possible in the late twentieth century. But rather than reassessing the secularization narrative, some spoke as if horror movies had *broken modernity*, undoing progress that had been underway since the Enlightenment. Dr. James L. Foy was a psychiatrist at Georgetown University. Georgetown was inundated with calls about demonic possession, and at least one person was admitted to the university's hospital after watching *The Exorcist*. Dr. Foy declared: "It suddenly seems ironical that the profession has labored for the past 400 years persuading troubled persons that the Devil hypothesis is pure hokum and that they had better examine more closely the hidden motivations and consequences of irrational acts . . . . The rising epidemic of cases of possession will find its natural explanation in brain disorders, hysterical phenomena, dissociated mental states, and just plain psychoses. Freud and Jung, where are you when we really need you?"[41] Predictably, these jeremiads linking horror movies to the decline of Western civilization only generated further interest in the films. In fact, condemnations from psychiatrists likely primed audiences to have more extreme reactions, fueling the very phenomenon they claimed to oppose.

Rosemary's Baby

By 1967, Satanic conspiracies were already an established trope featured in the novels of Dennis Wheatley and such horror films as *The Seventh Victim* (1943). What made *Rosemary's Baby* stand out was its realism. Truman Capote called Ira Levin's 1967 novel "a darkly brilliant tale of modern devilry that, like James's *The Turn of the Screw*, induces the reader to believe the unbelievable."[42] When William Castle was offered the movie rights, he asked his wife, Ellen, to read the novel. Ellen told him, "You're going to have trouble with the Church," to which Castle replied, "Even if they ban it, Catholics will go."[43] Castle had a reputation for promoting gimmicky horror films, such as *The Tingler* (1959), about a parasite that attaches itself to the spine and must be killed by screaming. For this film, Castle installed special vibrating theater seats that activated when actor Vincent Price turned to the audience and yelled, "Scream! Scream for your lives!" Castle saw *Rosemary's Baby* as his opportunity to direct a "serious" film. Although the studio would not let him direct, he was able to form an amicable partnership with Polanski. *Rosemary's Baby* premiered on June 15, 1968, and it soon generated $30 million.

Historian W. Scott Poole noted that this film "managed to place in a single, disturbing package many of America's cultural and religious anxieties."[44] The tragedy of birth defects caused in the 1950s and 1960s by the anti-nauseant thalidomide likely informed the film's reception. But the film also stoked religious fears about Satanism, the Devil, and the Antichrist. In fact, the first reviews called it "the best advertisement for Satanism ever made."[45] The journal *Sight and Sound* noted that belief is what drives the story: "The film is about a girl who is trapped in a reality which she cannot believe. She must choose between not believing what appears to be real or believing what cannot be real." But Rosemary's choice was really the audience's choice: "Yet at the same time the audience cannot accept what is being presented as real, because for centuries we have believed that the birth of the anti-christ is a detestable lie."[46] This comment demonstrates how the secularization narrative raised the stakes around the unholy trinity: Science was supposed to render films like *Rosemary's Baby* laughable, yet somehow the narrative of triumphant science only made them more compelling. Hal Lindsey's apocalyptic book, *The Late Great Planet Earth* (1971), would soon become a bestseller, proving that many people never stopped taking the idea of the Antichrist seriously.

As predicted, the Catholic Church did not like the film. The National Catholic Office for Motion Pictures—formally the League of Decency—gave *Rosemary's Baby* a "C" for Condemned even as they praised Polanski's directing:

> Because of several scenes of nudity this contemporary horror story about devil worship would qualify for a condemned rating. Much more serious, however, is the perverted use which the film makes of fundamental Christian beliefs, especially the events surrounding the birth of Christ, and its mockery of religious persons and practices. The very technical excellence of the film serves to intensify its defamatory nature.[47]

And in London, the film was censored on the grounds that it contained "elements of kinky sex associated with back magic."[48]

In his memoir *Step Right Up! I'm Gonna Scare the Pants Off America*, William Castle described how he began to receive as many as fifty death threats a day, containing such statements as, "You have unleashed evil on the world. You will not live long enough to reap your rewards"; "*Rosemary's Baby* is filth and YOU will die as a result. Lover of Satan, Purveyor of Evil, you have sold your soul. *Die. Die. Die.*"; and "Bastard! Believer in Witchcraft. Worshiper at the Shrine of Satanism. My prediction is you will slowly rot during a long and painful illness which you have brought upon yourself." On the night of Halloween, Castle fainted and had to be hospitalized—the result of uremic poisoning caused by kidney stones. After the first surgery, he awoke shouting, "Rosemary, for *God's sake*, drop that knife!" While at the hospital he learned that Christopher Komeda, who composed the film's score, had died from injuries suffered while skiing.

Then came the Manson family murders. In addition to the murder of Polanski's wife, a number of strange coincidences seemed to link the events to the film. One of the victims had been named "Rosemary." The group's senseless crimes implied some ritualistic motivation. Polanski told Lt. Earl Deemer of the Los Angeles Police, "I wouldn't be surprised if I were the target . . . It could be some kind of witchcraft, you know."[49] In a negative review that appeared in *Film Quarterly* a few months before the Manson murders,

Robert Chapetta complained that the witches were "not frightening, but an absurd lot, rather like a small far-out California religious sect."[50] But the Manson family *had* been a far-out California sect, and they *were* frightening. In fact, *Rosemary's Baby* seems to have shaped the way the public interpreted the Manson family—not as a confused group of drug-addled criminals, but as an organized Satanic cult. Within a month of Manson's arrest, the *Los Angeles Herald Examiner* ran the front-page headline, "Hippie Commune Witchcraft Blood Rites Told." The accompanying article contained rumors about witchcraft cults and animal sacrifices and marked an important step in the beginning of the Satanic Panic.[51]

Castle wrote of the murders, "Again life was imitating the picture. When would it stop?"[52] He linked the murders with his health problems and Komeda's death to suggest that the film was cursed—possibly by literal witches. He told writer John Brosnan:

> That sort of thing never happened on any of my other horror films, but the ones I had made before *Rosemary* were on a superficial level. They didn't deal with the devil or the occult, they were cheap, *fun* films. But I am super-stitious and I do believe in the devil. If one believes in God, and I do very strongly believe in God, one must automatically believe in the devil. And I do believe that the film, which I lived through and almost *died* through, was controlled by some unexplainable force which was rather frightening. And having spoken to the people who worked on *The Exorcist* I heard that apparently the same thing happened there.[53]

Castle's claims of a curse can fairly be interpreted as yet another gimmick to promote a horror film, and it is impossible to know how much of his story in *Step Right Up!* is exaggerated. But his interview with Brosnan is a master class in transtextual anchoring: Castle offers a metatextual reflection on his film, before anchoring this story to legends about *The Exorcist*. For good measure, he suggests those who believe in God are obliged to heed his story. These sorts of maneuvers blurred the lines between film and reality and enhanced the cultural influence of supernatural horror films.

The most obvious consequence of *Rosemary's Baby* was that it helped to spark the Satanic Panic. In his review, Chapetta opined, "To begin with, any reasonable person's response to the ending is likely to be: but there are no witches."[54] Chapetta complained that witches are only believable in a fan-tastic or exotic setting. But increasingly, Americans were worried that a conspiracy of witches might be living among them. On *The Tonight Show Starring Johnny Carson*, Polanski explained that the film was having trouble getting past British censors because "there is quite a lot of this particular kind of witchcraft going on in Britain today."[55] In 1985, ABC's *20/20* aired a special entitled, "The Devil Worshippers," raising the alarm of Satanic Panic. It showed a full minute of footage from *Rosemary's Baby* while the narrator intoned, "The zeal of these fictional devil-worshippers is strikingly similar to that of real-life Satanists." David Frankfurter notes that an important effect the film had on the popular imagination is that it migrated demonological themes from the sphere of religion to that of secular authorities such as therapists, psychiatrists, and police.[56] And because Rosemary's husband, Guy Woodhouse, strikes a deal with the witches in exchange for success as an actor, it also linked Satanic conspiracies with celebrity. In 2020, QAnon conspiracy theorists began to claim that Tom Hanks was part of a Satanic cabal engaged in child sex trafficking. Hanks, according to these rumors, was essentially the real-life Guy Woodhouse, harming the innocent in exchange for fame.

Another consequence was its influence on Western occulture. Nikolas Schreck wrote that "*Rosemary's Baby* became a kind of blueprint for the occult renaissance of the late 1960s, quite unintentionally placing the Hollywood seal of approval on the Black Arts. Putting the cart before the horse, both occultists and Christians of different stripes have looked in the film for hidden magical messages and authentic Satanic lore."[57] In 1970, writer Arthur Lyons published *The Second Coming: Satanism in America* based on his encounters with self-described Satanists. Lyons describes going with a Satanist to purchase lard and then returning to his home where the coven put "tannis root" in an electric blender: Tannis root and lard produced a hallucinogenic "flying ointment."[58] Whatever Lyons witnessed was not the grinding of tannis root because there is no such herb: it was invented by Ira Levin. This was likely a form of pseudo-ostension, bringing the film to life for the author's benefit.

In a 2006 interview for *New York* magazine, serial killer David Berkowitz reflected on his teenage years, "I was obsessed with 'Rosemary's Baby.' I felt like it was speaking directly to me."[59] He attributed his fascination with the film to a demon that "has been with him since birth" and is ultimately responsible for his crimes. Here, the lore surrounding *Rosemary's Baby* and Berkowitz's own fascination with it became evidence in this narrative he told about himself.

Malachi York, founder of a black new religious movement called the Nuwaubian Nation, took the idea that *Rosemary's Baby* contains occult secrets to its logical conclusion by claiming it was not fiction at all. In his book *Leviathan: 666* (1984) York wrote:

> In June 6, 1966, Satan gave birth to his son in the western hemisphere (right here in New York). We the black and Latin populace did not even know what was going on. The Devil has camouflaged these factual events in a series of movies, and has told you the truth without you even realizing it! The first movie that dealt with the birth of his son was *Rosemary's Baby* . . . . Rosemary was not a fictitious character, she was a real Amorite. The name Rosemary (Satan's Mother) was chosen because it symbolizes the ancestral background of the physical Devil, the Amorites.[60]

Although York's book is an obscure text, this fact–fiction reversal is a profound example of *The Exorcist* effect.

The Exorcist

The Exorcist emerged as a Catholic rebuttal to *Rosemary's Baby*. Throughout the process of writing his novel and creating the film adaptation, Blatty was encouraged and supported by Catholic priests who took offense at Polanski's depiction of Satan triumphing over a godless world. These priests wanted to remind the public that both God and demons really existed, and they influenced how Blatty articulated "the message" of his story as a statement about "the mystery of goodness." Prior to *The Exorcist*, Blatty wrote comedies, but he had harbored an interest in exorcism since 1949 when he was a junior at Georgetown University and *The Washington Post* reported on an exorcism of a young boy in nearby Mount Rainier, Maryland. Father Eugene Gallagher discussed the case in Blatty's New Testament class. On May 10, 1950, Georgetown hosted a talk by Edward Hughes, a Catholic priest from Mount Rainier who had participated in one of the boy's exorcisms. This would have been around the time of Blatty's graduation.[61] Today, it is known that the boy was Ronald Hunkeler (1935–2020) and that he was from Cottage City, not Mount Rainier. Hunkeler's problems were serious enough to warrant hospitalization and, after an unsuccessful exorcism at Georgetown University Hospital, his family visited relatives in St. Louis, where a second round of exorcisms conducted at the Alexian Brothers Hospital was deemed successful. It was repeatedly stated that these exorcisms were "the basis" of Blatty's story, but this is only partly true. *Rosemary's Baby*, combined with a downturn in the market for comedy writing, inspired Blatty to finally write something about exorcism. In 1967, the year that *Rosemary's Baby* was published, he met Mark Jaffe of Bantam books at a New Year's Eve party. He pitched a novel about a child who kills an adult and makes a courtroom plea of demonic possession.[62] As Blatty recalled, it took Jaffe less than two minutes to reply, "I'll publish that."[63]

Blatty was given a small advance and began researching demonology and exorcism. He reached out to Thomas V. Bermingham, who agreed to help with his research but warned, "I don't want another *Rosemary's Baby*."[64] Bermingham went on to be a technical consultant for the film and was given a small role. Through the Jesuits, Blatty was put in touch with William S. Bowdern, a Jesuit from St. Louis and one of the lead exorcists in the Hunkeler case. In an interview, Blatty explained, "Fr. Bowdern wanted to help me because he felt that a book about the reality of possession would be beneficial to the public, whether it was a non-fiction account as I'd once suggested or a novelized version."[65] However, Bowdern's cardinal, as well as the Hunkeler family, made clear that they did not want a non-fiction account of the exorcism written: it had to be a novel. Blatty also told the *St. Louis Post-Dispatch*, "Had I not heard from (Bowdern), I don't think I would have written the book. I was a comedic writer then, 'A Shot in the Dark,' that sort of thing."[66]

After completing his research, Blatty retreated to a cabin in Lake Tahoe where he wrote *The Exorcist* in just ten months. (According to one source, he was aided by amphetamines.)[67] The novel was initially a flop until Blatty received a last-minute invitation to appear on *The Dick Cavett Show*. The other guests all either canceled or gave poor performances such that that Blatty was given forty-five minutes to pitch his novel. As a result, *The Exorcist* became an overnight bestseller, moving four million copies before the release of the film adaptation. It has since sold over thirteen million copies.

Some Catholics embraced Blatty's novel as an alternative to *Rosemary's Baby*. Father William O'Malley was a drama instructor at a Jesuit high school in New York. He wrote a review of Blatty's novel, praising the theme of transcendence hidden in the horror, and sent Blatty a copy. Blatty was so flattered that O'Malley was cast in the film adaptation as Father Dyer. (O'Malley required the approval of his Jesuit provincial who agreed, in part, because *The Exorcist* was presented as a spiritual film.)[68] O'Malley explained, "'Rosemary's Baby' treated evil like an interesting anomaly in a dull city. [*The Exorcist*] raises large questions, and leaves them open."[69]

The idea that demonic evil suggests the possibility of a merciful God—even in the face of scientific skepticism—is an important theme of *The Exorcist* and part of what makes it a good novel. However, as first Blatty and then Friedkin continued to emphasize the "spiritual" dimension of *The Exorcist* there is a sense that this was a form of metatextual reflection; like the rumors that the film was "cursed," this became a story about the story that functioned to heighten interest in the film—especially in response to such critics as *Time*'s R. Z. Sheppard, who deemed it "a pretentious, tasteless, abominably written, redundant pastiche of superficial theology, comic-book psychology, Grade C movie dialogue and Grade Z scatology."[70] When the Jesuit magazine *America* put out a special issue on *The Exorcist* in 1974, Blatty contributed an article entitled "There is Goodness in The Exorcist," explaining that the mystery of goodness is "the point all critics miss."[71] Friedkin told *The Los Angeles Times*, "Blatty wrote 'The Exorcist' to persuade those who do not believe that there is a case to be made for the supernatural and to offer the possibility that there is a supernatural force of evil in the universe whose game plan is to convince us that he does not exist."[72] In a 2011 interview Blatty stated, "I have no recollection of intending to frighten anyone at any point in time."[73] However, there are some signs that Blatty wrote *The Exorcist* primarily for money and only later came to interpret it as a spiritual manifesto. In a 1975 interview for *Literature/Film Quarterly*, Friedkin stated bluntly, "[*The Exorcist is*] not literature, it's a commercial book; Billy Blatty wrote it to write a best seller, and he did . . . . Trash makes the best movies."[74] When we asked Grady Hendrix about this discrepancy, he answered, "Everyone buys into their own hype."[75] It is significant, though, that Blatty's brand of "hype" was inspired by priests such as Bermingham, Bowdern, and O'Malley.

Every studio in Hollywood turned down the movie rights to *The Exorcist*. Producer Paul Monash made Blatty an offer, but Blatty snuck into his office and discovered Monash had already drafted a contract selling the rights to Warner Brothers. Monash also wanted to make major changes, including cutting out all the priests. Blatty copied the contract and used it to cut a deal directly with Warner Brothers for $641,000. He also retained creative control.[76] By this time, *The Exorcist* was selling about seven thousand copies a week. It was also around this time that Blatty acquired a journal written by Raymond Bishop, one of the priests who had assisted Father Bowdern in St.

Louis. Although it describes the exorcism and the symptoms of possession in detail, Blatty told interviewers it had little influence on the screenplay.[77]

It was Blatty who picked Friedkin to direct. Friedkin stated that *The Exorcist* "had to be a totally realistic view of inexplicable events. It had to be absolutely flawless in its presentation of real people against real backgrounds."[78] In *The Exorcist*, Jesuits are depicted drinking beer and smoking along with other humanizing activities. Some real-life priests found this portrayal refreshing. Father Thomas J. Dove commented, "Of all the Hollywood films I've seen that include priests—usually they are a 55-year-old Irishman with a pot, the typical Hollywood monsignor—in this film, the priests are human beings."[79] In addition, three Jesuit priests were hired as consultants: Bermingham, O'Malley, and John Nicola. At the time Nicola was completing a doctoral thesis on exorcism in Rome. He reportedly suggested Blatty revise the script because the demon's language was not sufficiently obscene. Nicola went on to advise psychiatrists who believed their patients needed exorcism.[80] The involvement of these priests lent authenticity to the film, but it was also part of a long tradition of horror films deploying "experts" as a strategy of metatextual reflection to blur the boundaries between film and reality.

There were critics of Friedkin's adaptation. Jack Nitsche, who composed most of the soundtrack for *The Exorcist* commented, "William Friedkin doesn't give a shit about the occult—it's just a hot commodity as far as he's concerned."[81] Georgetown faculty member Edward Ingebretsen opined, "What is theological meditation in Blatty is technological *Grand Guignol* in Friedkin."[82] But overall, *The Exorcist* was a runaway success. It was released the day after Christmas in 1973, and in January 1974 it accounted for fourteen percent of all box office sales. It was the first horror film ever to be nominated for best picture. It also received Academy nominations for best director, best actress, best supporting actor, and best supporting actress. It won academy awards for best sound and best screenplay adaptation. Blatty claimed that *The Exorcist* also won an award for best special effects but that opponents of the film canceled the category rather than cede a third award.[83] Despite his Oscar wins, he commented, "The Academy should fold its tents and go back to baking apple strudel or whatever they can do well."[84]

Before discussing the phenomenon that formed around *The Exorcist*, it is necessary to discuss metatextual reflection surrounding this film. Friedkin once stated, "The only thing that causes people to go to the movies is word of mouth."[85] There may be no other film where the audience was responding to the story *about* the film to the same degree as with *The Exorcist*. Shooting for *The Exorcist* began on August 14, 1972, by which time Warner Brothers had already teamed up with publishers Harper & Row on a promotional campaign to keep interest in *The Exorcist* at a fever pitch. In doing so, they were inadvertently aided by Pope Paul VI, who on November 15, 1972, gave a speech to an audience of over six thousand that began: "What are the greatest needs of the Church today? Do not let our answer surprise you as being over-simple or even superstitious and unreal: one of the greatest needs is defense against that evil which is called the Devil."[86] The pope went on to warn that Satan is "a living spiritual being, perverted and perverting" whose power was growing due to both popular interest in the occult and scientific rejection of Christianity. For some, it seemed the pope was endorsing the upcoming film. David Bartholomew of *Cinefantastique* opined, "With these words, the Pope shifted from the spiritual into the secular ad-pub business."[87]

Press releases for the film emphasized that *The Exorcist* was based on a true story that occurred in 1949.[88] This idea was repeated in two books published in 1974: *William Peter Blatty: On The Exorcist from Novel to Film* and *The Story Behind The Exorcist* by Peter Travers and Stephanie Ann Reiff, respectively. There have since been dozens of books and documentaries claiming to depict "the true story" behind *The Exorcist*. Blatty stated that since Ronald Hunkeler's family had not wanted the story to be novelized, he had changed the possessed character from a boy into a girl. But *The Exorcist* was really an original story that borrowed only a few elements from the Hunkeler case.

The idea of a possessed child was certainly derived from the Hunkeler case, as was the use of a Ouija board. Hunkeler had been exposed to the Ouija board by his "Aunt Tillie" who had an interest in Spiritualism. Tillie died shortly before the Hunkeler family began experiencing what they interpreted as poltergeist activity. Before concluding that this was a case of demonic possession, some family members speculated that Tillie's spirit might be causing the disturbances. Catholic authorities had warned that the Ouija board was spiritually dangerous as early as 1919. However, Blatty experimented with a Ouija board and had conversations with ghosts that lasted for hours.[89] Modern associations of the Ouija board with occult danger are owed largely to *The Exorcist*.[90]

The other element derived from the Hunkeler case is the trope of messages appearing spontaneously on the possessed person's skin. In the film, the words "Help Me" appear on Regan's torso. Hunkeler repeatedly had messages appearing on his body in the form of anomalous scratches that spelled out such words as "Hell." These messages often functioned as an indirect way for Hunkeler to advise his family and the exorcists. For example, when they discussed returning Hunkeler to school, scratches appeared on his chest that read "No School." On at least one occasion, William Van Roo, a St. Louis Jesuit who assisted in the exorcism, saw Hunkeler scratching words into his own chest and noted how long his fingernails were.[91] However, Blatty called the messages "unquestionably paranormal," noting that some messages appeared on the boy's back, suggesting he was not creating them himself.[92] Skeptics Joe Nickell and Robert Bartholomew counter, "Such feats are well within the realm of possibility by a determined youth—with or without a wall mirror."[93]

The other case that influenced Blatty occurred in 1928 in Earling, Iowa, and involved a woman described as Anna Ecklund or Emma Schmidt.[94] An account of this exorcism was published in Germany and translated into English in 1945 as *Begone Satan! A Soul-Stirring Account of Diabolical Possession*. The story became a sensation and it was featured in *Time* magazine the following year. Many tropes in *The Exorcist* are found in *Begone Satan!*. Schmidt (who was in her mid-forties by 1928) had to be tied to a bed during exorcisms. She was described as being able to leap to impossible heights and cling to walls in ways that bordered on levitation. *Begone Satan!* also dedicates a great deal of description to her vomiting, which she did ten to twenty times a day. The author comments, "These came in quantities that were humanly speaking impossible to lodge in a normal being."[95]

Blatty wrote of the pamphlet, "I instinctively felt it could not have been invented," but also that, "The tone of the pamphlet seemed so overly credulous, so replete with pietistic asides and exclamations, that it turned me off."[96] However, Blatty could not have claimed his story was inspired by this case even if he wanted to because another novel—*The Case Against Satan* (1962) by Ray Russell—had already done this. Russell's novel was apparently written a decade too soon. Nevertheless, audiences were able to make the connection between *The Exorcist* and the Earling case. Michael W. Schwartz, pastor at St. Joseph's Catholic Church in Earling, told reporters, "At the time [1928], it wasn't considered to be a big thing. Now that the movie and book versions of 'The Exorcist' have focused attention on exorcism, however, I've been receiving letters and phone calls asking about it."[97] (Inevitably someone did base a film on the Earling case. The forgettable *The Exorcism of Anna Ecklund* premiered in 2016.)

The Exorcist also refers to specific books read by Father Karras, suggesting that Blatty researched them, too. These include *The Devils of Loudun* by

Aldous Huxley (1952), *A Seventeenth-Century Demonological Neurosis* by Sigmund Freud (1922), and *Possession* (1921) by psychologist Traugott Konstanin Oesterreich. Oesterreich's work is cited several times throughout *The Exorcist*. Richard Woods accuses Blatty of abusing his sources, noting that Oesterreich did not believe in literal possession.[98] It seems the real purpose of mentioning these texts is as a form of transtextual anchoring: alluding to non-fiction work on possession suggests to the reader that such things really happen. Blatty also noted that the film's ending—in which the demon exits and Regan enters Father Karras, was precedented by exorcisms at Loudun, France, in 1634.[99] In that case, Jesuit Jean-Joseph Surin believed that he had himself become possessed and even leapt out of a second-story window. Unlike Father Karras, he survived.

Most of the other elements of the story simply came from Blatty's own imagination or personal experience. He had learned of the Mesopotamian entity Pazuzu while working for the United States Information Agency in Lebanon. Chris McNeil was based on his friend, the actress Shirley MacLaine. Lankester Merrin was based on the Jesuit paleontologist Tielhard de Chardin. (De Chardin never wrote on exorcism but among the Jesuits was rumored to have had a lifelong interest in the subject.)[100] And Damian Karras was based largely on Blatty himself.

John Nicola told reporters that *The Exorcist* was, essentially, a faithful account of the Hunkeler case, claiming the novel and film were both "pretty near the truth and, though dramatized, about 80 percent accurate."[101] But William Van Roo, who witnessed Hunkeler's exorcism, told *St. Louis Today*, "I didn't read Blatty's book; I didn't want to. I personally felt that the movie was utterly disgusting, utterly false and quite dangerous because of the effect it might have on emotionally disturbed persons. The movie has been melodramatized, especially the ending, which was utterly absurd."[102] Similarly, Andrew Kelly, an English professor from UCLA who once aspired to be a Jesuit and wrote a book on the devil, opined, "I think it's really important to bring out the truth behind this because as I get the publicity, the film is based on a real case and everyone jumps to the conclusion that everything that goes on in the film, all the strange happenings, were really verified. In reality, the film is nothing like the case at all."[103] In 1988, Blatty conceded, "I, in fact, did not base my book on either of the publicized North American cases [Schmidt and Hunkeler]."[104] But this admission suggests that the narrative that *The Exorcist* was "based on a true story" was always more of a promotional device than a literal reality.

The other story about *The Exorcist* was that the film was cursed. In part, the curse legend began as an attempt to turn numerous setbacks in filming into an asset rather than a liability. There was a fire of unknown origin that destroyed a set causing a six-week delay. The statue of Pazuzu was lost in transit to Iraq and ended up in Hong Kong. There were also several deaths and injuries connected to the film, most notably actor Jack McGowan, who died shortly after performing the role of Burke Dennings. Of course, the longer it took to complete filming, the more opportunity there was for accidents. By the time filming ended, *The Exorcist* was three months behind schedule and as much as $6 million over budget.[105] As Blatty recalls, the legend began when a *Newsweek* reporter asked Friedkin whether the film was cursed: "Well, Billy [Friedkin] couldn't believe his incredible luck. He was being offered some amazing—and free—publicity and promotion for the movie, and he instantly responded, 'Yes, I do. Exactly.' "[106]

At one point, Friedkin asked Bermingham to do an exorcism on the set. Bermingham explained that he could not do an exorcism and that these were, after all, just accidents. In an interview he recalled thinking, "I guess they want me to do a Catholic thing" and performed a blessing. He also told the cast and crew that they were made in the image of likeness of God and their efforts "mirror the creativity of God."[107] The story more often told, though, is that the set had to be exorcized because of the curse.

Another rumor was that the film's soundtrack contains the actual voices of demons that had been recorded during an exorcism. In an interview, Friedkin explained that a Jesuit provincial in New York had given him a cassette recording of an actual exorcism of a fourteen-year-old boy in Rome.[108] Friedkin did not say he actually put these sounds in *The Exorcist*, only that he tried to emulate them. Either way, this story reinforced the idea that actual supernatural events closely resembled Friedkin's film.

There were also numerous rumors about Linda Blair, who played Regan: she was literally possessed, her parents made a pact with the devil, her mother had been struck blind and her father dumb, she'd given birth to a child born without eyes, and that she keeps a room in her basement where she performs black masses.[109] Others—aware of Blatty's connection to Shirley MacLaine—claimed that MacLaine or her daughter, Sachi, were possessed. MacLaine reported that she had to take her daughter out of school because other children feared she had demons.[110] These rumors were another metanarrative layer blurring the boundaries between fiction and reality.

Religious figures began ascribing supernatural significance to the film. Hal Lindsey told *Newsweek*, "It is setting the stage for the future attack of Satan."[111] Joe DeLouise, a Chicago-based psychic who claimed to have performed several demonic exorcisms, warned the tabloid *The Tattler* that the film was so realistic that viewers might "open themselves up psychically" to demonic attacks.[112] Ed Fitch, the high priest of a Gardnerian Wiccan coven, told an interviewer that spirit entities really exist and that they could use this film as "a catalyst" to possess people. He explained, "We who are involved in the occult believe that 'like attracts like'—the film is vivid and convincing, and the audience sympathizes and empathizes with the innocent girl. What happens to her could happen to them . . . . The film is entirely too effective. It is enough to cause serious psychoses or actual possession in some cases. Frankly, it's very dangerous."[113] Fitch advised viewers to bring religious objects and other forms of spiritual protection with them to the theater. All this discourse primed audiences to have extraordinary experiences when they finally saw the film.

The Exorcist was first released in only twenty-four cities, mostly in art house theaters. Initially, the studio thought it might be better received as an art house offering. However, the demand was so great that it was soon shown in theaters all over the country—especially after crowds of urban, working-class people arrived at posh art theaters, demanding to see the film. Only hours after the film premiered, movie critics in Washington, DC, watched theater employees remove a young girl from the audience and place her in an ambulance.[114] Similar incidents happened all over the country in what Stephen King described as a "two-month possession jag."[115] People stood in line for hours to buy tickets. In Los Angeles, Blatty and Friedkin began paying $600 a night for caterers to deliver coffee to those waiting in line. In New York City, people in line started fires on the sidewalk to keep warm. In February, when New York's Paramount theater canceled their last showing, the crowd mobbed the theater in protest.[116] In Chicago, police had be stationed outside the Gateway Theater to keep order before each showing.[117] On New Year's day 1974, Washington, DC, became the first city ever to ban minors from seeing an R-rated film after the US District Attorney's office barred anyone under seventeen from being admitted to see *The Exorcist*. Officers from the police department morals division warned the management of the Cinema Theater that arrests would be made if any more tickets were sold for use by minors.[118] Executive producer Noel Marshall stated, " 'The Exorcist' is a 'happening,' not a picture."[119]

Theaters all over America reported people fleeing the theater, fainting, or vomiting. While some of these reports were exaggerated, many incidents were well documented. A reporter for *The Los Angeles Times* interviewed a man who had left the film to seek refuge in the lobby. He tried to explain his experience: "I guess I let it get to me. It just psyched me out. I've never walked out of a movie in my life, but this one keeps building and building— relentlessly. There's no relief. I just had to get out of there."[120] In Berkeley, a man charged the screen in an attempt to fight the demon.[121] In Denver, a man walked straight from the theater to the Cathedral of Immaculate Conception, arriving barefoot and shirtless. Pastor James W. Raspy recalled, "We called an ambulance but he was so upset that it took the police, the attendants and two priests to get him into it."[122] One viewer attempted to sue Warner Brothers after he fainted and hit a theater seat, breaking his jaw. He claimed subliminal messages in the film were responsible for his fainting and Warner Brothers settled out of court.[123]

Even in 1974, many people speculated that these reactions had less to do with the film itself and more with the fact that audiences were primed to behave this way. A cartoon in the Associated Press depicted a couple waiting to buy tickets to *The Exorcist*; the box office attendant tells them, "Sorry the seats are all taken, but we're selling tickets to the lobby to watch the audience."[124] In response to claims that the film induced psychiatric problems, film critic Hollis Alpert explained, "The thing is, *The Exorcist* became a sensation and a fad. A few of the more suggestible heard about the fainting and the vomiting (much played up by television talk shows) and promptly fainted and vomited."[125] Eugene Kennedy, a priest and psychologist at Loyola commented, "As to the celebrated passing out and throwing up that occurred during the picture's well-advertised horrors, a group of college students laughingly told me, 'If you had to wait in line for two hours in a lobby where everybody was smoking grass you'd get sick and pass out too.'"[126] Lending evidence to these theories, a letter to *The Los Angeles Times* stated, "I have not seen 'The Exorcist' but when I do I will be totally prepared to clutch my stomach and be shocked out of my skin. Anything less will be disappointing as hell."[127] And Ted Fishman, a man found standing in line in zero-degree weather told reporters, "We're here because we're nuts and because we want to be part of the madness."[128] The fan magazine *Cinefantastique* pointed out that similar reactions were reported when *Frankenstein* was screened in 1931: Ambulances allegedly awaited outside theaters and smelling salts had to be given to fainting audience members. However, the fact that the reaction to *The Exorcist* had precedent does not negate its sociological significance. The phenomenon surrounding the film resembled what sociologist Émile Durkheim called "collective effervescence." The social reality—as much as the film itself—inspired people to act and think differently. Some church authorities viewed these responses favorably, while the medical community reacted with alarm.

Several Protestant denominations picketed the film. In Washington, DC, Methodists passed out leaflets to the crowd asking whether "you will be controlled by the spirit of darkness or by the spirit of God?"[129] In Rock Island, Illinois, the Bethel Assembly of God Church held a public book burning of *The Exorcist* and other "Satanic" texts.[130] In Boston, a coalition of Protestant leaders sought to stop screenings of the film. Mrs. Rita Warren filed suit with the state Supreme Court, arguing that theaters must be prohibited from screening *The Exorcist* because it is blasphemous and obscene. Warren was arrested for protesting in front of Boston's Sack 57 theater and charged with trespassing.[131] Rev. A. Patterson Lee of Boston's Fremont Temple Baptist warned, "This kind of shock therapy could easily convert our theaters into brain-washing boxes, where the audience is no longer spectator, but guinea pig to be turned on, worked up and gone over."[132] This quote is significant because it demonstrates that discourse around *The Exorcist* was colored by larger debates about "brainwashing," which had come to the fore in the 1970s as a result of a panic about new religious movements. Interestingly, Steven Hassan, who dropped out of college to join the Unification Church before leaving that group and becoming a "cult deprogrammer" recalled that the church rented a movie theater to show *The Exorcist* to the congregation: according to Hassan they were told that this was what would happen to them if they left the Unification Church.[133]

The Catholic Church, while divided, was far more supportive. The US Catholic Conference's Division of Film and Broadcasting gave it a rating of "A-4," meaning it was suitable for adults, but with some reservations. *Catholic News*, the official newspaper of the Archdiocese of New York, described it as "a deeply spiritual film" and applauded its "well-researched authenticity" and its characterization of Karras and Merrin as "powerful, holy men." *The National Catholic Register* entered it into a list of pro-Catholic films.[134] John Nicola, one of the priests who served as a technical advisor, vacillated on the value of the film. Initially he stated, "The Devil's greatest asset is the doubt people have about his existence. If this movie makes people more aware of the supernatural, or spiritualism, of the possibility of possession, it will do great good."[135] But after the film became a social phenomenon he reflected, "If it were up to me now to decide whether to release the film to the general public, I don't think I would do it because of the danger of hysteria. I think it could rival what we had in Europe in the Middle Ages with St. Vitus's dance."[136]

Whether religious leaders praised or condemned the film, there were wide reports of people being frightened back to church. Many of these church visits seem to have been motivated by curiosity rather than religious conversion. Georgetown University was flooded with *Exorcist* fans. Executive vice president Edmund G. Ryan commented, "People are coming from all over to see the chapel, to hear mass, to discuss exorcism."[137] Arthur Dekruyter of Christ Church in Oak Brook, Illinois, gave a sermon on *The Exorcist* and reported that hundreds had to be turned away.[138] Maxwell Whyte, a United Apostolic pastor from Scarborough, Ontario, Canada, suggested that God had permitted this film to be made so that people would return to church. By 1974, Whyte had already been casting out demons in deliverance ministries for twenty-five years. He added, "The effect of this film could launch a new inquiry into demonic powers and what they do to people."[139]

While religious authorities were divided over the significance of *The Exorcist*, medical authorities almost universally condemned it. The excitement surrounding the film was frequently described in medicalizing language as a fever, an infection, and an epidemic. Psychiatrists at Georgetown declared that watching the film was more damaging than hardcore pornography.[140] (One wonders whether they took offense at the way medical science and Georgetown hospital in particular are depicted in *The Exorcist*.) Louis Schlan, a psychiatrist and medical director of Riveredge Hospital in Forest Park, Illinois, told *Time* and *Newsweek* that the film was driving people mad and causing people to believe they were possessed. He described admitting six patients "straight from the theater," two of which had to be put under restraint. Schlan claimed none of these people had a history of psychiatric problems but now either thought they were possessed or had developed "a continuing fear of demons in their children."[141]

Psychiatrist James Bozzutto published an article in *The Journal of Nervous and Mental Disease* arguing that *The Exorcist* had necessitated a new diagnosis called "cinema neurosis." The article profiled four individuals who sought medical help after viewing *The Exorcist*. "Norman," eighteen, was discovered by his father at four or five in the morning, clutching his Bible in the dark, afraid he would be possessed by the devil. Uncertain what to do, his father brought him to the emergency room. "James," twenty-three, sought the help of a priest a month after watching the film; the priest referred him to a psychiatric outpatient clinic. "Martha," twenty-two, sought psychiatric help because she was suffering from insomnia. She seemed torn between her strict Catholic upbringing and her decision to cohabit with her boyfriend and the film had somehow aggravated this tension. "Lyle," twenty-four, was the only black person profiled. He had made three visits to the emergency room in the month after viewing *The Exorcist*, before being referred to a psychiatric clinic. He feared his daughter might be possessed and—echoing *Rosemary's Baby*—suspected his therapist "may be involved with the Devil." He had also suffered neck pains since watching *The Exorcist*, which he felt were connected to watching Regan's head spin around. Bozzuto concluded that the film was "directly related to traumatic neurosis in susceptible people."[142]

Hilde Mosse, a child psychiatrist from Manhattan, raised a different set of concerns about *The Exorcist*: "The idea that we can solve our problems by magic instead of by rational solutions is destructive. I lived through this before Hitler came to power. He said, 'Listen to the language of your pure Germanic blood, your unconscious.' The Jews in Germany then became the devil to be exorcized. The only thing *The Exorcist* can do is to pull young people down to a primitive level."[143] While more measured, Mosse also equated the excitement over *The Exorcist* with atavism.

An odd feature of this psychiatric literature is that the psychiatrists cannot seem to help themselves from diagnosing Regan. Bozzuto notes the similarity of Regan's case with Freud's analysis of Christoph Haizmann, an actual seventeenth-century demoniac.[144] In a letter to *The Journal of the American Medical Association*, another psychiatrist noted the girl in Blatty's novel had symptoms resembling Tourette's syndrome.[145] Not only were these psychiatrists analyzing a *fictional* character, but within the story Regan is literally possessed by a demon. Apparently, the mental health threat posed by *The Exorcist* was such that even imaginary demons had to be explained away as medical problems.

With all the discourse surrounding *The Exorcist*, ostension was inevitable. Paulist fathers in Boston told *Newsweek* they were receiving an average of one call a day requesting an exorcism.[146] In Anaheim, a Pentecostal preacher began holding late-night services to cast demons out of people who had seen *The Exorcist*.[147] In Houston, workmen who had recently seen the film heard a house they had been hired to remodel had previously served as a Pagan church—they demanded an exorcism before they would complete the job. Richard Woods reported, "In less than six months, seven persons requested that I exorcize them, or rather, their demons, having been convinced (in at least four cases) that they were possessed after reading or hearing about *The Exorcist*." At the same time, students at Loyola were requesting more classes and lectures on demonology and the occult. Woods added, "Several of these people seemed to *want* to be possessed, as if that could make sense out of their lives."[148] He also related hearing about "informal" exorcisms from both his Catholic peers and Protestant pastors.

As with David Berkowitz and *Rosemary's Baby*, certain criminals were drawn to *The Exorcist*. The last letter the Zodiac Killer sent to *The San Francisco Chronicle* stated, "I saw and think 'The Exorcist' was the best saterical comidy [sic] that I have ever seen."[149] As a result, police staked out lines for the film, hoping the killer might reveal himself while waiting for a second viewing. In 1975, a British teenager named Nicholas Bell beat a nine-year-old girl to death. In explaining his senseless crime to the police, Bell stated, "It was not really me that did it, you know. There was something inside me. I want to see a priest. It is ever since I saw that film *The Exorcist*. I felt something take possession of me. It has been in me ever since."[150] After he was found guilty, Bell confessed that he had invented this explanation in the hopes he would be granted clemency.[151] Bell's defense was a form of pseudo-ostension that nevertheless contributed to the film's reputation.

Even today, *The Exorcist* functions as an ostensive text. Richard Gallagher is a psychiatrist on the faculty at Columbia University. He is also a member of the International Association of Exorcists and consults with the Catholic Church in cases of alleged possession. In 2020, he published his book, *Demonic Foes: My Twenty-Five Years as a Psychiatrist Investigating Possessions, Diabolic Attacks, and the Paranormal*, in which he states that Catholic demonology is essentially correct and that truly possessed people really do exhibit clairvoyance, levitation, and other supernatural abilities. Reflecting on his life, Gallagher identifies with Father Karras: "The personal transformation of Father Karras proved especially fascinating to me . . . . Like Father Karras, I have since walked in two worlds—the world of scientific psychiatric investigation and the world of exorcism."[152] *The Exorcist* is referenced extensively throughout Gallagher's description of actual events—diagnosed as either mental illness or actual demonic possession. This demonstrates how *The Exorcist* has become and remains a way of talking about and imagining the demonic in Western culture, even among highly educated people.

The Omen

In 1974, a group of fifty Baptists picketed a theater in Corpus Christi, Texas, where the lines for *The Exorcist* went around the block. One picketer bore a sign that said, "Today The Exorcist Tomorrow the Antichrist."[153] The youth minister who organized the picket admitted he had not seen the film; however, the sign's prediction was more right than he knew. Much as the Catholic Church sought to make a response to *Rosemary's Baby*, *The Omen* began as an effort to spread dispensationalist ideas about the Antichrist while simultaneously profiting on the coattails of *The Exorcist*. In fact, horror scholar Darryl Jones called *The Omen* "The Exorcist for Protestants."[154]

Robert Munger was an actor and advertising executive. He was also an evangelical Christian who had recently read Hal Lindsey's best-seller *The Late Great Planet Earth*. There was already a niche market of films, such as *A Thief in the Night* (1972), that were essentially horror movies but claimed to be accurate depictions of imminent tribulations predicted in the Bible. Munger approached producer Harvey Bernard about a film about the Antichrist. Munger's wife, Grace, later recalled, "He wanted people to know what the Bible said about the Antichrist." Similarly, Ted Baehr, founder of the Christian movie review site *Movieguide*, called Munger "a brilliant strategist," stating, "(He) wanted to communicate the good news of Jesus Christ in a creative way. 'The Omen' was his answer to doing that."[155] Bernard, in turn, tapped screenwriter David Seltzer to produce "a story about the devil."

Seltzer agreed to the project but was unenthusiastic. He described coming from an Orthodox Jewish family that did not believe in hell or the devil. He liked documentary filmmaking and acquiring new knowledge. He felt there was nothing to learn about the devil because, "The devil's not real."[156] In *The Omen*, diplomat Robert Thorn (Gregory Peck) learns that his son, Damian, is actually the son of Satan and destined to become the Antichrist. He consults an archaeologist who convinces him to ritualistically murder Damian by placing him on a church altar and stabbing him with an ancient set of daggers from the ruins of Megiddo in Israel. Thorn agrees to this plan after finding a birthmark on Damian's scalp resembling the number 666. Police shoot Thorn during the ritual and Damian is adopted by the president of the United States, bringing the world one step closer to the reign of the Antichrist. *The Omen* premiered on June 6, 1976 (6-6-6) and grossed over $4 million in its opening weekend, in part because it had a built-in audience. By the time it premiered, *The Late Great Planet Earth* had outsold every non-fiction book except for the Bible. A few weeks before the movie debuted, Seltzer wrote a noveliza-tion of his screenplay that sold 3.5 million copies.[157] *The Omen* inspired two sequels, which Seltzer refused to watch, as well as several forgettable made-for-television movies. There was also a re-make that premiered on June 6, 2006, and featured Mia Farrow, now playing Mrs. Baylock, the Antichrist's Satanic babysitter.

Regarding the first two films of the unholy trilogy, Seltzer stated, "I frankly don't think mine holds a candle to the other two, but I'm certainly honored to be in that company. I think that mine is derivative of both."[158] As with the other films, producers started a rumor that the film was cursed. Bernard took to wearing a cross on the set. He later stated, "I wasn't about to take any chances. The devil was at work and he didn't want that film made. We were dealing in areas we didn't know about and later on in the picture it got worse, worse and worse."[159] Similarly, Munger recalled, "I warned Harvey at the time. I said, 'If you make this movie you're going to have some problems. If the devil's greatest single weapon is to be invisible and you're going to do something which is going to take away his invisibility to millions of people, he's not going to want that to happen." There were, of course, incidents that could be attributed to a curse—namely the suicide of lead actor Gregory Peck's son, only two months before filming was scheduled to begin. (As a result, Peck had tremendous difficulty with the scene where his character attempts to murder Damian.) There was also a plane crash and a bombing by the Irish Republican Army that nearly harmed the cast and crew. Munger started a prayer chain for the cast and crew, ensuring that rumors of a curse were widely disseminated. A documentary entitled *The Curse of the Omen* (2005) featured exorcist Bob Larson, who warned, "The curse is still there and demons are still following everybody who was involved in it to this day."

Producers also invited metatextual reflection on the film with the poster's tagline: "If something frightening happens to you today, think about it: it could be The Omen." In other words, audiences were invited to use the film as a model through which to think about their own lives. The filmmakers agreed to have characters die in gruesome accidents, on the theory that the Devil does not want people to know he exists. But in making demonic ac-tivity look like coincidence, *The Omen* also opened audiences to the possi-bility that coincidences could be demonic in nature.

The Omen certainly influenced American religion but, despite Munger's intentions, it worked more to distort Biblical ideas than to spread them. In traditional Protestant dispensationalism, the reign of the Antichrist and the

apocalypse are part of God's plan, not something to be prevented. Prior to
The Omen, the Antichrist was not generally understood to be the son of the
Devil and there was less popular fixation on the number 666.[160] Certainly,
there is nothing in Christian tradition remotely like the daggers of Megiddo.

The Omen also invented Biblical prophecies. A priest named Father
Brennan attempts to convince Robert Thorn that his son is the Antichrist by
reciting a poem:

> When the Jews return to Zion / And a comet rips the sky
> And the Holy Roman Empire rises / Then You and I must die.
> From the eternal sea he rises, / Creating armies on either shore,
> Turning man against his brother / 'til man exists no more.

Then Brennan states, "The Book of Revelations predicted it all." In an interview, journalist Don Kaye told Seltzer, "[*The Omen*] also had me looking fe-
verishly through the Book of Revelation for that damn poem, until I found
out that you made it up yourself," to which Seltzer replied, "Yeah, I'm sorry.
I got in trouble with a lot of people for that."[161] The tradition of inventing
Bible prophecies continues in *The Omen III*, in which a prophecy is cited as
being from the Latin "Book of Hebron," which Damian calls "one of the more
obscure backwaters of the Septuagint Bible." Not only is there no such book,
but the Septuagint is written in Greek, not Latin.

There are also more subtle Biblical distortions. Thorn travels to the ruins
of Megiddo because "Armageddon"—a gathering of armies referenced in
Revelation—derives its name from "*Har Megiddo*." *Har* simply means mountain and *Megiddo* is the name of a settlement. Bible scholar Steve A. Wiggins
comments on this connection, "Megiddo is described as being south of
Jerusalem when it is actually well to the north. There seems to be no particular reason for this error other than failure to consult a map. [The archaeol-
ogist] also says Christianity started in Megiddo, which really isn't the case
since the final occupation of the site was nearly six centuries earlier than
Jesus."[162]

The greatest testament to *The Omen's* effect on Biblical literacy may have
come in 2019 when Amazon aired a television series based on the satirical
novel *Good Omens* (1990) by Terry Pratchett and Neil Gaiman. A far-right
Catholic group, called Tradition, Family, and Property, claimed the show
was mocking the Bible and making Satanism socially acceptable. They organized an online petition signed by twenty thousand people protesting the

show—which was erroneously addressed to Netflix, not Amazon. Despite this embarrassment, Tradition, Family, and Property declared victory after a second season of the show was not initially announced.[163] (The second season aired in the summer of 2023.) As religion scholar Philip Jenkins pointed out, *Good Omens* was never mocking the Bible. The events depicted in the novel—a child destined to become the Antichrist, a hellhound, a Satanic babysitter guarding the child, and so on, were all parodying *The Omen*. But many Christians were no longer able to discern between Biblical tradition and horror movie mythology. Regarding the petition, Jenkins opined, "That is what they are satirizing—not the Bible, not Revelation, not Judeo-Christian civilization, but a schlock genre of devil films . . . . When you are dealing with social idiocy on this scale, you can either laugh or cry. Gaiman and Pratchett decided to laugh."[164]

Disseminating The Devil

In 1974, William Friedkin told *Time*, "I think *The Exorcist* will be a bell-wether. If it wins a wide audience, that may give the studios courage to handle more ambitious themes with more graphic scenes."[165] Friedkin was certainly correct in that a slew of imitators emerged in the wake of the un-holy trinity that made these themes ubiquitous. Television began airing these films, which meant that a much wider segment of the population could see horror movies. In 1974, Anton LaVey commented, "Don't forget, those Catholics whose integrity forbade them from viewing 'Rosemary's Baby,' which would have necessitated violating their religion's ban, had to wait several years to 'accidentally' catch it on television."[166] A severely edited version of *The Exorcist* premiered on CBS on Tuesday, February 12, 1980, at 8:30 p.m. Eastern Standard Time.[167] Some local network affiliates prefaced the film with warnings by clergy and other experts about its offensive nature, which likely only heightened its influence. The migration of these films from theaters to television made them truly ubiquitous and likely contributed to the problem of source amnesia. Prior to this move, someone could say with relative certainty whether they had ever seen these films. But by the 1980s, even people who shunned horror films might have seen images of possession or Satanism while switching channels, in a bar, or anywhere that televisions were playing. The Sony Betamax VCR debuted in 1976 and VHS emerged the following year. By 1988, sixty-two percent of American homes owned a VCR.[168] Now children too young to see an "R" movie could finally watch horror films. The "unholy trinity" also entered heavy rotation on cable television. By 1982 unemployment had reached its highest level since the Great Depression, ensuring people had plenty of time to watch television.[169] This situation is portrayed in the Satanic Panic-themed comedy *The Burbs* (1989) in which suburbanite Ray Peterson (Tom Hanks) has taken a week off from work and is shown channel surfing and catching snippets of *The Exorcist* and *The Texas Chainsaw Massacre*. He falls asleep and dreams his neighbors are Satanists sacrificing him on a giant barbeque grill.

Beginning in the 1970s, there was a resurgence of interest in exorcism, which paved the way for the full-blown Satanic Panic of the 1980s. While these developments are not reducible to the influence of horror films, American culture was now freshly saturated with ready-made images and narrative tropes of Satanism and the demonic. The legacy of the unholy trinity provided a kind of cultural shorthand for discussing, imagining, and ultimately making claims about supernatural evil operating in the real world.

4

The Warren Cycle

"People have always been interested in the occult. But in the last ten years, the public has been exposed to *so much* information on the subject of spirits and the supernatural that they're trying to come to grips with it. Wherever we go, people have read *The Exorcist*."

—Lorraine Warren[1]

"Conjure spirits just by walking around / The devil hiding in the walls of your house / She can feel it in your head / possessing your mind and your heart from hell."

—Psychedelic Witchcraft "The Warrens"

The Exorcist created an unprecedented demand for demon expulsion, but, in 1973, the Catholic Church in America still regarded exorcism as an embarrassment and only a handful of priests were trained to perform this rite. These conditions created a seller's market for anyone who could deal with demons, leading to the unlikely rise of a husband-and-wife team of lay Catholic demon-busters. Ed Warren (1926–2006) and Lorraine Warren (*née* Moran, 1927–2019) earned a living as paranormal researchers, investigating cases, giving lectures, and doing countless media appearances. The couple had been ghost-hunting for decades before *The Exorcist*, but the film fundamentally changed their careers. For people who wanted a Catholic exorcism but could not get one, the Warrens acted as backdoor exorcism brokers. In the years following Vatican II (1962-1965), "traditionalist" Catholics who rejected the church's efforts at modernization led to the rise of "sedevacantist" groups that called themselves Catholic but rejected the authority of the current pope. The Pope is said to occupy the "Seat of Peter." *Sede vacante* means "with the chair empty," meaning no one legitimately occupies the seat.) Leaders of sedevacantist groups declared themselves bishops or even popes. This situation meant the Warrens were often able to connect people with priests

The Exorcist Effect. Joseph P. Laycock and Eric Harrelson, Oxford University Press. © Oxford University Press 2024.
DOI: 10.1093/oso/9780197635391.003.0004

and bishops who claimed to perform Catholic exorcisms despite having no formal affiliation within the Catholic Church.[2] Ed began describing himself as a "demonologist." This title, with its academic connotation, complimented his wife's identity as a clairvoyant or "light trance medium," who could supply data about the spirit world for Ed to interpret. But most importantly, *The Exorcist* changed the publishing market, creating a demand for books, like *The Amityville Horror* (1977) and *The Demonologist* (1980), that catapulted the Warrens into stardom.

The Warrens have enjoyed a surge in popularity over the last ten years since the release of *The Conjuring* in 2013. *The Conjuring* is now a multi-billion-dollar franchise. On Halloween weekend, 2022, we attended the second annual Seekers of the Supernatural Paracon at the Mohegan Sun Casino in Uncasville, Connecticut. The Paracon was a chance for fans of Ed and Lorraine Warren and those who carry on that work to enjoy a day of lectures, vendors, and meet-and-greets. Convention-goers could hear talks by ghost hunters and demonologists; have a Tarot reading; shop for vintage Ouija boards, magical charms and potions; buy horror movie inspired art, Jason Vorhees-hockey-mask-shaped bath bombs, or even get a tattoo. But the real attraction was the artifacts on display from Ed and Lorraine's Occult Museum. Each of these objects was recovered from one of the Warrens' investigations and is supposedly a source of tremendous supernatural danger if handled improperly.

The Paracon was organized under the auspices of the New England Society for Psychical Research (NESPR). NESPR is headed by the Warrens' son-in-law, Tony Spera, who is currently in charge of the Warrens' estate and legacy. Spera put together the first Seekers of the Supernatural Paracon in 2021. In 2022, the convention drew an estimated five thousand attendees willing to plunk down $89 to see objects from the cases that inspired *The Conjuring* movies. Some exhibit items were decidedly unimpressive. There was a Halloween decoration witch with a sticker on its chest that read, "Hello my name is Hannah Cranna"—a reference to an eighteenth-century Connecticut woman rumored to be a witch. There was a heavy book with a sign explaining that it was the "Necromonicin" (which we assume is an egregious misspelling of Necronomicon) and that, "Though fictional, it includes incantations and rituals that are considered objectionable to Biblical teachings." There was a plastic dinosaur said to have levitated during the alleged possession of eleven-year-old David Glatzel (described below). The dinosaur now sat in a wood and glass enclosure adorned with crucifixes, battery-powered plastic votive candles, and the inscription "Accept the Existence of the Devil." Not everyone seemed to take the stories about these objects at face value. But for some visitors they offered a sense of connection to the supernatural and to stories the Warrens fostered throughout their careers.

Families that called the Warrens about their paranormal problems found people who not only believed them, but who knew how to help. Whatever else they were, the Warrens were creators of stories who bestowed coherent narratives and supernatural authority onto people's anomalous experiences. These narratives would be reiterated in lectures given on college campuses and often resulted in book and movie deals, creating a growing mythology. The Warrens' investigations dotted the northeastern United States with houses famous for encounters with the demonic. They became film characters themselves, beginning with the made-for-television movie *The Demon Murder Case* (1983) and continuing with the billion-dollar *The Conjuring* franchise (2013–present). In this way, the Warrens were almost living exemplars of *The Exorcist* effect: They worked with people to construct narratives by drawing from cultural scripts that were widely accessible through horror films, and then they pitched these narratives back to the media for film adaptations.

Tracing the history of the Warrens is difficult. Gerald Brittle's *The Demonologist* (1980) is the closest thing to a published biography of their careers. Although Brittle did reach out to priests and exorcists for feedback, it is hardly a critical source. The Warrens did not write their own books, but publishers would commission writers to work with them. These books, as well as interviews with the Warrens, often contradict each other, sometimes on key details. But the biggest obstacle for historians is that the Warrens were masters of "impression management" and worked hard to present a certain image of themselves.[3] We interviewed Ray Garton, a horror author who was commissioned to write *In a Dark Place* about the Warrens' investigation of the Snedeker family. Garton recalled meeting the Warrens: "The initial impression they gave was almost Rockwellian; they seem like everyone's favorite grandparents or aunt and uncle, the ones you were always happiest to see show up at your house for Christmas dinner."[4] Many people described the Warrens as idealized parents, and this seemed to be a key ingredient to their success. A 1974 article reported, "They're regular folks, much like Mom and Dad, speaking with a great deal of sincerity about very irregular happenings."[5] *The Conjuring* films emphasize this aspect of the Warrens' story, portraying their love for one another almost as a superpower that can defeat demons.

There was also a dark side to the Warrens and their business of transforming the experiences of troubled families into marketable supernatural narratives. Several people we interviewed for this chapter felt they were cynical con artists who exploited the vulnerable. Belying the public image of a perfect Catholic couple were reports of abusive arguments and an affair with a teenage girl. It is not the goal of this chapter to evaluate the Warrens' character, but these critiques are as relevant to this study as their portrayal in *The Conjuring*. To understand how a new American mythology formed in the decades following *The Exorcist*, it is important to know as much as possible about who the Warrens were.

Ed and Lorraine

As large a role that film played in the Warrens' lives, it seems fitting that they met at a movie theater when they were both sixteen. Ed worked as an usher at the Colonial Movie Theater in Bridgeport, Connecticut. Lorraine's friends convinced her to meet him, and they became high school sweethearts. Ed joined the navy on his seventeenth birthday, in 1943, and served in the Pacific theater during World War II. They married in 1945 while Ed was still enlisted and recovering from a shipwreck. Their daughter, Judy, was born six months before Ed returned from the war. Ed briefly attended art school between 1951 and 1952 and both Warrens aspired to careers as artists.[6] For a while they operated "The Barn Door Studio and Art School" out of their home.[7] Ed's favorite subject to paint was "haunted houses." The couple began touring New England, selling paintings and seeking spooky New England houses for Ed to paint. Sometimes Ed would deploy Lorraine to use her "Irish charm" on a home's owners, getting the couple invited inside and to learn more about the house's history.[8] Garton recalled that Ed painted haunted houses on dinner plates that they sold door-to-door.[9] The common denominator of these accounts is that, like most artists, the Warrens struggled to turn their passion into a living.

Painting haunted houses gradually elided into a career as paranormal investigators. In 1952, the Warrens founded the NESPR. The American Society for Psychical Research (ASPR) had been founded in 1885 with the help of such luminaries as William James. ASPR sought scientific evidence of ghosts and mediumship. By 1952, laboratory experiments on purported psychic abilities had been conducted at Stanford University and Duke University.

The Warrens often framed their ideas in scientific terms, suggesting they were doing similar work to these groups. It is not clear that NESPR did much (many articles on the Warrens make no mention of it), but its existence gave the Warrens a certain authority as researchers.

We interviewed Jerry Solfvin, who conducted investigations for the Psychical Research Foundation based in Durham, North Carolina. He crossed paths with the Warrens while investigating the so-called "Bridgeport Poltergeist" case in 1974 and the "Amityville Horror" case in 1976. In 1976, Solfvin also joined the Warrens in investigating a reported haunting at an armed forces retirement home in Washington, DC.[10] Solfvin recalled, "It was clear from the beginning they had a different philosophy, but we respected each other. It was always a delight to see them." Solfvin felt that what the Warrens were doing was not psychical research but "ghost busting," and it was based on faith, not the scientific method. He added, "Lorraine was definitely not a scientist, nor of scientific mind."[11] A 1978 article from *The Philadelphia Inquirer* describes the Warrens operating an organization called "The Foundation for Christian Psychic Research," and the book *Satan's Harvest* (1990) calls NESPR "a Christian ministry."[12] As previously discussed, NESPR still exists today and is headed by the Warrens' son-in-law, Tony Spera. A recent NESPR logo features a large cross and the words "Saint Michael Protect Us."

At some point, Lorraine came to identify as a psychic. Some sources describe Lorraine as a skeptic before she married Ed and a "late bloomer" in developing her psychic abilities.[13] Others describe her as having had psychic abilities her entire life. In *The Demonologist*, Lorraine describes planting a seedling for Arbor Day at her Catholic girls school and being able to see it as a full-grown tree. When a nun asked, "Are you seeing into the future?" Lorraine replied in the affirmative. As punishment, she was sent away to a "retreat home" for a weekend of isolation and intense prayer. She recalled, "That taught me. After that, when it came to things involving clairvoyance, I kept my mouth shut."[14]

The Warrens also claimed that Lorraine's abilities were tested by a lab at UCLA and rated "far above average."[15] *Ghost Hunters*, written with the Warrens in 1989, states that Lorraine was investigated by a UCLA parapsychologist named "Viola Barron."[16] Their 2004 book *Ghost Tracks* states Lorraine was evaluated at a parapsychology laboratory run by Dr. Thelma Moss.[17] An actress-turned-academic who studied psychic and paranormal phenomena, Dr. Moss had a PhD in psychology and ran UCLA's

Neuropsychiatric Institute, which studied parapsychology from 1968–1978.[18] Significantly, Moss's research was popularized through a horror film. Moss's team investigated Doris Bither, a woman who claimed she was being sexually assaulted by a poltergeist. Bither's story became the basis for a 1978 novel, and then the film *The Entity* (1982), which will be discussed further in Chapter 6. We could find no confirmation that Lorraine was tested at UCLA or that a Viola Barron ever existed. Jerry Solfvin, who knew Thelma Moss, would not say Moss never tested Lorraine, but cautioned, "I wouldn't put weight on that."[19] Barry Taff, a parapsychologist who worked closely with Moss at UCLA, claimed he had never met the Warrens and would not want to, stating, "These people are nuts. They're religious zealots."[20] This discrepancy suggests shifting stories about Lorraine's psychic talents are another form of impression management, connecting the Warrens to a famous poltergeist case.

Art and "psychic research" continued hand-in-hand into the 1960s. In 1968, a banker friend suggested Ed hold a charity art show featuring paintings based on his "cases." This was the year *Rosemary's Baby* came out, marking heightened interest in all things occult. This show effected a pivotal shift for the Warrens. Now, instead of seeking out spooky houses, people with ghost stories came to them, and their number of cases accelerated rapidly.[21] *The Demonologist* reports that this was also the year the Warrens gave their first public lecture. A 1972 article from *Connecticut Magazine* describes the Warrens as lecturing around the country and having already accumulated two thousand cases, including working with teenagers whose dabbling with Satanism had caused them to become blood-drinking vampires. Significantly, this article does not describe Ed as a demonologist and states, "On the other side of the spirit world [Ed] Warren has investigated a demon possession. (Lorraine, a clairvoyant, does not get involved in these.)."[22] This suggests that, in 1972, the Warrens had not yet branded themselves as demon-busters. At most, they were ghost-hunters whose work occasionally stumbled across the demonic.

Another curious detail of the 1972 article is a photo with the caption, "Ed and Lorraine attending a witch's ceremony."[23] The Warrens are depicted outdoors at night, clad in black. Ed is holding a lantern and they appear to be leading a procession of four other people wearing black capes and white druid-like robes. When asked about this image, Jerry Solfvin recalled that Ed was very much interested in witchcraft lore and may have even identified for a time as a witch.[24] The Warrens' first book, *Deliver Us From Evil* (1973), contains a very sympathetic discussion of Wicca, stating that it is the oldest religion in the world and that historically practitioners were persecuted for the psychic abilities they cultivated through its rituals.[25] Despite their eventual identity as Catholic demon busters, the Warrens always professed beliefs and practices that seemed at odds with traditional Catholicism. Lorraine described herself as a medium and held séances, while Ed once told a crowd at the University of New Hampshire, "Everyone in this room has been reincarnated."[26] It may be that prior to *The Exorcist*, the Warrens professed a far more eclectic approach to magic and the supernatural.

Later in 1972 they were mentioned in *The New York Times* after they gave a lecture on haunted houses to cadets at West Point Academy. Not long after, underclassman began reporting an apparition haunting the dormitory. According to *The Demonologist*, West Point asked the Warrens to help. Lorraine used her powers to speak with the ghost of a black soldier named "Greer" who had falsely been accused of murder and asked him to pass on.[27]

By 1973, the Warrens had constructed their famous museum in their basement. Visitors can view "haunted objects" recovered from their cases, many of which are said to be too spiritually dangerous to be stored by the uninitiated. They had also hired Philip A. Douglass of Douglass Associates as their talent agent, who organized tours of colleges all over the country. A receipt from Texas Christian University indicates they were paid $600 for their visit—the equivalent of $4,000 in 2022. (Presumably, Douglass Associates took a cut of these earnings.) Colleges felt they got their money's worth. An assistant director of activities at Texas Tech wrote to Douglass to say, "Please let me take this opportunity to say how much everyone at Texas Tech enjoyed the Warren's visit. Their visit is undoubtedly one of the highlights of our programming this year as evidenced by the large crowds drawn to their lectures."[28] An article in the University of New Hampshire campus paper featured a photo of one of their lectures and reported that two thousand people were in attendance.[29] The Warrens taught a course on the paranormal at Southern Connecticut University. The lure of the Warrens seems to have primarily been entertainment. In the days before the Internet, their lectures allowed college students to see slides and films of alleged hauntings. For some, the lectures seem to have been an opportunity for romance and to perform gender roles, one of the social functions of horror movies. A campus paper reported that a show at Baldwin-Wallace college was so frightening that several female audience members "had to find escorts to take them back to their rooms."[30] Despite success on the lecture circuit, a 1973 article from *The National Enquirer* still describes the Warrens as "artists by profession."

With this success, the Warrens shifted from being primarily ghost-hunters in the tradition of the ASPR to Catholic warriors battling the demonic. To some extent, the Warrens acknowledged shifting their focus. An article from March 1974 writes of Ed: "His emphasis of late has been on the non-human variety, he says, because his audience interest has been focused on the demonic."[31] This rebranding seems to have occurred around the time *The Exorcist* came out in December 1973. Asked about this connection, Garton noted, "The Warrens started out investigating ghost stories . . . Immediately after the phenomenal success of first the novel and then the movie *The Exorcist*, the Warrens changed their approach, and from then on, it was always demons."[32] The earliest instance we could find of Ed Warren being described as a "demonologist" appears in an article about *The Exorcist* that appeared in *Focus* magazine in October 1973. It stated, "The secret church files of the case on which 'The Exorcist' is based are open to very few people. One of those allowed to see them is Ed Warren, a demonologist, who is considered a leading expert on ghosts and spirits."[33] This claim was repeated in a 1974 letter from the Warrens' agent seeking an endorsement from a Catholic exorcist: "With the release of the film, "The Excorcist" [*sic*] there is renewed interest everywhere for the Warrens lectures since Ed was one of the few people authorized to see the church files."[34] Now that documents from this case are publicly available, it seems clear from Ed's account that he never saw any secret church files.[35] Much as Lorraine claimed a special connection to the story behind *The Entity*, Ed claimed a special connection to *The Exorcist*.

Despite calling himself a "demonologist," Ed admitted having no formal training, stating, "My knowledge of demonology does not come from a university. There is no college course that can teach me the fantastic and incredible ways in which these negative forces of darkness work their malign deeds."[36] The Warrens effectively created their own demonology, including theories of what demons are and how they behave. Instead of spirits of the dead with unfinished business, demons are inhuman spirits "who have never walked the Earth in human form"[37] and their goal is "to corrupt, harm, and eventually kill, taking over a person's soul.[38] Bible scholar Steve A. Wiggins notes this is an original take on what exactly demons are and that the Warrens "gave the world an entity that acts like a ghost, only worse."[39] When the Warrens diagnosed haunted houses as being infested with demons, this raised the stakes considerably. It also made for better horror movies.

Aside from movie trends, the other factor that likely steered the Warrens toward the demonic was ongoing frustration in the Catholic community following Vatican II. In the 1970s, the demonic became a site where traditionalist Catholics could voice their resentment.[40] Ed told the tabloid *The Tattler*, "I'm a Roman Catholic but the liberalism in the Catholic Church has made me lose faith in the priesthood. All they want to do is live like laymen . . . . One Bridgeport, Conn. priest I asked to perform an exorcism practically told me there was no such thing as Satan. I'm sick and tired of telling men of God that there IS a devil!"[41] Paradoxically, while the Warrens complained about "liberalism" undermining the Church, they often expressed pluralist attitudes. Ed stated, "I've worked with exorcists from every major religion . . . Usually they have no other title than monk, priest, rabbi, minister, or yogi, but they all seem to embody a combination of wisdom, kindness, and compassion that you don't see in ordinary people."[42] However, such surprising combinations of elements—traditionalism, ecumenism, scientism, folk magic—are surprisingly common in Christian spiritual warfare practices.[43]

By 1974, the Warrens had a weekly column about their adventures in *The Tattler*, where they offered a cash prize to the reader who submitted the best report of an encounter with the supernatural for them to investigate. In 1975, they investigated the story known as "The Amityville Horror," and the films based on this case made them almost a household name. In the 1980s, the Warrens experimented with operating the "New England School of Demonology" from their home. Reporter Michael Lasalandra describes a class of mostly high school and college students watching Ed prepare to lecture by playing a tape of Gregorian chants and setting out a display of swords, skulls, and other occult props.[44] Significantly, this description mirrors accounts of "occult crime" seminars during the Satanic Panic, that featured similar props.

The Warrens continued to conduct investigations and lecture well into the 1990s. They formed contacts in the film and television industry, and they became regular guests on paranormal shows. From 1998 to 1999 they even had a local cable access show called *Seekers of the Supernatural*, in which their son-in-law, Tony Spera, interviewed them about their investigations. If nothing else, their ability to turn ghost-hunting into a full-time vocation was impressive.

Even after they stopped traveling, they still welcomed guests into their home for lectures and tours of their museum, almost until Lorraine's death in 2019. They also never charged the people who requested their services. Catholic theology professor and exorcist Alphonsus Trabold wrote of the Warrens, "Speaking as a Catholic priest, I feel that Ed and Lorraine are continuing the healing ministry of Christ by bringing peace and comfort to many souls suffering from evil forces that they cannot control. Whether these demons are objectively real or only the subjective creation of their own minds, we can never be sure. Nevertheless, the relief and healing that the Warrens bring these troubled souls is real."[45]

But not everyone thought the Warrens were helping people. Horror author Grady Hendrix pointed out that some of the families who consulted the Warrens seemed to be experiencing serious trauma and, in some cases, physical or sexual abuse. By interpreting the family's problems as demonic, the Warrens raised the stakes around these problems while concealing their actual cause. As Hendrix put it:

> For the record I could not have a lower opinion of a human being than I have of Ed and Lorraine. I don't think they were well-intentioned. I don't think they were good people. I don't think they were in over their heads. I think they saw situations and exploited them and I think they did untold harm to people. I think they caused great psychological and emotional distress. You can't go into a place where people are undergoing the kind of emotional and psychological and even physical trauma that people who are in some of these situations are . . . and say "Oh yeah, well I know the answer. Here's what's happening. These are demons." And they did that, over and over again. They went in and they said that again and again and again and, you know, who the hell are they to know if demons exist or not? . . .
>
> I think there are a lot of other causes that are a lot more compelling before we get to demons. That said, they don't know, but they go in pretending they do. And they're bulls in emotional china shops and people get hurt.[46]

There were also accusations that the Warrens routinely lied to get book and movie deals. Ray Garton met the Warrens and the Snedeker family and concluded both parties were engaged in a hoax. He described being told that the Warrens had a videotape of "an actual demonic materialization" on the Snedeker's staircase. He asked to see it and the Warrens fumbled around for a few minutes only to tell him the tape had been misplaced. Garton told Ed he was having a problem writing the book because the family members' stories seemed contradictory. According to Garton: "He said (and this is very close to a quote because I can still hear him saying it in my head), 'These people are crazy. All the people who come to us are crazy, otherwise they wouldn't come to us. Just use what you can and make the rest up. You write scary books, right? That's why we hired you. Just make it a good, scary story and it'll be fine.'" Garton had been hired to write a "true story," but he concluded that neither the Warrens nor the publisher cared whether the Snedekers were telling the truth. He could not get out of the contract he had signed, but the contract also gave him no royalties. He recalled, "So I decided to go ahead and write it as if I were writing a horror novel. I tried to make it as entertaining and scary as I could. Then, when the book was published, I immediately began to denounce it. I knew how easy it was going to be to debunk it, with stories that were wobbly at best and zero evidence to back it up. And I also knew that it simply wasn't true, that it was an attempt to stir up a movie or TV deal."[47]

We also interviewed Matt Baxter, a paranormal researcher who accompanied Ed and one of his colleagues on an investigation in Black Forest, Colorado, in 1995. The investigation was portrayed on the paranormal show *Sightings*. Baxter reportedly witnessed the entire team, as well as the family who asked for the investigation, faking evidence. He watched an investigator singe a rose using a lighter while the cameras were not looking and then claim it had been spontaneously burned by supernatural forces. He saw a father scratch his own arm and then, as welts rose, summon the camera crew to film "demon scratches" manifesting. He also reportedly saw a rock tumble down the roof of the house, followed by Ed Warren striding around from the opposite side of the house. Baxter said Warren later told him that he had the rock analyzed and that it was actually highly compacted feces conjured by demons. Echoing Garton, Baxter said that when he told Warren this was not a serious investigation, Warren answered that "all these people are crazy" and urged him to simply play along.[48]

Baxter concluded that the people who asked for the Warrens' help were often exhausted and suggestible, and that Ed asked them leading questions such as, "How did you feel when the demon did X?" "The people were very vulnerable, and eager to glom onto you as their savior," he said, "And the Warrens were only too happy to present themselves as that savior." As far as Baxter was concerned, Ed and his associates were "con men, flat out."

He added, "You can't be around Ed Warren for long without him revealing himself."[49]

Jerry Solfvin also noted that Ed asked leading questions of witnesses, and that their investigations were not objective. However, he strongly disagreed that they were motivated by money, remarking, "I think they totally believed in what they were doing . . . . I have no doubt they were doing it from the good of their hearts."[50] Solfvin noted that the Warrens' work did not seem especially lucrative compared to the time and energy it took. He also pointed out that belief becomes more concrete as more people participate in it. The Warrens affirmed each other's interpretations, as did a close circle of their friends, and the experiencers who called them. Within such a community, supernatural beliefs likely seemed plausible or even self-evident. It may be significant that Solfvin knew the Warrens earlier in their careers than did Garton or Baxter, and that the Warrens seem to have looked up to Solfvin and the scientific authority he represented.

Solfvin could not recall an incident in which Ed lost his temper, but both Garton and Baxter described him as quick to anger. Garton recalled, "I quickly learned that it was a mistake to say anything that might suggest to Ed that I questioned or doubted his story, because he would get angry fast . . . . I later learned he had a reputation for being irascible, sometimes to the point of violence."[51] In 1992, the Warrens appeared on an episode of *The Sally Jesse Raphael Show* entitled "I Was Raped by a Ghost." Other guests included the Snedeker family and skeptic Joe Nickell, who engaged in an angry exchange with Ed. According to Garton, "After the Sally show finished taping, Ed tried to physically attack Joe Nickell backstage and had to be restrained."[52]

Baxter's first interaction with the Warrens came after reading Garton's book. He was interested in the paranormal and decided to give the Warrens a call. Lorraine answered the phone but seemed "absurdly annoyed." She handed off the phone to Ed, who said that Lorraine had gotten "bad vibes" from him. He asked about *In a Dark Place*, to which Ed replied it contained "zero exaggeration." After putting down the phone, Baxter suspected the Warrens had been in a heated argument when he called and that their image as the perfect couple was just for show. He described Ed as "a raging anger management case" whose face would "turn red like a cartoon character" when angered.[53]

In fact, Baxter suggested that at least part of the reason Ed sought self-employment—first as an artist, then as a ghost-hunter—is because his temper made it difficult for him to hold down a job in which he had to answer to a boss. He felt that while the Warrens probably started with gen-uine interest in the paranormal, what they were doing was about wealth and fame. We pointed out that the Warrens' work seemed exhausting and asked whether there was not an easier way con artists could have made a living. He answered, "You try to figure out how to make money without having to work. Then you end up working twice as hard."[54]

The biggest hole in the narrative the Warrens presented about themselves did not concern their research methods or Ed's anger, but a young woman named Judith Penney. In November 2014, following the financial success of *The Conjuring*, Penney gave a sworn statement alleging that in 1960, when she was fifteen, she began a sexual relationship with Ed, who would then have been more than twice her age. At the time, Ed was working as a city bus driver. Lorraine accepted their relationship and Penney came to live with the Warrens for nearly forty years. In 1963, she spent the night in the North End Prison in Bridgeport while the police urged her to sign a statement admitting to her relationship with Ed. When Penney refused to cooperate, the court or-dered her to report to a delinquent youth office for the next month. Ed picked her up from school every week and drove her to her meetings. When Penney became pregnant with Ed's child in 1978, Lorraine bullied her into getting an abortion. Penney claimed Lorraine's Catholic piety was just an act and that her "real god is money." She recalled, "They wanted me to tell everyone that someone had come into my apartment and raped me, and I wouldn't do that. I was so scared. I didn't know what to do, but I had an abortion. The night they picked me up from the hospital after having it, they went out and lectured and left me alone." Penney also reported abuse and hoaxing. She said Ed would slap Lorraine and once hit her so hard that she lost conscious-ness. She also reported that a famous video of a ghost called "The White Lady," shot by Ed at Union Cemetery in Easton, Connecticut, was actually her wearing a sheet. Ed justified this deception saying he wanted to show what the White Lady "would look like."[55]

There is independent confirmation for some of Penney's testimony. *The Demonologist* mentions a "Judy Penney," describing her as "a young woman who works as a liaison when Ed and Lorraine are out of town."[56] The Warren's daughter and son-in-law admit Penney stayed with the Warrens but that they took her in because she had nowhere else to go. New Line Cinema paid Lorraine Warren $150,000 to serve as a consultant on *The Conjuring*. However, her contract specified that the films could not "show her or her husband engaging in crimes, including sex with minors, child pornography, prostitution or sexual assault," and that, "Neither the husband nor wife could be depicted as participating in an extramarital sexual relationship." A talent attorney interviewed by *The Hollywood Reporter* noted that while she had never seen these specific clauses before, there is precedent for contracts that prohibit "depictions of certain types of odious behavior."[57]

Penney's story would likely never have been known had *The Conjuring* franchise not earned $1 billion in its first five years. Tony DeRosa-Grund, a producer who worked on the first film, felt he was unfairly shut out of the various sequels and spin-offs. DeRosa-Grund's Internet Movie Database page states that he wrote the original story and treatment and came up with the name "The Conjuring."[58] In September 2013, a few months after the film came out, DeRosa-Grund sent an email to the production studio and the distributors warning that he had met a woman who was "mortified" by the film's inaccurate portrayal of Ed and Lorraine Warren and that no actor would want to portray the Warrens if they knew the truth. This email preceded a protracted legal battle between DeRosa-Grund and the studio. Gerald Brittle also entered the fray, claiming *The Conjuring* ripped off his book, *The Demonologist*, and suing for $900 million. The studio noted that historical events cannot be copyrighted, but Brittle countered that the stories in *The Demonologist* are *not* historical—he believed they were when he wrote it, but he had since come to believe the Warrens were frauds. The plaintiffs used Penney's testimony as leverage in their efforts to get a settlement from the studio. Penney was not involved in settlement discussions, although one deal proposed the studio pay her the same amount given to Lorraine Warren in exchange for her life rights and a confidentiality agreement.

Regarding the decision to portray the Warrens as they wanted to be seen— a loving, monogamous, Catholic couple—attorney Lincoln Bandlow stated the obvious: "It's a less enjoyable film if the ghost hunters are a bunch of assholes no one likes. You have to have your protagonists be likable."[59] Writer Gabrielle Moss grew up in Connecticut hearing stories about the Warrens and their collection of haunted objects. A few months before *The Conjuring* came out in 2013, the Warrens occult museum was reopened and Moss went to meet Lorraine. Reflecting on the discrepancy between the image of the Warrens as demon-busting, idealized parents and the accusations raised by their contemporary critics, Moss reflects:

Maybe I feel about the Warrens the way other people do about their parents: I know they're probably really messed up, but I imprinted on them when I was young, and now they mean something to me as symbols. When I see the Warrens, I don't see two individuals who may or may not have harmed some very real people in very real ways; I see archetypes, abstracted figures, folk tales in extremely uptight plaid outfits who somehow set my spirit free . . . . In a place where I struggled—and failed—to fit in, everyone somehow just left the Warrens alone, free to be weirdos in the basement of their suburban house at the end of the street. Hoaxers or not, creeps or not, they were the only thing in my childhood that suggested that being confident in your weirdness was as important as fitting in.[60]

In this sense, the myth of Ed and Lorraine Warren—to the extent it has influenced culture and inspired paranormal seekers—is just as real as the Ed and Lorraine described by Solfvin, Garton, Baxter, and Penney.

We turn now to some of the specific cases that the Warrens investigated (or in some instances, inserted themselves into) and their cinematic adaptations. These incidents are arranged chronologically by the original case to highlight the trajectory of the Warrens' career.

Annabelle

The prize exhibit of the Warrens' occult museum is a Raggedy Anne doll named Annabelle. It is kept behind glass in a special box with a sign that reads, "Warning: Positively Do Not Open." Rather inexplicably, a Tarot card of The Devil is attached to the outside of the box. At the Seekers of the Supernatural Paracon, Annabelle was the star of the convention, a true unholy relic. We arrived Saturday morning and joined a line of thousands that wound through the Mohegan Sun casino, past shops and restaurants, finally terminating somewhere near the Michael Jordan sports bar and grill. Over an hour later, we were in a casino ballroom that had been converted into a museum of Warrens' artifacts. But Annabelle was the only thing everyone wanted to see. The line hugged the wall, forming a spiral around Annabelle's enclosure that was reminiscent of Muslim pilgrims circling the Kaaba. When we were finally yards away, a conference organizer called for everyone's attention and announced that there was no need to wait in line. "Crowd around, everybody!" he urged, "Crowd around!" Apparently, the line was causing congestion for the entire casino. Anarchy ensued as conventioneers began scrambling to take selfies with the possessed doll.

Later, we learned we could purchase special "Annabelle Vodka," a special run of only 666 bottles that had been aged for a month next to Annabelle in the Warrens' Occult Museum. The bottle came with gloves to provide spiritual protection while handling it. This seemed to be a product for people who were not content to merely see Annabelle, but who wanted to ingest her essence.

The story about a haunted doll that terrorized a pair of student nurses and their male roommate in 1970 gave rise to the first *Conjuring* spin-off, *Annabelle* (2014), and two sequels: *Annabelle: Creation* (2017), and *Annabelle Comes Home* (2019). In these films, Annabelle is a far creepier looking Victorian doll, whose design is not trademarked by Hasbro. As told in *The Demonologist*, the doll was given to one of the nurses, Deidre, by her mother. The students noticed the doll acting strangely: It would move on its own, reposition itself in the apartment, and leave notes written in pencil for the three roommates. The students called in a medium, who concluded that the doll was being moved by the spirit of a little girl named Annabelle Higgins. The spirit asked for permission to inhabit the doll and the young nurses consented. But the Warrens had a different diagnosis: "Annabelle" was the alias of a demon who had tricked the nurses into inviting it into their home. According to what Ed called "The Law of Invitation," demons always require some sign of approval to work their mischief. The doll supposedly clawed the young man, Cal, leaving a mark on his chest. The Warrens called in a priest to exorcize the apartment, undoing the demon's invitation.[61] But the demon remained inside the doll, so the Warrens took it to their museum for safe keeping.

Unlike the Warrens' other cases, no details of the Annabelle story can be confirmed. The student nurses, the priest, and the apartment where these events occurred have never been identified.[62] There seems to be no record of this story in print prior to the publication of *The Demonologist*. This raises the question of whether Annabelle is simply a mass-produced doll that the Warrens used as a prop to tell a ghost story. In one of their columns for *The Tattler* published in 1973, the Warrens described performing a séance for one Judith Liberto of Brandford, Connecticut, whose house showed signs of a haunting. Liberto became possessed and stated that her name was Cynthia Nesbitt and she was a child who had died in the home. The Warrens concluded Cynthia was a confused earthbound spirit, but cautioned, "We are still uncertain as to if the spirit was really that of Cynthia Nesbitt. Many times inhuman spirits—demons—try to confuse investigators of the supernatural by adapting such sympathetic case histories."[63] This seems like an early itera-tion of the Annabelle legend.

Annabelle also seems derivative of similar stories of haunted dolls pop-ular in the early 1970s. In 1970, there was already a legend of a haunted doll named "Robert" that belonged to an artist named Robert Eugene Otto of Key West, Florida. Children claimed Robert would inexplicably change po-sition. Some claimed the doll had been given to Otto by a Caribbean woman who practiced black magic—a story that influenced the horror film *Child's Play* (1988). Like Annabelle, Robert is currently on display in a museum and receives many visitors annually. Also around 1970, a self-described Satanist from Toledo named Herbert A. Sloane began doing interviews with para-normal writers such as Hans Holzer and Brad Steiger. Sloane operated a Satanic coven out of his barber shop where he housed a special doll named April Belle Llodgar ("ragdoll" spelled backwards). Sloane said he had April Belle commissioned after learning about life-sized dolls used in Spiritualist séances, that he communicated with her telepathically, and that she served as "mascot" for his coven. One interviewer described it as "a red-headed rag doll about twenty-four inches tall."[64] And before both these legends, there was *The Twilight Zone* episode "Living Doll" (1963), in which a woman named Annabelle gives her daughter a "Talky Tina" doll that proceeds to ter-rorize the family.[65]

Regardless of the story's origins, the chance to encounter a demon face-to-face—even one trapped in a Raggedy Anne doll—brought people to the Warrens' museum and jump started their careers as demonologists. Annabelle has also continued to generate more stories. According to Lorraine, a young visitor once banged on Annabelle's enclosure and mocked her until Ed evicted him. After he and his girlfriend rode off on his motor-cycle, he lost control of the bike and fatally crashed into a tree. There is no independent confirmation for this story, either.[66]

Annabelle is not the only haunted doll in the Warrens' museum collec-tion and Ed Warren seemed rather preoccupied with evil dolls. In the 1980s, "Cabbage Patch" dolls became a cultural craze, and *The National Enquirer* ran an article in which Ed Warren declared, "We face a plague of devil infestations and possessions because women are treating these dolls as if they were real children."[67] The Warrens reported multiple cases of possessed Cabbage Patch dolls levitating, informing their owners they are "lords of hell," and other ne-farious deeds. Their solution was to bury the dolls in backyards and sprinkle holy water onto the "graves."

The Perron Family, Bathseba Sherman, and *The Conjuring*

Before it was adapted into *The Conjuring*, the alleged haunting of the Perron family in Harrisville, Rhode Island, was one of the Warrens' lesser-known cases. It is not mentioned in *The Demonologist* or *Ghost Tracks*, nor was it discussed on *Seekers of the Supernatural*. This lack of detail arguably made it better fodder for a film adaptation, giving writers more flexibility while still being able to claim the film is "based on a true story."

In 1971, Roger and Carolyn Perron and their five daughters moved into an old property called the Arnold Estate and began experiencing poltergeist-like activity and visits from spirits of the dead. A local historian told Carolyn about Bathsheba Sherman, a Rhode Island woman who died in 1855. According to legend, a baby died while under Bathsheba's care, apparently from a needle driven into its neck. The baby's parents claimed Bathsheba had sacrificed it to Satan. Although Bathsheba was acquitted, she was still ostracized.[68] Carolyn concluded that Bathsheba's ghost was haunting her home. A friend put Carolyn in touch with the Warrens, who met the Perrons in October 1973 and made several visits to the home. Carolyn told the Warrens about Bathsheba and gave them her notebook with her research on the case (which she said was never returned.)[69] The Warrens expanded on this mythology, confirming that Bathsheba had been a witch who sacrificed multiple children to Satan and that her ghost was responsible for several deaths and suicides on the property.

The alliance between Carolyn and the Warrens soon became strained. As would happen in Amityville, curious people started showing up on the property. Carolyn discovered that the Warrens had been describing her home in their lectures, including the name of the property.[70] In 1974, the Warrens arrived for a séance, followed by a priest, a researcher from Duke University, and a camera crew. During the séance, Carolyn began screaming and—according to one of her daughters—levitating in an apparent bout of possession. At this, Roger—a long-haul truck driver who had been absent for much of his family's growing preoccupation with spirits—punched Ed in the nose and ordered everyone out of the house.[71]

The Conjuring took liberties with this story, greatly enhancing the legend of Bathsheba Sherman as an undead, child-murdering, Satanic witch. Investigative journalist J'aime Rubio examined town records from Burrillville, Rhode Island, and concluded that while there was indeed a Bathsheba Sherman, there was no documentation to support claims she killed children. She did not hang herself, as depicted in *The Conjuring*. She was buried next to her husband in a Baptist cemetery and her obituary made no mention of witchcraft or murder. She also never lived on the property of the Arnold home, nor was there any record of suspicious deaths on the property, as the Warrens claimed. Rubio did find evidence of a local murder that occurred during Sherman's lifetime, and an account of a manor where a mentally ill woman resided.[72] It is possible these incidents coalesced into a regional legend, but the Bathsheba in *The Conjuring* most closely resembles another story about a New England witch the Warrens discovered and embellished around the same time they worked with the Perron family.

In one of their columns in *The Tattler*, the Warrens described their investigation of the Phelps mansion in Stratford, Connecticut. They discovered the house was haunted by Goody Basset, a woman executed for witchcraft in 1651.[73] There are colonial records of a Goody Bassett hanged for witchcraft in Stratford, although where the hanging occurred is unknown. This column appeared in 1974—the same year the Warrens did their séance for the Perrons. This connection gives an insight into how the Warrens spun legends—taking contemporary paranormal experiences, cursory research into local history, and impressions from Lorraine's clairvoyant sessions, and then binding it all together into a narrative of supernatural evil.

Unfortunately, after *The Conjuring* came out, Bathsheba Sherman's grave was repeatedly defaced—presumably by people who had seen the movie and assumed she had been a witch. Local historians began a fundraiser to restore her headstone and a campaign to correct the horror movie version of local history.[74] It seems unlikely the Burrillville Historical and Preservation Society will have much success asserting their version of history against a billion-dollar juggernaut like *The Conjuring* franchise.

The Amityville Horror

In July 1979, *The Amityville Horror* opened in 810 theaters. It was the second most profitable film of the year, beating such films as *Alien*, *Apocalypse Now*, and *The Muppet Movie*. It earned $86 million that year, a sum that—adjusted for inflation—surpasses *The Matrix*, *The DaVinci Code*, and *The Lego Movie*.[75] All this from an independently produced movie shot in seven weeks on a budget of $4.7 million.[76]

The Amityville case begins with a gruesome real-life massacre. In the early morning hours of November 13, 1974, a twenty-three-year-old car mechanic named Ronald DeFeo, Jr. walked from room to room in his family's Dutch Colonial home at 112 Ocean Avenue, Amityville, in Long Island, and used a .32 caliber Marlin rifle to murder his entire family, including his parents, two brothers, and two sisters. DeFeo's motive remains a mystery. He changed his story several times: He claimed his family had been murdered by a mafia hitman, that his sister Dawn committed the murders, and, finally, that supernatural forces had driven him to kill. A jury was unconvinced, and DeFeo received six life sentences. The house sat empty until it was purchased by the Lutz family in December 1975 at a considerable discount. According to the Lutzes, they experienced all manner of supernatural occurrences. They heard voices and the sounds of a large marching band at all hours of the night, the walls would "bleed" unknown liquids, and the house was plagued by thousands of flies. Father George Lutz claimed he was awakened every night at 3:15 a.m.—allegedly the time at which DeFeo murdered his family. Soon objects, and even George's wife, Kathy, were seen levitating. Doors were ripped off their hinges. The children reported seeing a red-eyed pig monster they named "Jody." A priest brought in to bless the home was slapped in the face by an unseen force and ordered to "Get out!" Twenty-eight days after moving into their dream home, the Lutzes fled, never to return, abandoning their personal belongings.[77]

The media homed in on the story and the Warrens were among many psychics and investigators approached for comment. On their show, *Seekers of the Supernatural*, Ed recalled that a New York news anchor, who had "been involved in a haunting" the Warrens investigated, called them about the Lutzes' home.[78] In February 1976, with news cameras rolling, the Warrens began a series of three séances to discern the source of the trouble. Lorraine's conclusion: The house had a negative spirit that had never "walked the earth in human form."[79]

Jerry Solfvin recalled that in 1976 he was driving from North Carolina to Massachusetts to see his family. George Lutz had been calling the Psychical Research Foundation for weeks, so he stopped in New York and gave him a call. Lutz invited him to meet for coffee and give him a key to explore the Amityville house. As soon as Solfvin pulled into the driveway, the Warrens arrived behind him accompanied by three or four television trucks. Solfvin refused to participate in the Warrens' séance and did his best to duck camera crews as he investigated the home. After everyone left, Solfvin and one cameraman decided to spend the night. Solfvin considered this a "non-case" and was more anxious about driving late at night than staying in the Amityville house. After an uneventful night, he resumed his journey.[80]

In September 1977, writer Jay Anson published *The Amityville Horror: A True Story* with Prentice-Hall. Solfvin and the Warrens' séances are mentioned briefly near the back of the book. Anson's book allegedly drew on thirty-five hours of taped testimony from George and Kathy Lutz, as well as interviews with police and historians. But skeptics Joe Nickell and Robert Bartholomew found numerous factual errors. According to Anson, the Amityville Historical Society reported that the house was built on a site that the Shinnecock tribe believed to be "infested by demons" and where they left their dead and dying. But the Historical Society told Nickell and Bartholomew they had said no such thing and that the Shinnecock never lived in Amityville. Similarly, Anson described police being called to the house and witnessing paranormal activity. But no record could be found of police visiting the home while the Lutzes lived there.[81] Other researchers arrived at similar conclusions. Ed Lowe, a neighbor and son of Amityville's police chief during the Lutzes' stay, reported that not only had police never visited the house but that the day after the Lutzes supposedly fled the home, George Lutz returned to hold a garage sale.[82] Likewise, in November 1977, the local Catholic diocese declared *The Amityville Horror* a false report and their lawyers prepared a list of inaccuracies for the publisher.[83]

Anson sold the film rights to CBS, who planned to adapt the story into a TV movie with a budget of $800,000. But a bookstore owner in San Fernando Valley showed Anson's book to Samuel Z. Arkoff, founder of American International Pictures, an independent production label known for making schlock. Arkoff took the book, went on vacation, and forgot about it. But his daughter discovered it and convinced him to read it. Arkoff liked it so much he called CBS, bought the rights, and began pre-production immediately. But Arkoff found that everyone involved in *The Amityville Horror* was quarrelsome and litigious, especially Anson's agents and the Lutzes. Arkoff mused, "I often thought that if I could conjure up the demons of Amityville, I'd turn them loose at the homes of those individuals who had tormented us throughout making the picture!"[84]

As with *The Conjuring*, the film's success triggered lawsuits, which led to revelations about "what *really* happened." The day the film premiered, newspapers reported that DeFeo's lawyer, William Weber, claimed the story was a hoax perpetrated by himself and the Lutzes. Weber said George and Kathy Lutz approached him about alleged supernatural activity in their home. Weber was already looking to parlay DeFeo's story into a book deal and decided a haunted house story was even better. He told the papers, "We created this horror story over many bottles of wine that George was drinking."[85] Weber fed the Lutzes information about the murders, such as the detail that they occurred around 3 a.m. Kathy allegedly replied, "I can say I'm awakened by noises at that hour of the day and I could say I had dreams that hour of the day about the DeFeo family.'" As Weber put it, "We were really playing with each other. We were creating something the public would want to hear about."[86] Solfvin felt this story was believable, although it was unclear exactly how much of the story Weber was responsible for. He recalled that George Lutz had called the Psychical Research Foundation nearly every day and had even asked for a certificate verifying that his house was haunted. (In a press release, the Foundation stated that there was "nothing for science to investigate" in the Amityville case.)[87]

Weber's conspiracy with the Lutzes could not survive the story's financial success. In March 1976, Weber had sent the Lutzes a contract proposing a corporation to write the story, find a publisher, and share the profits. Each partner would get twelve percent, except for author Paul Hoffman, who would get forty percent. Instead, the Lutzes signed a contract with Jay Anson that gave them fifty percent of the profits. But Hoffman still sold articles about the haunted house story to *The New York Sunday News* and *Good Housekeeping*. In May 1977, the Lutzes sued Hoffman, Weber, and the various news outlets for $4.5 million, citing invasion of privacy, mental distress, and other charges. Weber and Hoffman countersued for $2 million, charging the Lutzes with fraud and breach of contract. It was in this context that Weber told the media the entire thing was a fraud.

In 1977, the new owners of 112 Ocean Avenue sued Jay Anson, the Lutzes, and publisher Prentice-Hall, charging that *The Amityville Horror* was a hoax and that they could no longer enjoy their home due to throngs of tourists—up to one thousand carloads of them every weekend—whom the town dubbed "the Amityville Horribles."[88] None of this controversy embarrassed Prentice-Hall. Instead, the success of *The Amityville Horror* inspired the publisher to commission Gerald Brittle to write a book about the Warrens. That book, *The Demonologist*, came out one year after the film. In a letter to a Catholic exorcist who was consulted on the manuscript, Brittle wrote, "The first draft came back to me [from Prentice-Hall] X'd-out all over the place with a comment—'this is not a book for Catholics, this is a mass-market book for all the Jews, Indians, and taxi drivers who read The Amityville Horror. Change the ms. or forget it.'"[89]

The Amityville Horror inspired over forty works of fiction including novels, prequels, sequels, remakes, spin-offs, and knockoffs. Because "Amityville" is the name of a town, anyone can make a horror movie with "Amityville" in the title. One of the less ridiculous installments was *Amityville II: The Possession* (1982), loosely adapted from a book by paranormal researcher Hans Holzer, arguing that DeFeo was literally possessed when he murdered his family. The Warrens were brought in as advisors for this film and went to work promoting it. An article in *The Chicago Tribune* reported that while the Warrens warned Ouija boards and rock music were spiritually dangerous, it was important to watch films like *The Exorcist* and *Amityville II*. Ed explained that everything in the film was an accurate depiction of "what happens" when dealing with the demonic.

The connection to Amityville cemented the Warrens' reputation as national authorities on the demonic. After 1979, news articles almost never described the Warrens as artists or anything other than full-time demon-busters. A 1985 flyer for one of the Warrens' lectures called them, "Chief investigators of the Amityville Horror."[90] By 1986, they were making as much as $1,800 for a lecture—the equivalent of over $5,000 in 2022.[91] It seems the Warrens spent the rest of their careers seeking a haunted house story that could replicate the success of Amityville.

In 2022, Netflix aired a reality show hosted by Tony Spera called *28 Days Haunted*, in which teams of paranormal investigators are locked in allegedly haunted locations for twenty-eight days. Spera and journalist Aaron Sagers watch them on cameras from what appears to be a bunker and comment on their progress. According to the show, the Warrens hypothesized that supernatural activity occurred in a twenty-eight-day cycle and that observing a location for the entire cycle could result in a breakthrough for investigators. We are unaware of the Warrens ever saying such a thing, and many of their investigations seem to have lasted only a day. The show seems to have settled on twenty-eight days because this is the amount of time the Lutz family allegedly stayed in the Amityville house before fleeing for their lives.

The Enfield Poltergeist and *The Conjuring 2*

The second *Conjuring* film is based on a well-documented claim of poltergeist activity that took place in the Brimsdown neighborhood of Enfield, on the outskirts of London, between 1977 and 1979. The case is known to paranormal researchers as "The Enfield Poltergeist." Single mother Peggy Hodgson lived in Enfield with her four children: Margaret, aged 13; Janet, aged 11; Johnny, aged 10; and Billy, aged 7. The family claimed they were tormented by all manner of inexplicable phenomena, including furniture moving on its own, loud noises, voices, thrown toys, and even Janet being levitated.[92]

Guy Lyon Playfair, a British paranormal researcher and member of the Society for Psychical Research, traveled to the home. He and his assistant, Maurice Grosse, spent many hours recording and documenting incidents. Playfair and Grosse were convinced the phenomenon was genuine and centered around Janet, who always seemed to be present when the activity occurred. Skeptics concluded this was because Janet perpetrated a hoax. Even Anita Gregory, of the Society for Psychical Research, concluded that while there may have been genuine paranormal activity in the beginning of the case, "It had turned quickly into a farcical performance for investigators and reporters desiring a sensational story."[93] American stage magician Milborne Christopher was more skeptical, declaring the phenomena the antics of a "very very clever" little girl.[94]

In *The Conjuring 2*, the Warrens' help is requested, and they are shown consulting with Grosse and Gregory. In reality, the Warrens seem to have simply showed up at the Hodgson residence for one day. In a 2016 interview, Playfair recalled "[The Warrens] did turn up once, I think, at Enfield, and all I can remember is Ed Warren telling me that he could make a lot of money for me out of it." He added, "Nobody ever mentioned them. I mean, I don't think anybody in the family had ever heard of [Ed] until he turned up. Uninvited."[95] It is possible the Warrens hoped that by inserting themselves into the situation, they could replicate their success with Amityville. *The Conjuring 2* takes the story in a very different direction, introducing a demon named Valak that has long sought to destroy Ed. The actual Warrens never mentioned anything like this, but Valak gave *The Conjuring*'s Ed a demonic foil, much like Pazuzu is to Lankester Merrin in *The Exorcist*.

The Glatzels, Arne Johnson, and *The Conjuring 3*

In 1973, Ed boasted, "If our proof was given the same credibility in a court of law as any other case, we would have no trouble proving our case."[96] Ed got a chance to test this claim in 1981 when he argued that Arne Cheyenne

Johnson was not guilty of murder by reason of demonic possession. The so-called "Demon Murder Case" resembles an ostensive performance of *The Exorcist*, which was originally conceived as a courtroom drama. The case began not with Johnson, but eleven-year-old David Glatzel of Brookfield, Connecticut. In 1979, David began exhibiting odd behavior, including alleged hallucinations and violent outbursts. The Glatzels were Catholic, and they contacted Father James Dennis of St. Joseph's Catholic Church for help, who referred them to the Warrens. In 1983, Gerald Brittle wrote the Warrens' version of the story in *The Devil in Connecticut*. According to this account, the Warrens witnessed all manner of demonic activity in the Glatzel home, including strange knocks, lights flashing on and off, and vibrations that rattled the house. The source of this activity was an entity the family called "The Beast." The Beast had forty-two subordinate demons who would assault David with invisible fists. Eventually David became possessed by The Beast. He would become violent, spout obscenities, and even attempted to strangle his mother.[97] The Warrens recommended an exorcism.

Johnson was in a long-term relationship with David's older sister, Debbie. During one of David's episodes, Johnson allegedly tried to help by telling the demon, "Come into me—leave the little lad alone."[98] According to the Warrens, the demon obliged and entered Johnson. On February 16, 1981, Johnson and Debbie had lunch with Debbie's boss, Alan Bono, from whom the couple was renting a small apartment. Bono was intoxicated and reportedly tried to stop Debbie from leaving. An altercation ensued and Johnson fatally stabbed Bono. Johnson claimed to have no memory of the argument or the stabbing. The Warrens and Debbie insisted that he had been possessed and was not responsible for his actions.[99] According to one source, a book contract for what would become *The Devil in Connecticut* was signed on March 3, only fifteen days after this incident.[100]

Johnson's attorney, Martin Minella, made the unusual decision to plead not guilty by reason of demonic possession. The Warrens began marshaling evidence about David's exorcism. The Bridgeport chief of police confirmed that the Warrens had reached out to him in October to warn him that they were dealing with a demonic situation and that violence might ensue. The local Catholic diocese confirmed that four priests had taken action to help David, but they claimed none of them had sought the bishop's permission for a formal exorcism. Ed disagreed, claiming that he knew priests who went directly to the bishop and that he would subpoena them if necessary.[101] Judge Robert Callahan ruled that there was no such defense and that it would be "irrelative and unscientific" to allow discussion of possession or exorcisms in the courtroom.[102] Minella switched to a claim of self-defense while prosecutors argued that Johnson had been motivated by romantic jealousy toward his girlfriend's boss. The jury convicted Johnson of first-degree manslaughter. He served only five years before being released early on parole for good behavior.[103] While serving his sentence, he married Debbie.

Some time after the trial, the Warrens connected the Glatzels with an exorcist in Canada (because the local diocese would not grant one), who concluded that young David had been possessed through no fault of his own but as the result of a curse. According to this interpretation, some friends with whom the family had a falling out must have been Satanists and this misfortune was their doing. The curse was likely placed during a snowmobile trip that took place exactly one year before the murder. It had likely been meant to kill someone, and its conditions were met when Johnson murdered Bono.[104]

At the time of the trial, Dudley Clendinen of The New York Times noted that the Glatzel family seemed predisposed to interpret David's behavior as possession. Debbie had attended "at least one" of the Warrens' lectures before her brother's unusual behavior started. The entire Glatzel family had also recently watched The Exorcist on television.[105] The story of Johnson challenging a demon to leave a child and enter into him is, of course, exactly what happens at the end of The Exorcist. David's brother, Carl Glatzel, Jr., later claimed that David had suffered from a mental health episode that was misinterpreted as demonic possession. The Warrens, he claimed, "saw a goldmine." They encouraged the family's belief that their son was possessed and brought unwanted attention to what should have been a private health crisis. One source quoted David, reflecting on his behavior during the episode: "Ed and Lorraine told me I was possessed, so I fed into it. They told me how to act so I acted that way. I wanted attention and I got it, but it wasn't possession."[106] After The Devil in Connecticut was re-printed in 2006, Carl— who had been a teenager when the book was first published—sued Lorraine Warren and Gerald Brittle for invasion of privacy, libel, and intentional infliction of emotional distress. In a press release, Glatzel stated, "The Warrens told my family numerous times that we would be millionaires and the book would help get my sister's boyfriend, Arne, out of jail. I knew from day one it was a lie, but as a child, there was nothing I could really do about it."[107]

The same year The Devil in Connecticut was published, Dick Clark Productions adapted the story into the NBC made-for-TV movie "The

Demon Murder Case." The names and locations of the story were changed. A young Kevin Bacon played "Kenny Miller," the young defendant. Ed and Lorraine became "Guy and Charlotte Harris," with Andy Griffith playing Ed. The plot sticks very closely to the story as reported in the papers and leaves it ambiguous whether anything supernatural is actually occurring. The Warrens/Harrises are presented as well-meaning, but not necessarily helpful. In one scene, they leave the Glatzel residence with a priest, who reprimands them for encouraging the family to believe they are dealing with the demonic. Guy Harris responds, "All we did was arm this family against the Devil in a very small way. If the Devil isn't here, then no harm's been done." To which the priest replies, "But there *is* harm done. You lead them to believe that they're making sense!" This argument—that the Warrens were harming families rather than helping them—would later become a common critique among skeptics. Attorney Martin Minella was so proud of this publicity that the website for his law firm still mentions that one of his cases "became a TV movie starring Kevin Bacon." It does not specify the case or the movie.[108]

When Carl Glatzel, Jr. sued Lorraine Warren and Gerald Brittle, he remarked, "If there is anything I can do about it, there is no way there will be a movie about me and my family based on these lies."[109] But the case was still adapted into *The Conjuring III: The Devil Made Me Do It* (2021). This film deviated far from the original story, focusing more on the element of a curse placed by Satanists. In the film's *denouement*, the Warrens confront the witch responsible for the curse and smash her Satanic altar, causing the demon she summoned to turn on her instead. This ending builds on the belief that the murder of Alan Bono fulfilled the requirements of a curse meant for someone else. In another example of *The Exorcist* effect, both the interpretation of how David's possession led to the death of Alan Bono and the plot of *The Conjuring III* are derivative of *Night of The Demon* (1958) and the Hammer Classic *The Devil Rides Out* (1968), both discussed further in Chapter 7. Those films also feature evil magicians slain by their own conjured demons.

Maurice Theriault and *Satan's Harvest*

The case of Maurice "Frenchie" Theriault, a farmer from Warren, Massachusetts, is the most disturbing of the Warrens' cases. It was adapted into the book *Satan's Harvest* (1990), co-authored with the Warrens by

Michael Lasalandra and Mark Merenda. The story has not yet been depicted in any of the *Conjuring* films; however, footage of Theriault's exorcism appears in *The Conjuring* when Carolyn Perron visits Lorraine. Maurice Theriault is a main character in *The Nun* (2018), a spin-off of *The Conjuring II*. However, the film character has little in common with the actual man.

Maurice's father pulled him from school in the third grade to work on the family farm in rural Maine. His father abused him physically and sexually, and allegedly once forced Maurice to participate in bestiality with him. Despite this trauma, Maurice married and acquired a farm of his own. In 1982, Maurice's father murdered Maurice's mother and then killed himself. Sometime after this, Maurice came to believe he might be possessed. In addition to other unexplained phenomena, a series of anomalous fires had started on his farm. He reached out to a local priest, who put him in touch with the Warrens. On February 24, 1985, he entered the police office in Warren, Massachusetts, with his wife and attempted to surrender all his firearms— something the Warrens had advised him to do. Police Chief Jerry Seibert suspected a scheme in which Maurice was trying to burn down his own farm for insurance money and blame his actions on possession.[110]

The Warrens approached the Church about an exorcism and were denied. Numerous tabloids began covering the case. Finally, the Warrens obtained an exorcism from Bishop Robert McKenna, a sedevacantist priest who broke away from the Catholic Church following Vatican II. The Warrens videotaped the exorcism, which appears to show blood oozing from Maurice's eyes and stigmata appearing on his body. Theriault's sister, Dana Daviau, claimed this was staged, stating, "Maurice was not possessed; Maurice was an actor." Daviau claimed she had seen Theriault rehearse the oozing blood effect by placing blood under his eyelid.[111]

Although the exorcism was deemed a success, Seibert was alerted by a child abuse investigator that Maurice had repeatedly raped his thirteen-year-old stepdaughter. Furthermore, he had previously pled guilty to a charge of child rape in 1976 and served five-years' probation. Maurice was arrested for rape. But Ed Warren asserted that an incubus—and not Maurice—had been raping the stepdaughter. Video of the exorcism was shown to the attorney general's office. Although Maurice was deemed competent to stand trial, the stepdaughter refused to testify, and he was never convicted.[112]

Satan's Harvest was cited in the 1992 book *Satanism: Is it Real?* by Catholic priest Jeffrey J. Steffon. Steffon does not comment on allegations of rape or incubi, but he does cite it as an example of possible true possession. This book received a *nihil obstat* and *imprimatur* from Catholic authorities, indicating that it contains nothing contradictory to Catholic faith and morals.[113] This connection is significant because it shows the Warrens leading Catholic authorities, rather than the other way around.

After *Satan's Harvest* was written, Maurice and his wife separated. In 1992, Maurice returned home with a shotgun, cut the phone line, and waited for his wife. When she arrived, he shot her in the arm before turning the gun on himself.[114] Theriault's situation may have been a mix of delusion, conscious deception, and genuine belief in the demonic. But, in this case, the Warrens' approach of always believing those who contact them was demonstrably harmful. It seems unlikely this story can be incorporated into *The Conjuring* films.

The Smurl Family and *The Haunted*

The case of the Smurl family of West Pittston, Pennsylvania, in 1986, became the basis for the book *The Haunted*. In 1991, *The Haunted* was adapted into a Fox made-for-TV movie, giving the Warrens their first screenwriting credit. Jack and Janet Smurl moved into a double-block house with Jack's parents in 1973. While living in the home, the Smurls experienced an escalating series of supernatural experiences, culminating in Jack's experience of being sexually assaulted by a succubus. The Warrens were asked to investigate in January 1986. They reported ample evidence of demonic infestation: bad odors, inexplicable noises (screaming, pig grunts, and others) at all hours of the night, physical assault of pets and family, and levitation. Ed himself claimed to have felt "a drop in temperature of at least 30-some degrees," followed by the appearance of a swirling black mass accompanied by a rattling sound.[115] In August, the Smurls turned to the diocese of Scranton, who would not perform an exorcism. The Warrens turned again to Bishop Robert McKenna, who exorcized the home. However, McKenna's efforts were deemed unsuccessful.

Skeptics were unconvinced. In 1986, Paul Kurtz, a philosophy professor at the State University of New York at Buffalo, and chairman of the Committee for the Scientific Investigation of Claims of the Paranormal, called the entire affair a hoax, comparing it to the Amityville case and noting that the Warrens' investigation was not objective. Also in 1986, a mentalist named George Joseph Kresge Jr. (also known as "The Amazing Kreskin") used stage illusions to replicate some of the alleged demonic activity. There were also concerns that Jack's problems could be medical. In 1983, Jack underwent a procedure to remove water from his brain. He also admitted that prior to this he had experienced memory loss, likely due to the effects of a meningitis infection he suffered as a child.[116]

Scranton Tribune staff writer Robert Curran worked with the Smurls and the Warrens to write *The Haunted*. Reviewers slammed it for being too uncritical. Although the book's film adaptation did not become another *Amityville Horror*, Ed Warren said of *The Haunted*, "I also would like to mention that this was a movie of the week. That movie was done beautifully. The Smurl family insisted that there be no fabrication in that movie at all. No Hollywood hype."[117]

The Snedeker Family and *The Haunting in Connecticut*

In 1986, Allen and Carmen Snedeker rented an old residence known as the Hallahan House in Southington, Connecticut, to be closer to the hospital where their son, Philip, was being treated for Hodgkin's lymphoma. Soon after moving in, the family discovered a box of coffin handles, a chain and pulley casket lift, and a blood drainage pit in the basement of their home. These relics had all been left over from the house's previous business, the Hallahan Funeral Home.[118] The Snedekers reported all manner of paranormal occurrences during their two-year stay in the home. First, Philip began seeing ghosts and other terrifying visions. Carmen claims a mop bucket full of water turned blood red while she was cleaning, and it had the stink of decaying flesh.[119] The family also suffered apparitions, noises, and other physical attacks, but none so harrowing as the alleged repeated sexual assaults. Carmen, Al, and their young niece all claimed to have been sexually assaulted, raped, and sodomized by unseen forces on multiple occasions during their stay in the house.[120] The family contacted the Warrens, who arrived with their team and stayed in the house the better part of two months.[121] The Warrens experienced cold spots; knocking; and an oozing, stinking green slime. They (again) concluded that this was a case of demonic infestation. The Snedeker family had an exorcism performed, and eventually left the home.

Garton said that when he interviewed the Snedekers for his book *In a Dark Place*, they seemed nervous: "I'm not sure why, but there was some tension in the air. Carmen kept returning to the subject of a movie adaptation. She wanted to know how much money they'd make from a movie sale." He recalled that a bit later, "I overheard her saying something to Al about a lottery, and then she turned to me and said 'You weren't supposed to hear that. Please don't tell anyone, okay?'"[122] When questioned, Carmen offered a vague explanation about some kind of out-of-state lottery scheme. While Garton was unclear on the details, Carmen insisted that he not mention it to anyone. This exchange set the tone for Garton's interaction with the Snedekers, and when he questioned them about their experiences, he began to find numerous inconsistencies: "Carmen went on at length about the many times she was anally raped by an invisible demon while doing things around the house—washing dishes, doing laundry, that sort of thing—and she and Al told me about his experience with the anal raping demon."[123] Garton says that after his book was published, Carmen accused him of creating the stories about the rape, but Garton maintains that it was discussed when they met. (Carmen also referenced sodomy on the episode "I Was Raped By A Ghost" of *The Sally Jesse Raphael Show*.) Garton concludes, "She changed her mind when she saw how people responded to those stories while promoting the book."[124] The Snedeker story became the basis for *The Haunting in Connecticut* (2009), which had moderate success at the box office.

The Warrens had numerous other cases, ripe for film adaptations. In addition to haunted houses, the Warrens described encounters with all manner of mythological creatures, most of which were folded into a larger cosmology of the demonic. It was originally announced that *The Conjuring III* would tell the story of William Ramsey—a disturbed man from Southend, London, who believed he was a werewolf. In 1983, Ramsey was admitted to a hospital, where he bit a nurse. In a subsequent incident he entered a police station and asked to be locked up, then entered a frenzy and had to be restrained. He was committed to a mental institution for twenty-eight days. The Warrens learned of the case through the tabloids and flew to London where they diagnosed Ramsey as possessed by a "werewolf demon." They brought him back to Connecticut where Bishop McKenna performed an exorcism that was declared successful.[125]

The Warrens even tried their hand at Bigfoot hunting. In 1972, Charles B. Pierce's docudrama *The Beast of Boggy Creek*, about a Bigfoot-like creature that has been spotted near Fouke, Arkansas, since the early twentieth century, became a drive-through hit. It was one of the highest grossing films of the year and sowed Bigfoot mania across the country. In 1976, twenty-six-year-old Jennie Robertson of Flintville, Tennessee, reported seeing an eight-foot hairy monster carrying away her four-year-old son before she intervened and snatched him away. Her husband reported the incident to the local paper. Soon, other witnesses reported similar sightings and parties of monster hunters were combing the forests. Lorraine Warren visited the area to try to help.[126] While exploring the forest with some monster hunters, Lorraine received a psychic vision of a creature that "appear[ed] to be a fusion of ape and man" and whose eyes "shone with intelligence, compassion, and fear." Lorraine reported that she experienced a psychic connection with an injured Bigfoot: "He was hurt . . . . his hairy, splayed foot scabbed with still-seeping blood. During his travels that day, he had somehow injured his foot. Afraid that his injury would keep him from returning to his secret cave, the creature now projected great fear." Lorraine attempted to soothe the beast by projecting images of benevolence and friendship at it. Then a member of the search party blasted a horn, severing their mental connection. The Bigfoot reportedly ran into the woods. Lorraine followed a trail of blood to the edge of a cliff, but no sign of the creature could be found.[127]

Ed expressed belief in "cryptid" creatures, including Bigfoot and the Loch Ness Monster. But, perhaps influenced by paranormal researcher John Keel, he claimed these were not flesh and blood animals but "tulpas" or thought forms that had acquired a form of physical reality. He explained, "They are Tulpas, physical manifestations that are projections of the mind. They are creatures of black magic as practiced throughout the world, but most notably by the monks in Tibet."[128] It is significant that where Lorraine imagined a wounded Bigfoot in need of compassion, Ed saw a demonic menace. The idea of the tulpa in paranormal discourse is only tangentially related to anything in Tibetan Buddhism.[129] And even in paranormal discourse, tulpas are not normally associated with black magic. But Ed's brand emphasized his role as a warrior against demons and black magic.

The Legacy of the Warrens

Whatever we might think of the Warrens or their strange career, they have had a significant impact on the way Americans imagine and experience the supernatural. By some counts, there are now as many as three thousand paranormal investigation groups in the United States. While psychical research dates to the nineteenth century, the work these groups do resembles the investigations of the Warrens far more than the experiments of the ASPR. Like the Warrens, paranormal investigators go hunting for spooky houses. They use a variety of scientific gadgets, but their approach is rarely scientific. More often it is an eclectic mix of Christianity, fringe scientific discourses, and magical practices—an approach pioneered and popularized by the Warrens. More importantly, their goal is not really to assess evidence for the existence of ghosts, but to generate compelling experiences and stories. Marc A. Eaton has argued that contemporary ghost hunting is really a spiritual practice that "creates within participants a sense of being connected to and aware of some transcendent, perhaps divine, reality beyond our world."[130] This sense of a transcendent reality, we argue, is what the Warrens were actually selling to their audiences—not protection from demonic dangers. Furthermore, religion scholar Daniel Wise notes that ghost hunters seem increasingly preoccupied with the possibility of encountering demons in their investigations, and that their ideas of what demons are and do are often heavily indebted to the Warrens. Why would an investigator want to encounter a demon? Wise argues that demon encounters—even more than ghost sightings—provide the witness with evidence of a supernatural order that is not only transcendent, but moral.[131] This idea that an encounter with a demon could prove the existence of the divine was, of course, popularized by The Exorcist.

In addition to modeling a new spiritual practice, the Warrens also helped transform twentieth-century America into an enchanted landscape dotted with haunted houses, cursed objects, and portals to hell. Daryl Caterine has argued that America, as a country colonized by Europeans, has no traditional religious pilgrimage sites. Instead, Roswell and other paranormal sites have become locations where travelers can feel uniquely connected to an unseen order.[132] The Warrens presentation of themselves as traveling investigators, crisscrossing the country and discovering the supernatural forces lurking under the surface of America, became a kind of media aesthetic, in which the romance of travel works to fuse together landscape, history, and the supernatural. This trope of the traveling American paranormal investigators has echoes in such television shows as The X-Files, American Horror Story, and, especially, Supernatural, in which the show's protagonists, the Winchester brothers, roam the country in a muscle car slaying ghosts and demons. Like the Warrens, demon-hunting is the Winchester "family business," and they employ a medley of Catholic sacra and folk magic to accomplish their goals.

Regarding *The Exorcist* effect, it is possible that the Warrens could still have made careers for themselves, even if Blatty and Friedkin had never made *The Exorcist*. But it is undeniable that the Warrens were uniquely aided by the film industry. In 1982, a reporter for the *Philadelphia Inquirer* opined, "One reason for the campus popularity may be the incredible proliferation in the last 10 years of horror films dealing with possession and the occult."[133] Horror films helped the Warrens in several ways. First, they primed audiences to interpret anomalous experiences as demonic. This was certainly the case with the Glatzel family, who watched *The Exorcist* before interpreting their child's mental health crisis as demonic. The priming effect in this case was likely reinforced by the fact that the family was Catholic and interested in the supernatural. Second, horror films provided a kind of cultural shorthand for talking about things like hauntings, witches, curses, and demons. This enabled the Warrens to visit families like the Perrons, Glatzels, Smurls, and Snedekers, and quickly negotiate a narrative of what was happening, why, and how to fix it. The end of *The Conjuring* quotes Ed Warren, "The fairy tale is true." In other words, supernatural forces—of which we know primarily from movies and other media deemed fiction—actually exist. Third, the market for horror films based on true stories clearly created a financial incentive for the Warrens to do their work and—at least in some cases—for experiencers to collaborate with the Warrens. The lawsuits surrounding *The Amityville Horror* and *The Conjuring* demonstrate that film adaptations of these stories can be highly lucrative, and that people will go to great lengths to get a share of their profits.

Even more significantly, the Warrens changed the way some people think about supernatural horror. Ed Warren once stated, "These things are real and we would rather have the kids see it in a movie than have it in their lives . . . . I think people are far more open-minded about the subject than they used to be. When we talk at a college now you can hear a pin drop."[134] Far from being something Christians should avoid, the Warrens suggested that watching horror movies is a pious activity that inculcates belief in the supernatural and may even protect the viewer from demonic perils.

The Hayes brothers, who wrote *The Conjuring*, have continued this line of thought, asserting that *The Conjuring* is not a horror film but a "religious supernatural" film.[135] In our interview with the Hayes brothers, they explained they did not belong to any denomination but that they believed in God and their movies were alerting Americans to the real possibility of the demonic. The brothers recalled that when they were consulting with Lorraine on the phone, there would be strange interference on the call. Lorraine said this was caused by demons trying to interrupt their conversation. She uttered some prayers and the interference ceased. We asked why demons would try to stop Lorraine from talking to screenwriters. They answered that the demons probably did not want anyone to see *The Conjuring* because it would alert people to their activities. This anecdote should probably not be interpreted as a tenet of faith for the Hayes brothers, but as part of a long tradition of metatextual reflection. Like Friedkin's hints that *The Exorcist* was cursed, the phone demons are a story that enhances a story about Lorraine.

The Warrens began as artists and, in a way, they remained artists their entire lives. Their medium became stories rather than paintings. It is not an understatement to say that the Warrens invited clients to experience starring in their own horror movie, with the hope of transforming this experience into an actual film. In the process, they changed the way many people thought about religion, media, and the supernatural. None of this mitigates the disturbing stories of Judith Penney, Carl Glatzl, Jr., Maurice Theriault, and others, but neither does ignoring the significant impact the Warrens had on American culture.

5

The Martin Cycle

"Satanism is all around us. We deny it at our peril. I could point out places only minutes from here where black masses are being celebrated. I know of cases of human sacrifice—the sacrifice of babies. I know the people who are doing these things."

—Malachi Martin[1]

"No, I'll never forgive Martin. He wrote about demonic possession and I think he had an inside track."

—Robert Blair Kaiser[2]

In 1996, near the end of his life, an article appeared on Malachi Martin's website, describing his work as an exorcist:

The dark shadows of skyscrapers are falling across New York as an elderly white-haired priest leaves the reassuring comfort of his home and heads through the streets towards the apartment block where the others are waiting. He walks quite slowly, carrying a small black case filled with the essential paraphernalia of the ritual he is about to perform.[3]

This image of an elderly priest setting off to an exorcism, case in hand, literally appears on the movie poster for *The Exorcist*. Once a Jesuit priest and Vatican insider, Martin (1921–1999) was released from his vows in 1964 following an affair with the wife of a prominent journalist. He ended up in New York, where he supported himself as a writer. Of his seventeen books, the most influential was *Hostage to the Devil: The Possession and Exorcism of Five Living Americans*. *Hostage* was published in 1976, just two years after *Exorcist* mania swept the country. The original cover boasted, "It's not like The Exorcist or The Omen . . . Because It's True." Drawing on his background as a priest, Martin claimed his book was not fiction; instead, it was

The Exorcist Effect. Joseph P. Laycock and Eric Harrelson, Oxford University Press. © Oxford University Press 2024.
DOI: 10.1093/oso/9780197635391.003.0005

based on recordings of actual exorcisms of which he had personal knowledge. Although Martin never wrote another book on possession, he became known as a famous exorcist and the rest of his life became a sort of ostensive performance of Lankester Merrin's character. In the wake of Vatican II, Martin was uniquely positioned to appeal to the grievances of traditionalist Catholics, and he gained a cult following that has continued after his death in 1999. In an ironic reversal of influences, a 2017 article in *The New York Post* declared that "Martin's decades of work as a spiritual healer inspired the cult classic 1973 movie 'The Exorcist.' "[4]

Of all the people whose careers rode the wave made by *The Exorcist*, Martin may have been the most influential. Unlike Ed and Lorraine Warren, Martin was highly educated, a prolific writer, and knew numerous languages. But whereas the Warrens embellished stories about their experiences investigating hauntings and holding séances, Martin invented stories entirely from his imagination. He was a notorious liar and his own accounts of his involvement with exorcism are inconsistent. In fact, he likely never witnessed an exorcism prior to writing *Hostage*. Yet his influence on the culture of exorcism in the last twentieth century cannot be understated. Through his books, interviews, and a series of appearances on the late-night radio show *Coast to Coast AM*, Martin effected at least four important changes to contemporary demonology.

First, whereas Blatty presented exorcism as incredibly rare, Martin alleged that it is actually common, and that Church authorities were engaged in a conspiracy to cover it up. In a 1987 appearance on *Oprah* he stated, "I've met the heads of state hospitals . . . who tell me that fifty percent at least of the people they have behind bars, tied down, in padded cells are certainly beyond repair by psychiatry because they're really possessed."[5] Martin loved to invent statistics like this. For example, in the foreword to the 1992 edition of *Hostage to the Devil*, he stated that eight hundred to thirteen hundred major exorcisms are performed every year and that the number of exorcisms has increased 750 percent since the period between the early 1960s and mid-1970s. A few pages later, his original 1976 text states, "The truth is that official or scholarly census of possession cases never been made,"[6] raising the question of how the figure of a 750 percent increase was calculated.

Second, Martin quite literally re-invented Catholic demonology. For all his appeals to clerical authority, Martin seems to have known surprisingly little about exorcism, as several contemporary reviewers of *Hostage* pointed out. Instead of researching what figures such as Thomas Aquinas or any number of early modern theologians or Church councils had already stated about demons, possession, and exorcism, Martin invented an entirely new demonology from his imagination. And in many ways, Martin's demonology was superior to that of his predecessors. Pre-modern demonologists had to contend with the messiness of conflicting Bible verses and religious doctrines, ambiguous cases where both exorcist and demoniac may be engaged in fraud, and the politics of Europe's wars of religion. Martin could ignore all this and approach demonology like a fantasy author, creating an imaginary world that feels real because it is internally consistent. Unlike pre-modern witch-hunting manuals, *Hostage* is concise, practical, and accessible. Armed with this advantage, Martin's ideas superseded centuries-old teachings almost overnight. Eventually Martin's demonology was applied in actual exorcisms and appeared in horror films.

Third, Martin's demonology bridged the gap between exorcism and contemporary conspiracy theories. Martin often presented himself as someone with secret insider knowledge about the Vatican and world governments. Even before his departure from the Jesuits, he enjoyed telling tales that implied he had been on secret missions.[7] In her memoir *Disguised as a Man*, Sarah Colwell describes her experiences having a years-long romantic relationship with Martin when he lived in New York in the 1980s. In this account, Martin told the much younger Colwell that he was privy to "the third secret of Fatima"; that he worked with various intelligence agencies; and that during the Iran hostage crisis, he was part of a cabal that undermined the Carter administration by encouraging the ill-fated rescue mission, knowing that a sandstorm would down the helicopters. Martin also told Colwell that the Third Prophecy of Fatima predicted an alien invasion and that he had once been brought to a debris site in Mayhill, New Mexico, so that he could use his linguistic knowledge to translate script from an extraterrestrial craft. Rome and Washington had a pact to keep the public from ever learning about the alien threat. In fact, reports of a 1947 crash at Roswell were a disinformation campaign by Martin's associates to distract from the *actual* spaceship that Martin investigated. Colwell reflects, "He lied when the truth would do, when honesty would have been a better policy. He lied just to hear himself talk."[8]

After *Hostage*, Martin wrote a series of conspiracy-driven books claiming that his former order, the Jesuits, were playing a key role in undermining the Catholic Church so as to render it a tool of the New World Order—a perennial villain in 1990s conspiracy theories. Along with the Jesuits, Satanists,

Freemasons, pedophile rings, the Soviet Union, and liberation theology were all agents of the New World Order. Martin claimed that the power elite of both church and state were "perfectly possessed"—a term he invented to describe demoniacs who can never be exorcised because they have willingly offered themselves over to demons. He also claimed that elite bloodlines raise their children from a young age to achieve perfect possession. In many ways, Martin's writings anticipated QAnon, which likewise frames political and religious differences in terms of a monolithic conspiracy of absolute evil.

Fourth, Martin wrote novels as well as non-fiction books, and his lies and distortions eventually took *The Exorcist* effect to its logical conclusion by intertwining truth and fiction to the point where they ceased to be meaningful categories. Michael Cuneo called Martin's work "a twilight zone where fact bleeds into fiction, history into myth, and where trying to sort out the differences is a tortuous business."[9] Martin's final novel, *The Windswept House* (1996), describes traitorous Vatican officials performing a Satanic ritual called "The Enthronement of Lucifer" in Saint Paul's Chapel in the Vatican on June 29, 1963. When asked how much of this story was "true," Malachi replied with more statistics: "To speak in percentages, roughly 85% of the fictional characters mirror real people, and roughly 85% of events in the book mirror real events . . . We are talking about real events and real people masked in the form of a novel; nowadays it is called faction, a term coined by Norman Mailer, but an art form really created by Taylor Caldwell."[10] At least some of Martin's contemporary followers have expressed certainty that the Enthronement of Lucifer ceremony occurred, exactly as described in the novel.[11] It is ironic that Martin condemned "postmodern" thinking as sophistry, when his own deployment of "faction" invites readers to believe whatever they prefer or intuit as true. This demolition of any shared reality is another way in which Martin's writings anticipated QAnon.

From the Vatican to Manhattan

Constructing a biography of Martin is difficult because so many details of his life are contested or contradict each other. Martin has been called many things. A *New York Times* reviewer called him "a lapsed Irish cleric half in love and half in hate with God"[12] and *The Washington Post* dubbed him "as powerful a caster of spells as Rasputin."[13] Willam van Etten Casey, a Jesuit professor at the College of the Holy Cross in Worcester, Massachusetts, described him as "a poetic con man."[14] Journalist Michael Novak, who worked alongside him at the second Vatican council, called him "a brilliant man whose playfulness outruns his brilliance."[15] M. Scott Peck, a psychiatrist who became Martin's protege after coming to believe some of his patients were demonically possessed, described Martin half-seriously as "a leprechaun." Another psychiatrist, Frank Ayd, diagnosed him as a likely sociopath.[16] But by all accounts, Martin was well-spoken and gregarious, a consummate charmer who especially enjoyed taking friends to dinner to engage in conversation and storytelling.

Martin was born on July 23, 1921, in Ballylongford, a village in County Kerry, Ireland. He had ten brothers and sisters. His mother was Irish, his father was an obstetrician who had emigrated to Ireland from Britain. One legend told about Martin is that he was baptized before he was born: Martin had been a breech baby and while his father was delivering him, he performed a baptism.[17] All of Martin's brothers went to seminary and Martin became a Jesuit novice at the age of eighteen. He received a bachelor's degree in Semitic languages and Oriental history from the National University of Ireland, and he studied Assyriology at Trinity College in Dublin. He taught classical languages for several years and was ordained as a priest in 1954. The Jesuits sent him to the University of Louvain, in Belgium, where he earned a doctoral degree. He studied further at Oxford and the Hebrew University in Jerusalem.[18] He also spent some time in the Middle East doing archaeological work and, in 1958, he produced his first book, an interpretation of the Dead Sea Scrolls. Martin took a teaching position at the Vatican's Pontifical Biblical Institute. By the time the second Vatican Council was convened in 1962, he had become a close friend of Cardinal Augustin Bea, a German Jesuit and an important progressive voice at the Council. Through Bea, Martin had access to Pope John XXIII's inner circle of advisors.

Bea's chief goal at the council was to produce an official declaration advancing Jewish and Catholic relations and condemning antisemitism. These efforts eventually resulted in *Nostra aetate*, a declaration on ecumenism promulgated in 1965. Bea faced opposition from both conservatives and Middle Eastern nations, who were wary of the Vatican lending political support to Israel. Bea began holding secret meetings with the American Jewish Committee (AJC) to better coordinate their efforts. Martin inserted himself into this situation, becoming the AJC's "mole" in the Vatican. He offered advice and leaked restricted and secret documents to the AJC. In the process, he made friends with Abraham Heschel, a theological consultant to the AJC. Reports from AJC director Zechariah Shuster refer to Martin variously as "Forest," "Puskin," and Heschel's "young friend." Historian Edward Kaplan suggests Martin helped the AJC out of "a mixture of motives, lofty and ignoble."[19] He seems to have genuinely cared about Catholic–Jewish relations while also relishing the chance to have a role in Vatican intrigue.

Through his work with the AJC, Martin was introduced to Roger Straus, a publishing magnate and member of the Guggenheim family. When Pope Paul VI succeeded John XXIII in 1964, the odds of a declaration on ecumenism seemed imperiled. So, Heschel decided to rush out a book about the internal workings of the Ecumenical Council in the hope that this would help Bea's case. He persuaded his friend Straus to publish it through the publishing house Farrar, Straus & Giroux, and tapped Martin to write it under the pseudonym "Michael Serafian." Martin cranked out *The Pilgrim* in only six weeks. In typical Martin fashion, it mixed fact with fiction, praising Paul VI while simultaneously casting him as indecisive and weak. It took one month for *Commonweal* to publish a review outing Martin as the author. *The Pilgrim* was removed from circulation at a loss to the publisher, eventually leading to the end of Straus's and Heschel's friendship.[20]

The events leading to Martin's departure from Rome and the Jesuits began when *Time* sent journalist Robert Blair Kaiser to Rome to cover Vatican II. Kaiser had been a Jesuit novice himself before leaving this vocation and his Jesuit connections had helped him land this dream assignment. He moved into a spacious villa near St. Peter's Square with his wife, Sue, and their first child. Martin befriended Kaiser in the same way he had befriended the AJC, by offering insider information. As Kaiser told it in his memoir *Clerical Error*, Martin offered to be "a kind of research assistant" and in return occasionally asked for travel money.[21] He used the same alias, "Pushkin," in some of his memos to Kaiser. Between 1962 and 1964 Martin became a close friend of the family. When Sue became pregnant with her second child, Martin offered to predict the child's sex by tying a string of Sue's hair to her wedding ring and dangling it over her belly: if the ring spun clockwise it meant a boy, counterclockwise, a girl. But despite his Irish charm, the information Martin supplied to journalists proved inaccurate. One colleague told Kaiser, "I think Martin just makes things up. I think the man's crazy."[22]

When Sue tried her hand at writing reports on the council, Martin was eager to assist her, too, while her workaholic husband was away. Kaiser became increasingly suspicious of their relationship. He found that Martin had annotated Sue's copy of *The Feminine Mystique* and underlined comments disparaging husbands. Then he discovered that Sue had been secretly taking birth control.[23] As Kaiser sought evidence of an affair, he hired detectives and hid a recording device in his phone. He was briefly committed to a mental institution for paranoia—a move that Martin had secretly encouraged using mutual friends.

As the situation deteriorated, Sue announced she no longer loved her husband, took the children, and went to Nevada where she could obtain an expedited divorce. When Kaiser was able to visit the children, he discovered love letters Martin had written to Sue, pledging to leave the priesthood and marry her. Excerpts from the letters are salacious and undeniably Martin's writing style: "I can summon up the memory of your glistening limbs on that first eve, your raven locks shining in the moonlight, your moist, half-open eyes, your moist, half-open lips, my love, my dove, my panting doe . . . ."[24] In June 1964, Kaiser copied the letters and sent them to Martin's superiors on both sides of the Atlantic. Sue warned Martin, who intercepted one of the copies sent to Rome. But knowing other copies were coming, Martin resigned from the Biblical Institute. He left a note for his supervisor stating, "Since persons unknown—maybe the Arab Christians who wanted to scuttle the *schema* on the Jews—are making an attempt on my life, I will have to leave the Biblical immediately."[25] Kaiser believed that Martin often exaggerated opposition to Bea's declaration on the Jews to make the AJC feel more dependent on his help.

Kaiser's version of events is supported by a letter from his friend William Van Etten Casey, a Jesuit professor at Holy Cross College, to the Apostolic Delegate of Great Britain dated November 1, 1965. The letter makes the case for an annulment. Casey describes a meeting with Sue after her divorce in which she admitted to the affair and to Martin's plans to marry her. Mail from Martin was delivered during their meeting that included Kaiser's intercepted letter along with another letter written in a cipher Martin had devised. Casey wrote, "I now knew all the facts and their inescapable conclusion: Bob Kaiser was the innocent victim of a cruel liaison between a devil and a fool."[26]

Martin never met Sue in Nevada, and he eventually stopped answering her letters. She finally tracked down his brother in Dublin who explained that three other women, as well as "one rather attractive young man," had all come to him, believing Martin was in love with them, only to be discarded.[27] Martin might have gone on like this indefinitely had Kaiser not had numerous connections with the Jesuits and stumbled on indisputable evidence of the affair. In May 1965, Martin was granted a provisional release of his vows and on June 30, 1965, Paul VI approved an agreement in which Marin would be dispensed from his vows of poverty and obedience, but not celibacy.

The circumstances of Martin's departure from the Jesuits and his exact status as a priest remain contested to this day. Although Martin had begun his career championing Bea's progressive agenda, he now claimed that Vatican II had rendered the Church too liberal and that he could no longer in good conscience obey the Jesuits, or even a bishop. In one interview, he stated that the Vatican begged him to stay and promised to make him a cardinal.[28] This version of events instantly made Martin popular with traditionalist Catholics upset by the Church's reforms. In New York, Martin never wore priestly garments in public and never performed the sacraments publicly. However, he claimed he said mass privately every day and was still a priest under the agreement approved by Paul VI.

Martin left Rome for Paris to plot his next move. He called on his friend Roger Straus and told him that he had to flee Rome due to plots against his life.[29] Straus paid for Martin's airfare and asked his uncle, Harry Guggenheim, to give Martin a Guggenheim grant. That summer, the Harry Guggenheim Foundation awarded Martin $7,350 to study "the role of the motive of dominance in the historical development of Christianity, Islam, and Judaism."[30] This research would eventually result in *The Encounter* (1969), published by Farrar, Straus & Giroux. Curiously, from 1965 until 1967, Martin used his mother's maiden name and identified himself as "Malachi Fitzmaurice-Martin" in all his communications with the foundation. Sometimes he used his middle name "Brendan" and signed documents "B. Malachi-Fitzmaurice-Martin."

Soon after Martin's arrival, Straus and his wife Dorothea held a dinner party and invited Martin and Kakia Livanos, a wealthy widow. Livanos's husband, a Greek shipping magnate, had died in 1964. According to Boris Kachka's history of Farrar, Straus & Giroux, Martin went home with Livanos that night. In the morning, Livanos called Dorothea and asked, "Is he a devil or is he a god?"[31] Martin went on to live with Livanos, and she acted as Martin's benefactor for the rest of his life. A handwritten note from Livanos to Dr. Henry Allen Moe, director of the Guggenheim foundation explains, "We are looking around for an apartment for Malachi. We know it is the right thing for him so we will do the best we can."[32] Martin's defenders claim their relationship was platonic and that Cardinal Terrence Cooke had advised Martin to live with Livanos as her family's adopted priest.[33] This claim seems unlikely, though, as Livanos was Greek Orthodox and remained so for the rest of her life. There were also rumors that O'Connor, Cooke's successor, asked Malachi to stop cohabiting with Livanos but backed off when Martin responded with a letter from his attorney.[34]

In 1967, the foundation awarded Martin another grant for $5,000. But the grant money was not enough to make ends meet. To earn a living, Martin worked at a diner named Schrafft's, and then at Twin Donuts. He worked as a cab driver. He worked at a public relations business, and then for Encyclopedia Britannica. He started an antiques business called Collectors Founding.[35] All this must have seemed unglamorous to a former Vatican insider. The archives of Henry Allen Moe contain letters from various influential people speculating about how to help Martin and wondering why he did not simply seek a job as a theology professor. A letter from Livanos states:

> If I had the choosing and the giving of the ideal position for this man, I would automatically attach him to some very, very busy, very, very big man, as the latter's quiet, unrelenting, spade-work man . . . . He has learned how to serve and there must be someone, somewhere needing the services of a man who prefers to be in the background, who has thoroughgoing scholarship, and who has the rare gift of being able to identify with the person he serves, for writing, thinking, speech-drafting, conduct of social affairs, political commentary and interpretation.[36]

Livanos seems to have been seeking something similar to Martin's former position under Cardinal Bea—perhaps with Harry Guggenheim. In November 1968, Martin sent a pleading letter to Moe explaining that he was broke and had used his advance from *The Encounter* to pay off outstanding debts. He wrote: "I have actively sought employment since August. In all I have had 11 interviews, left my 'bio' with 5 agencies, combed classified advertisements and notices, and endeavored to find avenues of approach through my friends and my friends' friends. To date, nothing concrete has resulted."[37]

In 1970, Malachi Martin became a US citizen. Through friends in Long Island, he met Wanda Jablonksi, a journalist famous for covering the global petroleum industry. In 1972, the two had a brief affair and were spotted traveling together in Egypt and Saudi Arabia. But when Jablonski returned to New York, she was no longer enamored with Martin.[38] He wrote one more book with Farrar, Straus & Giroux, but the publishing house passed on his book *Jesus Now* (1973), finding the proposal "incoherent and anti-Semitic."[39] This ended Martin's relationship with his former patron. But Lila Karpf, a subsidiary rights director, left Farrar, Straus & Giroux in protest over their rejection of Martin. She became Martin's literary agent and has defended him to this day. By 1973, Martin needed another best-seller, Warner Brothers's promotional campaign for *The Exorcist* was well underway, and Karpf had a keen eye for what would sell. The stage was now set for Martin to write *Hostage to the Devil*.

Hostage to the Devil

Many conservative Catholics—notably Cardinal O'Connor and Gabriele Amorth, who founded the International Association of Exorcists—loved *The Exorcist*. Martin, however, conspicuously dismissed it. Paradoxically, this may have been the greatest evidence that *Hostage* was derivative of Friedkin's film. When Martin first appeared on *Coast to Coast AM* on October 18, 1996, one of the first things host Art Bell said to him was, "Many years ago . . . the movie *The Exorcist* came out. It was the first of its kind really, of major movies. And it scared the hell out of me, to be honest with you, as no movie—even with all their horrible little monsters—ever has since. And I'm not sure why." In response, Martin sniffs, "Isn't that funny? Isn't that interesting? I find that really curious, I really do. Even more than any of the *Dracula* and the *Frankenstein* films?" In another interview—featured in Marty Stalker's documentary about Martin, *Hostage to the Devil*—Martin says of *The Exorcist*, "It makes out exorcism to be a sort of combination of Frankenstein and Dracula with a lot of green goo and windows breaking and bodies flying, and it's much more terrible and lethal than that."[40] *The Exorcist* is, of course, so unlike *Dracula* or *Frankenstein* that one wonders if Martin has ever seen any of these films. This critique seems like a case of projected inversion. Instead of acknowledging that *Hostage* is derivative of *The Exorcist*, *The Exorcist* is derivative of clichéd horror films. Martin's comparison also functions to reinforce the central conceit of his book, that *The Exorcist* belongs in the category of fictional horror films while his book is describing reality.

Hostage, first published by Reader's Digest in 1976, consists of a brief introduction, five lengthy stories each describing a different exorcism, and a "manual of possession" containing Martin's theories about possession. An appendix features prayers used in exorcism. Martin states that exorcism generally proceeds in six phases that he dubs: presence (an uncanny sense of the demon's presence), pretense (the possessing demon pretending to be unpossessed innocent), breakpoint (where the pretense ceases), the voice (in which the demon emits inhuman noises), the clash (in which the exorcist pits his will and faith against the demon), and finally expulsion. We are unaware of any text predating *Hostage* describing these six phases. Martin attributes them to an experienced exorcist named "Conor."[41] William Peter Blatty reported that he was sent an advance copy in which the experienced exorcist was named "Damian"—the name of the protagonist in his novel. He called the publisher demanding an explanation and they responded that they had "caught it" and changed the name to Conor.[42]

The five cases are essentially horror stories that contain even more salacious and scatological detail than *The Exorcist* (a fact for which Blatty expressed gratitude). To give just one example, one tale describes a priest being raped by an invisible demon: "Gerald felt one claw was now totally sunk in his rectum. Another claw held his genitals, stretching his scrotum away from his penis, jerking at him brutally . . . . Gerald staggered in spasms, stumbling over his feet, doubled up, flaying the air helplessly, leaving a thin trail of semen, blood, excrement, and screams."[43] *The New York Times* wrote that *Hostage* "reads more like the diary of a cleric who trips on mescal while leafing through the pages of a medieval bestiary."[44]

Each story is also a morality tale emphasizing how the wrong ideology or spiritual practice can result in possession. "Zio's Friend and the Smiler" concerns a college student who is seduced by a philosophy of exaggerated subjectivism. "Father Bones and Mister Natch" describes a priest who begins reading the works of progressive Jesuit Teilhard de Chardin, resulting in conversion to a form of pantheism and, finally, possession. "The Virgin and the Girl-fixer" concerns a transgender person who becomes possessed after rejecting traditional ideas of gender and embracing sexual taboos. "The Rooster and the Tortoise" is a comparatively stock tale about the spiritual dangers of exploring psychic abilities. "Uncle Ponto and the Mushroom-Souper" describes a disk jockey harassed by a familiar spirit named Uncle Ponto. This is perhaps the most like a traditional horror story. Echoing the racism of H. P. Lovecraft's "The Horror at Redhook" (1925), it is implied that the protagonist somehow inherited a familiar spirit by being the son of Greek and Armenian immigrants, raised amidst the ethnic diversity of New York. As Martin puts it, "European and Middle Eastern pagan instincts were never rooted out; they were adopted, sublimated, purified, transmuted. In that mildewed baggage of morals, ritual practices, folk mores, social and familial traditions, the new Americans surely transported the seeds and traces of ancient, far-off powers and spirits which once had held sway over the Old World."[45] Another of Martin's contributions to modern demonology was popularizing the idea that demons have intergenerational relationships with families, an idea featured in Ari Aster's film *Hereditary* (2018).

Many reviewers found the heresiological nature of these stories suspicious. John Nicola, a Jesuit who acted as a consultant for *The Exorcist* called *Hostage* "a sermon of admonition to modern man."[46] In fairness, Martin admitted this, writing, "I have chosen these five cases from among a greater number known and available to me because, both singly and taken together, they are dramatic illustrations of the way in which personal and intelligent evil moves cunningly along the lines of contemporary fads and interests, and within the usual bounds of experience of ordinary men and women."[47] A review in *Commonweal* opined, "In this book's world, conformity is of the essence of the spiritual."[48]

It can reasonably be assumed that all the events described in *Hostage* are fiction. As *Newsweek* stated, "I very much enjoyed former Father Martin's stories, and I don't doubt them, but I don't believe them, either."[49] Priests who read *Hostage* were skeptical that one person could know of so many exorcism cases. Nicola commented, "Over a twenty- to twenty-five-year period I was asked by various bishops to examine about twenty cases of alleged possession, and in only two of these were exorcisms actually performed . . . . I'm not saying that Malachi Martin invented his case studies, but if they're true, it means that there were more exorcisms taking place in the United States."[50] Benedict Groeschel, a Franciscan friar based in New York and an expert on Christian mysticism, reported, "This is very baffling to me . . . . Several of the exorcisms that Martin reports were supposed to have taken place in the New York area, and I'd like to think I was in a position to have been informed—or at least to have heard—of any exorcisms in the vicinity. But I heard nothing, and I know of no one who has been able to corroborate Malachi Martin's case studies. I'm not telling you that he faked them, but they certainly are a mystery."[51] *The Los Angeles Times* contacted the archdiocese of New York, who confirmed that there had been no official exorcisms since the diocese was founded in 1808. To this, Martin simply told the *Times*, "They won't admit it."[52] But if Martin's response were true, then his book would be deliberately undermining a decision made by his Church.

It also seems impossible that the events described in *Hostage* could occur without producing substantial corroborating evidence. For example, the possessed priest in "Father Bones and Mister Natch" creates his own church in a loft in Greenwich Village called "The Shrine of New Being." The shrine began ordaining men and women, held services every Wednesday, and had a community of nearly 150 people. Even assuming Martin changed the name of this church, with so much written on new religious movements and breakaway Catholic groups in New York City during this period, there would surely be a record of such a group existing. "The Rooster and the Tortoise" described a psychic who could levitate and perform other feats, all under laboratory conditions. Martin writes, "To help our understanding of how these experiments went, we have the films, tape recordings, and the minutes of the laboratory log, together with Carl's own recordings made after each session."[53] Not many laboratories did this sort of research, and it seems unlikely that scientific evidence of levitation could be kept a secret. In "The Virgin and the Girl-fixer" a transgender person is sexually ravaged at a party held by eighty Satanists who were "drinking and eating a cold buffet around an open-air pool."[54] In addition to the absurdity of Satanists enjoying a cold buffet to fuel up for their poolside orgy, this scene is classic Satanic Panic literature. Scholars who study religious Satanism know a great deal about organized Satanism during this period and there is no evidence that gatherings of Satanists of this size were occurring in the early 1970s. Compare this absence of evidence to the 1928 exorcism described in *Begone Satan!* or the Mount Rainier case that inspired *The Exorcist*. Those cases involved far fewer people than the stories in *Hostage*, but there were still enough clues for determined investigators to eventually uncover the identities of nearly everyone involved.

Perhaps the greatest evidence of fraud comes from the experts who were asked to review the book. Nicola noted that Martin never described asking a skeptic to investigate alleged cases of possession, which he considered a standard practice. He also objected to Martin's graphic descriptions of deviant sexuality, noting that while these things certainly happen during exorcisms, most exorcists do not discuss them out of respect for those they are trying to help. Nicola concluded, "For the reader who wants information that will help him arrive at his own conclusions about the credibility of possession and exorcism, *The Exorcist*, despite some appeal to sensationalism, is a far more valuable resource than *Hostage to the Devil*."[55]

Richard Woods, a Dominican priest who had helped to interpret the social phenomenon surrounding *The Exorcist*, was also sent an advance copy for review. He concluded that "Martin's five 'cases' were fabrications of an inventive but disturbed mind, lacking all psychological, historical, theological and pastoral credibility." Later, Woods interviewed Martin on television, recalling, "In person, I found Martin to be a clever, charming, engaging Irish rogue who evaded every effort to document the instances of possession he so graphically described. In the end, my earlier suspicion that Martin was a deeply disturbed individual was strongly reinforced."[56]

In a three-page review for *The Los Angeles Times*, Blatty slammed *Hostage* as a shoddily researched fraud meant to capitalize on his novel, declaring, "Malachi Martin, to put it bluntly, doesn't know a demon from a troll in the ground."[57] He especially objected that one of Martin's characters used the expression, "banal as graves in a row." Blatty wrote, "I sniffed and assumed my suspicious look; for with the possible exception of John Simon reviewing the Resurrection, no living human ever could have said that."[58] But Blatty was wrong: someone had said that, or at least something near it. In a 1972 article for *Harper's* entitled "The Scientist as Shaman," Malachi Martin denounced the cultural authority of science as dogmatic and destructive to wonder. The essay concluded, "This promises a boredom as great as the universe and an ennui as deathly as a row of gravestones."[59]

Blatty communicated with Reader's Digest and was told no one had heard any of the alleged tapes on which Martin's stories were based. Additionally, no one at the publisher had been given real names nor had direct contact with anyone depicted in *Hostage*. Martin did show "blind affidavits" to the publisher's attorneys, but he held his hand over the names of the signatories. When the publisher brought Blatty's concerns to Martin, he produced testimony from an anonymous Catholic priest who asserted that there had been eleven exorcisms in America in the last ten years, but he could not say where they happened or who was involved. Blatty then reached out to several bishops, but could find no official church records that would substantiate any of the cases in *Hostage*: the only documented case of exorcism anyone knew of was the Mount Rainier case. Blatty also reported that the copy he was first sent contained an endorsement attributed to "a high Vatican source." He wrote, "It was determined with absolute certainty that the 'high Vatican source' who had commended the book was not Pope Paul. The quote is being cut."[60]

The Los Angeles Times reached out to journalist Michael Novak, who had been in Rome during Vatican II and knew both Martin and Robert Kaiser. Novak offered this context for *Hostage*: "May I be playful and just say that I knew Malachi as a pixie-like, mischievous, whimsical person when he was a Jesuit in Rome. He loves to surround himself with mystery—dropping hints of intelligence activities in the Middle East . . . . He lives in a very fertile imaginative world." In a possible allusion to the Kaiser affair, he added, "I think he does feel possessed. He has to explain his at times incredible behavior to himself." *The Times* raised this possibility in an interview with Martin: "Martin said he has never thought or felt he was possessed, and of the possibility that all the characters in the book are known to him, because they are, in fact, him, he was silent for one angry moment and then said, 'That would be the biggest goddamn lie in the world.'"[61]

For the rest of his life, Martin gave interviews in which he explained how he became involved in so many exorcisms and why they are apparently being done without the approval of the archdiocese of New York. These explanations were inconsistent. In 1976, he told the *Los Angeles Times* that he had never been involved in an exorcism before leaving the Jesuits and coming to New York in 1965. Martin stated, "If someone had asked me in 1961, 'Do you believe in the devil?' I would have said, 'Look, we have to be very careful about these things because there is a lot of hokum and I'd finally end up saying, 'No.'"[62] In this version of the story, Martin got a call one night from a priest friend who needed some pinch-hitting to complete an exorcism as his assistant had collapsed. Later, Martin told Michael Cuneo that this occurred in the Bronx in 1972, and his friend had been "a bit of a maverick" who performed exorcisms without the permission of a bishop.[63] In 1987, in an appearance on *The Oprah Winfrey Show*, Martin explained that he only assisted in exorcisms and was never the chief exorcist because he is too intellectually curious and prone to making conversation with the demons instead of commanding them.[64]

But around 1996, he began telling a new story: the first exorcism he had participated in was not in the Bronx but in Cairo, when he had been doing archaeological work for the Jesuits. Martin told versions of this story both to Cuneo and on *Coast to Coast AM*. The most thorough version of it appears in an article on Martin's website where Martin states this occurred in 1958, and that the exorcism was of an Egyptian youth who had taken to murdering his sisters as sacrifices to Satan.[65] Of course, this story directly contradicts his earlier statement that he did not believe in the devil in 1961.

There is similar confusion about the exorcisms Martin was allegedly involved with after writing *Hostage*. In 1976, he told the *Los Angeles Times* that he worked with "a group of about 42 people from different Protestant, Catholic and Orthodox Christian religions who are engaged in exorcism on the East Coast, mostly in and around New York."[66] According to Martin, this anonymous group received about five thousand applicants a year, conducted physical and psychological tests, and then exorcized about two hundred of them. Martin also stated in 1975 that there had been over 120 major exorcisms in the United States, most of which had been performed on non-Catholics. However, when psychiatrist W. Scott Peck became convinced one of his patients needed an exorcism, Martin refused to do it, claiming he was suffering from a detached retina. When Peck asked if Martin could recommend anyone else, he answered, "I'm afraid I just don't know any other exorcists. At least none who would be able to handle a case such as this. You have to realize exorcists don't just grow on trees, and they work alone. Oh, when they do an exorcism, they assemble a team to help them, but basically they operate alone. There's not exactly a directory of them, you know."[67] (Peck subsequently learned that Martin had lied about suffering a detached retina but decided that Martin, in his wisdom, had deliberately orchestrated a situation in which Peck had no choice but to perform the exorcism himself.")

The 1996 article from Martin's website stated that Martin performed at least one exorcism a month, always after all medical options had been exhausted and with "permission of his bishop."[68] Of course, Martin did not answer to any bishop, as he publicly told Art Bell on Coast to Coast AM. John Grasmeier, a traditionalist Catholic, finally called James LeBar, who had been the chief exorcist for the Archdiocese of New York during the 1990s, to see if any of Martin's claims could be verified. LeBar emphasized that all authorized exorcisms in the diocese were performed by him and his team. Martin had occasionally referred people who were seeking exorcisms to him, but the two had never discussed exorcism. LeBar reported that, "He has no knowledge whatsoever of Martin ever taking part in any exorcism, at any time, in any way in the state of New York or anywhere else."[69] Grasmeier's conclusion was that if Martin ever witnessed an exorcism in the diocese of New York, it was not an authorized one.

Or perhaps not. In May 1998, Martin stated on Coast to Coast AM that he had special authority directly from the Vatican to perform exorcisms within the tri-state area.[70] There is no precedent for such an arrangement and it would go against the well-established rule of leaving such matters to the discretion of bishops. It is also not clear why the Vatican would recognize state borders instead of dioceses. Martin's most stalwart defenders have gone even further, claiming that Martin had secretly been a bishop since the 1950s. According to this implausible story, during the Cold War, Martin was sent behind the Iron Curtain to Prague, where a priest had become heretical. Martin was made a bishop in secret specifically so that he could laicize this

priest. In retaliation, the now ex-priest turned Martin over to the Czech secret police and he spent time in prison before being released through the in-
tercession of Vatican officials.[71] If Martin truly was a "secret bishop" without
a diocese than perhaps he could authorize his own exorcisms. This story is
another example of projected inversion: Martin was not rogue priest who
was laicized by church authorities for his indiscretions; instead, he was a
church authority laicizing rogue priests for *their* indiscretions.

The Demonology of Malachi Martin

Martin re-wrote Catholic demonology almost overnight and his ideas
influenced practicing Catholic exorcists, misguided psychiatrists, Hollywood
horror movies, New York City police officers, and even serial killer David
Berkowitz. In 2005, a peer-reviewed article in *The Journal of Religion and
Health* called *Hostage* "the most convincing and authoritative book available
on the subject."[72] This was after Cuneo and Kaiser had published damning
indictments of Martin. Today, Martin's influence continues to grow. To give
one stark example, in the fall of 2021, one of the authors of this text received
an email from a colleague which included a recording of a guest lecture
delivered over Zoom by an "independent Catholic bishop," who performs
exorcisms and calls himself a demonologist. The professor asks, "When you
study demonology, what are we talking about? Are you reading Thomas
Aquinas? Are you reading early modern texts? Are you reading psychiatric case studies? What's involved in the study of demonology for an exorcist?" The bishop replies, "All of the above, all of the above. You know, Father
Malachi Martin, of course. *Hostage to the Devil* is a fantastic book. He was a
Roman Catholic exorcist. He was actually the primary exorcist in Rome. And
he left the Roman Catholic Church. He wrote a fantastic book on demonology." This bishop *had* in fact read Aquinas, who wrote a theory of demons
and how they can influence people in the thirteenth century. But Aquinas
now takes a back seat to Malachi Martin.

Theologians who studied demonology before *Hostage* could spot the
discrepancies. Richard Woods, who taught courses on the occult at Loyola
University stated bluntly, "Malachi Martin had no discernible training, expertise or even adequate knowledge of the history or ministry of exorcism
in—or out of—the Catholic faith he once professed but which he bitterly
turned against at the end of his unhappy life."[73] Similarly, Blatty, who did

research traditional demonology to write his book, objected to Martin's claim that, "In the records of Christian exorcism from as far back as the lifetime of Jesus himself, a peculiar revulsion to symbols and truths of religion is always and *without exception* a mark of the possessed person." Blatty points out that in Mark 5:6, when the Gerasene demoniac saw Jesus from the distance, he "ran and adored him."[74]

One of its most impressive selling points when *Hostage* was published in 1976 was a blurb on the front cover by Harvard theologian Harvey Cox. When the *Los Angeles Times* asked Cox about this endorsement, he described inviting Martin to lecture on the demonic to his graduate students:

> It was a catastrophe. He was terrible. Everything was so prepared. He was evasive, trying to be spectacular, very anecdotal. He avoided the hard questions, hinting darkly that he knew a lot more . . . He was very ill-read . . . . For all his credentials he was a loser. I didn't allow myself to think it while he was there, but I became suspicious that the whole thing is a big fiction. I'm feeling a little bit like I got stung. If I could withdraw the blurb, I would.[75]

True to form, Martin told the *Times* that Cox was simply retaliating against him because he had gotten hold of an unpublished manuscript in which Martin had criticized a theological conference Cox had attended.

The suspicions of Woods, Blatty, and Cox seem vindicated by a call that came at the very end of Martin's first interview on *Coast to Coast AM*. The caller had a specific question concerning a friend whose household was troubled by demons: "Uh, there is two particular demons that—I don't know what the names of them are—but he has stated that he has seen one that attacked his wife in a sexual manner. There's one for men and then one for women. What are those names please?" Significantly, the caller was not asking for a good story but for specific information that could potentially be disproven after the interview. Martin responded, "I don't know. I don't know. I only know the name of two demons: One is Lucifer and the other is Satan. They're distinct demons." The names the caller is seeking are obviously "incubus" and "succubus." These are sexual demons that Aquinas discussed in some detail and are common in popular culture. Martin's statement that Satan and Lucifer are distinct demons is not unprecedented in the lore of exorcisms, but it is a rather embarrassing claim for a former faculty member of the Pontifical Biblical Institute to make.[76]

Martin quietly gives himself license to rewrite demonology in the beginning of *Hostage* when he states that demons have adapted to the times and that knowledge of whatever came before him is obsolete: "No fourteenth- or fifteenth- or sixteenth-century case, for all its possible romantic appeal, would have any relevancy for us today."[77] Besides, Martin's demonology lacked the messiness of tradition. Peck, one of Martin's advocates, praised *Hostage* as, "the first book ever, to my knowledge, to outline and define the different stages of real exorcisms . . . . In doing so, Malachi was the first to offer exorcists a map."[78] Significantly, Nicola commented that *Hostage*'s "greatest shortcoming is that it fails to assert how much we do not know."[79]

Martin's biggest break with traditional demonology concerns free will. According to *Hostage*, possession involves "the voluntary yielding of control by the possessed person to a force or presence he clearly feels is alien to himself and as a result of which the possessed loses control of his will, and so of his decisions and actions."[80] For Martin, demoniacs may not be responsible for what they do while possessed, but they are responsible for getting possessed in the first place. Nicola regarded this as a serious error:

> His thought is compatible with that of the Church except on one important point: the culpability of the possessed. While Martin alleges that there is a moment at which the energumen [possessed person] must freely admit the invading spirit—an implicit argument for culpability—the introduction to the rite of exorcism in *The Roman Ritual* avers that possession is not necessarily a divine retribution visited on a grievous sinner; sometimes the victim is entirely without fault. An obvious case of this sort is the boy in the ninth chapter of Mark's Gospel who has been afflicted by an evil spirit from infancy. It is my personal experience that in most cases the energumen is a good and innocent person, the spiritual "big fish" who draws out all the venom of the diabolical angler.[81]

Martin repeatedly described demons claiming the will of the possessed. This claim was anathema to Catholic theologians of the medieval and early modern periods who reasoned that while demons can tempt, they cannot remove free will. Most theologians resolved this problem by concluding that demons could control the bodies of the possessed, thereby controlling the brain and the mental faculties. This allowed them to indirectly control (but not claim) the will. This is why demoniacs were not morally responsible for what they did in a state of possession.[82]

By contrast, Martin assumed the possessed were always guilty of some failing—often heresiological or ideological in nature—that could be rooted out and identified. In fact, a reviewer for *The Washington Post* noted, "Behind his Gaelic charm, Malachi Martin has all the witch-hunting instincts of a Torquemada or a Commie-baiting Joe McCarthy."[83] This divergence from medieval and early modern theories of possession may be owed in part to the fact that many classic demonologists were dealing with real people who might live or die depending on how their alleged possession was interpreted, whereas in *Hostage*, Martin was imagining what a possessed person might be like.

Martin also introduced the category of the "perfectly possessed," those who have willingly given themselves over to demons. Because demon and host are in perfect harmony, these people cannot be exorcized and have no susceptibility to holy water or other religious objects. In terms of early modern demonology, the perfectly possessed effectively erased the line between a demoniac and a witch—a person whose powers came from a pact willingly made with demons.[84] This move, in turn, lent itself to conspiracy theories. In 1996, when Martin explained to Art Bell that certain politically powerful figures are perfectly possessed, Bell immediately asked whether Bill Clinton was perfectly possessed, to which Martin replied, "no comment."

The Influence of *Hostage to the Devil*

Hostage may have been written by an impecunious ex-Jesuit seeking to capitalize on a horror movie, but its influence has led to serious consequences. One of the first people to invoke *Hostage* to frame real life events was David Berkowitz. Berkowitz was apprehended in 1977, one year after *Hostage* was published. In his prison diaries he wrote, "After reading the book *Hostage to the Devil* by Malachi Martin I now have no doubt that I am a person who had been visited by an alien force or being. The evidence is overwhelming . . . . There were even times after my arrest in which I doubted the reality of the demons, thinking of myself to be a person hallucinating or living in a delusion but now, after reading Mr. Martin's work, I am convinced beyond my own doubt about demons."[85] Martin did not let this opportunity go to waste. He claimed he visited Berkowitz in his cell and determined that he was perfectly possessed.[86] According to some accounts, Berkowitz asked Martin to write his autobiography, but Martin declined. Then publishers offered Martin vast sums to write a book about his relationship with "The Son of Sam," which he also declined. Journalist Steve Fishman interviewed Berkowitz, but he was unable to find any record of Martin having visited him due to a fire that destroyed prison records.[87]

By the 1990s, Catholic exorcists had begun to adopt Martin's terminology. In 1991, when *Nightline* showed an exorcism performed by James LeBar and "Father A," Father A can be heard narrating the footage and explaining, "Now we're heading into the clash, which is what we call the confrontation stage where we clash together." In 2014, Father Michael Maginot performed an exorcism on Latoya Ammons of Gary, Indiana, after her children had to be hospitalized. When *Vice* asked Maginot about a Satanist and a witch who also offered to perform ritual exorcisms, Maginot suggested that these people might be "perfectly possessed" and that they were under demonic control without realizing it.[88] One detailed analysis of the case on which *The Exorcist* is based, speculated that it may not have been an authentic case of possession because witnesses did not report a demonic "presence," one of Martin's key phases of exorcism.[89]

More disturbingly, psychiatrists began to use *Hostage* in experimental and unethical forms of therapy. In 1997, a media story broke about Nadean Cool who sued her psychiatrist, Kenneth Olson, and received a settlement of $2.4 million. Using a combination of drugs and hypnosis, Olson convinced Cool that she had repressed memories of abuse and now had 123 distinct personalities. In fact, Olson had convinced several women that they were suffering from multiple-personality disorder and charged exorbitant amounts for treatment. What made Cool's case especially significant is that Olson tied her to a hospital bed and attempted an exorcism, claiming that one of her personalities was actually Satan. Olson used *Hostage* to perform his exorcism.[90]

Psychiatrist M. Scott Peck became so influenced by Martin that he dedicated his book *Glimpses of the Devil* to him. Peck described "devouring" *The Exorcist* over two nights, but he regarded it as entertainment. Then, in 1978, he published his first book, *The Road Less Traveled*, and the publisher found only one person willing to write a promotional comment: Malachi Martin. Peck went out and bought *Hostage*, then set up a phone call with Martin, and finally arranged lunch. Peck was going through his own spiritual crisis during this period and was deciding whether to be baptized Christian. The two became friends and dined together every few months. Around 1980, Peck was baptized and Martin began referring people to him to determine whether they were mentally ill or in need of exorcism. Peck diagnosed several patients as suffering from mental illness, but he encountered two (both women) whom he came to believe were genuinely possessed. He finally described exorcizing these patients using Martin's techniques in his final book, *Glimpses of the Devil*, published in 2005. In that book, Peck called for the medical community to accept the reality of possession and make demonology "an incipient subspecialty of psychiatry and psychology."[91]

Glimpses is a profoundly disturbing book. The first patient, "Jersey," was initially referred to therapy because she was immature, self-absorbed, and neglecting her husband and children. She was also preoccupied with Spiritualism and the New Age, and she had started to entertain the idea that she might be possessed. In therapy, she described having her appendix removed at the age of twelve; for weeks afterward, her father would "check to make sure she was OK" every night after dinner by inserting his finger in her vagina. Jersey initially denied that this had been sexual abuse. Her father had a PhD and she incorrectly claimed he had been a medical doctor. This was a clear case of denial, but Peck—following Martin's demonology—believed no one is possessed without somehow asking for it. In an interview with Cuneo, Peck stated, "At some level they have cooperated with demonic evil; they have invited it into their life. In such cases there is always—perhaps at an unconscious level—some kind of sellout to evil. *Hostage to the Devil* dissected this dynamic beautifully."[92] With coaxing, Peck got Jersey to admit that while she had only been twelve and was the victim of a predator, she had to an extent *chosen* to believe her father's lie. Then he told her, "It was natural for you to believe the lie. But in doing that, by not exercising your precious little choice, you left a tiny little crack where the devil could get in."[93]

"Beccah," the second patient, was married to an abusive husband, had taken to cutting herself, and was suicidal. Peck reports that during her exorcism everyone could see her face transform into that of a snake—yet this effect was not captured on film. When the exorcism appeared to be a failure, Peck began making arrangements to have her involuntarily committed to a state psychiatric hospital. Upon hearing this, Beccah began screaming that Peck had promised he would not commit her and demanding to review the forms she had signed. Peck again drew on Martin's theory of exorcism and interpreted this reaction as "the clash" phase. Peck fully understood that what he was doing involved coercion: "Even before the exorcism, it had occurred to me that the process could be considered a form of brainwashing—or, more accurately, a variety of deprogramming, which in those days was used to rescue a number of young people from their involvement in cults."[94] Beccah suffered from a bone disease that she treated with morphine and, some time after her exorcism, she died after administering an overdose to herself.

Peck describes being warned repeatedly about his association with Martin. A New York cleric he calls "Canon Brewster" told Peck, "You've been led down the garden path by Malachi Martin. He's an evil man. Somehow you've fallen under his spell. But I don't blame you. I blame him. Everybody knows he's evil. He's the one that's possessed. He's more possessed than anyone he's written about, and now he's somehow managed to take over your mind."[95] There is a strange cognitive dissonance throughout *Glimpses* in which Peck knows Martin is lying outrageously and yet still trusts him. He writes, "Many of the accusations about him—that he was a manipulator, sometimes a liar, the seducer of another man's wife, a publicity hound, and especially a proponent of possession and exorcism—are undoubtedly true."[96] But Peck somehow looked past all of this and declared Martin "the greatest expert on the subject of possession and exorcism in the English-speaking world."[97] Perhaps this is because he wanted the demonology of *Hostage*, with its consistent internal logic and lack of loose ends, to be true. Richard Woods wrote of *Glimpses*, " 'Beware the man of one book!' said Thomas Aquinas (perhaps). Here, clearly, it would have been wiser by far for Dr. Peck to consult more widely than *Hostage to the Devil*."[98]

The Death and Legacy of Malachi Martin

After *Hostage*, Martin found a ready audience for his work among traditionalist Catholics, resentful over the changes of Vatican II. He wrote a series of books—some presented as non-fiction, some as "faction" novels—outlining a secret plot by Satanists who had infiltrated the Vatican to overthrow the Catholic Church and use it as a tool of the New World Order. Fears of communism, as well as liberation theology, played a major part in this conspiracy theory. In a 1997 interview with the John Birch Society, Martin claimed to have knowledge that the Soviet Union had not collapsed on its own but had been ordered to do so by a sinister entity he called "the capstone." Martin also invoked perennial enemies of conservative conspiracy theories, such as the Bilderberg Group and the Council on Foreign Relations.[99] And he alleged that the Satanic clergy were involved in "gay sex cults" that regularly engaged in pedophilia and used brainwashing to keep their victims compliant.

Ironically, there were grains of truth hidden in Martin's conspiracy theories. He described dioceses covering up pedophile priests by moving them to different parishes and, by some accounts, he named Boston's Cardinal Bernard Law as a chief offender as early as 1996.[100] In 2002, following an expose on sexual abuse in diocese by *The Boston Globe*, Law resigned and moved to Rome.

In the final years of his life, Martin held a series of interviews on *Coast to Coast AM*, each lasting about three hours. These interviews, perhaps more than any of his writings, cemented Martin's influence on American paranormal discourse. He fielded calls from psychics, witches, people experiencing recovered memories of Satanic abuse, and a self-described lycanthrope. He never expressed skepticism of the callers and often collaborated with them, adding details and interpretations of their narratives.

The *Coast to Coast* interviews are also saturated with references to horror films. Art Bell's very first remark to Martin concerns *The Exorcist*. About twenty minutes into the interview, Bell states, "Well you've already done it to me. You're already giving me chills."[101] This comment is telling because it suggests that the nature and function of a Catholic priest—and Martin repeatedly emphasized to Bell that he was a priest—is to frighten people. While Martin was dismissive of *The Exorcist*, he validated as somehow true every other horror film he was asked about. *The Amityville Horror* (1979) was true, and the house was definitely still infested with demons. Even though Martin had not seen *The Craft* (1996) when Bell asked about it, he declared it an accurate depiction of nefarious witchcraft currently being conducted throughout America. Large portions of the interviews could be interpreted as Martin bestowing his priestly authority on people's favorite horror films and giving these narratives a greater degree of reality.

Martin passed away on July 27, 1999, at the age of seventy-eight. He fell in his Manhattan apartment and injured his head. He had been taking medication following a series of strokes that likely increased intercranial bleeding. Doctors attempted to treat the injury with surgery, but Martin lapsed into a coma and died.[102] He was buried in Gate of Heaven Cemetery in Hawthorne, New York. When Kakia Livanos passed, on May 12, 2002, she was buried with Martin. They share one headstone.

One of Martin's friends, a Wisconsin priest named Charles Fiore, was likely the first to suggest that Martin had actually been killed by demons by suggesting that he had been preparing for an exorcism at the time of his fall.[103] In 2016, a documentary about Martin called *Hostage to the Devil* featured interviews with Robert Marro, a former CIA officer who had befriended Martin and often acted as his driver.[104] Marro stated that shortly before Martin's fall, he had driven him to Connecticut to exorcize a four-year-old girl. In fact, it had not been a "fall" at all: Martin had been pushed by an invisible force.

Although it has not yet manifested, a Malachi Martin horror film seems inevitable. In a way, the first Malachi Martin film was Brian Hegeland's *The Order* (2003), which *Philadelphia Weekly* called a "throwback to all those ponderous, dogma-laden 'religious thrillers' that cashed in on *The Exorcist*."[105] Heath Ledger plays Alex Bernier, an attractive young exorcist who inexplicably still says mass in Latin with his back to the congregation. Alex belongs to a fictitious order called "The Carolingians," about which a shady dealer in occult books states, "You exceed the Jesuits in your search for heretical knowledge." Alex becomes disgusted with the corruption of his church and decides to leave the priesthood so he can succumb to his desires for a young woman he once exorcized. In an incredibly convoluted plot, Alex learns he has been manipulated by Cardinal Driscoll, an American who will stop at nothing to become Pope so that he can remake the Church in his image. In fact, Driscoll maintains a secret identity as "Chirac," a "dark Pope" who holds court in catacombs beneath Rome. There, he dresses in a black hood, brokers secret deals with the Vatican elite, and murders people in Pagan, necromantic rituals. Although no longer a priest, Alex manages to expose Cardinal Driscoll's secrets to Church authorities, destroying his plans before sending him to perdition. Had Martin lived to see *The Order*, he would likely have identified with Father Alex Bernier—a misunderstood, traditionalist, renegade priest fighting a secret war against Satanic corruption in the Church. The trope of Satanists infiltrating the Curia had been part of traditionalist Catholic conspiracy theories since Vatican II, but Martin fleshed out this idea in such books as *The Windswept House* and combined it with a dark prophecy in which the Church will become a tool of the New World Order. Even if Hegeland never read any of Martin's books, it seems unlikely this film would have come about without Martin popularizing this milieu of religious conspiracy theory in the 1990s.

Martin also had several protégés, one of whose careers has already been adapted into a horror film. Ralph Sarchie is a retired NYPD sergeant, a traditionalist Catholic, and a self-described demonologist. His 2001 book, *Beware the Night*, describes his career as a police officer while moonlighting in what he calls "The Work," dealing with ghosts and demons. The parallels between

Sarchie's approach to demons and his attitudes toward suspected criminals are sometimes disturbing. For example, he writes, "Their [demons'] terrorism is an offense against humanity and God. So exorcism is the spiritual equivalent of an arrest. The trouble is, you can't grab a demon, throw him down, and punch the daylights out of him if he resists."[106] In 2014, Sarchie's memoir was given a very loose film adaptation as *Deliver Us From Evil*. The title of Sarchie's book was altered by the publisher to match the film, a change he found irritating.

Sarchie confesses, "One of my earliest memories is going to the Queens Center Mall and seeing the book *The Exorcist*."[107] He eventually met Ed and Lorraine Warren and formed a friendship with them. With their support, he founded the New York City Chapter of the NESPR. But Martin had an even greater influence on him. Sarchie refers to Martin as a Jesuit, even though he met him years after he left the order. He also had Martin baptize one of his children. Like Marro, Sarchie began driving Martin to lectures and other appointments. During one of these drives, Martin told him, "There's something important God wants you to do," which Sarchie took to be his call to "The Work."[108] Sarchie's demonology is heavily indebted to Martin. He calls *Hostage* "the best I've ever read on demonic possession"[109] and he interpreted people's paranormal experiences by comparing them to Martin's fictional cases. He also describes Martin's six phases of exorcism and the concept of "perfect possession."

Beware the Night demonstrates direct links between Martin and Satanic Panic. Sarchie writes:

> What most people don't realize, until they're threatened by it themselves, is how common Satanism really is. By some estimates, there are over 8,000 Satanic covenants in this country. In just about every American city, black masses are now available on a weekly basis, in a choice of locations; some covens have become so specialized that they limit their membership to pedophiles from the clergy or lesbian ex-nuns.[110]

There is only one "estimate" that eight thousand Satanic covens exist in America—Malachi Martin's estimate in his preface to the 1992 reprint of *Hostage*.[111] The description of separate covens for pedophile and lesbian clergy also appears in this source. There seems to be a significant cluster of demonologists associated with the NYPD. Sarchie describes other officers who assisted him in "The Work." In 2021, the media began covering

Christopher DeFlorio, another NYPD officer who moonlights as a demonologist in the tradition of the Martin and the Warrens.[112] It is unclear whether
demonology shapes the way these officers perform their duties or how their
status as officers shapes their demonological investigations.

The film *Deliver Us From Evil* begins with a title card explaining that
this film is "inspired by actual accounts of NYPD sergeant Ralph Sarchie."
But other than depicting Sarchie being mentored by a priest in "the Work"
and performing an exorcism, it has little to do with the book. Even though
Sarchie's book was published before the terrorist attacks of September 11,
2001, the film opens with a scene of American soldiers in Iraq who become
possessed after entering an ancient tomb. This opening gives the story struc-
tural similarities to *The Exorcist* and plays on a horror trope that demons
manifest in Africa and the Middle East before possessing Americans.[113]
Sarchie's mentor is named Father Mendoza, a sexy Latin priest with a history of drug addiction. In the denouement, Mendoza explains that an exorcism always has six stages, and these are depicted cinematically more or less
as described in *Hostage*. The final scene shows Mendoza baptizing Sarchie's
baby followed by a title card explaining that Sarchie "continues to work with
Father Mendoza to this day"—despite Mendoza being a fictional character
inspired by a priest who died in 1999.

The 2017 film *The Crucifixion*, a story written by the Hayes brothers and
inspired by a Romanian nun killed during an exorcism in 2005, features another sexy priest—this time Romanian Orthodox—explaining the stages of
exorcism. The stages are shortened to four (presence, breakpoint, clash, and
expulsion), but the terminology is still Martin's. The more exorcism films use
Martin's language to give the story a sense of authenticity, the more difficult it
is to recognize this language as Martin's invention as opposed simply a taken-
for-granted fact of exorcism lore.

In 2017, it was announced that the film rights to *Hostage to the Devil*
had been purchased by Penchant Entertainment. The deal was brokered by
Martin's literary agent and defender, Lila Karpf. Penchant announced plans
for a series of projects adapted from the book, possibly creating a franchise
similar to *The Conjuring*.[114] In 2019, rumors began swirling that Lionsgate
Studios was working on a film called *Incident at Fort Bragg* depicting a
"true story" in which the US government brought Malachi Martin to a military base at Fort Bragg, North Carolina, to exorcize a soldier. Beau Flynn,
who had previously produced *The Exorcism of Emily Rose* and *The Rite* was
scheduled to produce.[115] Robert Marro wrote a treatment about this alleged

episode for the studio, but he became frustrated with the script. Marro never specified which military base this alleged episode occurred on, and it was the producer's decision to set the film at Fort Bragg. Sarchie said he had heard of this incident, but he had not been involved. He told *The Times of London* that Martin would not have been upset by the film: "He never shied away from exposing the devil. Just as long as Hollywood don't turn the case into complete junk."[116] Sarah Colwell recalled Martin asking her to read the novel *The Final Temptation of Christ* and summarize it to him, because he had apparently discussed some involvement with the 1988 film adaptation. Colwell felt Martin was always looking for ways to enhance his celebrity and hoped to cultivate connections in Hollywood.[117]

Martin's stories not only live on in various Hollywood films but in endless debates on obscure websites dedicated to conservative Catholic conspiracy theories. Martin pretended to have ties to the intelligence community and to possess all manner of secret knowledge that—for various reasons—he could not share with the public. One of his favorite claims was that while at the Vatican he had seen the "third secret of Fatima," a prophecy derived from a Martian apparition that occurred in Fatima, Portugal, in 1917. Naturally, Martin swore an oath that we would never reveal its contents, but that never stopped him from dropping dark hints about its apocalyptic contents. In 2000, the Vatican released the rather anti-climactic contents of this prophecy, but Martin's followers naturally concluded that this was not the *real* prophecy because it did not match Martin's clues.

One wonders how Martin would have shaped contemporary "conspirituality" had he lived into the twenty-first century. In an interview for the *Hostage to the Devil* podcast hosted by Marty Stalker, Robert Marro said that had Martin lived to see social media, he would definitely have used it. In many ways, Martin was "Q" before there was QAnon: Like "Q" his *modus operandi* involved making appeals to authority, dropping hints of dark conspiracies and hideous Satanic enemies, and then letting others formulate what conclusions they would. With both Martin and Q, there is a sense of an individual unleashing chaos simply to see if they can. Colwell commented, "If he were alive today, I shudder to think what sort of pernicious nonsense he might inflict on the credulous right-wingers."[118]

6

Exorcism

> "A lot of people probably are going to get into the exorcizing business now that the movie is calling everyone's attention to it."
> —psychic Joe DeLouise (1974)[1]

> "People think God is dead, but how can they believe that if I show them the devil?"
> —*The Exorcism of Emily Rose* (2005)

When *Time* ran the "Is God Dead?" cover in 1966, many assumed that exorcism was a relic of the dark ages. In 1969, Swiss Jesuit Herbert Haag published *Abscheid vom Teufel* ("Goodbye to the Devil"), arguing that a literal devil does not exist. But in hindsight, this period represented the calm before the storm. Reported cases of demonic possession rose starkly beginning in the late 1960s and early 1970s.[2] Today, exorcism is far more mainstream than in 1966. And while many clergy still regard exorcism as embarrassing nonsense, there are no longer many voices like Haag's willing to publicly question exorcism or belief in the devil. In this sense at least, the exorcists have won.

Father Gabriele Amorth (1925–2016), who founded the International Association of Exorcists and probably did more than anyone else to facilitate the Catholic revival of exorcism, stated, "It is thanks to movies that we find a renewed interest in exorcisms."[3] Most historians of exorcism believe that horror films, starting with *The Exorcist*, have played an important role in the return of exorcism, but there is a debate as to exactly how much credit is owed to Hollywood. Michael Cuneo argued that the entertainment industry was primarily responsible for this shift. Historian Brian Levack pushes back against this thesis, noting that while films certainly played an important role, "People do not need the entertainment industry to suggest that either they or others are possessed by the Devil."[4] This chapter traces the long relationship between horror films and reports of actual demonic activity. In doing so, we

The Exorcist Effect. Joseph P. Laycock and Eric Harrelson, Oxford University Press. © Oxford University Press 2024.
DOI: 10.1093/oso/9780197635391.003.0006

offer three insights into how exactly horror films have influenced the religious imagination and aided the return of exorcism.

First, the relationship between exorcisms and their cinematic depictions becomes clearer once we acknowledge Levack's thesis that exorcism—whatever else it may be—is a kind of performance in which both the demoniac and the exorcist follow "scripts that are encoded in their religious cultures."[5] Levack argues that while some historical cases of possession may have involved mental illness or fraud, they always involved people "acting possessed" in ways their culture prescribed and expected possessed people to act. This is why, during the early modern period, possessed Catholics responded violently to crosses and holy water, whereas possessed Protestants had no aversion to these objects but were unable to read from the Bible. Levack cites the printing revolution as one of the factors that fostered the wave of exorcisms during this period because printed pamphlets, sermons, and other materials created an abundant supply of scripts for demoniacs to follow.[6] It is reasonable to assume that horror films have likewise functioned as a form of mass media that introduced the public to scripts for demonic possession. The scripts in themselves did not inspire exorcisms, but they provided a cultural resource for how to "act possessed" and for diagnosing certain behaviors or experiences as possession.

Second, horror movies based on actual exorcisms shape the narratives about these events in ways that are often favorable to exorcists. These historical revisions are a reflection of the genre, which typically demands that supernatural forces are real and that exorcists, while they may be flawed, are ultimately heroic. These demands of storytelling become problematic with films based on cases where people died during exorcism. The death of Anneliese Michel in 1976 inspired three films, and the death of Maricica Irina Cornici in 2005 inspired two more. At worst, these films become apologies for exorcists who were convicted of negligent homicide. It is unclear whether such revisionist history affects the political calculus of church authorities, but it likely emboldens would-be exorcists who might otherwise view these cases as cautionary tales.

Third, successful exorcism movies inspire additional media, such as news segments, documentaries, talk show interviews, and DVD featurettes, that create a media platform for exorcists. Platforming exorcists has significant consequences for institutions, such as the Catholic Church, where clergy are normally subject to a hierarchy that tries to carefully balance its position on exorcism. When Christianity began, the perceived ability to perform exorcisms was a source of personal charisma. That charisma was routinized by the church, which eventually placed strict regulations on who may perform exorcisms, under what circumstances, and what may be reported about them. But when horror movies send the media in search of practicing exorcists for human interest stories, enterprising clergy are effectively provided an opportunity to "do an end run" around church authorities, platforming their stance over and against the more nuanced position of their church. Like Ed and Lorraine Warren, some clergy seem to perform exorcisms with the hope that this will lead to book and movie deals. Often such dalliances with the media are justified on the grounds that showing the reality of demonic activity will bring people to God. This relationship between horror films, exorcists, and news media seems to have a cumulative effect that has gradually worked to transform exorcism into an exciting asset for the modern church, rather than an embarrassing liability.

Exorcism Films Before *The Exorcist*

Le Manoir du Diable (1896) by Georges Méliès is generally considered the first horror film. It is also the first exorcism film. It features a bat that transforms into a Mephistopheles-like devil (played by Méliès) who torments a pair of cavaliers with magic tricks portrayed using stop motion animation (which Méliès had discovered by accident when his camera jammed while filming traffic in La Place de l'Opera).[7] A cavalier finally defeats the devil by brandishing a cross. In 1899, Méliès followed this up with *Le Diable Au Couvent*, in which a bat-winged devil takes the form of a priest and seduces nuns into sin. In 1919, Swedish director Benjamin Christensen encountered a copy of the witch-hunting manual the *Malleus Maleficarum* in Berlin. He studied the book for two years before making *Häxan* (1922), the most expensive Swedish film of the silent era. Described as a "cultural and historical presentation," it featured elaborate scenes of witches fornicating with demons. It was banned in the United States for nudity and scenes of torture.[8] Like *Häxan*, several subsequent exorcism films presented themselves as having anthropological or historical value to justify salacious material.

In 1963, Brunello Rondi, an Italian director, famous for collaborations with Federico Fellini, produced *Il Demonio*. The film portrays a lonely, young Italian peasant named Purificata (Dahlia Lavi) who attempts to win the love of a young man using witchcraft. The village ostracizes Purificata as a witch, causing her mental state to deteriorate further and eliciting more abuse. She is beaten by her father, raped by a shepherd, molested by a *mago* (folk healer), subjected to an exorcism, and finally murdered. The film leaves it ambiguous whether actual supernatural events are taking place, Purificata is mad, or she has been driven mad by the superstitions of the village. Several features make *Il Demonio* significant to this study.

First, although Rondi denied that his film was a horror movie, it has been cited as an early forerunner of the "folk horror" genre.[9] Rondi based his story on anthropologist Ernesto de Martino's book *Sud e Magia* (1959) about folk magic traditions in southern Italy. Rondi collaborated with De Martino and images from the book were directly recreated as shots in the film.[10] In fact, the plot of *Il Demonio* is primarily a vehicle for portraying southern Italian folk traditions.

Second, it is sometimes claimed that *Il Demonio* was an influence on *The Exorcist*.[11] The film contains an exorcism scene, based on De Martino's ethnography, in which Dahlia Lavi performs an impressive "spider walk." However, there is little evidence that this inspired Regan's spider walk in *The Exorcist*. In an interview, Lavi was asked about this connection and recounted that she had been improvising: "At the time, they asked me if I could do anything unusual like that, and I said, 'Well, I am a dancer, I'm flexible, let me show you what I can do.' I showed them that and they said, 'Oh, yes! That looks good!'"[12] This position had been associated with female demoniacs at least since French neurologist Jean-Martin Charcot's book *Les demoniaques dans l'art* (1887). Charcot and his student Paul Richer reproduced images of possessed women in a position Charcot called "the hysterical arch" to support his thesis that they had actually suffered from hysteria. Both films were borrowing scripts for possession, but from historical sources rather than from each other.

Third, and most importantly, *Il Demonio* began with a title card declaring: "The producer would like to thank Professor Ernesto De Martino of the University of Cagliari whose funding made possible our ethnological studies in the south of Italy. This film is based on a recent and tragic true story. The rites, spells, and demonic possessions you will see are scientifically verifiable and are a fact of life in Italy, just as they are anywhere else in the world." Lavi described being taken to a hospital and meeting a young woman about whom the story was based.[13] Title cards announcing the true basis of the story are now a cliché in exorcism films. In this way, *Il Demonio* represents a transition from the documentary approach deployed in *Häxan* into modern horror films.

Ken Russell's *The Devils* (1971) was another important exorcism film that split the difference between horror and "historical presentation." The film was based on Aldous Huxley's *The Devils of Loudun* (1952), a novelization of actual events that occurred in 1634, when an entire convent of French nuns became possessed, and a local priest was burnt as a sorcerer. Huxley's novel was adapted into a stage play that was performed in London in 1961 and the United States in 1965.[14] The film adaptation, which depicted nuns engaged in orgiastic blasphemy, was banned in Italy and Ireland in 1972. Like *Il Demonio*, *The Devils* begins with a title card declaring, "This film is based upon historical fact. The principal characters lived and the major events depicted in the film actually took place." This time, the card is black with red font, anticipating *The Exorcist*.

The 1970s: "Getting Into the Act"

In 1974, Anton LaVey of the Church of Satan predicted that, as a result of *The Exorcist*, exorcism was about to become a new American pastime:

> There will be a chance for everyone to get into the act; for as well as exorcists and the possessed, there will be plenty of room for detectors or spotters, who, like parlor psychoanalysts of a generation ago, will have a literal field day. *The Exorcist* has become America's No. 1 cocktail party conversation opener, even surpassing astrology. Soon, as with astrology, comparing possessions will become the main topic of conversations at block parties. In each crowd will be a graven-faced neighborhood expert, and he will serve as mediator or emcee. Of course, if the gathering is fortunate enough, the parish priest will be the guest of honor.[15]

LaVey's prediction was correct: More people did "get into the act," as mass media disseminated cultural scripts to fuel a renewed culture of exorcism. But this process was already underway before *The Exorcist*.

In April 1971, one month before Blatty's novel was published, NBC Chicago aired an exorcism on live television. Newlyweds Edwin and Marsha Becker had experienced a series of disturbances upon moving into their new home. Camera crews arrived to film William Derl Davis, a reverend from the Independent Spiritualist Church in Chicago, and medium Joe DeLouise as they exorcized the home. The crew were given crosses to wear for protection and Derl-Davis administered communion. DeLouise entered a trance and assumed the persona of an old woman whose spirit could not rest. The spirit was offered communion and the exorcism was declared a success. The Beckers's story was adapted into more horror media. In 2012, an episode *Paranormal Witness* called "The Tenants" featured a re-enactment of the experiences of the Beckers, and in 2022, a film adaptation, *True Haunting*, was announced. Although a media oddity in 1971, similar segments would soon follow, drawing exorcists from more mainstream churches.

Soon the networks were courting a Jesuit to perform a televised exorcism. Another couple—this time in Daly City, California—were reporting all manner of strange paranormal activity: explicable fires, knives and other objects flying across the room, a bite mysteriously disappearing from a sandwich they had just made, and a pot of hot soup vanishing from the stove. The husband was a twenty-nine-year-old airline mechanic raised in an Orthodox Jewish household, and the wife was a twenty-six-year-old from a Catholic family. They also had a two-year-old child. The wife sought help from her parish priests, who did a cursory investigation of the phenomena but decided not to intervene. She turned to the prioress of a local Carmelite convent, who directed the family to Father Karl Patzelt.

Patzelt was born in the Austrian Empire during World War I. While in seminary, Germany invaded, and all the seminarians were conscripted into military service. Patzelt served as a medic until he was captured by the Soviets. He learned Russian and upon his release he was ordained as a Jesuit and a Byzantine rite priest. He relocated to San Francisco and became the director of the Catholic Russian Center. Patzelt met with the family in July 1972 and suggested they move. The married couple said they had already tried this but the phenomena had pursued them. Patzelt then sought his bishop's permission for an exorcism and, the following summer, he performed fourteen exorcisms in English, Latin, and Old Slavonic. In September 1973, the exorcisms were declared successful, and the husband converted to Catholicism.[16]

Although up to twenty people witnessed the Daly City exorcisms, the event did not make national news until *The Exorcist* hit theaters. In December 1973, *The National Jesuit News* published an account of the exorcism. In January 1974, CBS radio picked up the story.[17] A CBS producer phoned Patzelt from New York to ask if they could film his next exorcism, but Patzelt refused.[18] However, he did agree when NBC asked him to appear on *The Tomorrow Show* alongside three other priests who had been working "*The Exorcist* circuit": Richard Woods of Loyola; Edmund G. Ryan, the vice president of Georgetown; and William O'Malley, who appeared in *The Exorcist*. Assembling these four priests further destabilized the status of *The Exorcist* as fiction. A parishioner who assisted Patzelt in the exorcism told *The Los Angeles Times* that it was "unfortunate" the exorcism coincided with the film because "it sounded like the whole thing was cooked up." They added that no one involved had seen the film, but that Patzelt eventually saw it and "thought it was a junky movie."[19] Patzelt later stated the film was unrealistic because God would not allow exorcists to be killed and one of the characters was not "sturdy" enough to attempt an exorcism.[20]

The Tomorrow Show was also significant because it demonstrated that in 1973 there was still public debate between priests about exorcism. Woods framed this discussion as a conflict between "the old-line Catholic establishment," which believed in literal spiritual warfare, and a younger generation of Catholics, who see evil active in humans rather than demons. Patzelt argued that the church should publicize exorcism so that people suffering from demonic attack know help is available. Other panelists countered that this could cause suggestible people to wrongly believe they are possessed and so exorcism should continue to be kept in strict secrecy. O'Malley described being "agnostic" as to whether demons even exist. *The New York Times* quoted priests who condemned the exorcism as "devil wizardry" and "a return to Paganism." The bishops seemed caught in the middle. Bishop John Ward said of the panel that the current fascination with exorcism "borders on hysteria" but added, "I'm not approving or disapproving of exorcism. It's a fact that the devil does exist and there is a Roman Catholic ritual using prayers to exorcize the devil."[21]

Although Patzelt never allowed an exorcism to be filmed, he did give a series of talks at universities, visiting the University of San Diego in February 1974 and the University of California-San Francisco the following month. In 1980, he gave a lecture at Fordham University where he stated that several hundred exorcisms a year are performed around the country. He also stated, "In most cases anyone can perform the ceremony," and referenced a woman in Seattle who "drives out devils left and right."[22] Significantly, Patzelt was able to platform his views on exorcism at Fordham because the networks were seeking an exorcism story.

The media paid less attention to the surge of exorcism among Pentecostals and charismatic Christians that began in the 1960s, but these groups were also getting into the act on both sides of the Atlantic. In 1973, the Church of England's Archbishop of York asked a charismatic prelate named Morris Selby to head an advisory committee to make guidelines for the diocese on exorcism. The committee was given three years to complete this task, but in March 1974, Selby sent an interim report citing, "The news that the film called 'The Exorcist' was about to cross the Atlantic, tornado-like, leaving a trail of damage behind it, together with an apparent increase of demand here for such a ministry."[23]

Selby's warning was prescient. In October 1974, thirty-one-year-old Michael Taylor of Ossett, England, was diagnosed as possessed by his charismatic Christian fellowship group, led by twenty-two-year-old Marie Robinson. He was subjected to an all-night exorcism held in a Church of England church, during which ministers bound him to a cross, inserted crucifixes into his mouth, and doused him in holy water. The exorcism was halted at dawn, whereupon he returned home and murdered his wife with his bare hands, tearing out her eyes and tongue. He was discovered walking the streets naked, covered in blood, shouting, "It is the blood of Satan." Taylor was found not guilty by reason of insanity. Psychiatrist William Trethowan diagnosed the episode as "hysterical pseudo psychosis" brought about by the exorcism. The Bishop of Wakefield immediately banned exorcism and established an investigative commission. The Archbishop of Canterbury announced new guidelines requiring a bishop's permission to perform an exorcism and requiring advice from medical professionals and continued pastoral care.[24]

Notre Dame held a symposium on demonic possession in January 1975. Naturally, The Exorcist was discussed as "but one example" of contemporary fascination with the devil.[25] The following April, a faculty member submitted a dossier concerning a group of about sixty Notre Dame students who had been engaging in unauthorized exorcisms and "spiritual coercion." True House, a "Catholic Pentecostal" movement, was accused of so-called "breakthrough ministries" in which student lay leaders would rouse members from their beds late at night and take them to a darkened room to confess their sins. Student lay leaders would then perform the Roman rite of exorcism over the individuals and order them to not mention these sessions to their priests.[26] This episode is indicative of changes to Catholic culture that were occurring after The Exorcist, as well as how the return of exorcism presented

complete Barbara Weigand's work. This shift from demoniac to mystic was fairly common among Catholic women, going back to early modern Europe.[33] Michel requested that the exorcisms go on and she ate less and less, explaining that she was "not allowed to." At her death, she weighed only seventy pounds. Extreme fasting is also precedented among female mystics and some historians have argued that mystics such as Catherine of Sienna suffered from *anorexia nervosa*. Catherine Walker Bynum has argued fasting allowed medieval women to exercise control over their environments, assert the significance of the spirit over the body, and fuse their suffering with that of Christ.[34] Michel's reported inability to eat seems rooted in her desire to emulate female saints rather than a neurological disorder. In fact, the exorcists may have been following Michel's lead. Rodewyk concluded that this was a "penance possession" in which God had ordained that Michel suffer to atone for the sins of others. This interpretation explained why the exorcisms had not been successful. Father Renz believed Michel's visions and concluded that the Virgin Mary's prophecy meant Michel could not die during the exorcism.[35] Likewise, Father Rodewyk stated in his 1963 book that demons are not permitted to kill the people they possess, citing the story of Job.[36] Others were less sure. Peter, a boyfriend Michel met in college, encouraged her to seek medical help, but she believed doctors could not help and she feared the state mental institution.[37] As late as June 30, Michel's sister urged her to see a doctor. On July 1, Michel was suffering from a fever. Her father put her to bed, and she never woke up. Authorities concluded that she had died of malnutrition combined with the strain of the exorcisms.

The trial went beyond proving negligence and put the entire practice of exorcism on trial.[38] A psychoanalyst pronounced the defendant's belief in exorcism abnormal. A psychiatrist examined Father Renz and concluded that he was psychologically normal, save that he seemed incapable of critical evaluation when it came to the topic of exorcism. This was attributed to a "small calcification" detected in his brain.[39] In 1979, the German Bishops Conference set up a commission to investigate exorcism to prevent similar events from happening in the future.

The story also triggered a resurgence of Catholic piety in Bavaria that transformed Michel into a folk saint. The death of this pious young girl raised a problem of theodicy: unless the demons won, then she must have been a holy martyr. There was a report of a priest playing tapes of her exorcisms in a local tavern.[40] In 1977, a Carmelite nun described a vision that Michel's body was incorruptible and demanded that it be exhumed. On February 25, the family had her body transferred to a more expensive casket and a large crowd gathered, including news crews, to see if her body was indeed miraculously preserved. The body was transferred to a new casket by a mortician, who told the family that it had putrefied, and recommended they not view it. Father Renz reported he was skeptical of the mortician but was not allowed to see the body. Others recalled that Renz had been free to see the body but chose not to. Afterward, conspiracy theories formed about what happened on February 25. Some claimed that if the body had really putrefied, the secular newspapers would have printed pictures of Michel's corpse; therefore, the absence of contradictory evidence proved a miracle had occurred.[41] Today, buses of pilgrims from Holland and other countries visit the grave and leave notes, petitioning Michel for help or thanking her for her sacrifice.[42]

The first film based on this case was *The Exorcism of Emily Rose* (2005), written and directed by Scott Derrickson, who also wrote *Deliver Us From Evil* (2014). This film was similar to *Il Demonio* in that it was based closely on the work of anthropologist Felicitas Goodman (1914–2005). Goodman is listed in the opening credits as a consultant and her 1981 book, *The Exorcism of Anneliese Michel*, was reprinted with a new cover declaring it "The Story that Inspired the Major Motion Picture *The Exorcism of Emily Rose*." Goodman's book was immaculately researched but put forth a controversial argument. Goodman was born in Hungary and had studied at Heidelberg University. Her niece was an attorney in Germany and helped her to obtain court documents. She listened to the tapes of the exorcisms, read letters between Michel and Father Alt, and interviewed those involved. In addition, Goodman studied Pentecostalism and specialized in researching altered states of consciousness. But Goodman also believed the Klingenberg case was an example of mystical experiences that had been medicalized by the psychiatric establishment to the detriment of Michel and those who tried to help her. She wrote, "I felt something had to be done to help the persons involved."[43]

Goodman cast doubt on the claim that Michel was epileptic, noting that she only had five seizures between 1968 and 1972 and that, in court, experts did not express certainty of this diagnosis. In addition, Michel's autopsy did not find evidence of brain damage associated with epileptic seizures. She also doubts that Michel died of malnutrition, noting that her organs seemed healthy and that there was an absence of decubitus ulcers (bedsores) normally associated with starvation.[44] Instead, Goodman hypothesized that Michel died when she went off the anti-seizure drug Tegretol. Withdrawal is known to cause fever and hypoxia (loss of oxygenated blood). Thus, she effectively suffocated rather than starved.[45]

More controversially, Goodman suggests that Michel was actually undergoing a type of shamanic process seen across cultures that she dubs "religious altered state of consciousness" (RASC), and that the exorcism *would have worked* had Michel not been given psychiatric medication. Goodman argues that Michel's fasting, self-abuse, and choking were all natural parts of this process that she was doing instinctively to alter her own body chemistry. But because her brain chemistry was already altered by psychiatric medication, these behaviors continued to escalate with no benefit. Goodman admits her theories are a construction of events, but counters that the psychiatrists were likewise offering a construction that was presented as fact.

The Exorcism of Emily Rose begins with the title card, "This film is based on a true story." It replaces Michel with an American college student and takes place after Emily Rose (Jennifer Carpenter) has already died. The opening scene references *The Exorcist* by showing a man with a black hat and bag staring up at the front of a house; however, this is not an exorcist but a medical examiner who informs the family that Emily Rose's death cannot be attributed to natural causes. The film is as much a courtroom drama as a horror film. The protagonist is Erin Bruner (Laura Linney), a skeptical and ambitious defense attorney who represents exorcist Richard Moore (Tom Wilkinson) and who is stalked by demons for her efforts. Anticipating the Hayes brothers' viewpoint that *The Conjuring* films are not horror movies, but "religious supernatural" movies, executive producer Clint Culpepper told the *Los Angeles Times*, "I never saw this as a 'horror' movie. I always saw this as an art-house treatment of a horrible story."[46] Co-writer Paul Harris Boardman explained his intention to use the courtroom to tell a Rashomon story with competing versions of what happened to Emily Rose. While the story leaves some ambiguity, it strongly pushes an interpretation that combines Father Rodewyk's theory that Michel's was a "penance possession" with Goodman's theory that psychiatric medication caused Michel's death by interfering with a natural process.

At one point, an anthropologist named "Dr. Sadira Adani" (Shohreh Aghdashloo)—an obvious stand-in for Goodman—takes the witness stand and presents Goodman's theory almost verbatim, even citing Carlos Castaneda, a fraudulent anthropologist who had not yet been discredited when Goodman's book was written. The subplot involving Bruner is also based on a detail from Goodman's book. In the actual trial, the defense called one Dr. Roth, hoping he might use his medical expertise to show the defendants had not been negligent. But Roth's statements proved unhelpful. Father Alt told Goodman that Dr. Roth met him outside of the trial and told him that he could not testify differently "because people who spoke against Satan would be punished for it."[47] This is the basis of a scene where a physician who believes Emily Rose was possessed tells Bruner he cannot testify because the demons will punish anyone who interferes. He is then inexplicably run-over in an accident reminiscent of *The Omen*. A detail not based in Goodman's book is that demonic activity is repeatedly shown as recurring at 3 a.m. Father Moore tells Bruner that this is "the demonic witching hour" favored by demons because it mocks the tradition that Jesus died at 3 p.m.[48] The association of the demonic with this hour was popularized by the DeFeo murders that preceded *The Amityville Horror* story.

The presentation of Emily Rose as a martyr was also calculated to appeal to Christians. Culpepper stated, "There's a huge faction in this country that we call the red states who I think will respond to the fact that [Emily Rose] made a choice based on her belief and on her faith."[49] This interpretation upset skeptics, who felt the film was covering for the crimes of negligent exorcists. A reviewer for *Philadelphia Weekly* wrote, "Kneeling down to suck off religious fanatics everywhere, the movie derisively shrugs off the scientific method for the sake of cheap scares."[50] The conservative website "Free Republic" interviewed exorcist James LeBar about the film and asked, "Isn't there a danger that it will lead people to see demons where none exist?" Rather than answer this question, LeBar replied, "One of the reasons I'm willing to do interviews like this is so that this phenomenon comes to the attention of people, Catholic and non-Catholic, and they will be informed that a: The devil exists, b: He tries to trouble people, and c: If he troubles people so much that he possesses them, they can be helped through exorcism."[51] This is another example of an exorcist advancing their cause in the wake of a horror movie. Further evidence of the film's legacy and influence is a story that surfaced in 2020 describing some anomalous experiences reported by Jennifer Carpenter during filming and speculating that the film is cursed.[52] This rumor replicates similar claims about *The Exorcist* and *The Omen*.

Whereas *The Exorcism of Emily Rose* takes place after a fatal exorcism, the German film *Requiem* (2006) portrays a troubled young woman and ends with her decision to undergo exorcism. The opening title card states, "Requiem is based on true events. However, the characters and their actions are fictitious." The protagonist is named Michaela (Sandra Hüller) but otherwise it is the most accurate film depiction of Michel's life. *Requiem* is shot in a documentary style and is not a horror movie. It does not suggest that the protagonist is experiencing literal demonic assaults, nor does it reduce her problems to misdiagnosed epilepsy. Rather, it seeks to locate Michaela's experiences within the larger context of a young college student with epilepsy transitioning between family life in a rural, religiously conservative household to college life, with its secular and libertine values. It explores her complex relationship with her family and her faith and portrays her having agency in what happens to her. The final scene shows Michaela sitting on a hill with a friend from college who tries to talk her out of an exorcism. Michaela answers that she must go her own way. There is a final shot of Michaela in the car headed home with a knowing expression on her face, then a title card stating, "After a series of several dozen exorcisms, Michaela Klingler dies of exhaustion in her parents' house."

Anneliese: The Exorcism Tapes (2011) was made on a budget of $100,000 and released straight to DVD. Whereas the other two films portray the aftermath and lead-up to the exorcisms, *Anneliese* claims to be documentary footage of the exorcism itself. A title card states, "The material contained in this film is real" and actors (some with barely passable German accents) assume the roles of Michel, her parents, Alt, and Renz. Despite this premise, this film distorts the story far more than those merely "inspired" by Michel's case. A skeptical American camera crew has come to film the exorcism as part of a "medical experiment" and Michel kills them all off, one by one. In an extreme form of the "realist montage," the bogus documentary is interspersed with actual audio recordings from the Michel exorcisms, which can be found online. It seems unlikely many viewers would be fooled by the conceit of this film, but it may well distort awareness of what actually happened in Klingenberg in 1976.

The 1990s: Exorcism Goes Primetime

The 1980s was an important decade for horror, but it had a surprising dearth of exorcism films purporting to be based on true events. In part this was because the trend moved toward elaborate special effects and more fantastic stories, such as Sam Raimi's *Evil Dead* (1987) and John Carpenter's *Prince of Darkness* (1987). One notable exception is *The Entity* (1982), based on a case that began in 1974 in which Doris Bither, a single mother of three from

Culver City, California, reported being harassed and raped by an invisible entity. The case was investigated by a team of parapsychologists affiliated with UCLA consisting of Barry Taff, Thelma Moss, and David Gaynor. The story was adapted into a 1978 novel by Frank De Felitta, and finally into a film with the tagline, "based on a true story that isn't over yet."[53] Bither came from an abusive home and one of her sons reported that she had been experimenting with a Ouija board and self-medicating with drugs and alcohol before her experiences began.[54] There is no way of knowing whether her story would have taken the shape that it did in 1974 had *Exorcist*-mania not been sweeping the country. Skeptic Benjamin Radford draws connections between the investigation conducted by Taff's team and those of the Warrens. Both involve "experts" going into an emotionally troubled household and massaging reports of paranormal activity into a coherent narrative fit for book and movie options. There have been rumors of a remake of *The Entity* that will stick more closely to the Bither case.[55]

A renewed culture of exorcism expanded in 1990, especially in the Catholic Church. Three events happened in this year: Blatty's sequel to *The Exorcist* came out, which he directed himself; Cardinal O'Connor gave his sermon on *The Exorcist*, setting the stage for an exorcism to be shown on network television; and Father Gabriele Amorth published *Un Exorcist Raconta* about his experiences as the exorcist for the Diocese of Rome. This book underwent twelve Italian editions before it was published in English as *An Exorcist Tells His Story*.

Exorcist II: The Heretic (1977) was made with no input from either Blatty or Friedkin. William Goodhart was commissioned to write a script and he developed a story based on the theories of Teilhard de Chardin, who had inspired the character of Lankester Merrin: Pazuzu did not possess Regan because of a Ouija board, but because the demon attacks special children on the cusp of humanity's spiritual evolution. The film was poorly received, in part because Goodhart's story lacked a sufficient basis in traditional Catholic demonology. In 1983, Blatty published *Legion* as a sequel to *The Exorcist*. It is a detective story in which Lieutenant Kinderman, a character from the first novel, discovers a series of gruesome murders are being carried out by Father Karras—or rather, the spirit of a dead serial killer that demonic forces have allowed to reanimate Karras's body. Blatty named his antagonist "The Gemini Killer." Recall that in 1974 San Francisco police received a letter from "The Zodiac Killer" praising *The Exorcist*. The film adaptation from studio Morgan Creek Entertainment was titled *The Exorcist III: Legion*, although it ignored the previous sequel. It is more sadistic than the original, with elaborate descriptions of how the Gemini killer inflicts maximum suffering on his victims. Serial killer Jeffrey Dahmer became obsessed with the film and engaged in a sort of ostensive performance of Blatty's villain. At his 1992 trial, forensic psychiatrist Park Dietz testified that Dahmer purchased yellow contact lenses so that he could more closely resemble the possessed character when visiting clubs in search of victims, and he would often play *The Exorcist III* to his victims before attacking them.[56]

While audiences were thrilling to the Gemini killer, the ABC network—inspired by O'Connor's sermon—was working with James LeBar to finally achieve what the networks had sought since the 1970s—a televised Catholic exorcism, not of a house but of an individual. On April 5, 1991, *20/20* showed an exorcist known only as "Father A" casting demons out of "Gina," a sixteen-year-old girl from Palm Beach, Florida. Producer Rob Wallace remarked on this event, "I came away believing that possession was possible, and that it can happen, and, in fact, we may have witnessed possession and the exorcism of demons."[57] But the segment was painful for many Catholics, who already regarded exorcism as embarrassing. In a particularly cringe-worthy exchange, Father A tries to learn the identity of the ten entities inhabiting Gina. Gina explains, "Zian is African." Father A asks, "Is he an African of this type—of today's age? Or is he an African in the jungle?" LeBar looks into the camera and explains that the devil plays a game of deception, trying to convince the exorcist he is not there. This comment caused Jesuit Thomas H. Stahel, in *America* magazine, to question why such a deceptive devil chose to appear on national television at all.[58]

The *20/20* episode was followed by a *Nightline* episode in which Ted Koppel interviewed a panel of priests. LeBar emphasized the reality of possession and encouraged viewers to read Malachi Martin's *Hostage to the Devil*. But Father Richard McBrien, a Notre Dame theologian, countered that regardless of any agreement between ABC and the family, this was a violation of Gina's privacy. He added that the segment could cause disturbed people to falsely believe they are possessed, and that the entire affair held the Catholic faith up to ridicule. McBrien followed up on this critique in a column for *The Catholic Courier*, in which he reported that every priest he spoke with was against televising an exorcism. He stated that O'Connor's 1990 sermon, as well as the *20/20* segment, were part of "hidden agenda": "The real objective of that project, I submit, was to help bring back that old-time religion when everyone, women especially, knew their place, when Catholics obeyed without question every directive from on high, and when there was never any question that the Catholic Church was the one, true church with all the answers to all the important questions we have about life, both here and hereafter."[59] But McBrien's column was met with a fierce reply from a lay Catholic who claimed he was insulting the intelligence of those who believe Catholic teachings about demons. In a statement that says a lot about the role of media in religious culture, the respondent wrote, "My faith tells me that the devil is real and the '20/20' program was allowed by God to show that reality. The show proved that Jesus is more powerful than Satan."[60] McBrien might have been in the majority of American Catholic priests in 1991, but this was one of the last instances of a priest publicly condemning the practice of exorcism. Meanwhile, exorcists like LeBar continued to use the media spotlight to advance their cause. LeBar described receiving up to twenty phone calls a day after the episode aired. As a result, O'Connor, LeBar's bishop, appointed four diocesan exorcists. In a direct way, LeBar created his own office within the church through skillful manipulation of the media.

LeBar's enhanced status as an exorcist in turn drew more attention from Hollywood. When *The Exorcist* was re-released in 2000, LeBar had a prominent photo published in *Time* magazine under the headline "If You Liked The Movie[61] . . . ." The same day *The Exorcist* premiered in 2000 also marked the premiere of *Lost Souls*, for which LeBar served as a consultant. This exorcism movie concerns a talented true crime author who discovers he is fated to become possessed by Satan, becoming the Antichrist. It begins with a bogus Bible verse about the Antichrist attributed to Deuteronomy 12. *Lost Souls* did terribly at the box office, being mostly a rehash of tropes from *Rosemary's Baby*, *The Omen*, and even *The Devil's Advocate* (1997). After his death in 2008, LeBar's name appeared on an Archdiocese of New York's list of clergy who were credibly accused of sexually abusing a minor.[62]

The year 1990 also marked the rise of Gabriele Amorth as a public advocate for exorcism. Like LeBar, Amorth was very much a creature of the media. He was a member of the Society of St. Paul, a group whose mission is to "evangelize with the modern tools of communication." In Italy, he hosted a radio show where callers could describe their problems with demons. He told *The Sunday Telegraph* that *The Exorcist* was his favorite film, commenting, "Of course, the special effects are exaggerated, but it is a good film, and substantially exact, based on a respectable novel which mirrored a true story."[63] Amorth was ordained in 1954 but did not become an exorcist until 1986—only four years before his book was published. Jean Young notes that Amorth's book would likely not have received as much attention were it not for *The Exorcist* and the panic over Satanic ritual abuse that was near its peak in 1990.[64] As an advocate for exorcism, Amorth claimed that Hitler and Stalin were demonically possessed, and that an increase of demonic possessions was due to the popularity of yoga and the *Harry Potter* novels. In 2013, he boasted of having performed 160,000 exorcisms over the course of his career.[65]

In 1990, Amorth formed the International Association of Exorcists (IAE) with five other priests and, in 1992, they held their first meeting in Rome. Two years later, the group elected Amorth as their president. Today, the IAE has an international membership of over five hundred, and it lobbies the church to loosen restrictions on exorcism. Its first skirmish with the Curia occurred in 1999 when the 1614 rite of exorcism was revised. The revision had been scheduled since Vatican II and was the last ritual to be updated. In 1984, a group of German theologians, disturbed by the death of Anneliese Michel, had petitioned the Vatican to remove the practice of speaking "imperatively" to the devil during exorcism. They argued that addressing the patient as the Devil in a commanding voice might falsely convince someone that they were, in fact, possessed. The new rite still calls for speaking directly to the Devil, to the disappointment of some German theologians.[66] However, the revised language emphasizes faith in God's providence rather than commands to the Devil.[67] In the aftermath of the *20/20* debacle, a clause was added stating, "No space may be given to any of the social media of communication while the exorcism is being performed, even before the exorcism is performed and, when it is completed, the exorcist and those present, preserving their duty of discretion, may not give notice of it."[68] Amorth immediately condemned the revised ritual as ineffective. Like Malachi Martin before him, Amorth hinted at a Satanic conspiracy within the Vatican, stating, "Their intention was to arm us with a blunt sword."[69] In 2000, Amorth retired as IAE president, but remained honorary president for life.

2005: The Tanacu Exorcism

In June 2005, global headlines again reported on a young woman killed in an exorcism. Twenty-three-year-old Marcia Irina Cornici died following an exorcism at an Orthodox monastery in Tanacu, Romania. Initially it was reported that she had been tied to a cross for three days. In reality, the cross was an improvised stretcher of rough boards to which arm supports were eventually attached. The nuns untied and fed Cornici, but she fainted. They called an ambulance and reported she was alive when placed in it. However, she was declared dead upon arrival at the hospital. Some reports speculated that the ambulance drivers administered an overdose of insulin. BBC reporter Tatiana Niculescu Bran researched the story and wrote two Romanian-language non-fiction novels about the case: *The Confession* (2006) and *The Book of Judges* (2007). Bran found that Cornici had been abandoned as a young girl by her alcoholic mother and raised in an orphanage where the production of child pornography and rape were regular occurrences. She adapted to this abusive environment by becoming violent herself and formed a homoerotic relationship with Anghel, another orphan. She may also have suffered from hallucinations from an early age. After Anghel became a nun, Cornici visited her and became a guest of the monastery. Cornici was frustrated that Anghel had no desire to leave the monastery or engage in a sexual relationship with her. She expressed this frustration with obscene, homophobic outbursts, which the monastery interpreted as evidence of demonic possession. In April, following a suicide attempt, the nuns tied her up and brought her to the hospital where she was diagnosed with major psychosis and leukemia. Bran notes that the hospital likely discharged her so that her impending death from leukemia would not affect the hospital's death rate. In May, Cornici became violent toward herself and set fire to her cell. Daniel Corogeanu, the twenty-nine-year-old priest in charge of the monastery, attempted an exorcism. Like some prominent Catholic exorcists, Corogeanu was often at odds with his diocese and invoked conspiracy theories to justify bending the rules. In 2003, his bishop read the church canon to him, which he dismissed as "freemasonry." The Romanian Orthodox Church limits the ceremony of exorcism to twice a year and requires that three priests are present to ensure safety, but Corogeanu ignored these protocols. He was charged with murder and depriving a person of liberty and sentenced to fourteen years in prison.[70]

Bran's novel was adapted into the play *Confession* by Andre Şerban, and then the Romanian-language film *Beyond the Hills* (2012) by director Cristian Mungiu. *Beyond the Hills* emphasizes the drama of the relationship between the two orphaned girls. In an interview, Mungiu explained that while the case garnered global media attention, no one seemed to have grasped the complexity of the situation: "People were either against the church, in an offensive manner and without spending one minute to understand why the nuns had acted in that way, or in favor of the church, arguing that everything was an unwarranted attack against the only individuals who had done something."[71]

The Crucifixion (2017), written by the Hayes brothers, avoids complexity in favor of a stark morality tale about the need for faith to protect us from demons. Structurally, this film closely follows *The Exorcism of Emily Rose*, in which a headstrong, secular female professional (this time a reporter) sets about investigating a woman who died during an exorcism, becomes the target of demonic attack herself, is mentored by a priest, and finally comes to believe in the reality of supernatural. Even more so than *Emily Rose*, this version of the story exonerates the exorcist and shifts the blame to skeptics. *The Crucifixion* suggests that the titular ritual would have been successful had it not been interrupted by a bishop embarrassed by exorcism.

The Aughts: Rome Embraces Exorcism

In the twenty-first century, the popularity of exorcism has continued to grow, both on the screen and among the Curia. In 2002, Morgan Creek Entertainment approved a script for a prequel to *The Exorcist*, but their director, John Frankenheimer, died of a stroke. He was replaced with Paul Schrader, an art house director known for films exploring morality and transcendence. But during editing, studio CEO James Robinson deemed Schrader's film was deemed "too cerebral," and he replaced Schrader with Renny Harlin, best known for *Die Hard 2: Die Harder*. Harlin persuaded the studio to start over and make a (mostly) new film. Schrader's version was slated to go directly to DVD, but he was able to lobby for a theatrical release by visiting horror websites and "starting a rumor" about his film.[72] In the end, Morgan Creek Entertainment released Harlin's film, *Exorcist: The Beginning*, in 2004 and Schrader's film, *Dominion: Prequel to The Exorcist*, in 2005. Adding to the confusion, Swedish actor Stellan Skarsgård agreed to play Lankester Merrin in both versions. Harlin's film caused a critic from the US Conference of Catholic Bishops Office for Film and Broadcasting to remark, "Saints and sages concur that nothing irks the devil's pride more than being mocked. That being true, Lucifer should consider investing in a pair of earplugs before seeing the laughably bad *Exorcist: The Beginning*."[73] Schrader's film was better received by critics and earned praise from Blatty himself. But Morgan Creek Entertainment's bet on back-to-back *Exorcist* prequels—and especially Schrader's ability to marshal horror fans to his cause—demonstrated there was still a significant market for exorcism movies.

Meanwhile, exorcism was continuing to gain ground in Rome. The 1917 Code of Canon Law mandated that each bishop appoint an exorcist for their diocese. But in North America, few bishops actually did this, and the requirement was removed when the code was updated in 1983.[74] In 2004, the Congregation for the Doctrine of the Faith sent letters to bishops around the world, starting with the United States, asking them to appoint an official exorcist in each of their dioceses. At the time, there were only seventeen exorcists in the United States.[75] The same year, the Pontifical Athenaeum Regina Apostolorum, a university affiliated with the Vatican, began offering a four-month course on exorcism. A chief part of the curriculum was how to distinguish between possession and mental illness, and the course drew on the expertise of the IAE. Hundreds of priests from around the world took the course. One such priest was Father Gary Thomas of California, who was sent by his bishop in 2005. While there, he met journalist Matt Baglio, who was doing research for his book *The Rite* (2009). While in Rome, Thomas also apprenticed himself under Capuchin exorcist Carmine De Filippis. Thomas's experiences became a theme of Baglio's book, which was adapted into a horror film from Warner Brothers the following year.

The Rite begins with a transtextual anchoring device—quoting a warning given by John Paul II in 1986, that "The devil is still alive and active in the world." The quote is followed by a title card, "What follows is inspired by true events." Thomas's stand-in in the film is named Michale Kovak (Colin O'Donoghue) and Carmine De Filippis becomes Lucas Trevant (Anthony Hopkins). Kovak is considering dropping out of seminary due to his lack of faith, but reluctantly agrees to travel to Rome to attend an exorcism course. He observes exorcisms with the eccentric Lucas Trevant, who asks him, "What did you expect? Spinning heads? Pea soup?" Finally, Kovak must rediscover his faith when Trevant himself becomes possessed and requires an exorcism. Gary Thomas spent a week on the set acting as a consultant and Colin O'Donoghue prepared for his role by observing an actual exorcism.[76] When *The Rite* premiered at a film festival, it was introduced by Gabriele Amorth.[77] *The Rite*, combined with Baglio's non-fiction book and Thomas's media appearances, sent a clear message to the public that the Catholic Church was still performing exorcisms.

In 2014, the Vatican suddenly announced that it was giving formal approval to the IAE, a group that had previously been snubbed by the Curia. However, in exchange for this recognition, the IAE was required to limit membership to priests who had been designated as exorcists by their bishops, and members were required to work with the needs of their diocese. There was also a stipulation that the IAE must promote cooperation with "medical and psychiatric experts competent in spiritual affairs." Upon this announcement an unnamed Vatican official was quoted, "They approved them so they could control them."[78] Still, this move demonstrated the Curia's acknowledgment that exorcists and exorcism were going to be part of Catholic culture in the twenty-first century.

Gabriele Amorth died in 2016. The following year, William Friedkin unveiled his documentary, *The Devil and Father Amorth*, which includes video footage of a ninety-one-year-old Amorth performing an exorcism on "Cristina," a young Italian woman. Some critics suspect Cristina's voice was altered in post-production to make it sound more demonic.[79] The last ten minutes of the film are bizarre: Friedkin explains that he had scheduled a meeting with Cristina, but there was an apparent miscommunication and he finally caught up with her on July 4, 2016, in a church in the small town of Alatri. He explains he did not bring his camera to this meeting and so he is recreating the event from memory. A shaky handheld video camera pans around an empty church in Alatri as shrieking violin music plays and Friedkin recounts how he found Cristina in a state of possession, along with her boyfriend, Davide, who threatened to kill Friedkin and his family if he did not return the film. But the possessed Cristina screamed that she wanted the film to be shown.[80] The following September, Amorth passed away before he could perform another exorcism on Cristina. It is hard to guess what Friedkin's intention was with this project, but one critic noted that it demonstrated the influence of *The Exorcist* on the culture of exorcism: "The movie has fed, like a loop, into religion, which is now feeding into the chaos of a world that, increasingly, needs the Devil to explain why everything appears to be spinning out of control."[81] In 2023, Sony Pictures released a film about Amorth called *The Pope's Exorcist* in which Russell Crowe played the titular role. While purporting to be based on true events, Crowe's Amorth wields a shotgun, explores ancient ruins, and discovers that demons were actually responsible for the Spanish Inquisition. International Association of Exorcists condemned the film as "unreliable splatter."[82]

2011: The 200 Demons House

The series of events sometimes referred to as the "200 Demons House" makes a fitting culmination to this chapter. In 2012, a Catholic exorcism was performed on a single mother of three in Gary, Indiana. The case was significant in that local authorities, including social workers and police, publicly endorsed claims of demonic activity. Gary is a rust-belt town with one of the highest murder rates in the country. As with some of the other cases explored here, there is a sense that demonic possession functioned as an "idiom of distress," through which women experiencing social deprivation signaled that they needed support.[83] It also seems that scripts from horror films played an important role in how events were interpreted, and how the story developed. Finally, as the case gained media attention, various actors swooped in seeking to control the narrative. Predictably, a film adaptation has been announced, completing the cycle of *The Exorcist* effect.

In November 2011, Latoya Ammons moved into a small house at 3860 Carolina Street in Gary, Indiana, along with her mother, Rosa Campbell, and her three children. While the names of the children are not known, there was a twelve-year-old daughter and two brothers, aged nine and seven. That December, Campbell reported an infestation of flies that swarmed the screened-in porch despite the cold. Campbell complained that the flies kept returning no matter how many of them she killed. This was followed by bumps and sightings of "shadowy figures" in the night and boot prints that seemed to appear spontaneously. Then, on March 10, 2012, Ammons's daughter was allegedly levitated off of her bed. In an interview on *Inside Edition*, Ammons described wrestling with an invisible force to pull her back down.[84]

Ammons and Campbell attended a Baptist church, but Campbell's mother, Ruth, put them in touch with a local church who believed in deliverance ministry. Ruth visited the house with someone from the church who advised the family to cleanse the home with bleach and ammonia and then use olive oil to draw crosses on every door and window, as well as the children's hands, feet, and foreheads. Two psychics were also contacted, who declared there were over two hundred demons living within the house. They advised Ammons to move out, but because she couldn't afford to move, they recommended another cleansing ritual, this time fumigating the house with sage and sulfur. They also had Ammons construct an altar in the house's basement with statues of saints.

There were three days of quiet and then the children began acting strangely, speaking in deep voices, and exhibiting "evil smiles." They reported hearing voices and being thrown around the house. Some nights the family slept in a hotel. The children's behavior became so severe that they stopped going to school, attracting the attention of authorities. On April 19, the family visited their physician, Dr. Geoffrey Onyeukwu. The children began cursing the doctor in demonic voices and then fainted. Someone called 911 and police and ambulances arrived. The boys woke up in the hospital and began screaming and thrashing. Meanwhile, someone called the Department of Child Services (DCS), speculating that Ammons may be mentally ill and was coaching her children to act possessed. DCS caseworker Valerie Washington, along with a nurse, attempted to interview the boys, who continued to growl threats. Campbell held one on the boy's hands and started praying, at which point the boy walked backward up the ceiling—bracing his hands on his grandmother—and flipped over her head. This was certainly an impressive feat, but not necessarily supernatural. However, Walker believed in ghosts and spirits and she fled the room. She later told police the boy "glided backward on the floor, wall, and ceiling."[85] When a doctor asked the boy to repeat the stunt, he refused, and Walker suggested he could only do it while demonically possessed. Ammons spent the night at the hospital and the next day DCS took custody of her children without a court order.

The hospital chaplain, a pastor at Unity African Methodist Episcopal Zion Church, decided the family needed the help of a Catholic exorcist. On April 20, he contacted Father Michael Maginot of St. Stephen Martyr Parish in Merrillville, Indiana, to request an exorcism. It was the first time Maginot had received such a request. Two days later, he visited the family for four hours. Campbell pointed out several phenomena that convinced him of demonic presence: the Venetian blinds seemed to move without an air current, seemingly inexplicable wet footprints appeared in the living room, and a flickering light bulb became steady whenever Maginot approached. Ammons complained of a headache and when Maginot pressed his crucifix to her head, she began to convulse. Maginot concluded that Ammons was possessed, possibly as the result of a curse placed on her. He blessed the house but advised the family to live with relatives.

Several days later, Campbell and Ammons returned to the house so their DCS worker could inspect the conditions of the home. Washington requested a police officer accompany her and two additional officers came out of "professional curiosity."[86] Like Washington, police captain Charles Austin believed in the supernatural, and the visit resembled a ghost hunt rather than a DCS inspection. A police report from the visit described malfunctioning electronic equipment, an anomalous cloud in a photo resembling a face, and a mysterious voice whispering "hey" on an audio recording.[87] Soon people who visited the house began keeping lists of any accidents or misfortune they experienced, citing it as evidence of demonic activity.

DCS petitioned a court to place a temporary wardship over the Ammons children, noting that they had not been attending school regularly. The agency had previously cited this problem in 2009. Ammons said some days the children could not attend school because they had been tormented by demons. The two older children were sent to St. Joseph's Carmelite Home in East Chicago, and the youngest was sent to Christian Haven in Wheatfield, Indiana, for psychiatric evaluation. Clinical psychologists concluded the children did not have psychotic disorders but had been induced into delusional beliefs by their family. DCS produced an action plan calling for all family members to cease talking about demons and possession. However, this plan was directly undermined by case managers who believed this was a case of demonic activity.

On May 10, another party toured the house consisting of Ammons, three police officers, Father Maginot, and a DCS worker. Samantha Ilic stood in for Washington, who refused to return to the house. They discovered an oily substance on the blinds, which Maginot interpreted as demonic. At Maginot's suggestion, the police excavated the dirt floor beneath the basement stairs. They discovered an assortment of detritus, including a pair of panties, candy wrappers, and what appeared to be a weight for a drapery cord. Maginot began spreading blessed salt, and the DCS worker experienced a panic attack and had to leave the house. After this, Maginot wrote a report to his bishop requesting authorization for a formal exorcism. He also performed a minor exorcism on Ammons, which did not require a bishop's approval. Ilic and two police officers observed the ritual and described sensing a demonic presence.

Ammons and her mother moved to Indianapolis and Maginot blessed their new home. On May 30, Maginot's request for exorcism was approved. Ammons was exorcized three times, twice in English and once in Latin. Two of the police officers assisted with some of these rituals. The exorcism was declared successful and, in November, Ammons regained custody of her children. The house on Carolina Street had become the object of local curiosity. The new tenant experienced no supernatural phenomena, but owner

Charles Reed had to ask the Gary Police Department to request that officers stop driving by the house.

Several news sources compared Ammons's experiences to *The Exorcist* and *Poltergeist*.[88] As skeptics were quick to point out, many aspects of this story seem derivative of horror movies. The trope of a family who moves into a new house only to discover it is haunted is well established. The first event interpreted as a demonic activity were anomalous flies, a detail from *The Amityville Horror*. When the action crescendos in that film, George Lutz falls through the basement stairs into a pit of supernatural black sludge. In Gary, Father Maginot suggested investigating under the basement stairs in search of a "portal" and the investigators found an "oily substance" on the blinds (which may have been the olive oil used to anoint the windows). The Protestant hospital chaplain's assumption that the situation required a Catholic priest also seems inspired by horror movie scripts. These connections do not mean that Ammons and her family were "making it up." Rather, this seems to be a case of quasi-ostension in which scripts of demonic activity, firmly established in horror movies, influenced how everyone involved interpreted what was happening. The result was a situation that resembled a "real-life horror movie."

In January 2014, *The Indianapolis Star* published a long article describing the case. Ammons was inundated with media requests and a scramble ensued to obtain movie rights. The speed with which media forces moved to transform this event into content was unprecedented. Four days after the article came out, Zak Bagans, executive producer for the show *Ghost Adventures* on the Travel Channel, purchased the house for $35,000.[89] Not long after, it was announced that Maginot had signed a deal for the movie rights with Tony DeRosa-Grund, the producer behind *The Conjuring* franchise. Maginot offered to prepare a report on the exorcisms that would have become property of the diocese, but the bishop instructed Maginot to keep the report for himself. Maginot took this response to mean he was at liberty to do as he wished with the story. He was assured the script would be true to life and not dramatized beyond recognition. He told reporter John Thavis that all he wanted was for the story to alert the public about the dangers of the occult.[90]

Bagans initially told *The Indianapolis Star* he was uncertain what he would do with his newly purchased haunted house, but stated, "It's not entertainment. I really do have a passion for this stuff and the research aspect of this stuff."[91] His documentary, *Demon House*, came out in 2018. In a move worthy of William Castle, it begins with a warning that "Demonologists believe that demons can attach themselves to you through other people, objects, and electronic devices. View at your own risk." This is followed by a kind of paratext, with footage of Bagans wandering around a ruined church and a voiceover in which he describes all the misfortune that occurred while making the film. He states, "I'm one of the world's leading researchers on ghosts and demonology and this is the case that really fucked me up. This story was huge. It was the next Amityville.... The truth is, this film is cursed."

Little happens in *Demon House*. There are re-enactments of the children acting possessed and interviews with Maginot, as well as the police and social workers involved in the case. Barry Taff, of *The Entity* fame, is brought in as an investigator. At one point, Bagans lunges at Taff, claiming he was inexplicably compelled to do so. As a finale, Bagans spends the night in the house with all the doors and windows sealed up. Then he has the entire house demolished, stating, "I wanted to make sure the house never harmed anyone again."

In an interview for *Insider Edition*, Maginot explained he was not informed that the house would be demolished and expressed concerns that occult rituals could be held over the vacant lot, adding, "It could be seven times worse."[92] Like LeBar before him, Maginot's cooperation with the media made him a famous exorcist, and people around the world have sought his expertise.[93] In 2021, after eight people died in a stampede at a Travis Scott concert at Astroworld in Houston, Texas, a conspiracy theory formed online that the accident had actually been a Satanic human sacrifice. For commentary, Fox News brought on Maginot and introduced him as "a Catholic priest and a renowned exorcist expert whose work was featured in the movie *Demon House*." Maginot commented that the imagery at the concert looked demonic and that demons enjoy whipping people into mob violence. However, he seemed to resist the interviewer's suggestion that Travis Scott is part of a Satanic conspiracy.[94] In 2022, it was announced that Netflix would air the film adaptation of the Ammons story, *The Deliverance*, directed by Lee Daniels.[95]

Other Exorcism Scripts

Historians of exorcism have noted that several decades before *The Exorcist*, a revival of deliverance ministry was already under way among Pentecostals and charismatic Christians that did not rely on the "sacramental" approach favored by the Catholic and Orthodox churches.[96] However, horror movies have focused heavily on the Catholic tradition, partly due to the legacy of *The Exorcist*. One of the most significant exorcism stories of the mid-twentieth century was that of Clarita Villanueva, a teenage Filipina girl imprisoned in Manilla in 1953. Villanueva's demons were cast out by Lester Sumrall, an American Pentecostal missionary. Filipino media was saturated with reports of Villanueva. Prison officials had reportedly seen bite marks appear on her body as if she was being bitten by an invisible force. Sumrall saw Villanueva's possession as a chance to prove the superiority of Pentecostalism to a predominantly Catholic nation. The exorcism was declared a success and afterward Sumrall founded Bethel Temple in Manila, where his family still ministers. In 2019, director Roderick Cabrido released the Tagalog-language film, *Clarita*, based on this case. However, Sumrall was replaced with two Catholic priests. As in America, the Catholic Church in the Philippines has become more open to exorcism. In 2022, the Manila archdiocese began construction of the "Saint Michael Center for Spiritual Liberation and Exorcism" to combat what they regard as rising rates of demonic possession.[97] One consequence of such a center is that future Pentecostal missionaries will have less ability to attract attention by casting out demons.

One of the few horror films to depict a charismatic exorcist is *The Last Exorcism* (2010), a "live-record horror" film in the tradition of *The Blair Witch Project*. Protagonist Cotton Marcus (Patrick Fabian) is an evangelical deliverance minister, who callously uses pyrotechnic props to convince his clients they are experiencing the supernatural. Marcus justifies this as a "pious fraud" that benefits the people he dupes. However, when he learns of a young boy who was suffocated during an exorcism, he agrees to perform one last exorcism and invites documentarians to film his deception, thus debunking the practice. (Naturally, Marcus's last exorcism pits him against actual demons and a Satanic cult.) For all its supernatural elements, *The Last Exorcism* is a surprisingly realistic film. Speaking to the camera, Marcus discusses the influence of *The Exorcist* and explains that exorcism is more popular than ever in the twenty-first century and that most modern exorcisms are not performed by Catholic priests, but by charismatic and Pentecostal ministers. The film's premise is inspired by the 1972 documentary *Marjoe*, in which celebrity preacher Marjoe Gortner invited a documentary crew to accompany him on one last revival tour and stated on camera he was a non-believer who took up preaching solely for the money. The detail of a child killed during an exorcism was apparently based on Terrance "Junior" Cottrell, an eight-year-old black child with autism, who was suffocated to death during an exorcism at a storefront church in Milwaukee in 2003.[98]

Also noteworthy is director Sam Raimi's *The Possession* (2012), in which a spirit from Jewish folklore, known as a dybbuk, is expelled by a Hasidic rabbi played by Jewish reggae singer Matisyahu. This film is inspired by a true story that began in 2001 when Kevin Mannis of Portland, Oregon, sold an antique wine cabinet on the online auction site eBay. A very long product description explained that he had purchased it at a yard sale from a woman who inherited it from her grandmother, a Holocaust survivor. The grandmother had called it "a dybbuk box," and when Mannis opened it, it contained ritualistic paraphernalia, including human hair. The product description added that the box was cursed and everyone who had been in contact with it had experienced disturbing paranormal activity. Mannis sold it to a college student, who in turn sold it to Jason Haxton, director of the Museum of Osteopathic Medicine at A. T. Still University in Missouri. Haxton's book, *The Dibbuk* Box (2011), describes the disturbing experiences he had after acquiring the box and speculates about its origins, including the theory that a cabal of Jewish mystics summoned a malevolent spirit to combat the Nazis but lost control of it before imprisoning it in a box. He finally had an ark constructed of gold leaf and acacia wood to contain the box's influence. Both Mannis and Haxton were hired as consultants for *The Possession*. Producer Sam Raimi, famous for the *Evil Dead* franchise, was raised in a conservative Jewish home. He told *Entertainment Weekly*, "I know the demonic lore of *The Exorcist*. But what does my faith believe about demonic possession?" Haxton offered to lend him the dybbuk box, but Raimi declined, stating, "I didn't want anything to do with it. I'm scared of the thing."[99] In truth, neither Mannis's story nor *The Possession* has much to do with actual Jewish folklore about dybbuks, which are generally understood to be wandering spirits who possess the living out of desperation. They are not trapped in boxes nor summoned through rituals. Polish director Marcin Wrona's *Demon* (2015) is a traditional dybbuk story.

In 2016, Haxton sold the dybbuk box to Zak Bagans, who made it an attraction at his Haunted Museum in Las Vegas—a collection of objects that seems inspired by the Warrens' museum. Bagans touted it as "the world's most haunted object." Mannis appeared on *Ghost Adventures* and revealed that there are ten dybbuk boxes known to exist, each containing a piece of the malevolent spirit summoned by desperate Jews during World War II, and that if all ten are ever assembled, a terrible evil will be unleashed. But in 2021, reporter Charles Moss of *Input* magazine coaxed Mannis into confessing what many long suspected—the dybbuk box was just an antique that he built a story around and filled with strange objects. It had not been passed down from a Holocaust survivor and there had been no curse. Mannis had even persuaded his mother to appear on the show *Paranormal Witness* and claim her stroke was caused by the box. Mannis made a meager profit selling the box on eBay but said his real motivation was for the box "to become an interactive horror story in real time."[100] Thus the dybbuk box is a profound example of what Anton LaVey called "getting into the act." The fact that a posting on eBay resulted in a book, a film, and a Las Vegas exhibit within such a short time frame demonstrates the speed at which supernatural stories can now transfer between mediums, mutating with each iteration.

There are also numerous foreign films based on folklore that depict non-Christian traditions of exorcism. The Thai legend of Nai Mak, a female ghost who is exorcised by a powerful Buddhist monk, has been the subject of numerous Thai films, going as far back as 1959. Turkish director Hasan Karacadağ's seven-film D@bbe franchise (2006–2017) takes its name from the *dabbe*, a strange beast referenced in the Quran that is prophesied to appear as an omen of judgment day. The series deals with jinn, exorcism, and other elements of Muslim mythology and is wildly popular in Pakistan and other Muslim-majority nations. In 2007, twenty-two-year-old Janet Moses of New Zealand was killed when her family attempted a traditional Maori exorcism to lift a *mākutu* (curse). No one administering the four-day ritual had proper training and so much water was poured onto Moses that her lungs became flooded and she drowned. In 2015, the docudrama *Belief: The Exorcism of Janet Moses* combined interviews with re-enactments. While not a horror film, it adds to a growing list of films about young women killed during exorcisms. A full analysis of global exorcism films and how they reflect and refract cultures of exorcisms still needs to be done.

Conclusions: The Banality of Evil

In January 2007, Netflix began offering a streaming service in which subscribers could watch films online and dozens of streaming services followed. One consequence of this new platform was a glut of cheaply produced exorcism films, often claiming to be based on true stories or presented as found footage. The ubiquity of this trope was parodied in the 2013 comedy *30 Nights of Paranormal Activity with the Devil Inside the Girl with the Dragon Tattoo*, which was released with the tagline "based on true events . . . that may not have happened." It opens with a sketch in which two women on the show *Storage Wars* purchase an abandoned storage facility and find a VHS tape simply labeled "Found Footage." This is only slightly less creative than the premise of many recent exorcism films.

While some Catholic clergy may still regard exorcism as embarrassing, the Church seems to have quietly conceded the fight to the exorcists. The Archdiocese of Washington, DC, maintains a website with information about obtaining an exorcism and their chief exorcist, Father Stephen J. Rossetti, created an exorcism application for smartphones. Rosetti has also warned that tattoos can lead to possession and devised a ritual to "decommission" demonic tattoos.[101] In part, the Church has embraced exorcism because it has become an asset rather than a reliability. There is a strong demand for the service and evangelical churches are happy to provide that service if the Catholic Church is not. But it seems likely that surging demand is also due to the prevalence of horror movies that provide scripts for demonic behavior and prime viewers to interpret mundane phenomena—being awake at 3 a.m., house flies, electronic disturbances—as signs of the demonic. A spike of requests for exorcisms was reported during the COVID-19 pandemic when much of the world was under lockdown.[102] No doubt, the financial and emotional stress of quarantine contributed to this pattern, but one also wonders how many of these people were stuck at home watching horror movies.

With less stigma attached to exorcism, it has become a political weapon, much as it was in sixteenth-century Europe. Increasingly, conservative Catholic clergy have begun to use public exorcisms to brand cultural opponents as demonic. In 2012, Father Earl Fernandez received permission from the Archdiocese of Cincinnati to perform an exorcism of an abortion clinic as part of a protest. Fernandez declared, "This prayer is said over a place that's infested with the evil spirits, to remove any evil that might happen to be there."[103] The following year, Bishop Thomas Paprocki of Illinois performed a public exorcism in protest of the state's acceptance of same-sex marriage. On October 17, 2000, following protests over the murder of George Floyd, Archbishop Alexander Sample performed a public exorcism in Latin to purge the community of evil. On the same day, Archbishop Salvatore Cordileone of San Francisco held an exorcism outside of a church where protestors had toppled a statue of saint Junipero Serra—a Spanish missionary whom some Native American groups regard as an accessory to violent colonization. Cordileone declared, "We pray that God might purify this place of evil spirits, that he might purify the hearts of those who perpetrated this blasphemy."[104] There remain some standards: In January 2020, Reverend John Zuhlsdorf of Madison, Wisconsin, claimed that the 2020 election had been stolen from Donald Trump and live-streamed an exorcism to banish the demonic power behind the alleged election fraud. Zuhlsdorf claimed he had the permission of bishop Donald Hying to do this exorcism, a claim Hying denied. Hying asked Zuhlsdoft to leave the diocese.[105]

In 1973, part of the appeal of *The Exorcist* was that such things were not supposed to happen—and yet it seemed possible that they could. *The Exorcist* captured the public's imagination because it presented the idea of a transcendent realm, beyond our quotidian, disenchanted world. Now the pendulum seems to have swung the opposite direction, such that the reality of demons is so taken-for-granted in some quarters as to seem banal. The demonic realm no longer points to the transcendent, but risks becoming one more front in an all-encompassing culture war. It remains to be seen whether horror movies can breathe new life into this overplayed genre and, if they can, how new cultural scripts might influence the public's experience of possession and exorcism. For now, though, the flood of cheaply made exorcism films shows no sign of abating.

7

Satanic Panic

"Did you ever hear of Satanism? The worship of the devil, of evil?"
—Dr. Vitus Werdegast (Béla Lugosi), *The Black Cat* (1934).

"A complete education in Satanic philosophy is available at your local video store."[1]
—Blanch Barton, Magistra Templi Rex of the Church of Satan

"The entire saga, said the judge, had stemmed from the fevered imagination of one six-year-old boy whose parents had allowed him to watch horrific videos."
—*Daily Mail*, following the 1990 Rochdale Satanic Ritual abuse panic.[2]

Exorcism and the Satanic Panic went hand-in-hand in the late-twentieth century. Ed Warren, Malachi Martin, James LeBar, and Gabriele Amorth all made wild claims about the danger of Satanic cults. The central claim of the Panic—that a conspiracy of criminal Satanists was all around us, abusing children in ways that could only be detected by special therapists—was a secular analog to claims that an invisible army of demons surrounds us and can only be countered by a trained exorcist. However, where exorcism claims remained a matter of private belief, accusations of Satanism sent law enforcement in search of criminal Satanists. The result was that innocent people were arrested and prosecuted for crimes that, in many cases, never even occurred.

Even more so than with exorcism, horror movies helped set the stage for the Satanic Panic. Following *Rosemary's Baby* (1968), there was a glut of movies depicting Satanists, most of which, like Rosemary's seemingly kind neighbors, the Castevets, hid in plain sight and performed evil rituals—often involving babies, children, or virgin women—for the purpose of attaining power. These films provided the public with a vivid model of what Satanic cults were and

The Exorcist Effect. Joseph P. Laycock and Eric Harrelson, Oxford University Press. © Oxford University Press 2024.
DOI: 10.1093/oso/9780197635391.003.0007

what they did. Furthermore, horror movie cults provided *a way of talking about* some of the anxieties and concerns present in American culture. In 1965, the Hart–Celler Act allowed immigration from Asia, setting the stage for new religious movements like the Unification Church and the International Society for Krishna Consciousness. These new arrivals, which appealed to the youth counterculture, contributed to growing fear of "cults" converting young people through nefarious means of mind control. Horror movies offered archetypal depictions of the "evil cult" using deception, mind control, and abusive ritual to achieve their ends. By the end of the 1970s there was a robust "anti-cult movement" that elided into a panic over Satanic conspiracies.

Journalist Debbie Nathan and attorney Michael Snedecker interpreted the Satanic Panic as a reflection of anxieties about family and sexual issues. Part of this was the realization that child abuse exists. In 1961, pediatrician C. Henry Kempe coined the term "battered child syndrome," acknowledging the medical reality of child abuse. By 1966, all fifty states had passed statutes against the abuse of children by their caretakers. In 1971, the senate passed the Comprehensive Child Development Act that would have created a national daycare system to aid single parents. President Nixon vetoed the act, warning that it would promote "communal approaches" to child rearing. Nathan suggests there was a sort of cognitive dissonance between the realization that children were being abused and a belief that the government should be prevented from intruding into the sphere of the family. The compromise, therefore, was to acknowledge child abuse but to attribute it to an imaginary group of evil outsiders—Satanic cults.[3]

David Bromley offers a similar analysis of the Panic, focused on the widespread suspicion that daycare providers were secretly Satanists. By the 1980s, two-income households had become standard, forcing parents to rely on childcare providers, as well as bus drivers, afterschool providers, and a variety of other strangers. Many parents experienced this situation like a kind of unwanted, invisible force usurping their ability to raise their own children, and Satanic cults provided a way of talking about this experience. As Bromley puts it, "Satanism claims may be metaphorically true even if empirically false."[4]

The influence of horror movies on the Panic became even more profound once the idea of "repressed memories" was introduced. People undergoing hypnosis suddenly "remembered" forgotten scenes from their childhood in which they were being tortured—often by their own parents—in Satanic rituals. It seems that in many accounts of so-called "Satanic ritual abuse" or SRA, horror movies provided a storehouse of images that the mind could summon in creating these scenes. Source amnesia caused patients to forget where exactly they had seen these things and therapists assured them that they had seen them with their own eyes, and that these were memories. In one stark example, an alleged survivor appeared on *The Oprah Winfrey Show* and said he could remember seeing a high priest impale a child with seven daggers, forming the shape of a cross. Another guest, Michael Aquino of the Temple of Set, asked him to identify this high priest so that he could be arrested for homicide. The first guest responded that he had partial amnesia and could not recall his name or face. The image of man placing a child on an altar and stabbing it with seven daggers in the shape of a cross appears at the end of the film *The Omen*, which is certainly the source of this "memory."[5] The ur-text of this phenomenon was the best-selling book *Michelle Remembers* (1980), a "non-fiction" book with clear influences from *The Exorcist* and other horror films.

But before the Satanic Panic, Hollywood depictions of Satanic cults also shaped religious culture in another way—they provided creative fodder for cinephile Anton LaVey, who founded The Church of Satan in 1966. Whereas moral entrepreneurs fueling the Satanic Panic claimed the sort of cults depicted in horror movies literally existed, LaVey engaged in a creative and lucid reading of these texts, using them as the foundation for a philosophy and (especially) an aesthetic for his Church. In turn, The Church of Satan inspired countless other Satanic groups and organizations.

Finally, whereas most Satanic horror movies do not claim to be "based on true events," some of the most influential films in this genre sought to be "realistic" by recruiting actual practitioners of magical religions or conducting "research" on actual magical groups. To this day, Satanists have enjoyed an almost symbiotic relationship with horror movies, often being recruited as consultants or commentators to give Satanic films a flare of authenticity. Thus, Satanic cult films provide another example of *The Exorcist* effect in which actual religious cultures become the basis for films that in turn influence religious cultures.

Country Cult, City Cult: Fearing the Past, Fearing the Future

Some of the films discussed in this chapter do not depict Satanists, but rather witches, Pagans, or practitioners of Afro-Cuban religions. This is not because we regard these traditions as synonymous or interchangeable. Rather it is because the Satanic Panic hinged on dark fantasies about the religious Other. Allegations of Satanic abuse in the 1980s were only the most recent iteration of a fantasy that David Frankfurter calls simply "evil ritual." The atrocities that Satanists were said to commit—infanticide, blood-drinking, sexual transgressions—are the same ones that early modern Europeans attributed to witches, medieval Europeans attributed to Jews, and Romans attributed to early Christians. They are also the same accusations that contemporary advocates of the QAnon conspiracy theory level against democrats, as well as celebrities like Tom Hanks. It is an enduring idea because the belief that somewhere people are performing evil rituals functions as a shield against anxieties about a changing world. The idea of monstrous opponents who are a living inversion of our values bolsters the idea that prevailing norms and values are unquestionably good and the way things must be.[6] At the same time, the thought of these dark rites is exciting and frequently erotic. In this sense, it makes little difference whether fantasies about the religious Other and their rituals resemble the savage inhabitants of Skull Island from *King Kong* (1933) or the elitist Order of the Silver Serpent from *The Ninth Gate* (1999).

However, there is one significant variation when analyzing fantasies of evil rituals, and this concerns whether the religious Other resides in the country or the city. The fantasy of "the country cult" invokes a fear of archaic religion that has somehow endured in parts of the world that modernity has never reached. In the fantasy of "the city cult," the cultists live among us and are often elites. They not only participate in modernity, but are largely responsible for it, having corrupted social institutions for generations. These categories manifest in both conspiracy theories and films. In 1970, the John Birch Society published an article entitled, "Satanism: A Practical Guide to Witch-Hunting." In this early manifestation of the Panic, the author explained, "For untold centuries nearly every nation has from time to time witnessed strange and demented cults whose chief preoccupation was Satan worship and black magic. While some of these groups were holdovers from some dim, pagan past, others were secret political organizations."[7] Similarly, in his analysis of claims of Satanic ritual abuse or SRA, David Frankfurter notes, "Ritual's evil seems to lie especially in two domains: on the one hand, the removal of moral and social constraints such as that participants become frenzied and, as it were, bestial; and, on the other hand, the repetitive dramatic program in which certain elite participants gain control over others through staging, robes, and secrets."[8] These two modes correspond roughly to the country cult and the city cult found in horror movies.

Of course, these are ideal types. Horror movies may feature elite Satanists slumming in rural America, as in *The Brotherhood of Satan* (1971), or primitive cults infiltrating high society, as in *The Believers* (1987). So, too, "superconspiracies" often posit a global conspiracy controlling less sophisticated cults.[9] But these two fantasies appeal to somewhat different sets of anxieties and gain popularity in different cultural moments. Country cult stories speak to a fear of rural people, but also a fascination with the past and a desire to uncover its secrets. City cult stories speak to anxieties about the future and a reactionary attitude toward modernity. At the same time, city cult stories elicit a millennial hope for the future after the conspiracy is defeated.

The Country Cult

Historian Philip Jenkins noted that before the Satanic Panic that followed *Rosemary's Baby*, there was an earlier wave of panic in the 1920s and 30s that was influenced by pulp stories about atavistic cults lurking in rural parts of the country. One factor that contributed to this was urbanization: 1920 was the first year that the census reported more Americans living in cities than rural areas. In the urban imagination, inhabitants of places like the Louisiana bayou or rural New England became objects of fear and fascination. Another factor was the book *The Witch-Cult in Western Europe*, published in 1921 by British archaeologist Margaret Murray. Murray's thesis was that a primordial religion had survived the advent of Christianity and that confessions taken from "witches" provided clues about the beliefs and rituals of a secret religion. (This theory appeared in the Warrens' first book *Deliver us From Evil* [1973].) In subsequent books, Murray suggested the witch-cult had survived into the present day. Murray was herself influenced by James G. Frazer's *The Golden Bough*, which theorized that ancient people held a near-universal belief in a god-king that must be sacrificed to ensure a good harvest. Frazer claimed traces of this cult could still be found in folk songs or such innocuous traditions as burning a yule log at the winter solstice. Murray's thesis has since been rejected by historians, who make the obvious point that accused witches would confess to *anything* because they were being tortured. Still, the idea of archaic religions offering sacrifices in remote parts of the country captured the imagination of modern people.

Between 1928 and 1929, a media story broke about three men in rural Pennsylvania who murdered an accused witch, crystalizing the idea that rural Americans still lived in a medieval world of witches and magic. Writers of "weird tales" made good use of this idea. Herbert S. Gorman's "The Place Called Dagon" (1927) and H. P. Lovecraft's "The Shadow over Innsmouth" (1931) built on Murray's theories to describe ancient cults surviving in America's backwoods. When the Great Depression began in 1929, struggling newspapers kept themselves afloat by publishing stories about murderous cults.[10]

The "country cult" is once again having a moment in contemporary horror movies. The rather nebulous category of "folk horror" is currently *de rigeur*, buoyed by Robert Eggers's *The Witch* (2015) and Ari Aster's *Midsommar* (2019). The term was popularized, but not invented, in 2010 by writer Mark Gatiss in an interview for the BBC series "A History of Horror." Gatiss offered his own "unholy trinity" of films that defined the genre: *Witchfinder General* (1968), *The Blood on Satan's Claw* (1971), and *The Wicker Man* (1973).[11] This trilogy fostered a "family resemblance" definition of the category, which has been extended backward to such media as Shirley Jackson's short story "The Lottery" (1948), and to several Asian horror films with folkloric elements, such as the Thai film *The Medium* (2021). At a conference on folk horror held in Belfast in 2014, filmmaker Adam Scovell offered four criteria that gave the category more substance: a rural landscape, isolation, "skewed moral beliefs," and a happening/summoning."[12] The criterion of "skewed moral beliefs" is broad enough to include both the zealous Protestantism of Matthew Hopkins (Vincent Price) in *Witchfinder General* and the murderous Pagans of Summerisle in *The Wicker Man*. It also means that folk horror is inherently about the wrong kind of religion. While the criterion of summoning/happening is not always some form of human sacrifice, it frequently is.

Part of the appeal of the folk horror label is that it implies a folkloric basis to the story—that the beliefs and rituals in the film were practiced by our ancestors. Folk horror tales play these connections up where possible. Matthew Hopkins and his henchman John Stearne were real witchhunters who may have condemned as many as one hundred people to death during the English Civil War. *The Witch* drew inspiration from an account of Elizabeth Knapp, a serving girl from seventeenth-century Massachusetts who claimed she signed a pact with the Devil. But this conceit can also work in the opposite direction, so that folk horror stories lend plausibility to claims about actual events. The acclaimed first season of *True Detective*

(2014) was essentially a folk horror story about an archaic religion lurking in rural Louisiana that sacrificed children, "The King in Yellow"—a reference to weird-tale author Robert W. Chambers. In an interview on *Entertainment Weekly*, writer Nic Pizzolato said, "You know, you can Google 'Satanism,' 'preschool,' and 'Louisiana' and you'll be surprised at what you get. But instead of having our Satan worshippers worship Satan, they worship The Yellow King."[13] As a good storyteller, Pizzolato did not say, "*True Detective* is a true story." Instead, he offered cryptic clues that sent journalists on a quest to discover the show's truthful basis. Pizzolato's hint led bloggers to a 2005 incident when pastor Louis Lamonica Jr. of Ponchatoula, Louisiana, made an unsolicited confession in which he claimed to have abused children in Satanic rituals. Lamonica's family and attorneys suggested he was mentally ill, noting his confession involved shape-shifting and other magical events. Lamonica was convicted of child molestation, but an FBI forensics team could find no traces of the bloody pentagrams he had described, nor any evidence of a Satanic cult, even after excavating the ground behind his church. This did not stop websites like *Jezebel* from running such headlines as "Did a Horrifying Real Satanic Abuse Case Inspire True Detective?" Several attorneys who had defended clients accused of Satanic abuse blamed the show for reigniting the panic.[14] While Pizzolato is partly to blame here, the more significant factor is the public's desire to believe rural Louisiana is a place out of time, where the savage rites of our ancestors never ended.

The City Cult

While country cults may horrify, they lack the resources to foment wars and revolutions or control the global economy. Misfortune on this scale requires someone more sophisticated to blame. Claims about Freemasons provided an early model of a global conspiracy, consisting of elites united in secrecy through evil rituals, bent on remaking the world in their image. The first third-party in American history was the anti-Masonic party, founded in 1828. Claims about the threat of Freemasonry rapidly mutated into claims about Zionists, The Illuminati, communists, Luciferians, and—eventually—reptilian aliens posing as politicians and celebrities. All of this made great fodder for fiction writers and films.

In 1891, Parisian novelist J. K. Huysmans published his novel, *Là-Bas*, about a Paris novelist who, depressed by the emptiness of the modern world, explores the occult underground of Paris in search of a Satanic mass. He finds one and, prefiguring *The Exorcist*, the Satanic horrors he witnesses suggest the claims of Catholicism may be true. *Là-Bas* contained a graphic, detailed description of a black mass, and it was rumored that Huysmans really had found an underground community of Satanists and was masking his discovery as fiction. Like Pizzolato, Huysmans employed misdirection, never giving a straight answer when asked if he had seen a real black mass.

The following year, another Parisian, Léo Taxil, along with some accomplices, began publishing their two-thousand-page book, *The Devil in the Nineteenth Century*. Published in serial form, it was purported to describe the adventures of one Dr. Bataille, a ship's surgeon in the French merchant navy. Bataille infiltrated the Masons, and his travels allowed him to witness evil Masonic rituals occurring all over the planet. He discovered that Hindus, Buddhists, and Spiritualists were all in league with Freemasons. The black mass described by Huysmans not only really occurred, but it was another part of this grand conspiracy. Furthermore, the Freemasons were led by an even more elite order, called "The Palladists," who worshipped Satan and regularly interact with demons. The Palladists were led by Albert Pike, a Freemason and former Confederate general who resided in Charleston, South Carolina. As the serial went on, it introduced a character named Diana Vaughn, a former high priestess of Palladism who had converted to Catholicism and was now on the run. Readers became fascinated with Vaughn and her whereabouts. In 1897, Taxil held a press conference that drew journalists from around the world. He informed the assembled crowd that there was no Diana Vaughn, that this had all been an elaborate hoax, and that he would like to thank the Catholic Church for helping him to perpetrate it. With that, he declared Palladism dead and left the building under police escort.[15]

Only this was not the end of Palladism because Taxil's mythology was too good a story not to be true. Some simply concluded that the conspiracy had gotten to Taxil and coerced him into saying these things. Others assumed Taxil had assassinated Vaughn. *Cult and Ritual Abuse Narratives, Evidence, and Healing Approaches*, a seminal text for SRA claims, first published 1995 and currently in its third edition, suggests Palladism existed. A footnote mentions this group was "described by Léo Taxil and later denied by him."[16] The Taxil hoax also influenced the conspiracy theories of Malachi Martin. In his last "faction" novel, *Windswept House*, Martin describes a ritual held in the Vatican on June 29, 1963, called "The Enthronement of Lucifer." Satanists in the Vatican coordinated via telephone with another black mass being held in South Carolina. In an interview for the John Birch Society's *The New American*, Martin affirmed that "The Enthronement of Lucifer" really occurred and took place in Charleston—Taxil's Palladist headquarters.[17] The endurance of the Taxil hoax demonstrates the powerful appeal of these stories and the inability of authors to recall them once they have been unleashed.

If Margaret Murray was the godmother of the country cult, the godfather of the city cult was not Taxil, but Dennis Wheatley, a novelist whose tales of Satanic conspiracies became the basis of several Hammer Film Productions horror movies. Over his long career, Wheatley wrote seventy-four books that sold over fifty million copies.[18] Whereas folk horror cultists were often out for little more than a good harvest, Wheatley's cultists were invariably wealthy elites, and their goal was world domination. Wheatley's occult stories were often colored by his politics. He suggested that Hitler, as well as Communists, were actually Satanists. Furthermore, modern music, art, "progressive education," and the Black Power movement were also components of a Satanic plot. A key appeal of Wheatley's novels was the conceit that they were based on "actual" occult practices. Wheatley suggested that he had a friendship with the magician Aleister Crowley. The only connection we know about between these two men is that they had lunch at the Hungaria restaurant on Regent Street in London, where Crowley gave Wheatley an inscribed copy of his book *Magick in Theory and Practice*.[19] Historian Ronald Hutton suggests that Crowley was impressed by the success of Wheatley's first novel and hoped this connection might boost his own literary career. Instead, Hutton concludes, "Crowley had, unwittingly, committed the greatest single disservice to himself and to his life's work that he was to produce in his whole career."[20] Wheatley's second novel, *The Devil Rides Out*, could now claim a true basis. The author's preface alludes to "conversations with certain persons . . . Who are actual practitioners of the Art," and warns that black magic is still practiced today in London and cities around the world.[21] In other words, the reader was invited to use the story as a model for imagining things that were really taking place. Wheatley's novels and their film adaptations became a key influence on Satanic conspiracy theories, as well as actual Satanic groups that emerged in the 1960s. Christopher Lee, who appeared in the 1968 film adaptation of *The Devil Rides Out* and considered it his greatest role, frequently endorsed the idea that Wheatley's novels described the activities of actual groups, stating, "Rather than fantasy, these books dealt with the absolute reality of Black Magic. There are cults and such people even today, at every level of society."[22]

In the end, both country and city cult stories endure because we desire to believe them. There is a social and psychological appeal to these stories that makes for good horror films. Whether we prefer folk horror or Wheatley's style of global Satanic intrigue is really a reflection of our prejudices: Do we feel more fascination and revulsion toward rural people and their benighted ways or toward the power elites who enjoy privileges that we lack? It seems the only people who might *not* be engaging in human sacrifices are those with the same level of cultural sophistication and political power as ourselves. But even this circle of trust can be broken during a moral panic.

Satanism on the Silver Screen

The oldest cinematic depiction of Satanism of which the authors of this text are aware is a seven-minute French "stag film" from 1928 called *Messe Noire: Réception et Initiation au Culte Satanique d'une Néophyte*. This silent film depicts a congregation of nude women kneeling before Lucifer—a rather ridiculous looking hirsute actor wearing false eyebrows and devil horns—and his consort, Astarte. A nude woman serves as an altar, Lucifer bites a woman's wrist and drains the blood into a chalice for the initiate to drink, and Astarte administers a whipping. Then a general orgy ensues. Two things are significant about this film. First, this bizarre scene requires no exposition: The intended audience of this film—presumably Parisian men—did not need to be told what a black mass is or what happens at them. This had already been well established by the likes of Huysman and Taxil. Second, there is a certain honesty to *Messe Noire* in that the black mass is presented as a sexual fantasy. The vicarious pleasure of recounting sexual transgressions is one reason stories about evil rituals are so persistent.

The first depiction of a black mass in mainstream cinema is *The Black Cat* (1934), starring Bela Lugosi and Boris Karloff. Newlyweds Joan and Peter Alison are traveling on the Orient Express where they meet Dr. Vitus Werdegast (Lugosi). In Hungary, the three transfer to a bus, which crashes. Werdegast leads them to the home of Hjalmar Poelzig (Karloff), which is built on the foundations of a fortress where thousands of soldiers died during World War I. In fact, Werdegast was captured in the war and has returned to murder Poelzig, who took his wife after telling her Werdegast was dead. Furthermore, Poelzig is a Satanist who decides to sacrifice Joan in the "The Rites of Lucifer." In one scene, Poelzig leads a congregation of Satanists chanting in Latin. A striking feature of this film are the sets, Poelzig's lair is not a typical gothic castle, but a high-tech, art deco fortress inspired by German expressionism. Poelzig prays to Satan surrounded by Egyptian obelisks and an abstract sculpture vaguely suggestive of a fallen cross. This was too much for British censors. In the British version, *House of Doom*, all references to Satanism were replaced with "sun worship."[23]

The Black Cat came out the same year as the novel *The Devil Rides Out*, and like that book, it was inspired by Crowley. Bohemian artist Nina Hamnett spent time at Crowley's "Abbey of Thelema," a farmhouse in Cefalú, Italy. In her 1932 autobiography, *Laughing Torso*, she wrote of her experience, "[Crowley] was supposed to practice Black Magic there, and one day a baby was said to have disappeared mysteriously. There was also a goat there. This all pointed to Black Magic, so people said, and the inhabitants of the village were frightened of him."[24] Crowley, who by 1932 was desperate for money, sued Hamnett for defamation. His attorney claimed Crowley opposed black magic and only practiced white magic. The defense brought in Betty May Loveday, who testified how she and her new husband, Raoul, had stayed at Crowley's Abbey in 1923. She witnessed a drugged Crowley stab a cat and then order Raoul to drink a cup of its blood. Raoul (who had been sickly before arriving at the Abbey) died from infection of the liver and spleen, which Betty May attributed to drinking cat blood. Crowley lost the case, and the testimony made good copy for newspapers. The original script for *The Black Cat* had been based on the 1843 short story by Edgar Allen Poe. But director and co-writer Edgar G. Ulmer decided Crowley's lawsuit made for a better film. The Alisons are based on the Lovedays and Poelzig's Satanic fortress is Crowley's Abbey of Thelema as it should have been (the actual Abbey was only a five-room farmhouse).[25]

The Black Cat ends with the newlyweds escaping Poelzig's lair just before it explodes. Back on their train, Peter, a mystery writer, opens a newspaper and starts reading a review of his latest novel to his wife: "We feel, however, that Mr. Alison has, in a sense, overstepped the bounds in the matter of credibility. These things could never, by the furthest stretch of the imagination, actually happen. We could wish that Mr. Allison would confine himself to the possible instead of letting his melodramatic imagination run away with him." The two exchange a stunned look, ending the film. This ending could be read as a wink to the audience, conceding the implausibility of the story. But it can also function as an argument that stories of Satanism may be true, no matter how far-fetched they sound.

The other significant depiction of Satanism in the black-and-white era was *The Seventh Victim* (1943). In this film, Mary Gibson, a student at a Catholic boarding school, learns that her sister and only living relative, Jacqueline, has disappeared. Jacqueline ran a cosmetics company in New York and Mary heads to the city to find her. Mary learns that Jacqueline had joined a Satanic cult called the Palladists. Jacqueline has been imprisoned by the Palladists for revealing their existence to her therapist. The cult's laws—handed down by Johann Rosenquartz—demand both non-violence and that anyone who betrays the Palladists must die. The previous six traitors in the group's history were all killed (thus the title of the film). Torn by these conflicting mandates, the Palladists spend hours attempting to persuade Jacqueline to drink poison. They eventually release her, but Jacqueline—who has apparently always had nihilistic tendencies—returns to a hotel room where she has left a noose waiting. The film ends with the thudding sound of Jacqueline hanging herself.

The Seventh Victim is the consummate "city cult" film in that it reflects anxieties about urbanization. Historian W. Scott Poole suggests it drew on a growing belief among conservatives that "modernity was being driven by a satanic conspiracy."[26] In particular, the film plays on anxieties about single women who had been moving to cities for work since the industrial revolution and were living on their own. When Mary embarks on her quest at the beginning of the film, a teacher warns her, "Mary, don't come back. No matter if you never find your sister, no matter what happens, don't come back. My parents died when I was a pupil. I left as you are leaving. I didn't have courage. One must have courage to really live in the world. I came back."

The story is heavily indebted to the Taxil hoax. Not only are the Satanists called "The Palladists," but Jacqueline resembles Diana Vaughn, an ex-cult member being hunted as a traitor. The founder of the Palladists, "Johann Rosenquartz," seems inspired by Christian Rosenkreutz, the legendary founder of the Rosicrucian order—another group featured in Taxil's byzantine conspiracy. But producer Val Newton wanted even more authentic occultism, so he sent screenwriter Dewitt Bodeen to see if he could attend a meeting "of one of those devil-worshiping groups." Bodeen described his search of devil worshippers to film historian John Brosnan:

They [RKO studios] had a marvelous office there in New York. I went to them and said, "Is there any chance of me going to a devil-worshippers's meeting?" And they started laughing, but they called me back and said

yes, it had been arranged. I would have to go under a pseudonym. The society would be glad to have me but I wouldn't be able to say anything—
just sit there and observe. They were exactly like the devil worshippers in
Rosemary's Baby. It was even in the same neighborhood on the West Side
that they used in that film. It was during the war, and I would have hated
to be Hitler with all the spells they were working against him. They were
mostly old people and they were casting these spells while they knitted and
crocheted. A bunch of tea-drinking old ladies and gentlemen sitting there
muttering imprecations against Hitler. I made use of the experience in that
the devil worshippers in *The Seventh Victim* were very ordinary people who
had one basic flaw, an Achilles heel which has turned against good and
towards evil.[27]

Indeed, *The Seventh Victim* may feature the most banal Satanists in all of
cinema. They are never shown engaging in any sort of ritual, wearing robes,
or chanting in Latin. They are only shown holding meetings over coffee, anx-
iously debating what to do, resembling a homeowner's association more than
an evil conspiracy.

Despite overly plausible cultists, the film had several consequences for
both Satanism and the Satanic Panic. The scene where the Satanists essentially try to nag Jacqueline into killing herself may seem absurd by the
standards of modern horror films. But this was one of the first cinema
depictions of "cult mind control tactics." Three decades later, hundreds of
thousands of dollars would be spent on lawsuits debating whether members
of religious "cults" were victims of brainwashing.[28] Another significant feature of the film is the Palladists' symbol, a parallelogram with a pyramid in
its center. Mary learns that Jacqueline's partner had planned to make this ancient symbol the new logo for the cosmetics company. The trope of Satanic
symbols hidden in corporate logos became a recurring fear in American culture. In 1982, the headquarters of Procter & Gamble, a company known for
its hygiene products, was receiving up to five hundred letters a day claiming
that its logo was Satanic. Conservative churches began passing out handbills
in shopping centers claiming the president of the company had made a pact
with the devil and that a percentage of all profits were donated to the Church
of Satan. People began to vandalize company cars. Eventually, Procter &
Gamble changed their logo, which they had used for over one hundred years.
The Palladist's parallelogram was also a likely influence on Anton LaVey, who
became preoccupied with a different quadrilateral.[29] His *Satanic Bible* (1969)

contains a cryptic reference to "The Order of the Trapezoid."[30] In 1976, LaVey wrote an essay for The Church of Satan newsletter "The Cloven Hoof" entitled "The Law of Trapezoid," suggesting that trapezoids make the viewer anxious because they are unfinished triangles. Such angles are "evil," but also powerful because they inspire change.

The Charles Walton Murder

Two years after *The Seventh Victim*, cult fantasies shaped an actual murder investigation in England. On Valentine's Day, 1945, the body of seventy-four-year-old farm laborer Charles Walton was discovered in Warwickshire, England. Walton's throat had been slit with his own bill hook, and a pitchfork was still lodged into his neck. There were also reports that a cross had been carved into his chest. It was a gruesome crime that was never solved. In 1950, at the age of eighty-seven, Margaret Murray took a holiday to Warwickshire disguised as an artist. Her real purpose was to ascertain whether a living witch-cult was active in the area. February 14 was not so far from the Pagan holiday of Imbolc, marking the beginning of Spring.[31] She later told a newspaper in Birmingham her conclusion that Walton had been sacrificed by "people who still believe in a religion practised in Britain before Christianity, whom we call devil worshippers."[32] Crime writer Donald McCormick described a conversation with Murray in which she related how local villagers expressed their indignation over her witch-cult theory, but only because they were engaged in a conspiracy to keep the cult secret. (Such a conspiracy is the very essence of a folk horror story.) McCormick also described Murray's theory that other unsolved murders were the work of "black witches" living in modern England.[33] One of the officers who investigated the Walton murder was Robert Fabian, whose memoirs were adapted into the BBC series *Fabian of the Yard*. Fabian increasingly played up the idea that Walton had been murdered by a cult, noting the crime's proximity to a neolithic site called the Rollright Stones.[34] In his book, *London After Dark* (1954), Fabian declared, "There is more active Satan-worship today than ever since the Dark Ages."[35] And in *Anatomy of a Crime* (1971) he warned, "I advise anybody who is tempted at any time to venture into Black Magic, witchcraft, Shamanism—call it what you will—to remember Charles Walton and to think of his death, which was clearly the ghastly climax of a pagan rite."[36]

Scholars of Paganism, such as Ronald Hutton, generally conclude there is no evidence to suggest Walton's murder was carried out by a Pagan cult. From a folkloric perspective, Murray and Fabian were engaged in quasi-ostension—misinterpreting data in light of a legend. The most likely suspect was always Alfred Potter. Potter employed Walton and they were in a financial dispute. Contemporary criminologist David Wilson proposed that Potter likely murdered his employee then alluded to local witchcraft conspiracies "to lay a false trail."[37] Wilson noted that works like *The Devil Rides Out* (1934) had already introduced the idea of cult murder to the public. If Wilson's theory is true, this would mean the murder was itself a form of pseudo-ostension—an action orchestrated to resemble a legend. In the 1970s, speculation about the Walton murder became the basis for the BBC radio play "Robin Red Breast," which in turn was an influence for subsequent folk horror films.[38]

In 1954, Gerald Gardner wrote *Witchcraft Today*, in which he claimed to have met members of the hidden witch-cult described by Margaret Murray. In 1951, Britain repealed the Witchcraft Act of 1735, which had made it a crime to profess magical powers. This, Gardner claimed, meant he was free to bring the teachings of the witch-cult into the open. He called his religion "Wica," which soon became "Wicca." Murray wrote a supportive forward to *Witchcraft Today*. Hutton called Murray "an almost literal godmother to modern pagan witchcraft."[39] And yet she is also one of the first examples of the modern "occult crime" experts who would play a significant role in the Satanic Panic of the 1980s. Her own 1954 book, *The Divine King in England*, suggested that several British royals had been witch-cult members and were ritually sacrificed, just as Frazer described in *The Golden Bough*.

In 1956, a ninety-three-year-old Murray was invited to an event to promote the upcoming film *Night of the Demon* (1957). This was an adaptation of M. R. James's story "Casting the Runes," and was another seminal film of the era featuring Satanic cults. The story's villain, Karswell, is a charming Crowley-esque occultist. He leads a "witch-cult" who believe "evil is good and good is evil." A community of skeptics has sworn to publicly debunk Karswell's claims of magic, so Karswell has been cursing them with runes that cause a demon to murder them within three days. In a scene that anticipates panics of the 1980s, Karswell not only presents as an English country gentleman, but also dresses as a clown and performs magic shows for children. American skeptic John Holden is cursed, but he concludes magic is real in time to save himself. The film opens with some onomastic anchoring by using a long shot of Stonehenge and narration about black magic. Deploying Murray—an archaeologist—added a form of metatextual reflection. These mechanisms enhanced the idea that witch-cults like Karswell's really existed.

The 1960s and the Church of Satan

Fantasies of Satanic cults grew exponentially alongside the counterculture in the 1960s. One significant artifact of this decade is *Mondo Freudo* (1966), a pseudo-documentary exploitation film purporting to be hidden camera footage of subversive subcultures from around the world. A poster for the film stated, "These scenes are too real for the immature" and advertised, "Witness a black mass performed in Manhattan by Peurto [sic] Rican immigrants."[40] The scene consists primarily of a Latina woman performing a topless dance to a soundtrack of Afro-Atlantic drumbeats before a rather bored-looking congregation. At various intervals, a dead chicken and a hog's head are incorporated into the performance. Then, a second Latina is brought out and the narrator, in a detached, clinical tone, explains that this seventeen-year-old girl is a human sacrifice and that her parents are honored she has been chosen. She is also rendered topless, laid in a circle, and (fake looking) blood is spilled on her. The congregation smears the blood, and the narrator announces that in their "frenzied state" induced by drumming and drugs, the celebrants believe Satan is caressing the woman. The scene then ends as the narrator explains they cannot show "Satan" claiming the woman's virginity. *Mondo Freudo* is significant because it indicates the idea of a Satanic cult holding human sacrifices in Manhattan was plausible in 1966—but somehow more plausible if these activities were attributed to immigrant people of color. The scene is a case study in the fantasy of the evil ritual, with its racist depiction of an ethnic minority, its conflation of Afro-Atlantic traditions with Satanism, and its pornographic appeal packaged as legitimate discussion of a social problem.

   In 1968, Hammer Film Productions made a film adaptation of Dennis Wheatley's novel *The Devil Rides Out*. Many considered it the best film the studio ever produced.[41] Wheatley's protagonist, the Duke de Richleau (Christopher Lee), discovers his young protege, Simon, had become involved in a Satanic cult led by a magician named Mocota, a figure Wheatley clearly based on Crowley. The duke, also knowledgeable of the occult, rescues Simon and a female initiate, Tanith, from Mocata's clutches. In retaliation,

Mocata launches a magical attack, forcing the heroes to spend the night in a magic circle of protection as various demons assault them. Needing to claim a soul, the thwarted demons turn on their summoner, killing Mocata. The film depicted actual rituals developed by The Golden Dawn, an occult order of which Crowley was briefly a member.[42]

The trope of rescuing naïve young people from a cult leader resonated with anxieties about cults at the end of the 1960s. The film's success also cemented Wheatley's authority as an "expert" on the dangers of the occult. In 1971, he published a non-fiction book on the occult called *The Devil and All His Works*. He began writing scores of forewords for re-issued mass-market paperbacks about the occult. Newspapers began seeking his advice on crimes that might have an "occult" dimension. He also lectured to clergymen and framed industrial strikes and anti-apartheid demonstrations as manifestations of Satanism. At one point, he claimed half of Britain's illegal drug trafficking was carried out by witch covens.[43] In this way, Wheatley pioneered the role of the occult crime expert that would come to the fore in the 1980s.

The same demand for all things occult that sent newspapers to Wheatley also led Anton Szandor LaVey to found The Church of Satan. LaVey held regular meetings at his San Francisco home with a group of bohemians called "The Magic Circle." In a forerunner to modern podcasting, LaVey would entertain his guests with lectures on witchcraft or various macabre topics. Eventually people were willing to pay $2.50 to attend weekly midnight lectures.[44] According to Nikolas Schreck (a former member of the Church of Satan, who became antagonistic toward LaVey) a local newspaper dubbed LaVey "the priest of the devil." A publicity agent named Edward Webber frequented a bar where LaVey worked and he suggested LaVey could use his expertise to start "some kind of religion."[45] LaVey founded his church on April 30 (Walpurgis night, a night associated with witchcraft), 1966.

A figure that is often left out of this story is Diane Hegarty, whom LaVey met in 1960. Hegarty became his long-time consort and bore his second daughter, Zeena. Michael Aquino's book, *The Church of Satan*, provides evidence that Hegarty played a critical role in organizing and leading the group and was key to its success. In fact, the Church of Satan lost nearly all public visibility after LaVey and Hegarty separated in 1980. As a "Satanic power couple" LaVey and Hegarty weirdly mirrored Ed and Lorraine Warren. Interestingly, Ed met Lorraine while working as an usher and LaVey met Hegarty when she was working as an usheress.[46] One wonders what

America's demonological landscape would look like were it not for romances forming in theaters.

By 1967, LaVey was working with Webber on events for the press, including a Satanic wedding ceremony, a Satanic baptism for Zeena, and even a Satanic funeral for a sailor who had joined his church. He painted his home black, using it as a headquarters and dubbing it "The Black House." For the public of 1960s San Francisco, the Satanic cults they had seen in movies finally existed—and in a way that seemed safe, and even charming.

The modern Church of Satan often describes Satanism as a "philosophy" created by Anton LaVey. LaVey's various writings, while provocative and sometimes insightful, do not quite add up to a coherent philosophy. Journalist and Church of Satan priest Gavin Baddeley described the Church of Satan as "a bizarre beast, sustained by a web of conflicting values and concepts. It is an anti-spiritual religion; a totalitarian doctrine of freedom; a cynical romanticism; a profoundly honest scam; a love of life garbed in the symbols of death and fear."[47] But what LaVey undoubtedly gave the world was an *aesthetic* that he articulated through his writings, music, and especially Satanic rituals held at The Black House. LaVey's gatherings, especially in the early days of his group, seem to have been one-part intellectual salon, one-part sex-positive party. He did not believe in a literal devil and discussion of "magic" was often shorthand for using popular psychology to empower the individual (and perhaps seduce other individuals). He described the black mass and other Church of Satan rituals as an "intellectual decompression chamber" that allowed for catharsis and promoted mental health. He drew openly from Huysman's *Là-Bas* and was likely influenced by Wheatley's novels, as well.[48]

LaVey was a consummate cinephile. Watching films was a ubiquitous activity for guests to the Black House. LaVey preferred to screen films on a 16 mm projector in a room called "The Purple Parlor."[49] Much of his aesthetic drew from his favorite films, especially the *film noire* genre of the 1940s. He studied the power of images to affect people and was particularly influenced by photographer William Mortensen's book *The Command to Look: A Formula for Picture Success* (1937). LaVey also saw no problem with choosing to live out fantasies derived from films. Whereas Gardner claimed his religion was passed down by a secret witch-cult, LaVey was comfortable admitting that he had invented his religion for his own purposes, drawing on his some of his favorite media. In *The Satanic Rituals*, he wrote, "Satanists can easily invent fairy tales to match anything contained in holy writ."[50]

In addition to *The Seventh Victim*, LaVey spoke highly of *The Black Cat*, commenting that it "portrays Satanists in a manner closer to the truth."[51] A rite in *The Satanic Rituals* called "Die Elektrischen Vorspiele" appears to be a homage to the Rites of Lucifer performed by Hjalmar Poelzig in *The Black Cat*, as well as the German films that influenced it. The ritual should resemble German *schaeurfilmen* (horror movies) of the interwar period and calls for "expressionistic" decor, as well as tesla coils, neon, and stroboscopic lights.[52] On June 6, 2006, The Church of Satan celebrated its fortieth anniversary by holding a ritual in Los Angeles with over one hundred celebrants from around the globe. Festivities included replicating the black mass scene from *The Black Cat*. Satanists read the Latin prayer uttered by Boris Karloff, even though they understood the filmmakers simply arranged a mishmash of Latin phrases.[53]

LaVey called *Rosemary's Baby* "the best ad for Satanism ever screened," adding, "For the first time, *Rosemary's Baby* presented Satanists as sophisticated, reasonable people, instead of stoned freak-outs."[54] He also praised producer William Castle, whose gimmicky showmanship seemed to resonate with LaVey's own flamboyant style. LaVey wrote *The Satanic Bible* in 1969, in part because an agent from Avon Books named Peter Mayer noted the market success of *Rosemary's Baby* and hoped LaVey could produce something similar.[55] But if the film was an ad for Satanism, LaVey also became an ad for the film. He was invited to attend the premiere—another instance of metatexual reflection. LaVey would later claim that Polanski hired him as a consultant and even promoted a rumor that he had an uncredited appearance in the film, playing the devil who rapes Rosemary during a psychedelic dream sequence. In fact, Polanski reported he had done "absolutely no research" on the occult, except for consulting a picture book to draw ideas for props and symbols, and the devil was played by Clay Tanner.[56] But by attaching himself to the film in this way, LaVey contributed to the idea that *Rosemary's Baby* was revealing actual secrets about Satanism.

One interview reports that LaVey claimed to have done consulting for *The Mephisto Waltz* (1971)—a film about an aging Satanic pianist who can transfer his consciousness into younger bodies.[57] He dismissed *The Exorcist* as "crap," but also predicted that it "will bring many allies into the satanic camp who previously had remained mute."[58] Michael Aquino recorded that the New York grotto of the Church of Satan had one member wait in line for four hours in the rain the buy tickets, "Then the entire Grotto—dressed to the teeth in red and black—had assembled to go on to the theater, no doubt terrorizing the already jumpy audience."[59] LaVey related that the studio producing *The Omen* had negotiated filming a scene in the Black House in which Damian receives a Satanic baptism, and that they could either fly child actor Harvey Stevens out from England or use a cardboard cut-out to represent Damian in the scene. LaVey turned the studio down, claiming he did not want to be bothered by tourists visiting The Black House "looking for Damien."[60] No confirmation could be found for this story.

Schreck suggested that LaVey hoped to parlay his role as head of the Church of Satan into a career as a Hollywood consultant.[61] This is speculation, but it seems plausible, and LaVey did have some success on this front. He appeared in the exploitation documentary *Witchcraft '70* (1969), and he was the subject of another documentary, *Satanis: The Devil's Mass* (1970). He briefly played Satan in Kenneth Anger's experimental film, *Invocation of My Demon Brother* (1969). He was a technical consultant on Satanic ritual for *Lucifer's Women* (1974). *The Car* (1977), perhaps to add some gravitas to a story about sentient killer Lincoln Continental, opens with a title card that reads, "Oh great brothers of the night who rideth upon the hot winds of hell, who dwelleth in the Devil's lair; move and appear. —Anton La Vey." The quote is from *The Satanic Bible*. *The Devil's Rain* (1975) was the film where LaVey was given the most creative influence. A card in the opening credits reads "Technical Advisor: Anton Szandor LaVey: High Priest of the Church of Satan." In a small southwestern town, Mark Preston (William Shatner) confronts a Satanic cult led by Jonathan Corbis (Ernest Borgnine). In a Satanic ritual filmed in Mexico, Borgnine performs "The Ceremony of Nine Angles" from *The Satanic Rituals*.[62] This scene also features an inverted pentagram within a trapezoid (LaVey's favorite shape) and a hooded figure playing the organ. Presumably, the organist is LaVey, who played the organ and the calliope in nightclubs and other venues. *The Devil's Rain* was John Travolta's first feature film, and LaVey allegedly poured him his first drink on his twenty-first birthday.[63] Furthermore, a special effect for this film required making a mask of Shatner's face. The mold was subsequently used to make "Captain Kirk masks," one of which was purchased and modified to serve as the face of serial killer Michael Myers in John Carpenter's *Halloween* (1978).

In an interview, Peter H. Gilmore, the current high priest of the Church of Satan, commented, "I always have fun looking through horror movies, to sort of say, 'These are pre-Church of Satan and these are post-Church of Satan.' Because that was a change. The imagery that he created for the pageantry of his rituals suddenly became the standard for what was Satanic and

Satanism, and it remains so. He aesthetically totally pushed a whole new paradigm into the culture that hadn't existed before."[64] Even if LaVey's influence is somewhat exaggerated by his followers, watching and discussing horror films remains a key practice of The Church of Satan. The Church still maintains a list of films they have endorsed as illustrating some aspect of their "Satanic philosophy."[65] The Church of Satan uses these films to think with, almost in the way that rabbis produce *midrash* by discussing stories from the Hebrew Bible.

LaVey's favorite film was *Nightmare Alley* (1947), adapted from a 1946 crime novel by William Lindsay Gresham. The protagonist, Stanton Carlisle, takes a job at a carnival. Zeena, the carnival's mentalist, teaches Carlisle how to deceive people into believing he can talk to spirits. Armed with this knowledge, he founds his own Spiritualist church and begins fleecing wealthy clients. In the end, Carlisle becomes blinded by his own hubris. He loses everything and becomes a homeless alcoholic. He again takes work at a carnival, this time as a geek. LaVey had a vintage poster of *Nightmare Alley* proudly displayed in the Black House.[66] He was born Howard Stanton Levey and, according to his daughter Zeena (whom LaVey apparently named after a character from the novel), he felt that his middle name signified "a magical or psychic link" with the character Stanton Carlisle. Gresham was named on the dedication page of early editions of *The Satanic Bible*.[67] In fact, LaVey's career followed a trajectory similar to Carlisle's: he started a religion and, for a time, enjoyed some celebrity. Several Hollywood celebrities joined the Church of Satan, including actress Jayne Mansfield, a fact LaVey was very proud of. Over time, however, he became increasingly reclusive, and the group's momentum slowed. In the 1980s, Hegarty left him, taking half his property, which began his slow decline. In 1990, he had a falling out with his daughter Zeena. He died in 1997 at the age of sixty-seven.[68]

In 2018, the long-running series *American Horror Story* featured an actor playing Anton LaVey. In the show, LaVey (Carlo Rota) is not a philosophical cynic or pop psychologist, but a murderer who is shown ripping a woman's heart out in a human sacrifice to usher in the Antichrist. The Church of Satan, having endured decades of libelous claims that they commit crimes, released a statement denouncing the show. In an interview, actor Cody Fern, who played the Antichrist, responded, "I really don't want to offend anybody, but I find all forms of religious fundamentalism frightening . . . . So, let them make statements."[69] It seems implausible that calling the Church of Satan "religious fundamentalists" was not calculated to offend, at least a little. LaVey's son, Xerxes, commented on the show's portrayal of his father, "I don't have a lot of justification to complain about him appearing in the pop-culture pantheon. I can certainly criticize individual portrayals. But . . . he's a public figure."[70]

Other Satanic religions have likewise borrowed from horror movies. One of the Church of Satan's earliest imitators was a group called The Brotherhood of the Ram, a name apparently borrowed from *The Devil Rides Out*. The group met above an occult bookstore in Hollywood where leader Don R. Blythe displayed a fetus in a jar that he named "Adrian"—a reference to *Rosemary's Baby*.[71] Michael Aquino, who acted as LaVey's right-hand man before forming his own group, The Temple of Set, first laid eyes on LaVey when he attended the premiere of *Rosemary's Baby*. Aquino told journalist Arthur Lyons that he had the number 666 tattooed on his scalp under his hairline—a trope from *The Omen*.[72]

The 1970s and Satanic Conspiracy Theories

By the 1970s, Satanic cults had become such a stock feature of exploitation films that often a second element was needed just to make an interesting story. Thus, the glut of Satanic films from this decade included the likes of *Werewolves on Wheels* (1971), featuring a lycanthropic biker gang battling a Satanic cult, and *Satan's Cheerleaders* (1977), in which a cheerleading team is abducted by rural Satanists, found unsuitable as virgin sacrifices, and finally usurps leadership of the cult. At the same time that Hollywood went through its Satanic cult phase, the Vietnam War and the Watergate scandal caused many Americans to lose faith in their institutions. It seemed to some that a subversive force was enervating society. There was also a growing panic about cults using "mind control" tactics. These three elements were ideal for creating a mythology of Satanic conspiracy theories, laying the groundwork for the Satanic Panic.

Like *The Black Cat* and *The Seventh Victim*, many Satanic films of the 1970s revolve around the theme of women in trouble—either because they have been selected as a ritual sacrifice or they are being seduced by the glamour of the occult. In *The Pyx* (1973) (also released under the title "The Hooker Cult Murders") a detective investigating the death of a heroin-addicted prostitute discovers she was murdered by elite Satanists in a black mass. George A. Romero's *Season of the Witch* (1973) featured a bored housewife who finds sexual agency by joining a local coven. And, in 1976, Hammer Film Productions released *To the Devil a Daughter*, based on a Dennis Wheatley novel. In this film another Wheatley-esque hero must use his occult knowledge to rescue a woman before a cult can transform her into the avatar of the demon Astaroth.

But the 1970s also saw a move toward young people and children being the target of the Satanists. As early as 1924, far-right conspiracy theorist Nesta Webster was spinning elaborate conspiracy theories about Luciferianism that involved "literally hundreds of children" disappearing to be sacrificed in Satanic rituals.[73] But it was several decades before Satanists corrupting youth or abusing children could be depicted in movies. *The Blood on Satan's Claw* (1970) is a period piece and part of the "unholy trilogy of folk horror." The corpse of a demon is uncovered in a field and nearly everyone who touches it undergoes a form of demonic possession. The demoniacs form a cult led by Angela, the village's teenage beauty. When not frolicking in fields or trying to seduce the parish priest, the cultists hold rituals to resurrect their demon master. In a finale that reflects the cult wars of the 1970s, the town's cantankerous judge restores order by intruding on the young people's ritual armed with a two-handed sword and impaling their master in front of them.

In *The Brotherhood of Satan* (1971), thirteen elderly Satanists gather in a small town and use their magic to mesmerize and control thirteen children. They then commit ritual suicide and transfer their consciousnesses into the children, a process they have repeated for centuries. This trope of Satanists possessing a young body (also depicted in *The Mephisto Waltz*) dovetails with anxieties about cult mind control. It is also a clear example of David Frankfurter's observation that evil conspiracies are frequently imagined as "intrinsically parasitical," needing our children to perpetuate themselves.[74] One scene from this film is especially germane to the Satanic Panic. The Satanists hold a birthday party in which entranced children wear hats and blow party horns, oblivious to the black robed Satanists attending to them. They are served a cake too black to be actual frosting that is cut open to reveal a blood-red interior. The camera cuts back and forth between the laughing children and crayon drawings of children participating in human sacrifices. Watching this scene today, it is impossible not to see the seeds of the SRA narrative.

The most significant film about evil ritual to emerge during this decade was *The Wicker Man* (1973). This is the folk horror film that defines the

genre, and it seems to have emerged as a direct result of Murray's interven-
tion in the Walton murder. Actor Robert Pinner had an idea for a film about
a puritanical police officer who investigates the murder of a child in a rural
village, only to uncover a conspiracy of Pagans engaged in human sacrifice.
Pinner's agent persuaded him to write a novel before the film adaptation and
Pinner published *Ritual* in 1967.[75] Pinner recalled, "*The Wicker Man* would
not exist but for my novel. At the time I wrote *Ritual*, there was very little
being written, other than Dennis Wheatley, on the subject of witchcraft,
Satanism and the occult, the Stephen Kings of this world come much later."[76]
Christopher Lee, along with writer Anthony Schaffer, approached Pinner
about a film adaptation. Schaffer eventually wrote his own film, directed
by Robin Hardy and starring Lee as the Pagan leader "Lord Summerisle."
The story is much the same: Sergeant Howie, a well-meaning if stuffy
Christian police officer, travels to a remote island in search of a missing girl.
The islanders are Pagans who lure Howie into an enormous wicker effigy,
which they light on fire as a sacrifice to their gods. The idea of sacrificing
people in this manner comes from Julius Caesar's description of druids in
Commentaries of the Gallic War. Whether there was any historical basis for
Casar's claim or it was merely propaganda, the story was repeated in Frazer's
The Golden Bough. Hardy and Schaffer made extensive use of Frazer and the
rituals described in his book can be spotted throughout the film. As Hardy
explained, "What we hoped would fascinate people is . . . That they would
recognize an awful lot of these things as sort of little echoes from either out
of childhood stories and nursery rhymes or things they do at various times
of the year."[77] In this way, by studying Frazer, the creators discovered a way to
use contemporary folkways as a form of transtextual anchoring to give their
story a sense of verisimilitude.

   Some have questioned whether *The Wicker Man* should be classified as a
horror movie at all.[78] It can be read as a Christian martyrdom story, an endorsement of Paganism, or a commentary on religion as an invented means
of social control. Just as Margaret Murray helped to inspire both the creation
of Wicca as a modern religion and conspiracy theories about ritual murder,
The Wicker Man has a cult following that includes many self-described
Pagans, but it also serves as a model for imagining what a murderous
"country cult" hiding in plain sight might look like. *Spellbinder* (1988) essentially repackaged the plot of *The Wicker Man* to involve a coven of Satanic
witches manipulating a Los Angeles police officer.[79]

One extremist group seems to advocate for an ostensive performance of the kind of sacrifice depicted in *The Wicker Man*. The Order of Nine Angles is a Satanic group with ties to neo-Nazism that formed at some time in the 1970s. It sneers at the law-abiding practices of the Church of Satan and claims "traditional Satanism" must involve "culling" or ritual murder. What is significant for this study is that the Order's literature specifies that before culling anyone, the victim (called an "opfer," German for "sacrifice") must be covertly tested to see whether they are worthy of death. An essay called "Guidelines for the Testing of Opfers" states, "It is a fundamental principle of traditional Satanism that all prospective opfers must be subject to several tests before becoming actual opfers either during a ceremony or otherwise. The purpose of the tests is to give the chosen victim a sporting chance and to show if they possess the character defects which make them suitable as opfers . . . . It is principle that no opfer under any circumstance be informed directly or indirectly that they are being tested for whatever reason as this would invalidate the test."[80] This idea of forming a conspiracy to test whether someone can be sacrificed seems derivative of *The Wicker Man*, where the Pagans offer Sergeant Howie a chance to lose his virginity before tricking him into willingly climbing inside a wicker effigy for sacrifice. Satanism scholar James R. Lewis interpreted the Order's rhetoric of human sacrifice as "macho posturing"; however, in recent years this material may have inspired crimes by neo-Nazi terrorist groups.[81]

Movies about Satanists and other conspiracies engaged in ritual murder became so ubiquitous that *everyone* knew what a Satanic cult was, whether they believed they existed or not. And reports on Charles Manson and LaVey lent themselves to the idea that groups like the ones in these films really existed somewhere. Writing in 1974, Dominican priest Richard Woods reflected:

> Along with television dramas, the filmed versions of *Rosemary's Baby*, *The Mephisto Waltz*, *The Devils*, and now, *The Exorcist* are bringing the message home to the viewing public. The occult revival of the late sixties spread pentacles and goats' horns throughout the counterculture, and Satanic cults are rumored (and occasionally reported in the daily press) to be flourishing in both suburbs and urbs. We find it difficult to forget the Manson slayings and the periodic if lesser outrages perpetrated by professing Satanists, same or otherwise. Perhaps it is easier in this way to forget the My Lai and Kent State "incidents." We appreciate the explicit pact.[82]

Woods is correct in that Satanic cults provided a shared imaginary that people could invoke in attempting to explain either social problems or personal misfortune.

By 1970, the John Birch's Society's "Satanism: A Practical Guide to Witch Hunting" had already assembled a full-blown Satanic conspiracy theory, declaring, "Next to communism, [Satanism] has become the fastest growing criminal menace of our time." The article connected Manson, Roman Polanski, and LaVey, incorrectly asserting that Polanski hired LaVey as a technical advisor for *Rosemary's Baby*. The article also noted that Polanski, "still travels on a Communist Polish passport" and referred to LaVey as "an ardent Socialist." (LaVey was staunchly anti-socialist, and his philosophy borrowed heavily from right-wing author Ayn Rand.) The article accepts Margaret Murray's thesis about the reality of "witch-cults," but adds, "Dr. Murray did more to influence the growth of modern Satanism than any other author this century."[83] In addition to anti-communist groups, the growing anti-cult movement in the 1970s also found rumors of widespread Satanism useful. In 1973, a group of strict Greek Orthodox parents in Arvada, Colorado, was upset that two of their adult daughters had left home and moved in together. They hired "cult deprogrammer" Ted Patrick to abduct them and end their involvement in "Satanism."[84]

By the early 1970s, several individuals had begun to claim they were themselves ex-Satanists who had seen the light. One of these was John Todd, whose claims are a profound example of a fact–fiction reversal. Todd spoke at evangelical churches where he said he was an ex-witch and solicited funds that he promised he would use to bring other witches to Jesus. Todd claimed he was born into a witch family, that his "witch name" was "Lance Collins," and that his ancestors settled in Salem, Massachusetts. Critics noted that this story seemed derivative of ABC's occult soap opera *Dark Shadows* (1966–1971), about the Collins family of Collinsport, Maine. Todd countered that before becoming a Christian, he had given Hollywood producers a copy of his family diary: He wasn't copying the show, the show was copying him. He also invoked horror films to make these claims more apprehensible to his audience. For example, he said the Lovecraftian film *The Dunwich Horror* (1970) was an accurate depiction of Satanism.[85]

In 1972, Mike Warnke published *The Satan Seller*, a seminal text of the Satanic Panic. Warnke claimed he had dropped out of college, become a drug dealer, and then a Satanist. The Illuminati, who Warnke claims control Satanic cults, promoted him and put him in charge of fifteen hundred

Satanists. Warnke led his flock in committing rapes and human sacrifice until his own Satanic sex slaves attempted to murder him with an overdose of heroin. He joined the navy to flee the Satanists, whereupon he converted to Christianity. Woods described Warnke's book as "a paranoid fantasy of Christian fascism."[86] But evangelicals loved it. It became a religious bestseller and was praised in *Moody Monthly* and *The Christian Century*. Warnke became a celebrity and began touring America in a "Witchmobile"—a trailer filled with occult artifacts. Visitors to the witchmobile could see and touch alleged Satanic objects, anchoring these stories in material reality. (It is not clear whether or not the Witchmobile preceded the Warrens' occult museum, or whether one was an influence on the other.) Horror films were not responsible for the careers of figures like Todd and Warnke, but the Satanic cults depicted in these films made their claims easy to imagine and even seem plausible. Warnke did not have to explain the premise that hundreds of criminal Satanists are active in California because this idea had already been thoroughly introduced to the public. Todd went further, actively invoking horror films to buttress his claims.

The evangelical magazine *Cornerstone* wrote an article debunking Todd's claims in 1979, and another debunking Warnke's in 1991. Warnke rebranded himself as a Christian comedian, while Todd was convicted of rape and eventually sent to the Behavioral Disorder Treatment Unit run by the South Carolina Department of Mental Health. But they inspired an entire genre of books by people claiming to be ex-Satanists. More importantly, Warnke demonstrated that such books were money makers. This set the stage for the next wave of the Panic: Satanic ritual abuse.

Michelle Remembers and "Satanic Ritual Abuse"

Michelle Remembers (1980) almost single-handedly ushered in an international panic over "Satanic ritual abuse." The events described in this book are derivatives of horror films and, were it not for the threat of a lawsuit, there would likely have been a film adaptation, completing the mobius strip of *The Exorcist* effect. As the discourse surrounding recovered memories and SRA went on, many therapists began to argue it was irrelevant whether their patients were describing actual memories or confabulations derived from movies and other media. This marked a new phase in the relationship between horror films and religious cultures: While films have always offered imaginary models of seemingly plausible realities, suddenly it was no longer clear whether "real" and "imaginary" were still meaningful categories.

Significantly, Ed and Lorraine Warren may have been among the first to use hypnosis to summon memories of Satanic rituals. One of their columns from *The Tattler* describes a woman named Leslie who claimed she had sold her soul to Satan to win back a former boyfriend. A friend brought Leslie to seek the Warrens' help following one of their lectures at the University of Hartford. According to the Warrens: "Under hypnosis, Leslie revealed the gruesome months during which she was the devil's playmate . . . . 'I wore a black veil, drew a circle around me (to confine the powers) and read incantations from the Satanic bible . . . . I can't get free now. I promised him I must do whatever he wants me to do. And I don't want to. He won't let anyone help me. He said I'm his now.'"[87] This column appeared in 1974, six years before *Michelle Remembers*, but the story shares many of the same themes: A young woman is desperate for help, believing she has a problem but does not know the full extent of it; using hypnosis, the victim and the (Catholic) expert construct a detailed fantasy of Satanic ritual together. Both stories are "captivity narratives" in which a woman is a prisoner in need of saving, and both are saturated with themes of sexual danger and the need to preserve sexual innocence.

Michelle Proby of Victoria, British Columbia, began seeing psychiatrist Lawrence Pazder in 1973. A Catholic, Pazder received a diploma in tropical medicine from the University of Liverpool in 1962 and spent time practicing medicine in West Africa, where he became preoccupied with reports of African "occult" practices.[88] Pazder was also interested in Satanic conspiracies. In 1976, Proby told him, "I know there's something I want to tell you, but I don't know what it is!"[89] That October she suddenly began screaming and did not stop for twenty-five minutes. Afterward, she began talking in the voice of a five-year-old and said a man named "Malachi" was hurting her. Pazder concluded that Michelle was reliving memories of some past trauma that she had forgotten for twenty-two years. Over the next fourteen months, he administered six hundred hours of hypnosis to help Michelle recover these "lost memories." The narrative resulting from these sessions was published as *Michelle Remembers*, a "non-fiction" book co-authored by Padzer and Michelle "Smith." Proby "remembered" that her mother, Virginia, had secretly been part of a Satanic cult. Between September and November 1955, the cult abused five-year-old Michelle more or less continuously for eighty-one days. She was forced to defecate on holy objects and stab a baby to death with a cross. She was sealed inside graves and inside a giant effigy of Satan that was then filled with spiders. She was made to watch dismembered limbs reassembled and then electrified to simulate reanimation. Horns and a tail were surgically grafted onto her body. All of this was meant to prepare Michelle for "The Feast of the Beast" where Satan physically manifested and took her on a tour of hell. But Michelle was saved by the archangel Michael and the Virgin Mary. Mary even miraculously healed Michelle's scars, leaving no physical evidence of the abuse.

In addition to the overt supernaturalism at the end of this tale, the narrative often lacks internal logic. For example, in one scene, the Satanists somehow kill Michelle's imaginary friend.[90] The year *Michelle Remembers* was published, a journalist for *Maclean's* magazine discovered ample contradictory evidence.[91] Proby's mother died of cancer when she was fourteen, but her father was alive and denied the entire story, telling one source, "It was the worst pack of lies a little girl could ever make up. The book took me four months to read, and I cried all the time. I kept saying to myself: 'Dear God, how could anyone do this to their dead mother?' "[92] Michelle also had two sisters, Charyl and Tertia, who are never mentioned in the book. The St. Margaret's School yearbook for 1955–1956 features a class photo taken in November 1955 in which Proby can be seen attending school and appears healthy (not in a dungeon being tortured by a cult).[93] But none of these discrepancies stopped the book from becoming a bestseller.

In 1980, Pazder spoke at the annual meeting of the American Psychiatric Association in New Orleans where he coined the term "ritualized abuse." He defined this as, "Repeated physical, emotional, mental and spiritual assaults combined with a systematic use of symbols, ceremonies, and machinations designed and orchestrated to attain malevolent effects."[94] Drawing on theories about "brainwashing tactics" that were popularized during the Cold War, Pazder argued that Satanists hurt children systematically as a form of "ego destruction" meant to convert them to Satanism. *Michelle Remembers* suggested this was being done to children on a large scale around the world. Soon, therapy patients all over America began remembering that they, too, had been tortured in Satanic rituals. Law enforcement specialist Robert Hicks found that neither Kenneth Lanning, an FBI agent who investigated allegations of Satanic abuse, nor Bennett Braun, a psychiatrist who has endorsed claims of recovered memories and Satanic conspiracy theories, could find any report of SRA that predated *Michelle Remembers*.[95]

In the infamous McMartin preschool trial (1983–1990), the McMartin family was accused of ritually abusing hundreds of children at the preschool they operated, possibly in the sort of Satanic ritual described in *Michelle Remembers*. Pazder was brought in to counsel children and to aid the prosecution in their investigation.[96] In many cases, therapists encouraged children to describe abuse and children who stated no abuse occurred were diagnosed as being in denial.[97] All charges were eventually dropped, although one defendant, Raymond Buckey, was jailed for five years awaiting a verdict. But the McMartin trial did little to stem a growing moral panic and similar cases occurred throughout the United States, as well as the United Kingdom and Australia. By 1990, Pazder reported having consulted in over one thousand "ritual abuse" cases.[98] By some estimates, the victims of false accusations of SRA number in the thousands worldwide.[99] At the same time, the panic drew resources away from investigating actual cases of child abuse.

Pazder and Proby went on a publicity tour together and even traveled to Rome, where they discussed evidence of a Satanic conspiracy with high-ranking Catholics. During this time, they began renting hotel rooms as "Mr. and Mrs. Pazder."[100] Eventually they divorced their spouses (the church refused them annulments) and married each other. A skeptical interpretation of Proby's "recovered memories" is that she was infatuated with her psychiatrist and was inventing stories to keep his attention. And what interested Pazder was Satanism. At one point he told Proby, "The only group I know about that fits your description is The Church of Satan."[101] (He reportedly backed away from this conclusion after LaVey threatened to sue for libel.)[102] Proby may have become a sort of gothic Scheherazade, spinning horrible stories to ensure Pazder always wanted another session. Pazder also believed Michelle's memories were cyclical, returning on the anniversary of the abuse. On Catholic holy days, Proby would urgently call Pazder because she was reliving a Satanic parody of the holy day from 1955. Pazder's first wife had a theory about this connection: These were normally days that Pazder spent attending church with his family, but the mythology of recovered memories gave Proby a way to ensure Pazder spent holy days with her instead.[103]

From the perspective of folklore studies, Proby's memories were a form of proto-ostension—reporting to have personally experienced a legend. Whether or not she was consciously inventing these stories, it is clear that horror films were a profound influence on them. Proby began her therapy with Pazder the year *The Exorcist* came out and popular fascination with the demonic continued throughout the sessions that became *Michelle Remembers*.

The most obvious influence can be spotted when the Satanists bring in a possessed woman and the child Michelle states, "She drools a lot and her head starts to go all funny and spins around."[104] This is a clear reference to the "head-spinning scene" in *The Exorcist* that Blatty thought was too unrealistic to portray. The scene of reassembled body parts being electrified is derivative of *Frankenstein*. The trope of a little girl being placed inside a sacrificial effigy is also found in *The Wicker Man*. When Satan appears, he utters goofy poetry about the end of the world such as, "Four times seven make twenty-eight/That's when the world will learn to hate./My fire will have burned for all those years./My fire will have burned out many ears."[105] Pazder showed these rhymes to Father Guy Merveille who claimed, "If you look up Satan in a theological dictionary, it will say that he is known to speak in rhymes."[106] Skeptics have yet to find any dictionary reporting such a thing, but Satan's prophecies in *Michelle Remembers* are highly reminiscent of the fake rhyming verse of Revelation invented by David Seltzer for the film *The Omen*, which came out a few months before Proby began experiencing recovered memories. Malachi Martin's *Hostage to the Devil* was also in print by October 1976. As a Catholic interested in Satanic cults, Pazder almost certainly read this book. One wonders if it was in his office when Proby first stated that someone named "Malachi" was hurting her. There is evidence of other influences, too. In one scene Satanists sever one of their own fingers to prove their loyalty. This trope appeared in *The Satan Seller*, suggesting Proby was exposed to Warnke's book. Pazder's tales of African rituals likely shaped the narrative as well.[107] In fact, he repeatedly suggests the Satanic rituals described by Prody are plausible because they "resemble" practices he witnessed in Africa.

Horror scholar Grady Hendrix locates *Michelle Remembers* within a larger glut of cheap horror paperbacks emerging during this period.[108] *Maclean's* compared *Michelle Remembers* to *Rosemary's Baby* and *The Exorcist* and even the publishers seem to have regarded it as a horror story rather than a claim about literal abuse. When confronted about discrepancies in Proby's narrative, the American publisher, Congdon and Latté, answered, "There are a lot of skeptical people, as well there probably should be."[109] *Maclean's* also described plans for a movie adaptation with Dustin Hoffman playing Pazder. This is plausible considering the publisher gave Pazder and Proby a $100,000 advance and it was standard practice in the 1970s for horror movies to be adapted from novels. But there never was a movie. Pazder claimed this was a matter of professional ethics: "This is a hard one because the media, the movie industry, everyone is very eager to capitalize on this and get the fear going and make it dramatic. I've seen all kinds of movies that do that. We've turned down millions from people who want to turn our book into a movie, because we can't get control over the final cut."[110] However, an alternative explanation comes from Proby's father, who stated, "I asked my lawyer if I could sue them. He said I would win, but it would cost me $5,000. So instead I took out a Notice of Intent against their publisher, which meant if they ever went beyond a literary contract I would sue. That meant they couldn't get their movie deal."[111]

One of the most disturbing features of the SRA panic is that claims-makers seemed to understand these stories could not be true and yet they continued to treat them as though they were. Pazder argued that Proby's experiences were "real to her" and that "in the end it doesn't matter" whether or not they really happened.[112] But, of course, when Padzer consulted in criminal trials, it very much mattered whether abuse really occurred. In this context, he acknowledged that children were describing fantasies, but paradoxically suggested this was evidence of actual abuse. He stated, "When we take these children before the court, and they start talking about their fantasy world that makes the judge think well this kid is making it up. But they have to retreat to the fantasy world to deal with the reality."[113] A similar argument was put forth following accusations that occurred in 1990 in Rochdale, England. The United Kingdom had censored *The Exorcist* in 1986 and was still wrestling with anxieties about "video nasties," or cheap horror films disseminated on VHS tapes. Some observers noticed children's descriptions of abuse sounded like scenes from horror movies and questioned whether their testimony might suffer from "contamination by video." Andrew Boyd, a journalist who defended claims of ritual abuse, suggested that Satanists could be deliberately abusing children in ways that seemed derivative of movies, so that no one would believe them. He wrote, "What more effective way to contaminate a child's evidence than by deliberately fostering such confusion, perhaps compounded by the use of drugs or hypnosis and blended with commercially available horror movies and video nasties?"[114] These sorts of arguments take evidence pointing toward the invented nature of these claims and attempt to use it to make the opposite conclusion. Horror has always claimed to be "based on true events," but in the logic of SRA, true events are based on horror stories. Or rather, reality is assumed to be so horrible that horror films may be a necessary tool for imagining it.

In addition to children and patients undergoing hypnosis, police also seemed to take cues from horror films. During the McMartin trial, police seized Peggy Martin's graduation gown. They described it as a "black robe" that could be evidence of participation in a Satanic cult. In the Rochdale case, police searched the homes of accused parents for anything associated with "black magic." Confiscated items included a book of erotic poetry, an Oriental statue of a couple making love, a child's letter to the tooth fairy, and a Guy Fawkes mask.[115] *Something* caused officers to identify certain objects with cult activity and not others. Where did the assumption that Satanic abusers might wear black robes or Guy Fawkes masks come from? It seems likely that law enforcement, along with the therapists and alleged victims, "knew" what Satanists looked like and what objects they used from horror movie tropes. By the end of the 1980s, this connection would have been enhanced by "occult crime" seminars in which police were sometimes told horror movies were "realistic" depictions of actual cult activity.[116] This means that police searching for evidence of Satanic crime were engaged in a form of quasi-ostension or misinterpreting evidence in light of a legend.

The Ongoing Legacy of Satanic Panic

Horror films depicting "country cults," "city cults," and lone Satanic killers continued through the 1980s and 1990s, but seemed to have less impact as the trend played itself out. Films such as *The First Power* (1990), *Hideaway* (1995), and *Bless the Child* (2000) all received terrible reviews and were quickly forgotten. Even Polanski's Satanic thriller, *The Ninth Gate* (1999), received surprisingly little attention. The Satanic Panic likewise began to lose momentum. In 1988, Geraldo Rivera hosted the infamous special "Exposing Satan's Underground"—discussed in more detail in Chapter 8. But on December 12, 1995, Rivera hosted a program on CNBC about false accusations of child molestation. He stated, "I want to announce publicly that as a firm believer of the 'Believe The Children' movement of the 1980s, that started with the McMartin trials in California, but now I am convinced that I was terribly wrong and many innocent people were convicted and went to prison as a result. And I am equally positive [that the] 'Repressed Memory Therapy Movement' is also a bunch of crap!"[117] The media began to lose interest in Satanic cults and law enforcement became more skeptical of claims of Satanic conspiracies. After September 11, 2001, the "War on Terror" gave Americans a more tangible enemy to fear. Eventually, the panic was either forgotten entirely or remembered as an odd phenomenon of the 1980s.

The 2015 psychological thriller *Regression* dealt with recovered memories of SRA. It opened with title cards explaining that in 1980 a moral panic started in which American communities began accusing their neighbors of participating in Satanic cults, followed by the line, "This film is inspired by real events."

Unfortunately, the Satanic Panic never really died. A 2012 study of legal cases found evidence suggesting allegations of Satanism still have a profound effect on juries and judges.[118] Ideas of repressed memory and ritual abuse are still promoted in some parts of the therapeutic community. The International Society for the Study of Trauma and Dissociation (ISSTD) was formed in 1984 and consists of health professionals studying "trauma-based disorders." Some of ISSTD's past presidents were leading figures in promoting claims of widespread SRA. ISSTD holds annual meetings and some members still encourage their patients to believe they are victims of the sort of cult rituals depicted in *Michelle Remembers*.[119] Meanwhile, QAnon, an online movement of right-wing conspiracy theorists, has accused numerous politicians and celebrities of torturing children. The rise of QAnon suggests that Satanic Panic is even more of a threat to democracy and public safety today than in the 1980s.

8

Heavy Metal

"There is a satanism problem in America. It involves teenage drug users who are instructed in satanic symbols and practices by the music recording industry and, to a lesser extent, the motion picture industry."

—*Religious Freedom Alert* (May 1989)[1]

"Demonic beasts. Whatever happened to the good old simple love song? 'I love you.' That's what good words use. Nowadays they have to write some sickness. It's just absolutely sick and bizarre, and I'm going to do my utmost best to try and stop it now."

—Reverend Aaron Gilstom (Ozzy Osborne), *Trick or Treat* (1986)

The Geraldo Rivera Show special, "Exposing Satan's Underground," was a high watermark of the Satanic Panic. It aired on October 25, 1988, and was watched in 19.8 million homes—about one-third of all Americans watching television between 8 and 10 p.m.[2] After a warning advising parental discretion, the show explodes into a heavy metal guitar riff that continues to play while Geraldo outlines the Satanic threat, and the audience is bombarded with a rapid montage of clips. The first image is lifted from a heavy metal music video: a pyrotechnic explosion reveals a fog-covered stage and a bass drum painted with an inverted pentagram. A camera effect then causes the pentagram to spin and fly out of frame. An alleged survivor of a Satanic cult describes making a blood sacrifice to Satan. Geraldo appears squatting in front of children from the McMartin preschool listening to them recite how they were threatened by Satanists. An "occult crime expert" warns that Satanists really exist. A clip from the documentary *Satanis: The Devil's Mass* (1970) shows Anton LaVey performing a ritual. A trio of teenage boys accused of murdering their friend in 1987 in Joplin, Missouri, are shown entering and exiting a courthouse.

The Exorcist Effect. Joseph P. Laycock and Eric Harrelson, Oxford University Press. © Oxford University Press 2024.
DOI: 10.1093/oso/9780197635391.003.0008

One of the three, Peter Roland, tells the camera, "It basically started out with the killing of animals. Then there's always the heavy metal music and drugs don't help." There is a shot of serial killer Robert Berdella. Then a snippet of an interview with Edward Spela, alleging that an acquaintance was a Satanist and was responsible for the murder of a homeless man in San Francisco. Then it cuts back to footage of a metal concert and young fans slam dancing before the stage while Geraldo intones, "Possessed by an obsessive fascination with sex and drugs and, yes, heavy metal rock and roll." This entire spectacle is only the first eighty-one seconds of the ninety-minute special. "Exploring Satan's Underground" is a master class in creative, sensationalized editing.[3]

The element that holds these eighty-one seconds together—visually, audibly, and narratively—is heavy metal music. A series of controversies in the 1980s gave rise to a folk devil that could be described as "the myth of the heavy metal Satanist." In 1984, heavy metal was implicated in the highly sensationalized coverage of seventeen-year-old murderer Ricky Kasso. The following year saw the arrest of serial killer Richard Ramirez. Ramirez had left a baseball cap for the rock band AC/DC at a crime scene and the media hypothesized that he had been driven to murder by the band's 1979 song "Night Prowler." That same year, Tipper Gore helped to form the Parents Music Resource Center (PMRC), which held congressional hearings over objectionable music. Beginning in 1985, there was a series of lawsuits in which bereaved parents blamed heavy metal musicians for their teenagers' suicides. One suit alleged a suicide was caused by satanic messages hidden subliminally in a rock album. All this controversy was equally useful for those seeking to entertain or sow moral panic—or both.

Because heavy metal seemed ubiquitous in the 1980s, it was ideal for those hoping to persuade the public of a hidden Satanic threat. Talk show hosts like Geraldo frequently juxtaposed discussions of heavy metal with coverage of "Satanically inspired" crime and serial killers. As with media coverage of drugs, there was a "routinization of caricature" in which the worst cases were framed as typical cases, and the episodic was framed as the epidemic.[4] This is a rhetorical strategy that sociologist Stuart Hall calls "convergence." Convergence links two or more activities in a way that falsely implies a connection between them so that "the danger implicitly is made to appear more widespread and diffused."[5] By conflating an entire genre of popular music with the most extreme and deviant of crimes, it was possible to create a sense that American culture was under a Satanic siege.

Once it was accepted that a sizable youth counterculture was "dabbling" in criminal Satanism, it was possible to allege even larger threats. In his book *Satanic Ritual Abuse: Principles of Treatment*, Colin Ross alleged that there are five levels of Satanism: (1) isolated criminal deviants, (2) teenage dabblers, (3) non-criminal public Satanic churches, (4) narcosatanistos (an entire category built around the murder of Mark Kilroy by a drug cartel in Matamoros, Mexico, in 1989), and finally (5) orthodox multi-generational Satanic cults.[6] The "teenage dabblers" were the lynchpin of this entire hierarchy because Americans could see them every day, either in person or on television. They were the only category of "Satanist" that Ross's audience was likely to ever encounter personally, but their demonstrable existence implied the other categories must also exist.

The theatricality of heavy metal—in its stage shows and counterculture clothing—was also useful to claims-makers who never lacked for album covers to use as props or shocking lyrics to pepper their lectures. These same elements lent themselves to horror films. Not only was heavy metal ubiquitous in the "slasher genre" marketed to teenagers, but a sub-genre of films emerged around claims of nefarious elements in rock music. Horror films became an arena through which popular fears and fantasies surrounding heavy metal were reflected and refracted. Some of these films poked fun at the claims-makers and others added novel twists to the mythology of heavy metal and the occult. Most simply capitalized on media discourse by telling stock stories about youth—invariably misunderstood teenage boys—being seduced by the occult power of evil music. Because of claims about heavy metal circulating on talk shows and other media, audiences could grasp the bizarre plots of these films with minimal exposition.

As with other manifestations of *The Exorcist* effect, these films seemed to amplify the behaviors they portrayed. Many bands saw the controversy as an opportunity for publicity and were happy to contribute songs to the soundtracks for these films or even play the part of a Satanic band. For example, W.A.S.P.—a band that seemed to have an almost symbiotic relationship of mutual antagonism with the PMRC—made a prolonged appearance in the 1984 film *The Dungeonmaster* (the title an appeal to controversy surrounding the role-playing game *Dungeons and Dragons*). An evil time-traveling wizard transports the protagonist to a W.A.S.P. concert where the heroine appears on stage shackled to a rack. He must fight his way past a throng of fans before she is decapitated while W.A.S.P. performs their song "Tormenter." As fictional films reflected claims being made in the media, this connection between metal, Satanism, and crime seemed less like an assertion coming from moral entrepreneurs and more like "common sense." By the end of the 1980s, heavy metal came to be framed as a manifestation of "the occult" and enjoying it came to be seen as evidence of criminal activity.[7]

In a pattern that David Frankfurter calls "the mimetic performance of evil," the hyperbolic rhetoric of the claims-makers helped to inspire the very behavior they claimed they were trying to prevent, bringing the myth of the heavy metal Satanist to life.[8] In 1993, Varg Vikernes, of the Norwegian black metal groups Burzum and Mayhem, murdered former friend and band manager Øystein Aarseth. Vikernes would claim self-defense, but commentators such as Michael Moynihan and Didrik Søderlind have suggested that the real motive was Vikernes's desire to prove he was "the most metal"—that he was actually engaged in dangerous criminal Satanism while similar musicians were merely "posers."[9]

More often, though, the victims of the panic were teenage boys who were unfairly targeted by law enforcement. The most famous such case was that of the West Memphis Three. In 1993, the small town of West Memphis, Arkansas, bore witness to a brutal crime: Three second grade boys were found murdered. Damien Echols, along with James Baldwin and Jessie Misskelley Jr., just teenage boys themselves, were tried and convicted of the murders, despite the absence of any physical evidence or reliable witnesses. The West Memphis Three spent eighteen years in prison essentially because Echols resembled the mythic heavy metal Satanist that had become familiar to law enforcement and juries through sensationalized media. Both these events have since been adapted into films, continuing the cycle.

Dangerous Music

Moral entrepreneurs such as Geraldo Rivera and Tipper Gore were far more interested in the alleged dangers of music than horror films. One reason for this is that by the 1980s there had already been several decades of conspiracy theories claiming that rock music was a tool of covert mind control. This discourse drew on Cold War paranoia, as well as fears of the religious other and racist anxieties about black music and the threat of atavism. In 1950, CIA operative Edward Hunter coined the term "brainwashing." During the Korean War, some American POWs refused to repatriate and advocated the virtues of communism. Hunter's books *Brain-washing in Red China* (1950) and

Brainwashing (1956) attributed this apparent conversion to a secret form of mental manipulation with ancient roots in Chinese religion.[10] Brainwashing was introduced to the American public through the film *The Manchurian Candidate* (1962), an adaptation of a spy novel by Richard Condon, published in 1959. It tells the story of Raymond Shaw, a veteran of the Korean War, who has been brainwashed and subconsciously programmed to work as a "sleeper agent." When given a certain "trigger," Shaw will commit an assassination and have no memory of it afterward.

Reverend David A. Noebel was among the first to use brainwashing as a cudgel against popular music. His anti-rock and roll treatise *Communism, Hypnotism and the Beatles* (1965), insisted that rock was a communist scheme to brainwash the youth of America using Pavlovian conditioning techniques and specific beat signatures hidden in popular music. Noebel claimed that communists were behind hypnotic music for all ages of American youth, including children's records produced by Young People's Records and the Children's Record Guild, the folk songs of Pete Seeger, and the rock and roll of the Beatles. He urged readers: "Let's make sure four mop-headed anti-Christ beatniks don't destroy our children's emotional and mental stability and ultimately destroy our nation."[11]

On January 13, 1968, Mel Brooks lampooned this scenario on his espionage-themed sitcom *Get Smart*. In an episode entitled "The Groovy Guru," a counterculture radio personality is actually an agent of the terrorist organization KAOS. He hypes a band that uses subliminal messages that program teenagers to destroy all government institutions when a certain song is broadcast. The trigger song includes the lyrics, "Bump off a square. That's what it's all about. Hate is in, Love is out." *TV Guide* voted "The Groovy Guru" among the one hundred best TV episodes of all time.[12]

Claims about the dangers of rock beats drew on racist fantasies about Africans using drums in frenzied Pagan rituals. One of exorcist Bob Larson's first books, *Rock and Roll: The Devil's Diversion* (1967), claimed rock music was a Satanic plot to corrupt American teenagers. Stories from African missionaries were a key piece of Larson's argument because he viewed American teenagers in much the way missionaries presented Africans: child-like, emotional rather than rational, and easily influenced by music. Larson offers the following anecdote:

A missionary in an uncivilized region of Africa told me of an experiment he conducted with music. One of his tapes was a recording of semi-classic

music. When he played this the tribesmen smiled and indicated in their
language that the sound was pleasing to their ears. They asked to hear more.
Then my friend played a tape of rock and roll music. In response, the natives
grabbed their spears as if intending to fight. They picked up stones to smash
the recording and destroy the music.[13]

Despite this reaction, Africans apparently *have* been seduced by the devil's
music and this is evident in their demonic religious practices. Larson
explains:

> There is no difference between the repetitive movements of witch doctors
> and tribal dancers and the dances of American teenagers. The same coarse
> bodily motions which lead African dancers into a state of uncontrolled
> frenzy are present in modern dances. It is only logical, then, that there must
> also be a correlation in the potentiality of demons gaining possessive con-
> trol of a person through the medium of the beat.[14]

Significantly, Larson had his own high school rock band, called "The Rebels,"
before becoming a minster and the dangers of Satanic rock music have been a
continuous focus of his ministry.[15]

Racist dog whistles continued in anti-rock literature into the 1980s. In
Satan's Music Exposed (1981), Lowell Hart equated rock music with "Voodoo
drums," claiming, "Rock has a heavy, incessant, throbbing beat, the same beat
that people in primitive cultures use in their demonic rites and dances."[16]
In his book *Backward Masking Unmasked* (1982), Jacob Aranza claimed
"rock and roll" was originally "a ghetto term describing premarital sex," and
described rock and roll rhythms as "jungle beats."[17]

As the utopian hopes of the 1960s faded into the pessimism of the 1970s,
Christian conspiracy theories about the dangers of rock continued to escalate. In 1978, evangelist Jack Chick published a full-color comic book called
Spellbound?. As Chick told it, rock music is a sinister plot against America
perpetrated not by communists, but by ancient druids. When the druids
were suppressed by the Romans, they survived in secret and continued to
cast spells using their music (played on drums made from human skin).
Modern record companies are run by secret druidic orders who gather in recording studios and cast spells over the records so that listeners will become
interested in Eastern religion and ideas such as reincarnation. In *Spellbound?*,
Druidism, Eastern religions, and the indigenous religions of Africa are all

presented as a monolithic opponent to Christianity. Although it is not credited to Larson, two panels depict a "true story" about a missionary whose children play rock records while in Africa—the Africans explain that before converting they had used these same rhythms in their demon summoning ceremonies. *Spellbound?* begins with a dedication: "My deepest appreciation to John Todd, ex-grand druid priest, for the authenticity of the occult information used in this story."[18] As discussed in the previous chapter, Todd was a disturbed individual and an early proponent of the Satanic Panic.

At the same time these conspiracy theories were brewing, a new genre of rock was emerging that drew on such elements as blues, psychedelia, Eastern religion, and sometimes Satanic imagery borrowed from horror films. In 1967, the Rolling Stones debuted their album *Their Satanic Majesties Request*. The following year, the opening track on their album *Beggar's Banquet* was "Sympathy of the Devil." In 1969, Chicago psychedelic rock band Coven took flirtation with Satanism much further in their album, *Witchcraft Destroys Minds and Reaps Souls*. The album featured such tracts as "Black Sabbath" and "Pact with Lucifer," and the final tract, "Satanic Mass," was a thirteen-minute performance of a Satanic liturgy. At stage shows, Coven would perform a black mass where the band's roadie was suspended on a cross. When the roadie was taken down, the cross would spin to an inverted position.

Coven was scheduled to play Detroit's Olympia Stadium on Halloween 1969 as part of a "Back Arts Festival" where Anton LaVey and Timothy Leary would appear as special guests. Newspaper and radio ads reported that a black mass would be performed in the stadium and that LaVey would give a Satanic benediction over the audience. The Detroit Council of Churches inundated the promoters with outraged letters that eventually led to the concert being canceled. LaVey, who had already flown to Detroit, settled for a few television appearances and a speaking engagement at the University of Michigan.[19] The cancellation of "Satanist's Woodstock"[20] can be read as an opening salvo in a battle between Christian opposition to rock and rock musicians seeking to capitalize on popular fascination with the occult.

By 1971, Coven had re-invented themselves as a more traditional folk band with their anti-war single, "One Tin Soldier." In an interview, Coven member Rick Durret recalled it had actually been Mercury Records who suggested the band "go satanic."[21] If this is true, Mercury likely hoped to capitalize on the success of *Rosemary's Baby*. The imagery in Coven's early music and stage shows was likely inspired by the success of the film *The Devil Rides Out* (1968).

Rock musicians in the United Kingdom were also flirting with Satanic imagery. In 1970, psychedelic band Black Widow produced its album *Sacrifice* and their stage shows included the mock sacrifice of a nude woman.[22] But it was Ozzy Osbourne's band Black Sabbath that *Rolling Stone* magazine described as "England's answer to Coven."[23] The band was originally called "Earth" and played blues music. But, in 1969, the band was renamed in reference to the 1963 film of the same name featuring Boris Karloff. Their first album has been described as the birth of heavy metal and it drew inspiration from Dennis Wheatley novels, as well as H. P. Lovecraft and J. R. R. Tolkien. In a 2017 interview, guitarist Tony Iommi stated, "We wanted to create a vibe like you get off horror films—try and create a tension within the music."[24] Despite these dark themes, Black Sabbath's lyrics warned that Satan was to be feared, not worshiped. Their song "War Pigs" (1970) compared generals to witches and prophesied that God would soon punish the war pigs while, "Satan, laughing, spreads his wings." When the band saw *The Exorcist* in 1974, they were so terrified they had to all sleep in the same hotel room afterward.[25] Nevertheless, many assumed that Black Sabbath was glorifying Satan. In his solo career, Ozzy Osbourne leaned further into this perception, playing with occult and demonic themes and imagery in his lyrics and music videos. Osbourne's first solo album, *The Blizzard of Ozz* (1980), featured the song "Mr. Crowley" about the life of magician Aleister Crowley. Less than two months after the release of the album, Ronald Reagan was elected, setting the stage for a culture war over heavy metal.

The PMRC and Backmasking

The Reagan administration saw a wave of conservative policies and the expansion of the Christian right. The conservative mood emboldened conservative culture warriors even as it drove the counterculture to seek new outlets for resistance and opposition. For suburban white males, especially, heavy metal offered an appealing alternative to the Reagan era's vision of law and order. In 1985, Tipper Gore, wife of then-senator Al Gore, formed the PMRC with the help of a group called the "Washington Wives," a circle of women married to influential and politically connected men. The Washington Wives included Susan Baker (wife of secretary of state James Baker), Pam Howar (wife of realtor Raymond Howar), Sally Nevius (wife of Washington City Council Chairman John Nevius), and eventually grew to twenty-two members. The PMRC is most famous for their push to force a rating system for music to give parents more control over what sort of music their kids were buying.

The PMRC drew up a list of songs they dubbed "The Filthy Fifteen" with lyrics they deemed objectionable. The Filthy Fifteen was presented in two columns, one listing the title of the song, the other a proposed label for the type of offense given: "profane or sexually explicit," "violent," "drugs and alcohol," or "occult." Notably the only two songs listed as "occult" were heavy metal songs: Mercyful Fate's "Into the Coven" and Venom's "Possessed." In her book, *Raising PG Kids in an X Rated Society* (1989), Gore wrote, "By using Satanic symbols on the concert stage and album covers, such as those employed by Ozzy Osborne, Ronnie James Dio, and groups like Venom, Slayer, Black Sabbath, Mötley Crüe, Celtic Frost, Mercyful Fate, W.A.S.P., and Iron Maiden, certain heavy metal bands lure teenagers into what one expert has called 'the cult of the eighties.' Many kids experiment with the deadly satanic game, and get hooked."[26] This image of the vulnerable teenager experimenting with "occult" music was the plot of several heavy metal films including *Trick or Treat* (1986) and *Black Roses* (1988).

On September 19, 1985, the PMRC used their Washington connections to schedule a hearing before the senate to lobby for their proposed label system. Three musicians spoke in opposition to the labels: avant-garde jazz musician Frank Zappa; lead singer of Twisted Sister, Dee Snider; and, surprisingly, country folk musician John Denver all testified that the label system amounted to artistic censorship and therefore violated the artists' civil liberties. But the PMRC was ultimately successful, and their efforts resulted in the adoption of the black and white "Parental Advisory" sticker still in use today.

The PMRC hearings also provided a platform for a new conspiracy theory about rock music known as backmasking. Backmasking refers to a process in which a message is recorded backward onto a track that is meant to be played forward.[27] The Beatles experimented with this technique on their album *Revolver* (1966). In 1969, a rumor surfaced that Paul McCartney had died and that this fact was being concealed from the public. The evidence of this conspiracy was allegedly hidden in The Beatles' experimental sound collage "Revolution 9" from *The White Album* (1968), which, played backward, revealed such messages as "turn me on, dead man," and "Paul is a dead man, miss him." Following this rumor, rock fans experimented with playing records backward to search for hidden messages. While bands occasionally did use backmasking for artistic purposes, normally the result was meaningless sound that functioned like a Rorschach test in which the listener could discern whatever message they wished.

The connection between backmasking and Satanic activity was planted in the popular imagination by *The Exorcist* (1973). When Father Karras takes a recording of demonic noises and plays it backward, he can hear the demon say intelligible messages, such as "I am no one" and "Fear the priest." Significantly, the backmasked message in this scene is a kind of "confession" from the demon in which its true nature and motivations are revealed. By the 1980s, Satanic cults had largely replaced communists in conspiracy theories about subliminal messages. Michael Millis was one of the first conservative Christians to allege Satanic messages were backmasked in rock songs. In a 1981 radio interview he explained:

> As I work with kids every day, I find sometimes a literal force field around them. A force field of the lyrics of the songs that they hear from AC/DC, from Black Sabbath, from Blue Oyster Cult, from the Rolling Stones. So many times we come to young people and tell them not to listen to rock music. Parents tell them not to listen to rock music and what they need is proof. That's why I want to research this so intently. I want them to know that we know what we're talking about with this.[28]

Note Millis's emphasis on "proof." Whereas Noebel essentially asked readers to trust him that rock beats were hypnotic, "backmasking" provided what appeared to be empirical evidence of a secret message—especially if the listener had already been psychologically primed to hear the message before listening to a reversed track.

In 1982, a self-described "neuroscientific researcher" named William H. Yarroll appeared on the Praise the Lord Network and claimed that, played backward, Led Zeppelin's "Stairway to Heaven" contained the phrase, "Here's to my sweet Satan."[29] According to Yarroll, rock stars were working directly with Anton LaVey's Church of Satan to implant these messages. California Republican Phil Wyman took Yarroll's claims seriously and assembled a state consumer protection committee on the subject. Wyman warned that backmasking "can manipulate our behavior without our knowledge and turn us into disciples of the anti-Christ."[30] When concerned citizens began playing rock records backward to find Satanic messages, they believed they found them. They heard "Satan moves though our voices" in Styx's "Snowblind" and "Yes, Satan organized his own religion" in The Eagles' "Hotel California." Yaroll's discovery in "Stairway to Heaven" was even expanded to, "I live for Satan . . . the Lord turns me off . . . there's no escaping it . . . here's to my sweet Satan . . . . there's power in Satan . . . he will give you 666."[31] Decades later, Led Zeppelin guitarist Jimmy Page gave an address at Oxford University. When someone asked about a hidden Satanic message in "Stairway to Heaven," he answered, "Oh gosh, it's hard enough writing the music one way round rather than backwards."[32]

The 1985, PMRC congressional hearings gave an air of legitimacy to these conspiracy theories. Dr. Joseph Stuessy, a music professor from the University of Texas at San Antonio, testified on the findings of "music psychology." He claimed that heavy metal was entirely unlike other forms of music because, "Its principal themes are, as you have already heard, extreme violence, extreme rebellion, substance abuse, sexual promiscuity and perversion and Satanism. I know personally of no form of popular music before which has had as one of its central elements the element of hatred." More importantly, heavy metal influenced behavior in a variety of ways, including through subliminal messages. Dr. Stuessy testified, "The message may also be covert or subliminal. Sometimes subaudible tracks are mixed in underneath other, louder tracks. These are heard by the subconscious but not the conscious mind. Sometimes the messages are audible but are backwards, called backmasking. There is disagreement among experts regarding the effectiveness of subliminals. We need more research on that."[33]

While admitting that "more research was needed," this testimony gave the impression that backmasking was real and taken seriously by scientists and the federal government. It is hardly surprising, then, that four months later, in December 1988, when Raymond Belknap, then eighteen, and James Vance, twenty, committed suicide with a shotgun after six hours of drinking, smoking marijuana, and listening to Judas Priest's album Stained Class (1978), the parents claimed their deaths were caused by subliminal messages in the album.[34] The alleged scenario was nearly identical to the plot of The Manchurian Candidate: hidden signals in the music had triggered Belknap and Vance, causing them to carry out a death pact. At trial, the prosecution played the album forward, backward, and sped up in an attempt to persuade the jury of the subliminal messages.[35] Although Judas Priest won their day in court, they did so only because the judge ruled that they had not intentionally placed messages in their songs that led to suicide. A noise that sounded a bit like the phrase "Do it!" was explained as a combination of singer Rob

Halford exhaling combined with the sound of a "Leslie guitar." The noise only became apparent when the guitar and vocals tracks were combined. Weirdly, the judge did *not* dispute the prosecution's claim that this sound was, indeed, a "subliminal message" that contributed to the suicide.[36]

Ironically, claims of backmasking inspired several bands to experiment with the technique. Electric Light Orchestra's album was accused of hiding backmasked messages in their album *Eldorado* (1974). So, in *Face the Music* (1975) they deliberately added a backmasked message to their song "Fire on High": "The music is reversible, but time—turn back! Turn back! Turn back! Turn back!" Pop band The B-52's included a message hidden in the song "Detour Through Your Mind" in 1986: "I buried my parakeet in the back-yard. Oh no, you're playing your record backwards. Watch out, you might ruin your needle." Prince even included a backmasked message about the re-turn of Jesus at the end of "Darling Nikki": "Hello, how are you? Fine, fine, 'cause I know that the Lord is coming soon. Coming, coming soon." "Darling Nikki" was among the songs listed among the "Filthy Fifteen" because of its references to masturbation. Ironically, the PMRC had missed an actual case of backmasking. The response from artists can be seen as a form of ostension in which rumors of backmasking inspired artists to engage in the very prac-tice they were suspected of doing.

The Heavy Metal Murders

Alongside rumors of backmasking and anxieties about the corruption of youth, the myth of the heavy metal Satanists was fueled by a handful of high-profile murders that were blamed on Satanic music. Chief among these were Richard Ramirez and Ricky Kasso, both of whom committed their crimes between 1984 and 1985. Sensationalized in the media, these figures appeared to prove that warnings about music that could transform young men into Satanic killers had finally come to pass. They were also parodied and pastiched in a slew of horror films.

Dubbed "The Night Stalker" by the media, Ramirez raped and murdered, seemingly at random, residents of neighborhoods across Los Angeles and the San Francisco Bay Area. Victims ranged from children to the elderly, and they came from varied ethnic and economic backgrounds. Ramirez dressed his crimes in Satanic symbols, often drawing pentagrams and other Satanic graffiti at the scene or on his victims. He sometimes ordered his victims (according to those who survived) to "swear on Satan."[37] At his arraignment in 1985, he famously scrawled a pentagram on his hand and yelled "Hail Satan." After being sentenced to death, Ramirez remarked, "Big deal. Death always went with the territory. See you in Disneyland."[38]

Ramirez was a fan of heavy metal and would occasionally give the rock sign of "the horns" for photographers. The discovery of an AC/DC hat at one of his crime scenes lent itself to a facile narrative that metal had led him first to Satanism and then to murder. This narrative served to distract from more significant factors that contributed to his pathological behavior. Ramirez suffered from seizures as a result of receiving blows to the head as a child. He was abused by his father and, at the age of twelve, began spending more time with his uncle, Miguel "Mike" Ramirez, an Army Green Beret and Vietnam veteran. Miguel showed his nephew graphic pictures of people he had murdered and women he had raped during his time in Vietnam. He also taught Ramirez supposed military skills, such as how to "kill with stealth."[39] In 1973, Miguel shot his wife, Jessie, in the face, in front of the young Ramirez. Later that year, Ramirez went to live with his older sister and her husband, a peeping Tom who took Ramirez with him on his nocturnal exploits. But these more entrenched problems of mental illness, child abuse, and the ongoing trauma related to veterans returning from Vietnam were not as exciting or simple as the idea of Satanic music transforming people into "night stalkers."

In 1984, seventeen-year-old Ricky Kasso of Long Island, New York, murdered his friend Gary Lauwers, in what the media dubbed the "Say you love Satan" murder. Kasso frequently spent nights on the streets after being kicked out of his parents' affluent home. He indulged in drugs, including LSD and PCP, and was known to his friends as "The Acid King." He enjoyed heavy metal and read LaVey's *Satanic Bible*. He was also charged with robbing a grave, allegedly in search of a skull for use in Satanic rituals. Kasso and a friend decided to celebrate April 30, 1984—a day celebrated by Anton LaVey as the Satanic holiday of Walpurgisnacht—by driving to the house featured in *The Amityville Horror* and attempting a Satanic ceremony on the lawn.[40] In May, Kasso was hospitalized for pneumonia and his parents tried to use this opportunity to have him forcibly admitted to a psychiatric hospital. They feared Kasso was becoming a threat to himself and others, but the hospital disagreed and Kasso was released.[41]

The following summer, Gary Lauwers angered Kasso by stealing ten bags of PCP from him while he was passed out. On the night of June 19, Kasso invited Lauwers along with two friends to get high with him in the woods. After taking doses of LSD and smoking PCP, Kasso confronted Lauwers about the theft: Kasso stabbed Lauwers thirty-two times and gouged out his eyes. As Kasso stabbed Lauwers he allegedly cried, "Say you love Satan!," a phrase that seemed derivative of reportage of Ramirez's crimes from the year before. Upon his arrest, Kasso was wearing an AC/DC shirt. He never stood trial because a few days after his arrest he hung himself in his jail cell.[42]

The most significant factors in the murder of Gary Lauwers appear to have been Kasso's undiagnosed mental illness combined with drug abuse. But even more so than Ramirez, Kasso appeared to be the perfect example of the dangerous influence of heavy metal. He came from a stable, white, affluent household, but he lived much of his life on the street, involved with drugs and heavy metal. In fact, Bob Larson lists Ramirez and Kasso alongside Charles Manson as a sort of unholy trinity that exemplifies a pattern of "Satanic slayings." For Larson, these crimes were directly related to the failure of parents to respond to dangerous youth subcultures: "Charles Manson, Richard Ramirez, Ricky Kasso, and other killers for Satan weren't born bad. They were bent bad by a society that neglected their basic human needs and substituted affluence for affection. In defiance, they became satanists, determined to exploit evil and get forcibly what they couldn't receive freely from those who should have loved them. A lack of self-esteem was the chief reason they exchanged virtue for evil."[43] Kasso's story inspired several forgettable films including *My Sweet Satan* (1994), *Black Circle Boys* (1997), and *Ricky 6* (2000).

The following year, seventeen-year-old Sean Sellers of Oklahoma City was arrested for the murder of his mother and stepfather. Sellers spent thirteen years on death row before his execution in 1999. During this time, he fully endorsed the narrative of a good teenager seduced by the Satanic forces of *Dungeons and Dragons* and heavy metal. At one point, he claimed that these activities had allowed a demon named Ezurate to possess him and commit the murders. He became a regular guest caller on Bob Larson's radio show and wrote his own book on the dangers of Satanism called *Web of Darkness*. In 1987, Sellers appeared in a film by Pastor Fletcher A. Brothers called *Escaping Satan's Web*. Brothers builds on Sellers's narrative, adding there is not one case where a person who has "committed a heinous crime because of Satanism [that] rock music wasn't involved."

In 1987, the FCC eliminated the fairness doctrine, which required that controversial issues be presented in a way that was honest, equitable, and balanced. This opened the floodgates to tabloid talk shows and other forms of "infotainment." As demonstrated by *The Geraldo Rivera Show*'s "Exposing Satan's Underground," talk shows loved stories about Satanism. These programs amplified the Satanic Panic, causing stories about Satanism to appear both urgent and credible.[44] Law enforcement began to echo these claims as well. Training manuals created for seminars on "occult crime" from the late 1980s and early 1990s typically ended with a list of "Satanic symbols" that police needed to be able recognize. These lists often included such innocuous symbols as the yin-yang or the Egyptian ankh. Invariably, they included band logos for KISS, Ozzy Osbourne, and AC/DC.[45] The associations between rock music and occultism continued into the 1990s. In 1993, pastor Joe Schimmel produced his video presentation *Rock-n-Roll Sorcerers of the New Age Revolution*. Other than its wacky title, there was little original in the video. It was the same medley of conspiracy theories associating rock music with Asian mysticism, the teachings of Aleister Crowley, and subversive political movements. But, as we will see, 1993 was an important year for the myth of the heavy metal Satanist.

Heavy Metal Horror Films

Horror directors have used heavy metal as metonymy for the dangers faced by modern youth for almost as long as metal has existed. One of the earliest examples is Wes Craven's *The Last House on the Left* (1972). The film begins with two seventeen-year-old girls embarking for a concert in the city, where they are abducted, raped, and killed. The band they hope to see is called "Bloodlust" and one of the girls' parents inquires, "Aren't those the guys who dismember chickens?" to which she responds, "They only did that once." This dialogue was likely a reference to Alice Cooper's performance at the Toronto Rock n' Roll Revival concert on September 13, 1969. Although there are varying versions of the story, Cooper hurled a live chicken from the stage, assuming it would fly away; instead, it plummeted into the crowd who—to Cooper's horror—ripped it apart.[46] Transplanted into Craven's story, Cooper's goofy antics are now part of a tableau of dangers threatening to murder the innocent and destroy the family.

By the 1980s, discourse about the dangers of heavy metal had developed into a sub-genre of "metalsploitation" films. For the most part, these were lazily written films that used metal bands as background for established slasher plots, as well as gratuitous nudity and violence. In some ways, they resembled exploitation films of the 1970s with stereotyped depictions of hippies and bikers. However, many of these films made implicit critiques of the hysteria over heavy metal. The ultra-low budget *Terror on Tour* (1980) was one of the earliest examples of the genre. It featured a band called The Clowns—an obvious parody of KISS—who play violent music and engage in debauched parties backstage. Someone begins to murder prostitutes while wearing the band's signature make-up. At the film's denouement, the killer is revealed to be not a member of The Clowns, but their manager, who is motivated by his hatred of prostitutes. Holding a bloody knife, he gives a speech on the sacrality of motherhood, stating, "I had to kill them. They had no moral values at all." While this speech is primarily meant to make a dull plot less predictable, it is significant that the film does not blame violence on transgressive music but rather on those espousing puritanical notions of "family values."

Rocktober Blood (1984) takes place during a planned reunion show for a band whose lead singer, Billy Harper, went on a killing spree and was subsequently executed for his crimes. As the reunion show approaches, the murders resume and Billy's ex-girlfriend, Lynn, is convinced that Billy is stalking her from beyond the grave. In fact, she is seeing Billy's twin brother, John, who framed Billy for the murders. John locks Lynn inside a prop coffin that is displayed on stage during the reunion concert and tells her he will murder her during the show's finale. Before he can do this, security rush in and John screams "I'm back!" as the credits roll. An actual rock band named Sorcery acted in the film and wrote the soundtrack.

Rocktober Blood pokes fun at some of the tropes of the panic. Mock human sacrifices had been incorporated into rock shows for over a decade. The plot of *actually* murdering Lynn on stage assumes the audience's understanding that the shocking aspects of rock shows are, in fact, just ridiculous attempts to entertain the audience. Sorcery also mocked claims of backmasking, writing a track for the film called "Kcab m'I" ("I'm back" backward.) Similar attempts to use heavy metal to enliven otherwise boring slasher plots included *Murder Rock* (1984), *Heavy Metal Massacre* (1989), and *Shock 'Em Dead* (1991).

Hard Rock Zombies (1985) built on the genre by adding elements of the supernatural. In a plot that parodies *Footloose* (1984), a band books a show in a small town that has outlawed rock and roll. In fact, the town is run by an aging Hitler, his wife Eva Braun (who is also a werewolf!), and a cabal of Nazi cultists. The Nazis murder the entire band, except the lead singer, who then uses lyrics he found in a medieval grimoire to resurrect his bandmates to wreak zombie revenge. *Hard Rock Zombies* is pure low-budget exploitation, but it provides an interesting twist on conspiracy theories about occult influences in rock music. The idea that rock songs are actually ancient spells appeared in Jack Chick's comic *Spellbound?*, but here the band is using this magic for sympathetic purposes while the opponents of rock are literally Nazis.

The first film that directly addressed the moral panic over heavy metal was Charles Martin Smith's *Trick or Treat* (1986). Smith's film not only shows the fear of rock music, but it also makes it a central theme. *Trick or Treat* portrays the life of Eddie, an outcast metalhead, nicknamed Ragman and bullied by the popular jocks at school. He is a devoted fan of rock star Sammi Curr, who attended the same high school as Eddie and is scheduled to perform a show there on Halloween. Because of his occult and violent performances, Sammi is banned from playing, and shortly thereafter dies in a mysterious hotel fire. His idol gone, a distraught Eddie visits his friend Nuke, a DJ at a local radio station (played by Gene Simmons of KISS). Nuke gives him the only copy of Sammi's final, unreleased album, "Songs in the Key of Death." After dreaming of Sammi performing a Satanic ritual in the burning hotel, Eddie plays the record backward, releasing Sammi's spirit to wreak havoc with his new Satanic powers. At first, Sammi helps Eddie seek revenge on Eddie's bullies, who are just like those who bullied Sammi during his time in high school. But soon the revenge escalates into murder. Sammi even uses his electrical powers to reach through the television and kill anti-rock evangelist Aaron Gilstrom (played by Ozzy Osbourne). Eddie eventually confronts and defeats Sammi at the Halloween dance.

The portrayal of heavy metal in *Trick or Treat* is ambivalent. Unlike many other counterculture horror exploitation films of the past, Eddie the metalhead is a good-hearted teenager, not a caricature. Moral entrepreneurs are soundly mocked in this film, as is evident by casting Osbourne, the father of heavy metal, as an anti-rock evangelist. *Trick or Treat* came out only one year after a family sued Osbourne for their adolescent son's suicide. One the other hand, the story of an innocent, misunderstood teenager who falls under the supernatural influence of heavy metal was essentially the same one told about Ricky Kasso and Sean Sellers. As a Satanic spirit, dead rockstar Sammi Curr is a stand-in for the idea of an insidious presence hiding within rock music, guiding young men to acts of evil. Curr's abilities all involve audio equipment—he grows stronger the more his album is played and the more people listen to his music. Then again, Eddie manages to defeat Sammi without renouncing metal fandom. In fact, Eddie plans on pursuing a career as a DJ. This is an unusual turn in a genre of films where teenagers who engage in illicit activities are typically murdered. At any rate, *Trick or Treat* was a box office success, earning nearly $3 million in its opening weekend.

While not able to capitalize on the financial success of *Trick or Treat*, writer John Fasano nonetheless made two attempts: *Rock and Roll Nightmare* (1987) and *Black Roses* (1988). Both these films locate heavy metal within a supernatural realm of demons and the occult, but on opposite ends of the spectrum. In *Rock and Roll Nightmare*, metal band Triton rents an old farmhouse to get away from the big city and work on new material, using a classic slasher trope of isolated young people. (*Monster Dog* [1984] and *Blood Tracks* [1985] also feature rock bands who travel to remote locations to record and meet gruesome deaths.) Sure enough, demons begin to pick members of Triton off one by one, eventually leaving only lead singer, John Triton. When Satan himself appears, John reveals that he is actually the archangel Triton and that his entire band had merely been illusions he created to lure Satan out of hiding. A ridiculous battle scene ensues in which Triton defeats Satan (represented by a slime-covered puppet) and banishes him to hell. *Rock and Roll Nightmare* is unique in that it preserves the idea of a Manichaean war of good and evil while presenting the metal band as agents of God.

Fasano's other heavy metal film, *Black Roses*, goes in the completely opposite direction. A band called The Black Roses arrives in a small town to play a series of concerts. The parents object until the sympathetic English teacher and principal argue that this is merely some harmless rebellion. Damien, the band's leader, invites the parents to see a show. The Black Roses play ballads about teenage love clad in white shirts. Satisfied, the adults leave and then The Black Roses tear off their disguises and rip into the real show. The band members are actually demons, who have come to corrupt and destroy teenagers with their evil metal. Eventually, the hip English teacher figures it out, and begins to fight back. He rids the town of the hellish menace, but not before the power of their demon rock turns quite a few unsuspecting teens into skeletons.

What sets *Black Roses* apart from similar films is that there is no intermediary between music and supernatural evil. There is no backmasking or occult rituals hidden in the lyrics: the band are literal demons, and their music is indisputably evil. Fasano credits Tipper Gore as direct inspiration for the movie, recalling in an interview, "Tipper got it into her head that teens were committing suicide after listening to heavy metal. She said it was the devil's music, and back in 1985 there was a huge movement against it. My ex-girlfriend Cindy Cirlle, who wrote the script, said, 'What if this band really was from hell?' "[47]

None of these movies were acclaimed horror films like *Rosemary's Baby* or *The Exorcist*. While some, notably *Trick or Treat*, achieved a cult following, these were mostly forgettable films marketed to a niche audience. However, they were significant for several reasons. First, these films provide a "sociophobic window" into how the public understood the heavy metal subculture in the 1980s.[48] It is significant that plots in which bands summon demons, conduct human sacrifices, or hide secret messages in their albums did not have to be explained to audiences because these ideas had already saturated the public's imagination. Second, these films contributed to an echo chamber in which heavy metal was associated with Satanism and criminal activity. Third, by portraying transgressive, Satanic bands as fodder for campy, low-budget plots, these films may have fueled escalation within the heavy metal subculture as some bands now had to go further to appear genuinely sinister. Certainly, this dynamic was at stake in the events that culminated in the murder of Norwegian heavy metal promoter Øystein Aarseth in 1993.

Becoming the Heavy Metal Satanist: Varg Vikernes

By the end of the 1980s, heavy metal had developed into numerous subgenres. Of these, "black metal" has been described as the "most extreme" and includes those bands that most openly embrace associations with Satanism and the sinister.[49] British band Venom, which drew inspiration from LaVey, is often credited with creating black metal. Subsequent black metal bands included Bathory, Hellhammer, and Mercyful Fate. Mercyful Fate's vocalist, King Diamond, even became a member of the Church of Satan. These bands often wore inverted crosses, black and white "corpse paint" on their faces, and sometimes black leather gauntlets covered in spikes. Their performances often began with dark soundscapes punctuated by funeral bells or Latin chanting and crescendoed into violent percussion and cries of "Hail Satan!" All this "evil" imagery was deemed necessary to distinguish black metal from "hair metal" or "glam metal" acts that celebrated sex and partying. Black metal bands wanted to be taken seriously and be feared, even as their excesses struck some as patently ridiculous. This resulted in a sort of race in which metal acts incorporated ever more extreme elements to distinguish

themselves from the "posers." In Norway, this spiral reached its logical conclusion with metal musicians engaging in actual murder.

Øystein Aarseth, also known by his self-applied nickname "Euronymous,"
owned a record shop in Oslo called Helvete ("Hell") that became the social
hub of the Scandinavian black metal scene. He also operated a record label,
Deathlike Silence Productions, and he founded a band named Mayhem.
Aarseth advocated Satanism, but he took issue with LaVey's Church of Satan
for being insufficiently dangerous and evil. He said of LaVey, "The Church of
Satan call themselves Satanists because they think it's funny and provoking."
In opposing what they saw as the injustices of Christianity, LaVeyan Satanists
understood themselves to be on the side of good. By contrast, Aarseth said of
himself and *true* Satanists, "We are against the Church of Satan because we
are against goodness."[50]

Mayhem, fueled by Aarseth's rhetoric, continued to push the envelope.
Lead singer Per Yngve Ohlin, known as "Dead," was the first musician to refer
to his black and white make-up as "corpse paint." He would bury his clothes
weeks before a show and then dig them up to wear on stage. Ohlin's stage
performance involved cutting himself as a "sacrifice to Satan."[51] In 1991, he
committed suicide by cutting his wrists and then shooting himself with a
shotgun. Upon discovering the body, Aarseth callously waited to alert police
so that he could take pictures of the corpse and collect pieces of Ohiln's skull
as souvenirs. One of the photos was later used in the cover art for Mayhem's
bootleg live album *Dawn of the Black Hearts* (1995).

Ohlin's suicide only emboldened Aarseth and his circle. Aarseth claimed
that Ohlin had taken his own life because metal was becoming "too commercial."[52] Mayhem preached anti-Christian hate and praised Mao, Hitler,
and Stalin as exemplars of Christian persecution. Religion scholar Massimo
Introvigne frames this rhetoric as sophomoric yet dangerous: "Most of
these musicians had only a primary school education and deep theological
considerations might hardly be expected from them. They mixed Satanism,
paganism, and radical politics in a sort of primitive cocktail. It was not culturally sophisticated, but it was dangerous."[53]

Mayhem was joined by Kristian "Varg" Vikernes, who had his own
black metal project, Burzum. Aarseth and Vikernes pushed each other further. In June 1992, they began burning Norway's historic stave churches
and encouraging others to do so. A wave of church arsons swept Norway,
outraging police, politicians, and the media. This publicity inspired others in
the Norwegian black metal scene to commit crimes to prove they were not

posers. In August, Norwegian drummer Bård G. Eithun, known as "Faust," stabbed a gay man to death in a park after having been solicited for sex. He planned to turn himself in to the police, and he told Aarseth and Vikernes the next day. Instead of turning him over, the two black metal leaders decided to burn the historical Holmenkollen Chapel in Oslo, and they took Eithun with them.[54]

Amidst this escalation, Vikernes sought to steal the spotlight by talking to one of Norway's largest papers, *Bergens Tidende*. In this interview, Vikernes admitted that he and others in the black metal scene were Satanists, responsible for the church burnings. He also claimed to have murdered a man in Lillehammer. This exposure led to numerous arrests within the black metal community, prompting Aarseth to close Helvete.[55] During this same period, Vikernes became involved with a neo-Nazi organization— the Norwegian Pagan Front—and he formally changed his name to Varg. Varg means "wolf" in Norwegian, but it has connotations of a lawless person. Vikernes and Aarseth had a falling out after the *Bergens Tidende* interview. Vikernes claimed that Aarseth threatened his life, although there is little evidence to suggest this was the case. In August 1993, Vikernes and another musician, Snorre Westvold Ruch, traveled to Aarseth's apartment where Vikernes murdered him, stabbing him twenty-three times. Vikernes was sentenced to twenty-one years in prison, the maximum sentence allowed by Norwegian law. Today he lives in France where he continues to make music.

The entire episode of Mayhem and the Norwegian black metal scene can be read as a case of ostension in which the myth of the heavy metal Satanist was truly brought to life. There were several dynamics at play in this process. One was an ongoing process of "dilution and distillation" within a radical subculture. As heavy metal became more mainstream, the symbols of being an insider to the subculture became "diluted," losing their signifying value. This drove figures like Aarseth, who prized their insider status, to seek ways to "distill" the culture by erecting increasingly extreme barriers to entry. This is a pattern that often happens in genres of music that celebrate authenticity and a transgressive outsider status. In their work on the idea of sincerity and its social consequences, sociologists Adam Seligman and colleagues argued that suicide by heroin—a fate that befell GG Allin, Kurt Cobain, and numerous other rock stars—is the logical conclusion to efforts to prove authenticity: "When all words are false, when even cutting yourself with broken shards on stage could simply be pandering to the market, suicide is the ultimate rejection of convention and evidence of sincerity"[56] We might quibble here that Mayhem's Per Yngve Ohlin took this slightly further, electing for an especially gruesome suicide rather than a drug overdose.

Another dynamic is what sociologist Ikuya Sato calls the "corruption of play." In his study of adolescent *bosozoku* biker gangs in Japan, Sato found that adolescents from affluent families formed biker gangs that committed gang rape and other serious crimes—a pattern similar to that of Aarseth. Sato concluded that these activities began as play, performing the role of a dangerous biker; however, if the play escalates into irrevocable consequences, the play-role becomes reality. Sato identifies three factors that contribute to this process: collective encouragement, intense involvement, and a challenge to reach the limit.[57] All these elements were present in the case of Aarseth and Vikernes: they received encouragement from peers in the black metal scene, including fan letters from around the world; their involvement in the scene became all encompassing; and they were competitive to see who could perform the most extreme act. One friend commented, "It sounds really silly, but I think there was a little bit of a contest between them to see who could be more evil. It created a very difficult situation, especially for Euronymous, who wanted the glamour and the showbiz."[58] Despite the tragedy of the murders, there was indeed something silly about the entire affair, pointing to its origins in play.

But did horror films contribute to these events in any way? While there is not a direct connection, it seems that the genre of heavy metal horror films aggravated the dilution of the heavy metal subculture while also contributing to the cultural script that played out in Norway. By the end of the 1980s, the most sinister elements associated with heavy metal—evil, occultism, and human sacrifice—had been reduced to hackneyed tropes in films marketed as entertainment to an increasingly mainstream audience. *The Gate* (1987) featured a metal band that hid demonic secrets in their lyrics and it was aimed at young children. How could metal musicians expect to appear sinister when the most "evil" elements of their music were being portrayed in this way? The answer to this question was also in films: *Terror on Tour* and *Rocktober Blood* showed musicians in black and white face paint who actually murdered people. Especially for Bård G. Eithun, murder seemed to be the only way to claim legitimacy as a transgressive musician. Even if no one from Aarseth's circle ever saw these movies (which seems unlikely), it is significant that "heavy metal murder" was depicted in film a decade before such things occurred in reality.

In 2018, these events were adapted into the film *Lords of Chaos*, based on the book by Michael Moynihan and Didrik Søderlind. Vikernes panned the film as "just a lot of made-up crap" and objected that he was portrayed by a Jewish actor.[59] While gruesome, *Lords of Chaos* is not, strictly speaking, a horror film. Critics complained that they could not tell whether the tone was meant to be tragic or comedic. But this ambiguity seems appropriate for a story about a subculture obsessed with media and their own image while also desperately striving for sinister authenticity.

Hunting the Heavy Metal Satanist: The West Memphis Three

The same summer that Vikernes murdered Aarseth in Norway, a murder trial was unfolding in West Memphis, Arkansas. Located firmly in the Bible belt, West Memphis sits across the Mississippi river from Memphis, Tennessee. According to 2010 census data, the town had a population of twenty-six thousand people, a low average level of education, and a high proportion of people living below the poverty line.[60] On the evening of May 5, eight-year-olds Stevie Branch, Michael Moore, and Christopher Byers of West Memphis were seen playing together and never returned. The following day officers discovered their bodies at the bottom of a water-filled ditch in some nearby woods. The bodies had been stripped naked and bound using the victim's shoelaces. There was also damage that law enforcement interpreted as bite marks on the bodies. Byers's testicles and the head of his penis appeared to have been removed. Details of what was assumed to be sexual mutilation were leaked to the press. On May 10, *USA Today* ran the headline, " 'Monstrous Evil' Haunts Town." According to FBI statistics, parents and stepparents are the most likely perpetrators in homicide cases with victims aged six to eleven.[61] But almost immediately, law enforcement began working on the theory that the children had been ritually murdered by cultists. The West Memphis Police Department assigned the case number "93-05-0 666" to the murders, linking the investigation to hackneyed notions of Satanism.[62]

On May 7, police interviewed eighteen-year-old Damien Echols because of his suspected involvement in "cult activity." To police, Echols *looked* like the mythic heavy metal Satanist: he was interested in occultism, wore black clothes, had a tattoo, and read Stephen King. He was a high school dropout and had been arrested for shoplifting. He had also been diagnosed with depression and spent several months in a psychiatric institution.[63] In an interview with Mara Leveritt of the *Arkansas Times*, Echols said that he was first teased about being a witch in the seventh grade. He claimed he changed his name from "Michael" to "Damien" after the nineteenth-century Catholic saint. However, locals assumed the name referred to the horror film *The Omen*. Years before the murders, county juvenile officers Steve Jones and Jerry B. Driver were already investigating possible teenage occultism in the county. Early in the investigation, Driver produced a list of eight teenagers believed to be involved with Satanism, including Damien Echols and Jason Baldwin. He declared that when the investigation was over, one or more of the teenagers on the list would be charged with the murders.[64]

Searching for evidence linking Echols to the murders, police recruited Vicki Hutchinson, a single mother who had a few run-ins with local police. Hutchinson sometimes hired seventeen-year-old Jessie Misskelley, an acquaintance of Echols, to babysit for her. Charges were dropped against Hutchinson, and she volunteered to "seduce" Echols to learn about his cult activities. Through Misskelley, Hutchinson succeeded in getting Echols to visit her trailer, where police had hidden a recording device. They also littered the living area with books on the occult. Hutchinson said she wanted to become a witch, at which Echols only laughed. She asked about rumors that Echols liked to drink blood and Echols answered he encouraged those rumors as a "mechanism" to keep people at bay. She asked, "What's a mechanism?" and Echols answered, "It means leave me the fuck alone."[65] Hutchinson listened to the tape and said the quality was excellent. But police claimed it was indecipherable and later reported the tape lost.

On May 28, 1993, Hutchinson made a statement to police that Echols had taken her and Misskelley to an "esbat" (a witch's gathering) where Echols bragged about committing the murders. This story fell apart almost immediately but it enabled police to proceed with their investigation by interrogating Misskelley. In 2004, Hutchinson told a reporter that this story had been a "total fabrication": Jerry Driver, who considered himself an expert on the occult, had essentially dictated to her what to say, including teaching her the word "esbat." Hutchinson believed she could lose custody of her son or even become a suspect if she did not cooperate. During the trials, she was also moved to a motel in Memphis so that attorneys for the defense could not question her. Hutchinson later spent time in prison for drug offenses and writing hot checks. She claimed that following a conversion experience in prison, she could no longer remain silent about her false testimony.[66]

The interrogation of Misskelley lasted nearly twelve hours. Misskelley was a minor, had an IQ of 72, and was questioned without a parent or attorney present. Police also tricked him into believing he had failed a lie detector test. Finally, Misskelley confessed that he, Echols, and sixteen-year-old Jason Baldwin had committed the murders. He was tried separately from Echols and Baldwin, and he pleaded not guilty to three charges of murder. There were numerous inconsistencies in Misskelley's confession, which he later recanted. The defense brought in social psychologist Richard Ofshe, who testified that Misskelley had given a coerced confession. Despite this testimony, a jury found Misskelley guilty, and he was sentenced to life in prison plus an additional forty years.[67]

The trial of Echols and Baldwin focused heavily on Echols's alleged involvement in Satanism. The prosecution brought in Dale W. Griffis as their star witness. A retired police captain, Griffis established a second career as an expert on "occult crime." Although he was addressed as "Doctor Griffis" in court, his doctoral degree came from Columbia Pacific University, an unaccredited distance-learning school that was finally closed by the state of California in 2000 for consumer fraud. However, the court ruled that Griffis's academic pedigree did not disqualify him as an expert witness. Griffis testified that there was evidence of occult activity in every detail of the crime: the location where the bodies were found, the date on which they were killed, the mutilation, and the method of restraint all had "occult" significance. Much of this was numerological: the victims were eight years old and eight is "a witch's number." The number of victims was also Satanic in Griffis's convoluted numerology: "One of the most powerful numbers in, in the practice of satanic belief is 666, and some believe the beast wrote a 6 as 3." Having testified that these crimes were Satanic, Griffis explained that Satanists often wear black T-shirts and repeated searches of Echols's home had found no fewer than fifteen black T-shirts.[68]

Misskelley refused to testify against Echols and Baldwin and his confession was deemed inadmissible. However, a transcript of the confession was leaked to the *Memphis Commercial Appeal*. On June 7, the paper printed parts of the confession with the headline, "TEEN DESCRIBES CULT TORTURE OF BOYS: MISKELLY TELLS POLICE OF SEX MUTILATION." Further evidence of a biased jury was uncovered in 2010, when attorney Lloyd Warford signed an affidavit that jury foreman Kent Arnold had already decided on Echols's guilt before the trial ever began, used deception to be selected for the jury, and then informed the jury about Misskelley's confession. Arnold had hired Warford in an unrelated criminal case and frequently discussed the case with him, remarking that if you looked into Echols's eyes, "you knew he was evil."[69] Echols and Baldwin were also found guilty of three counts of murder. Baldwin received a life sentence and Echols was sentenced to death.

This likely would have been the end of the West Memphis Three's story, were it not for documentarians Joe Berlinger and Bruce Sinofsky. They assumed Damien Echols was another Ricky Kasso, and they traveled to West Memphis to film a documentary about youth who had been transformed into murderers by heavy metal and Stephen King books. Instead, they found three boys who had obviously been scapegoated by a prejudiced justice system. Their documentary, *Paradise Lost* (1996), and its two sequels rallied national support for the West Memphis Three. Numerous celebrities voiced support for the Three, especially heavy metal acts such as Metallica, Henry Rollins, and Disturbed. Comedienne Margaret Cho became pen pals with Echols and called him "the heavy metal Nelson Mandela."[70]

In 2007, attorneys for the Three filed a motion in federal court to overturn the convictions in light of DNA evidence. Further investigation revealed unknown DNA on the victims, but no DNA from any of the Three. The motion also brought up the questionable testimony of Dale Griffis and the affidavit alleging jury misconduct. Furthermore, seven forensic scientists agreed that the sexual mutilation of one boy—the detail that seemed to prove the murders were "ritualistic"—was actually the result of animal predation after the bodies had been exposed to the elements. The Arkansas Supreme Court ordered Circuit Judge David Laser to consider this new evidence. Laser reached a deal with prosecutors in which a new trial would be held if the defendants offered Alford Pleas—a deal in which the defendant pleads not guilty yet concedes the state has sufficient evidence to convict. This arrangement protected the state of Arkansas from any legal fault. In 2011, the Three were freed but the actual murderer remained at large. Justice was not, and will likely never be, served.

The crimes of Varg Vikernes were a case of "ostension proper" in which Vikernes performed the legend of the heavy metal Satanist. What happened in West Memphis was a form of "quasi-ostension" in which law enforcement and the court misinterpreted data because they read it in light of this legend. The false accusation created by Driver and Hutchinson was a case of "proto-ostension" in which narratives are formed based on a legend. While there is plenty of blame to go around in this case, it is clear that sensationalized news media, as well as horror films, provided a cultural script by which nearly everyone approached the case. Peg Aloi cites this as an example of fictional texts influencing a criminal investigation. The murders were so gruesome that they demanded a context to make sense of them and horror films provided a ready-made framework for imagining how such a thing could occur. Aloi writes: "Grief, outrage, horror, indignation and a desire for revenge became a colored shade through which many onlookers viewed the case. In such an atmosphere, which itself resembled a horror film at times, it is not surprising that the players should become vulnerable to suggestion, rumor, innuendo and panic."[71]

This response was greatly aggravated by Jerry Driver and Dale Griffis, who played the role of "experts in evil"[72] with their investigation tactics and court testimony. Heavy metal had become the link between actual youth activities and the imaginary realm of "occult crime." During the trial, so much was made of Echols's and Baldwin's interest in the band Metallica that Aloi notes heavy metal became "a signifier of occult activity." Significantly, in her book *Raising PG Kids in an X-Rated Society* (1987), Tipper Gore praised nearby Memphis as a model community for its opposition to obscene music.[73]

Media also worked to change public opinion about the West Memphis Three through the *Paradise Lost* documentaries. The work of Berlinger and Sinofsky is an interesting manifestation of *The Exorcist* effect, located within several layers of true events and their fictional adaptations. They said of their original interest in the West Memphis Three, "Thinking we'd make a real-life *River's Edge*, we wanted to explore how three teenagers could be so cold-hearted as to brutally sacrifice three eight-year-olds to the Devil."[74] *River's Edge* (1987) tells the story of a group of teens whose friend murders his girlfriend and needs help disposing of her body. Some critics have classified it as a horror film. Ironically, there had already been a "real life *River's Edge*": the story was based on the 1981 murder of fourteen-year-old Marcy Renee Conrad, who was raped and strangled by a sixteen-year-old. Media coverage of the murder contributed to anxieties about amoral teenagers and *River's Edge* threw those anxieties into relief. *River's Edge* also featured a soundtrack with four songs by the heavy metal band Slayer. Had Berlinger and Sinofsky remained unwilling to question their assumptions, this narrative of amoral murderous teens would have been applied to the West Memphis Three as well.

The story of the West Memphis Three in turn became fodder for more films. While Berlinger was working on *Paradise Lost 2: Revelations* he also directed a poorly received sequel to *The Blair Witch Project, Book of Shadows: Blair*

Witch 2 reflected many of the themes of the West Memphis Three story. A group of young counterculture types have seen the documentary from the first film and traveled to Burkittsville, Maryland, to search for the Blair Witch. They hire a tour guide who, like Damian Echols, is the town outsider and has spent time in a psychiatric hospital. The people of Burkittsville are openly hostile to outsiders, especially ones dressed in black, and Burkittsville's "Sheriff Craven" is convinced that young people visiting the town to find the Blair Witch are troublemakers. Berlinger said that Craven's ponytail was intended as a reference to John Mark Byers, who appeared in *Paradise Lost*. Byers was the stepfather of one of the murdered children and exhibited bizarre behavior, including gifting the documentarians with a knife. As the characters are killed, it is unclear whether they are being murdered by Sheriff Craven, their mentally unwell tour guide, or an actual supernatural force.

Media reflections of the case changed further after the Three were released. In 2013, journalist Mara Levitt's book about the case, *Devil's Knot*, was adapted into a film. As Aloi notes, what we see here is an evolving dialogue between fictional texts about an event and changing attitudes about what actually happened. There was a sort of "narrative drift" in which heavy metal shifted from signifying adolescents who are dangerous to adolescents in danger of persecution.

The panic over heavy metal devolved into parody as Generation X came of age. Today, metal is no longer shocking, and metalheads are more likely to be seen as quirky than intimidating. *We Summon the Darkness* (2019) represents the most complete reversal of the myth of the heavy metal Satanist. Set on the night of a metal concert in 1988, a group of metalheads are captured and murdered by evangelicals: the plan of the evangelicals is to conduct indiscriminate murders and leave behind Satanic paraphernalia—just as Richard Ramirez had done—to sow Satanic panic and strengthen the political power of the church. While poorly received, the film's message seems clear: those preaching about the evils of rock music are the ones we must fear the most.

9

Conclusion

"Horror is radical. It can take you into a completely new world, new place, and just rattle your cage and say, wait a minute—look at things differently. That shock of horror is what horror's all about. But in most cases, at the end of the story, people try to bring everything back—the girl gets the guy and everything's fine and things go on just the way they were. Which is really why we are doing this in the first place. We don't want things the way they are or we wouldn't be trying to shock you into an alternative place."

—Director George A. Romero[1]

"Do you want to know the problem with places like this? With religion, in general? It's never known how to convey the anatomy of horror. Religion seeks discipline through fear . . . yet doesn't understand the true nature of creation. No one's ever believed it enough to make it real. The same cannot be said of my work."

—Sutter Cane, *In the Mouth of Madness* (1994)

This book has been an exploration of how horror movies have shaped and reflected American religious culture. The pattern we have dubbed *The Exorcist* effect describes a process in which films serve as models for what is possible, those models become frameworks for interpreting experiences, and narratives about those experiences become fodder for subsequent films. In closing, we make some observations about the current state of *The Exorcist* effect and what, if anything, to do about it.

The Exorcist Effect. Joseph P. Laycock and Eric Harrelson, Oxford University Press. © Oxford University Press 2024.
DOI: 10.1093/oso/9780197635391.003.0009

The Exorcist Effect, Social Media, and QAnon

It seems clear that the rise of social media has accelerated *The Exorcist* effect, simply because the amount of discourse about both films and the paranormal has increased exponentially. Christopher DeFlorio is a retired New York Police officer who has become a Catholic demonologist in the tradition of the Warrens. In a podcast interview, he remarked on the *overabundance* of voices now available to interpret paranormal experiences:

> You have to know who you're talking to because it's [demonic activity] very serious and you have, you know, plenty of people who really are, you know—they're being held hostages. Maybe in their home or somewhere, they're being attacked and they'll come onto social media and they'll post something and you'll have a comments section of, you know, thirty different ideas to try. And when I saw that I thought, you know, it's gotta be more personal. It's kinda like, you know, you have something happen to you and you call the police, you see the policemen come or you have a medical issue and the ambulance comes. You gotta know who is helping you.[2]

Part of why the Warrens were so successful in the 1970s is that people having paranormal experiences felt that no one would listen to them. But DeFlorio is describing the opposite problem: on social media *too many* people are eager to advise experiencers. It stands to reason that the more voices are brought in to interpret an experience, the more likely it is that ideas derived from media may influence the narrative that eventually emerges.

Social media also means that reports of demonic activity and Satanic conspiracies can spread exponentially faster. Communications professor Whitney Phillips commented on the role of the internet in a resurgence of Satanic Panic in the 2020s: "You can have an accusation that goes viral, be seen by millions of people by the end of that day. That was never possible before. You can almost foresee what is coming next. It's what we've seen before, but all of the bulwarks are gone."[3] This brings us to QAnon—an internet conspiracy theory turned social movement, alleging that the democratic party, as well as such public figures as Tom Hanks and Bill Gates, are part of a Satanic "deep state" conspiracy that is subverting society and that engages in the ritualistic torture of children. According to QAnons (as those involved in the theory are sometimes called), torturing children produces a chemical called "adrenochrome" that Democrats harvest and consume to rejuvenate their bodies. Furthermore, during the presidency of Donald Trump (2016–2020), QAnons believed Trump was engaged in a secret plan to eradicate this conspiracy, culminating in an event called "The Storm." Scholars of new religious movements have identified QAnon as a millennialist movement––a group awaiting collective salvation.[4] When insurgents, angry over Trump's 2020 election defeat, attacked the capitol on January 6, 2021, many were draped in QAnon garb or bore "Q" flags. In 2022, Trump shared a photo on his social media site, Truth Social, in which he is wearing a "Q" pin on his lapel with the caption "The Storm Is Coming."[5]

As many commentators have noted, there is nothing particularly new about QAnon. It regurgitates Satanic conspiracy theories found in John Birch Society publications from the 1970s, *Michelle Remembers* in 1980, and Malachi Martin's conspiracy theories in the 1990s. Pre-figuring the adrenochrome conspiracy theory, Ed Warren told a reporter that he knew of a Satanic group in Connecticut that kidnapped and killed a child, adding, "This is supposed to be the greatest sacrifice. These cultists believe that energy is released from their victim's fear. They believe they can harness this energy and use it in demonic rituals to obtain wealth, success and power."[6] Such claims about why evildoers feel compelled to murder children are, in turn, derivative of the medieval blood libel that Jews consumed the blood of Christian children.

What is different about QAnon is the way anonymous internet forums have allowed various parties to weaponize Satanic Panic for political and financial gain. Much of the groundwork for QAnon was laid by conservative resentment of the Clinton administration. In 1994, Patrick Matrisciana produced the documentary *The Clinton Chronicles* through his "Christian patriot" production company, Jeremiah Films. (Other titles from Jeremiah Films include *Satanic Cults and Ritual Abuse* [1990], and *UPC Codes and 666* [1994].) *The Clinton Chronicles* accused the Clintons of numerous scandals, including having people secretly killed. Jerry Falwell appeared in the documentary, and he promoted it on *The Old Time Gospel Hour*, where he claimed the Democrats were on the side of Satan.[7]

By the time Hillary Clinton became the Democratic presidential candidate in 2016, a miasma of Satanic rumors had swirled around her for two decades. In a series of events that came to be known as "Pizzagate," her campaign's emails were hacked and posted online, and a conspiracy theory formed that Comet Ping Pong—a pizzeria in Washington, DC, mentioned in the emails—housed a basement where Democratic "elites" engaged in child sex trafficking. On December 4, 2016, Edgar Maddison Welch drove from North Carolina to Washington, DC, where he invaded the pizza parlor, fired warning shots from an AR-15 rifle, and demanded to inspect the basement. He surrendered to authorities after learning there was no basement.

Incidentally, this episode inspired *The Pizzagate Massacre* (2020) by Austin, Texas, based filmmaker John Valley. This "horror/satire" film features an aspiring journalist who is fired from a far-right, conspiracy-driven television show hosted by "Terri Lee." To redeem herself, she decides to investigate a tip that an Austin pizza parlor is a front for a conspiracy of shape-shifting reptilians. For help, she recruits a militia member (who turns out to be the son of Branch Davidian leader David Koresh). *The Pizzagate Massacre* was filmed in Austin and the studio used as location for the Terri Lee show was once used by conspiracy theorist Alex Jones. The location for the titular massacre is East Side Pies. In the wake of Pizzagate, some claimed this pizzeria was also a front for child trafficking because its logo is an eye, and the initials "ESP" is a reference to the occult. Valley said the goal was to humanize the people who are susceptible to these kinds of conspiracy theories. However, he and the cast began receiving death threats from conspiracy theorists who believed Valley's film was a deep-state operation to discredit them.[8]

The Pizzagate episode of 2016 was only the beginning. In 2017, someone began posting on the anonymous message board 4chan calling themselves "Q." Q claimed to be a high-ranking intelligence officer with "Q level" security clearance. According to Q, Hillary Clinton's passport had been flagged and she was about to be arrested. Like all of Q's predictions, this was false. However, a community formed around Q's posts, or "Q drops," which were often vague and designed to elicit interpretation. Q migrated to the site 8chan/8kun—an even more disreputable version of 4chan—and from there, Q's predictions spread to Reddit, Facebook, and YouTube, attracting older, conservative followers who would never visit an anonymous message board. Filmmaker Cullen Hoback, in his documentary series *Q: Into the Storm* (2021), presents strong, but inconclusive, evidence that Q is actually Jim Watkins and his son Ron. Q migrated to 8chan shortly after Ron Watkins acquired it, and Hoback feels confident that the father–son team are at least "the lynchpin" behind Q. What is significant is not Q's identity but Hoback's conclusion about Q's motivations. He explained, "They also see the world as a game. There's a nihilism to it."[9] In fact, game designers who studied QAnon noted that the conspiracy seemed designed to "gamify" conspiracy theories in ways that would help far-right politicians win elections.[10]

Q's statements came to be called "breadcrumbs," and those who built significance around them became known as "bakers." Some people even made careers on social media as interpreters of Q, gaining an audience and endorsement money. The "game" of QAnon often resembles the maxim of "yes and" used in improvisational comedy, whereby actors can never deny a premise, but only build on it further. For example, one "Q drop" simply stated, "Act II, scene IV." Soon, someone concluded this must reference a scene in *Macbeth*, where two characters discuss seeing an owl kill a falcon—an omen of Macbeth's betrayal of King Duncan. From here, the poster surmises that "Act II, scene IV" means the Clintons are about to turn on the Rothschilds—a wealthy, Jewish family that is a perennial subject of antisemitic conspiracy theories.[11] In this way, QAnon became a process of collective myth-making, involving thousands of people. As it grew, the conspiracy came to include such elements as extra-terrestrials; the street plan of Washington, DC being part of a massive Satanic ritual; and "mole children," who have escaped Democratic torture dungeons and now inhabit the sewers beneath New York City.

This QAnon game of "breadcrumbs and bakers" resembles many of the examples of myth-making already described in this book. The Warrens acted as bakers, using their expertise to interpret and impose narrative onto the anomalous experiences reported to them by others. By contrast, Malachi Martin preferred to act like Q, dropping cryptic hints and implying he knew more than he was saying. Sarah Colwell reported that QAnon was triggering "flashbacks" to conversations she had with Martin. She wrote, "QAnon folks seem a bit rustic for someone as subtle and cosmopolitan as Malalchi.... But the mechanism feels familiar: make an outrageous, unverifiable hint about Satanism in the Vatican, or whatever else Malachi put forth, and watch what happens."[12] It is through this ludic aspect of constructing narratives together where popular culture can easily find its way into emerging beliefs and practices.

Q may not be a government agent with Q-level clearance, but he is definitely a cinephile. Many Q drops mention films by name, such as *Iron Eagle* (1986), *The Godfather III* (1990), and *Alice in Wonderland* (1951). Even more films are referenced, if not named, including *The Bourne Identity* franchise (2002–2016), *Snow White* (1937), *Speed* (1994), *Taken* (2008), and *The Matrix* (1999). Q is, of course, the name of a character that has appeared in twenty-two James Bond films, where he acts as quartermaster for spies. Significantly, Trump—the messianic figure of QAnon—has himself been described as having "a lifelong obsession with movies" to the point that aids played classic films to relax him during the 2016 election.[13] The QAnon slogan, "Where we go one, we go all," was taken from the film *White Squall* (1966) about a disaster aboard a fishing ship. For QAnon, it has become an expression of loyalty to the movement. On July 4, 2020, Trump's former National Security Advisor, Michael Flynn, released a video in which he pledges the *White Squall* slogan—a dog whistle meant to signal his affinity with QAnon. Flynn also runs an online store that sells t-shirts printed with the "hashtag" #WWG1WGA.[14] In some instances, QAnons are invited to use these films to "think with" or as plausibility structures to support the mythology of QAnon. In other cases, QAnons engage in "fact–fiction reversal," interpreting films not as fictional stories but as coded messages describing things that are actually happening.

The aspect of the QAnon conspiracy where the influence of horror is most apparent is the conspiracy theory about adrenochrome. Adrenochrome is a chemical compound produced by the oxidization of adrenaline that can also be cheaply manufactured in laboratories. Some countries prescribe adrenochrome as a coagulant. In the United States, adrenochrome is not approved by the FDA but it is readily available for research purposes. Santa Cruz Biotechnology, a laboratory in Dallas, currently charges $65 for 25 mg of adrenochrome.[15] A supply company in India charges 18 rupees for a 5 mg dose—about 22 cents.[16] The idea that adrenochrome is scarce or harvested from living humans appears to have arisen entirely from the 1998 film *Fear and Loathing in Las Vegas*, adapted from a 1971 novel by Hunter S. Thompson. In the film, Thompson's "lawyer," Dr. Gonzo offers him adrenochrome, claiming that it "makes pure mescaline seem like ginger beer."

Thompson likely fell upon the word "adrenochrome" in Aldous Huxley's *The Doors of Perception* (1954), which mentions the compound is derived from adrenaline and claims it has effects similar to mescaline.[17] In reality, adrenochrome does not have hallucinogenic properties.[18] In fact, Spanish psychonaut Eduardo Hidalgo Downing, in his drug memoir *Adrenochrome and Other Mythical Drugs*, described the experience as "absolute bullshit," adding that a cup of coffee provides a better high.[19]

But in the film, Thompson experiences vivid hallucinations and watches Gonzo morph into a demon with cat eyes, claws, horns, and six animal-like teats on his back. Gonzo explains that adrenochrome can only be harvested from the adrenaline gland of a living person. When Thompson asks who gave him the adrenochrome, Gonzo answers, "He's one of these Satanism freaks. He offered me human blood—said it would take me higher than I've ever been in my life."

This dialogue appears almost verbatim in Thompson's novel, which is itself a blend of fact and fiction. In 1971, the idea that "Satanism freaks" were murdering people to harvest hallucinogenic drugs seems to be a parody of conspiracy theories that followed in the wake of the Manson murders. Significantly, in the book, Gonzo immediately segues from relating how he bought drugs from a Satanist to a graphic discussion of a client accused of molesting children.[20] This links three core elements of the QAnon conspiracy: adrenochrome, Satanism, and pedophilia. The only thing missing is a political opponent to smear with these elements. Anyone can now watch the "adrenochrome scene" from *Fear and Loathing in Las Vegas* on YouTube, along with numerous comments elaborating on the "true" conspiracy surrounding adrenochrome harvesting.

As early as 2013, Thompson was being invoked by anonymous posters on 4chan promoting antisemitic conspiracy theories. Links to a video called "Jew Ritual BLOOD LIBEL Sacrifice is #ADRENOCHROME Harvesting" were repeatedly posted in threads about Pizzagate and Hillary Clinton.[21] In 2016, conspiracy theorists began to speculate that the children's film *Monsters, Inc.* (2001) was a coded discussion of adrenochrome harvesting. In that film, a society of monsters living in a parallel world rely on the screams of human children to power their technology. Every night they send monsters to emerge from closets and under children's beds to frighten them and harvest their screams. The monsters never harm children, believing them to be toxic. However, the film's antagonist seeks to harvest more energy by kidnapping children and attaching them to a device called a "Scream Extractor." In a fact–fiction reversal, conspiracy theorists claimed this was not a kids' movie, but rather Hollywood "telling on itself" about the actual torture of children. (In the film, the monsters discover that children's laughter is a more potent source of energy than screams, but this detail is not accounted for in the conspiracy theory.)

Predictably, these conspiracy theories became fodder for horror movies. The 2017 film *Adrenochrome*, directed by Trevor Simms, depicts a Satanic hippie cult, similar to the Manson family, that kills people to harvest the drug. The film's premiere in the United States came almost exactly one month before the first "Q drop" appeared on 4chan. Soon the conspiracy theory achieved a form of proto-ostension. In 2020, the talk show *Dr. Phil* featured a woman named "Sherrie" of Wenatchee, Washington, whose daughter disappeared. Sherrie explained to Dr. Phil her beliefs that cultists had murdered her daughter to harvest her adrenochrome. Dr. Phil said his producers contacted the Wenatchee police, who said they had never heard of adrenochrome or a crime connected to it. Sherrie countered that police were engaged in a coverup.[22] The exchange recalled episodes of *The Oprah Winfrey Show* and *Geraldo* that aired at the height of the Satanic Panic.

In 2018, the website "Your News Wire" posted a story alleging that a "snuff film" was circulating on the dark web in which Hillary Clinton and her aid, Huma Abedin, can be seen ripping off a little girl's face and then taking turns wearing it as a mask before drinking the child's blood in a Satanic ritual. The video was allegedly found on a laptop owned by Abedin's husband, Anthony Weiner, in a file labeled "Frazzledrip."[23] Your News Wire (now News Punch) is a literal "fake news" site that writes ridiculous partisan stories hoping they will go viral and generate web traffic. The "Frazzledrip" story spread on YouTube and was endorsed by Marjorie Taylor-Greene, who was voted into Congress in 2020.[24] Taylor-Greene was not alone in endorsing such claims. CNN reported that, in 2020, nearly two dozen Republicans who had publicly engaged with QAnon were on the ballot.[25] Frazzledrip is significant for this study because the idea of wearing someone's flayed face as a mask is a horror trope popularized by "Leatherface" in *The Texas Chainsaw Massacre* (1974) and subsequent films, such as *Dagon* (2001) and *House of a Thousand Corpses* (2003). So, Frazzledrip is indicative of a culture of online conspiracy theories in which horror films are being mined for wild accusations, which are then thrust into the political mainstream—all in a manner of months.

Conspiracy theories about evil rituals have been useful for vilifying one's political enemies at least since antiquity.[26] However, it is striking how much QAnon and related forms of far-right discourse have come to rely on popular culture, especially horror, to articulate their view of the world. For QAnons, Hillary Clinton and her allies are not just political opponents, or even spiritually evil: they slaughter children for drugs like the "Satanic freaks" in *Fear and Loathing in Las Vegas* and they wear children's faces as masks like Leatherface in *The Texas Chainsaw Massacre*.

It is also significant that self-initiation into QAnon shares similarities with the consumption of horror movies. QAnons are fond of the slogan "do your research," which for them often means watching conspiracy videos on YouTube. YouTube's algorithms ensure that watching one conspiracy video will cause similar videos to appear, instead of videos on other topics

236 THE EXORCIST EFFECT

or expressing different viewpoints. Going down such a rabbit hole can distort one's perspective, but it also offers certain pleasures similar to watching a horror movie: the content of these videos is often simultaneously exciting and gruesome, there are hideous revelations, and there is an intellectual satisfaction of guessing what will happen next. Often these videos will be accompanied by suspenseful music to heighten the entertainment value and the appeal to emotion.

One reason for this apparent affinity between horror and QAnon may be that the theme of *ambivalence* that permeates the horror genre resonates with the fundamental contradictions of the QAnon worldview. In 1979, film critic Robin Wood argued that one of the key themes of horror is ambivalence, in which the monster is simultaneously horrifying and sympathetic: "Central to the effect and fascination of horror films is their fulfillment of our nightmare wish to smash the norms that oppress us and which our moral conditioning teaches us to revere. The overwhelming commercial success of *The Omen* cannot possibly be explained in terms of the simple, unequivocal *horror* at the devil's progress."[27] For Wood, horror lends expression to the paradox of simultaneously desiring to break social norms and to repress those desires. This is why we are both excited to watch Damien's progress toward becoming the Antichrist and anxious to see him stopped.

It seems that many QAnons are racked with similar paradoxes: They are "patriots" who hate their government and large swathes of their fellow citizens. They invaded the capitol in an effort to overturn a free election, yet claim they are fighting for freedom and call their opponents "traitors." Many promoted the slogan "Blue Lives Matter," but their movement participated in assaulting police officers defending the capitol, with one insurgent shouting, "Kill him with his own gun!"[28] If Wood is correct, horror films provide a cultural resource for constructing narratives that help to articulate such a contradictory worldview while staving off the cognitive dissonance that arises from it.

Echoing Wood's theme of ambiguity, there is a vicarious pleasure inherent in inventing and disseminating claims like the Frazzledrip conspiracy theory. Religion scholar Jason Bivins calls this "the erotics of fear," or a fascination with that which is condemned.[29] Trump ally Steve Bannon openly expressed a degree of identification with Satanic villains shortly after the 2016 election when he told *The Hollywood Reporter*, "Darkness is good . . . . Dick Cheney. Darth Vader. Satan. That's power. It only helps us when they get it wrong. When they're blind to who we are and what we're doing."[30] Imagining one's political opponents killing children like a villain in a horror movie functions both to project one's own antisocial impulses onto someone else and to justify using violent, undemocratic means to achieve one's political goals. In sum, it may be that horror has become the mode through which QAnons talk about politics not only because they perceive their political opponents as monsters, but because it helps to simultaneously articulate and displace their sense of their own monstrosity.

Responding to *The Exorcist* Effect?

In his 2001 book, *American Exorcism*, Michael Cuneo wrote, "But can this be true? Am I really suggesting that the popular entertainment industry, with all its dreck and drivel, is capable of manipulating—actually manipulating—religious beliefs and behavior? Indeed, this is one of the main contentions of the present study, and there seems nothing (to my mind) especially far-fetched about it."[31] Twenty years later, Cuneo's contention appears truer than ever. Neuroscientists have now concluded that our "neural architecture" has evolved to evaluate new situations by comparing them to previous experiences—including the experience of watching movies.[32] We also know the average American now spends seven hours a day staring at screens.[33] It stands to reason that more media consumption means more of our behavior is shaped by the models of reality experienced through media. So the question arises: If horror movies are in a way "coming to life" through various forms of ostension, including exorcism practices and conspiracy theories, what should we do about it? Before answering this question, there are several important caveats.

First, as religion scholars we generally attempt to avoid making normative statements about the cultures we study. While it may seem shocking for a Catholic cardinal to read from *The Exorcist* or discuss Ozzy Osbourne's lyrics in St. Patrick's Cathedral, this is nevertheless an expression of Catholic culture. Popular culture has never been hermetically sealed from so-called ecclesiastical religion and "the sacralization of popular culture" is a normal part of the religious landscape.[34] However, as Americans we share a democracy with the people we study. Movements such as the Satanic Panic and QAnon draw their strength from horror films and cause demonstrable harm. We are therefore justified in diagnosing these movements as a social problem and proposing solutions.

Second, it needs to be acknowledged that using horror films as a model of reality is not, in itself, always a bad thing. Slasher films may be problematic in some ways, but watching the scenarios in these films has likely caused many young viewers to contemplate potential safety threats, leading to better decisions. In 2011, the Centers for Disease Control and Prevention produced a comic book entitled *Preparedness 101: Zombie Pandemic*, which presented the scenario of a zombie apocalypse to encourage readers to make emergency preparedness kits.[35] It may even be that supernatural tales provide a useful way of talking about experiences that cannot otherwise be expressed. This was the argument of physician David Hufford in his book, *The Terror that Comes in the Night* (1982). When that book was written, sleep paralysis was largely unknown in the United States. Hufford studied folklore in Newfoundland about "the night hag" who rides people in their sleep and drains their vitality. He concluded that people who reported "being hagged" at night were describing a real experience. Folklore allowed Newfoundlanders to talk about the experience of sleep paralysis with each other and to be believed, whereas many Americans who suffered from sleep paralysis were left with no way to understand or talk about the experience.[36] Like Hufford's night hag, horror films may sometimes provide a vocabulary or a cultural shorthand that is useful for narrativizing experiences in ways that are beneficial rather than harmful.

Third, it should be noted that aficionados of horror films—with some exceptions—are not the ones accusing innocent people of being Satanists, diagnosing their children as possessed by demons, or engaging in similar forms of problematic behavior.[37] More often, these claims appear to come from people who have indirect exposure to horror films. This makes sense considering what we know about source amnesia and "the sleeper effect."[38] Horror fans will remember where they have heard these stories and seen these tropes, whereas non-fans may be less likely to recall watching a film about cults or exorcism and are therefore unable to assess how it might have shaped their worldview.

Finally, and most importantly, in this study we have found that the mere existence of horror movies rarely leads to a heightened belief in demons or conspiracy theories. Instead, there are nearly always moral entrepreneurs and claims-makers who actively use these films either to gain a platform for themselves (as with the Warrens) or as plausibility structures to support their claims (as with Q). The moral entrepreneurs in this book fall on a spectrum from seemingly earnest to blatant manipulators. At one end are figures like

Ralph Sarchie, who seems to genuinely believe he and his team are combating demons. In the middle are Ed and Lorraine Warren, about whom religion scholar James M. Collins wrote, "Assuming they are serious, they are either crooked, deluded, or the world is a very much stronger place than most are inclined to believe."[39] Past the Warrens are figures like Mike Warnke, who simply invented a story out of whole cloth. And at the far end of the spectrum are figures like Malachi Martin and Q. If the Warrens and Warnke were liars, then these figures are "bullshitters." The difference, according to philosopher Harry G. Frankfurt, is that a liar is concerned about the truth and seeks to keep people from uncovering it, while a bullshitter has a fundamental disregard for truth. Martin did not seem to care whether a black mass was literally held in the Vatican or not, so long as his audience was paying attention to him. Q certainly does not care that virtually all his predictions were false. Lawrence and Michelle Pazder may also fall in the category of bullshitters because they claimed it was irrelevant whether stories of Satanic abuse are objectively true. Frankfurt argues that bullshit is ultimately a greater threat to truth, and therefore society, than is lying.[40]

For all these figures, horror has proved a useful cultural resource. Horror is inherently exciting and fascinating, and so allegations made in the horror mode will be circulated more widely, even by media sources that disbelieve them. Horror tropes frequently offer an appeal to emotion that can override logic and skepticism. Political scientist Joseph Uscinski noted that the tropes of Satanic cults popularized by horror were especially useful to QAnon because, "These are the worst things that you can accuse someone of. There's no redemption. So they make great cudgels to beat your political opponents with."[41] Horror writers and directors have already done their utmost to create plausible models of people doing the worst things imaginable. Moral entrepreneurs and conspiracy theorists have only to take this work and twist it to their own ends.

To return to our original question, the solution to *The Exorcist* effect should not and cannot be censorship. We believe horror writers should be free to make films about whatever subject they wish, and to enhance their stories with anchoring mechanisms, including claims that the film is "based on a true story" or even "found footage." Horror stories are important. At their best, they can call our attention to problems society has been unwilling to face or discuss. Instead of censorship, the focus should be on training the public to have greater awareness of how they know what they know. *The Exorcist* effect can be framed largely as a problem of information illiteracy.

The American Library Association's Report on Information Literacy states that a person who is information literate must "be able to recognize when information is needed and have the ability to locate, evaluate, and use effectively the needed information."[42] Information literacy can also inoculate the public against liars and bullshitters seeking to leverage horror movies for exploitative purposes. Library science has shifted toward the need for *critical information literacy*, or the ability to examine the social, political, and historical context in which a given piece of information was created.[43] Critical information literacy means the reader must try to be objective, even when the source is not. It also means understanding the difference between actual critical thinking and mere contrarianism or anti-intellectualism.

Put simply, the public ought to know better than to learn history, theology, and Biblical literacy from horror movies. When police are told by an "occult crime" expert that actual crimes are occurring that resemble the film *Rosemary's Baby*, they should automatically suspect that this person is not an expert. When social media claims that adrenochrome is harvested from tortured children, people should actually "do their research" to determine whether this claim is true. As they do so, they should understand the way internet algorithms tracking their search history are likely to direct them toward specific claims. Ideally, they should also have the self-awareness to realize graphic descriptions of tortured children are upsetting and that their emotional reaction to this claim might impair their information literacy.

As with all skills, raising levels of information literacy and critical thinking will require education. Education for information literacy could include basic research skills, training in what kinds of evidence would be needed to support a particular claim, and awareness of logical fallacies, confirmation bias, and other phenomena that can distort our understanding. Many of the concepts discussed in this book, such as confabulation, the sleeper effect, veracity mechanisms, and ostension would also be useful for a curriculum on information literacy. This kind of training cannot wait until college because many Americans never get the opportunity to go to college. Ideally, training for information literacy should begin in elementary school and continue to be reinforced throughout secondary education. In the meantime, it may be possible for grassroots organizations to promote information literacy. The alternative to creating a public that is information literate is for our culture to continue to drift into a "post-truth" digital age, in which the boundaries between reality, conspiracy theory, and fictional media become increasingly porous, and those seeking to manipulate the public become even more powerful. The stakes are no less than reality itself, at least as far as reality is socially constructed.

On January 7, 1974, Pauline Kael panned *The Exorcist* in *The New Yorker* asking, "Are American Catholics willing to see their faith turned into a horror show?"[44] After January 6, 2021, we might reverse this question and ask: Are Americans willing to see their horror shows turned into a faith? Because in a way this is what QAnon is—a haphazard assemblage of horror movie tropes that has evolved into a millennial movement. To mitigate the harm caused by groups like this, it is more important than ever that research on popular culture be taken seriously so that we can better understand the ways that film and media shape our understanding of the world.

Notes

Chapter 1

1. Gabriele Amorth, *An Exorcist Tells his Story* (San Francisco: Ignatius Press, 1999), 55.
2. S. Brent Plate, *Religion and Film: Cinema and the Re-Creation of the World* (London: Wallflower, 2008), 16.
3. United Press International, "Cardinal: Two Devil Exocisms [*sic*] Recently—Blames Heavy Metal," *UPI Archives*, March 5, 1990, https://www.upi.com/Archives/1990/03/05/Cardinal-Two-devil-exocisms-recently-blames-heavy-metal/1575636613200/; David Firestone, "N.Y. Cardinal Brings Exorcism to Open," *The Washington Post*, March 10, 1990, https://www.washingtonpost.com/archive/local/1990/03/10/ny-cardinal-brings-exorcism-into-open/8c994307-96f3-4b38-b18a-9edc57a18058/; Richard N. Ostling, "Religion: No Sympathy for the Devil," *Time Magazine*, March 19, 1990, http://content.time.com/time/magazine/article/0,9171,969630,00.html.
4. Leonard Primiano, "Vernacular Religion and the Search for Method in Religious Folklife," *Western Folklore* 54, no. 1 (January 1995): 37–56.
5. David D. Hall, *Lived Religion in America: Toward a History of Practice* (Princeton, NJ: Princeton University Press, 1997), ix.
6. Peter W. Williams, *Popular Religion in America: Symbolic Change and the Modernization Process in Historical Perspective* (Englewood Cliffs, NJ: Prentice-Hall, 1980), 3. Williams blamed the neglect of popular religion on the conditions of academia in North America, where scholars feel greater pressure to produce "serious" work in response to both American anti-intellectualism and a sense of inferiority to European scholars. He also cites the theological biases of religion scholars.
7. Hall, *Lived Religion in America*, 6.
8. Clyde Nunn, "The Rising Credibility of the Devil in America," in *Heterodoxy: Mystical Experience, Religious Dissent and the Occult*, ed. R. Wood (River Forest DEl.: Lisning Press, 1975), 84–10.
9. Matt Baglio, *The Rite: The Making of a Modern Exorcist* (New York: Random House, 1999), 7.
10. Associated Press, "Archbishop Performs Exorcism at Spot Where Protesters Toppled Serra Statue," *Los Angeles Times*, October 17, 2020, https://www.latimes.com/california/story/2020-10-17/archbishop-performs-exorcism-at-spot-where-protesters-toppled-serra-statue.
11. Sean McCloud, *American Possessions: Fighting Demons in the Contemporary United States* (New York: Oxford University Press, 2015), 10.
12. "Marine demons" are a recent sub-genre of Pentecostal demonology with several volumes on how to banish the influence of marine-dwelling demons. This literature

appears to have begun in West Africa where Pentecostalism brought by missionaries cross-pollinated with indigenous water-dwelling goddesses, such as Mami Wata. For an early example of the genre, see D. K. Olukoya, *Power Against Marine Spirits* (Lagos, Nigeria: The Battle Cry Christian Ministries, 1999).

13. Nunn, "The Rising Credibility of the Devil in America"; David Frankfurter, *Evil Incarnate: Rumors of Demonic Conspiracy and Satanic Abuse in History* (Princeton, NJ: Princeton University Press, 2006); Frederick Carl Mencken, Joseph O. Baker, and Christopher David Bader, *Paranormal America: Ghost Encounters, UFO Sightings, Bigfoot Hunts, and Other Curiosities in Religion and Culture*, 2nd ed. (New York: New York University Press, 2017).

14. On this connection see Darryl Caterine, "Introduction," in *The Paranormal and Popular Culture: A Postmodern Religious Landscape*, ed. Darryl Caterine and John W. Morehead (New York: Routledge, 2019), p. 5; Giuseppe Giordan and Adam Possamai, *Sociology of Exorcism in Late Modernity* (New York: Palgrave Macmillan, 2018), p. 5; and James R. Lewis, *Satanism Today: an Encyclopedia of Religion, Folklore, and Popular Culture* (Santa Barbara, CA: ABC-CLIO, 2001).

15. "Exorcist Fever," *Time*, February 11, 1974: 53.

16. Derek Malcolm, "The Exorcist," *The Guardian*, March 14, 1974, http://www.guardian.co.uk/film/1974/mar/14/derekmalcolmscenturyoffilm.mainsection.

17. Christopher Partridge, *The Re-Enchantment of the West*, vol. 2 (London: T&T Clark International, 2005), 240.

18. William Peter Blatty, *The Exorcist* (New York: HarperTorch, 2004 [1971]), 389.

19. Michael W. Cuneo, *American Exorcism: Expelling Demons in the Land of Plenty* (New York: Doubleday, 2001), 39–40.

20. Cuneo, *American Exorcism*; Giordan and Possamai, *Sociology of Exorcism in Late Modernity*, 5.

21. George Case, *Here's To My Sweet Satan: How the Occult Haunted Music, Movies and Pop Culture, 1966–1980* (Fresno, CA: Quill Driver Books, 2016), 35.

22. Cuneo, *American Exorcism*, 96.

23. Bob Curran, "Exorcist Wants to Cast Out Rumors," *The Buffalo News*, March 27, 1990, https://buffalonews.com/news/exorcist-wants-to-cast-out-rumors/article_8d486 61a-009e-5c88-9364-2a73be5840d4.html.

24. Brad Steiger and Sherry Hansen Steiger, *Demon Deaths* (New York: Berkley Books, 1991), 2–3.

25. Jason Bivins, *Religion of Fear: the Politics of Horror in Conservative Evangelicalism* (Oxford: Oxford University Press, 2008), 9.

26. Maynard Good Stoddard, "Billy Graham: The World is His Pulpit," *The Saturday Evening Post*, March 1986, https://www.questia.com/read/1G1-4151300/billy-gra ham-the-world-is-his-pulpit.

27. Colleen McDannell, *Catholics in the Movies* (New York: Oxford University Press, 2008), 202.

28. Billy Graham, *Angels: God's Secret Agents* (Nashville, TN: Thomas Nelson, 2009), 15.

29. Quoted in Margalit Fox, "Ira Levin, of 'Rosemary's Baby,'" Dies at 78," *The New York Times*, November 14, 2007, https://www.nytimes.com/2007/11/14/books/ 14levin.html

30. Quoted in Harry Medved and Randy Dreyfuss, *The Fifty Worst Films of All Time (And How They Got That Way)* (New York: Popular Library, 1979), 172.

31. Gerald H. Heisler, "The Effects of Vicariously Experiencing Supernatural Violent Events: A Case Study of *The Exorcist's* Impact," *Journal of Individual Psychology* 31, no. 2 (1975): 166.

32. John C. Lyden, *Film as Religion: Myths, Morals, and Rituals* (New York: New York University Press, 2003), 46.

33. Peter L. Berger, *The Sacred Canopy: Elements of a Sociological Theory of Religion* (New York: Doubleday, 1969), 41–43.

34. Christopher Partridge, *The Re-Enchantment of the West: Alternative Spiritualities, Sacralization, Popular Culture, and Occulture* (London: T&T Clark International, 2004), 124.

35. Jeff Zacks, *Flicker: Your Brain on Movies* (New York: Oxford University Press, 2015), 100.

36. Lewis, *Satanism Today*, 26–27; Robert D. Hicks, *In Pursuit of Satan: The Police and the Occult* (Buffalo, NY: Prometheus Books, 1992), 176.

37. Michael Barkun, *A Culture of Conspiracy: Apocalyptic Visions in Contemporary America* (Berkeley: University of California Press, 2003), 29–33.

38. Nikolas Schreck, *The Satanic Screen: An Illustrated Guide to the Devil in Cinema* (London: Creation, 2001), 137.

39. Rebecca Greenwood, *Let Our Children Go: Steps to Free Your Child From Evil Influences and Demonic Harassment* (Lake Mary, FL: Charisma House, 2011), 17–18.

40. Frankfurter, *Evil Incarnate*, 176.

41. Bill Ellis, *Aliens, Ghosts, and Cults: Legends We Live* (Jackson: University Press of Mississippi, 2003), 164.

42. Partridge, *The Re-Enchantment of the West*, 126.

43. James B. Twitchell, *Dreadful Pleasures: An Anatomy of Modern Horror* (New York: Oxford University Press, 1985), 65.

44. Gabriel Sanders, "Are We Still Afraid of 'Jaws'?," *The Tablet*, August 5, 2014, https://www.tabletmag.com/sections/news/articles/are-we-still-afraid-of-jaws.

45. Stephen King, *Danse Macabre* (New York: Gallery Books, 2010 [1981]), 139.

46. Barbara Creed, *The Monstrous Feminine: Film, Feminism, Psychoanalysis* (New York: Routledge, 1993), 35.

47. Douglas Cowan, *Sacred Terror: Religion and Horror on the Silver Screen* (Waco, TX: Baylor University Press, 2016), 50.

48. Quoted in Mark Kermode, *The Exorcist* (London: British Film Institute, 2011), 42–43.

49. Carlos Clarens, *An Illustrated History of Horror Films* (New York: Capricorn Books, 1968), 37.

50. Brandon Grafius, "Horror and Bible (Six Theses)" in *Religion, Culture, and the Monstrous: Of Gods and Monsters,* ed. Joseph P. Laycock and Natasha L. Mikles (Lanham, MDd: Lexigton Books, 2021), 36.

51. Mircea Eliade, *Occultism, Witchcraft, and Cultural Fashions: Essays in Comparative Religions* (Chicago: University of Chicago Press, 1976), 67–68. The other film Eliade cites is *2001: A Space Odyssey* (1968).

52. N. Katherine Hayles, *How We Think: Digital Media and Contemporary Technogenesis* (Chicago: University of Chicago Press, 2012).

53. Interview with Diana Pasulka, consultant on *The Conjuring* (July 7, 2020).

54. John C. Lyden, *Film as Religion: Myths, Morals, and Rituals* (New York: New York University Press, 2019). See also S. Brent Plate, *Religion and Film: Cinema and the Re-Creation of the World* (London: Wallflower, 2008).

55. Marcello Truzzi, "The Occult Revival as Popular Culture: Some Random Observations on the Old and the Nouveau Witch," *Sociology Quarterly* 13, no. 1 (Winter 1972): 30. Sociologist Peter Berger ("Secularization in Retreat," *National Interest* 46 (Winter 1996–1997): 3–12) coined the term "last gasp" thesis to describe theories that paradoxically dismissed signs of enduring religiosity as the death rattle before secularization. He described this interpretation as "singularly unpersuasive."

56. Peter L. Berger, "The Devil and the Pornography of Modern Consciousness," *Worldview* 17 (1974): 36.

57. Cowan, *Sacred Terror*, 51.

58. David Frankfurter, "Awakening to Satanic Conspiracy: *Rosemary's Baby* and the Cult Next Door" in *Deliver Us From Evil: Boston University Studies in Philosophy and Religion*, ed. M. David Eckel and Bradley L. Herling (New York: Continuum, 2011), 79–80.

59. Drew Beard, "Horror Movies At Home: Supernatural Horror, Delivery Systems and 1980s Satanic Panic," *Horror Studies* 6, no. 2 (2015): 211–223.

60. Robert D. Hicks, *In Pursuit of Satan: The Police and the Occult* (Buffalo, NY: Prometheus Books, 1992), 59.

61. Zacks, *Flicker*, 92–93.

62. Frankfurter, "Awakening to Satanic Conspiracy," 83–84.

Chapter 2

1. Diana Walsh Pasulka, *American Cosmic: UFOs, Religion, Technology* (New York: Oxford University Press, 2019), 140.

2. Quoted in Stephen Farber, "Film: New Scare Tactics, Low on Blood and Gore," *The New York Times*, January 11, 1998, 17.

3. Oscar Wilde, *The Decay of Lying and other Essays* (New York: Penguin Books, 2010), 26.

4. Emmanuelle Toulet, *Birth of the Motion Picture* (New York: H. N. Abrams, 1995), 15.

5. Pasulka, *American Cosmic*, 108.

6. Robert A. Orsi, *History and Presence* (Cambridge, MA: Harvard University Press, 2016), 159.

7. William Castle, *Step Right Up! I'm Gonna Scare the Pants Off America* (New York: G. P. Putnam's Sons, 1976), 210.

8. Mikel J. Koven, *Film, Folklore, and Urban Legends* (Lanham, MD: The Scarecrow Press, 2008), 150.

9. Peter Laws, *The Frighteners: A Journey Through Our Cultural Fascination with the Macabre* (New York: Skyhorse Publishing, 2018), 239.

10. Carey Hayes, Chad Hayes, and Diana Walsh Pasulka, "The Catholic Supernatural," *OUPblog*, October 29, 2014, https://blog.oup.com/2014/10/the-conjuring-movie-q-a-pasulka-hayes/.

11. Bill Ellis, *Aliens, Ghosts, and Cults: Legends We Live* (Jackson: University Press of Mississippi, 2003), 29.

12. Noel Carroll, "Why Horror?," in *Horror: The Film Reader*, ed. Mark Jancovich (New York: Routledge, 2002), 34.

13. Sigmund Freud, *The Uncanny* (New York: Penguin Books, 2003), 150.

14. Alison Gopnik, "Explanation as Orgasm," *Minds and Machines* 8 (1998): 102.

15. Annette Hill, *Paranormal Media: Audiences, Spirits, and Magic in Popular Culture* (New York: Routledge, 2011), 52.

16. Ibid., 75.

17. Lynn Schofield Clark, *From Angels to Aliens: Teenagers the Media and the Supernatural* (New York: Oxford University Press, 2003), 228.

18. Hayes, Hayes, and Pasulka, "The Catholic Supernatural."

19. Howard Phillips Lovecraft, *Selected Letters III: 1934–1937*. Ed. August Derleth and James Turner (Sauk City, WI: Arkham House Publishers, 1976), 193.

20. Adam Rockoff, *The Horror of it All: One Moviegoer's Love Affair with Masked Maniacs, Frightened Virgins, and the Living Dead* (New York: Scribner, 2015), 168–169.

21. "The Exorcist Haunts MDs at Georgetown," *American Medical News* 17, no. 9 (March 4, 1974), 14.

22. Pasulka, *American Cosmic*, 123.

23. Diana Walsh Pasulka, "'The Fairy Tale is True': Social Technologies of the Religious Supernatural in Film and New Media," *Journal of the American Academy of Religion* 84, no. 2 (June 2016): 542.

24. Steve A. Wiggins, *Holy Horror: The Bible and Fear in Movies* (New York: McFarland, 2018), 183.

25. Jeb J. Card, *Spooky Archaeology: Myth and the Science of the Past* (Albuquerque: University of New Mexico Press, 2018), 221.

26. Peter H. Gilmore, "Which Witch?" *Church of Satan News*, https://churchofsatannews.tumblr.com/post/138686035957/which-witch-magus-peter-h-gilmore-please.

27. Peg Aloi, "Rooted in the Occult Revival: Neo-Paganism's Evolving Relationship with Popular Media," in *Handbook of Contemporary Paganism*, vol 2, ed. James R. Lewis and Murphy Pizza (Leiden: Brill, 2009), 544. See also Adam McGee's analysis of DVD featurettes in horror movies about "voodoo" in "Haitian Vodou and Voodoo: Imagined Religion and Popular Culture," *Studies in Religion/Sciences Religieuses* 41, no. 2 (2012): 249.

28. Pasulka, "'The Fairy Tale is True,'" 536.

29. Hugo Munsterberg, *The Photoplay: A Psychological Study* (New York: Appleton and Company, 1916), 220–221.

30. Colin McGinn, *The Power of Movies: How Screen and Mind Interact* (Pantheon Books, 2005), 4–5.

31. Jeff Zacks, *Flicker: Your Brain on Movies* (New York: Oxford University Press, 2015), 7–8

32. Tom Valentine, "Audience Reactions Vary from Laughing to Fainting, But Nobody Can Ignore the Film," *The National Tattler* (Spring 1974): 6.

33. S. Brent Plate, *Religion and Film: Cinema and the Re-Creation of the World*, 2nd edition (New York: Columbia University Press, 2017), 108–109.

34. Douglas E. Cowan, *Sacred Terror: Religion and Horror on the Silver Screen* (Waco, TX: Baylor University Press, 2016), lx.

35. Zacks, *Flicker*, 96.

36. Ibid., 110–111.

37. G. A. Mazzoni, E. F. Loftus, and I. Kirsch, "Changing Beliefs about Implausible Autobiographical Events: A Little Plausibility Goes a Long Way," *Journal of Experimental Psychology: Applied* 7, no. 1 (2001): 51–59.

38. Holden Constance, "Possessed," *Science* 290 (November 3, 2000): 929

39. Paul Thomas, "New Religious Movements," in *The Routledge Companion to Religion and Film*, ed. John Lyden (New York: Routledge, 2009), 227–229.

40. Quoted in Mikita Brottman, *Hollywood Hex* (London: Creation, 1999), 152.

41. Ben Guarino, "The Creepy Clown Crisis: White House Defers to FBI; Stephen King Hits 'Hysteria,'" *The Herald News*, October 5, 2016, https://www.heraldnews.com/story/news/2016/10/05/the-creepy-clown-crisis-white/25259651007/; Alina Gorbath, "*IT* the Movie and Its Freakishly Good Marketing Campaign," *Awario.com*, October 29, 2020, https://awario.com/blog/it-the-movie-marketing-campaign/.

Chapter 3

1. William Castle, *Step Right Up! I'm Gonna Scare the Pants Off America* (New York: G. P. Putnam's Sons, 1976), 225.

2. Quoted in Dale Winogura, "William Friedkin," *Cinefantastique* 3, no. 4 (Winter 1974): 17.

3. Brian Baker, "The Occult and Film," in *The Occult World*, ed. Christopher Partridge (New York: Routledge, 2014), 453; Gregory A. Waller, "Introduction," in *American Horrors: Essays on the Modern Horror Film*, ed. Gregory A. Waller, (Chicago: University of Illinois Press, 1987), 2; David A. Cook, *Lost Illusions American Cinema in the Shadow of Watergate and Vietnam, 1970–197* (Berkeley: University of California Press, 2005), 222–223.

4. Peter Laws, *The Frighteners: A Journey Through Our Cultural Fascination with the Macabre* (New York: Skyhorse Publishing, 2018), 99.

5. Richard Eder, "The Screen: 'Omen' is Nobody's Baby," *New York Times*, June 26, 1976, 12.

6. Mikita Brottman, *Hollywood Hex: Death and Destiny in the Dream Factory* (London: Creation, 1999), 89.

7. Wingora, "William Friedkin," 17.

8. Carl Raschke, "Exorcizing the Devils of Watergate: Why the Prince of Darkness Is Having His Day," *Christian Century*, December 18, 1974, 1196.

9. Ralph R. Greenson, "A Psychoanalyst's Indictment of 'The Exorcist,'" *Saturday Review*, June 15, 1974, 43.

10. Hollis Alpert, "In Answer to Dr. Greenson," *Saturday Review*, June 15, 1974, 43.

11. Grady Hendrix, Interview with the authors, December 18, 2020.

12. Peg Aloi, "Rooted in the Occult Revival: Neo-Paganism's Evolving Relationship with Popular Media," in *Handbook of Contemporary Paganism*, vol. 2, ed. James R. Lewis and Murphy Pizza (Leiden: Brill, 2009), 549.

13. Sidney Gottlieb, *Hitchcock on Hitchcock* (Berkeley: University of California Press, 2014), 114.

14. Nikolas Schreck, *The Satanic Screen: An Illustrated Guide to the Devil in Cinema* (London: Creation, 2001), 133.

15. Quoted in Michael Newton, *Rosemary's Baby* (New York: Bloomsbury, 2020), 65.

16. William Peter Blatty, *If There Were Demons, Then Perhaps There Were Angels: William Peter Blatty's Own Story of the Exorcist* (Southwold: ScreenPress Books, 1999), 5.

17. Colleen McDannell, *Catholics in the Movies* (New York: Oxford University Press, 2008), 201.

18. Quoted in Mark Kermode, *The Exorcist* (London: British Film Institute, 2011), 66.

19. Don Kaye, "How *The Omen* Wrote the Bible on Satanic Horror," *Den of Geek*, October 22, 2019, https://www.denofgeek.com/movies/how-the-omen-wrote-the-bible-on-satanic-horror/?

20. Grady Hendrix, *Paperbacks from Hell: The Twisted History of '70s and '80s Horror Fiction* (Philadelphia: Quirk, 2017), 20.

21. Michael Collings, *Stephen King as Richard Bachman* (Mercer Island, WA: Starmont House, Inc., 1985), 140–141. It should be noted that Stephen King (*Danse Macabre* [New York: Gallery Books, 2010], 315) disdained *The Exorcist*, associating it with "the Dull, Thudding Tract School of horror writing."

22. Peter Hutchings, "By the Book: American Horror Cinema and Horror Literature of the Late 1960s and 1970s," in *Merchants of Menace: The Business of Horror Cinema*, ed. Richard Nowell (New York: Bloomsbury, 2014), 45–60.

23. "Law Suits, Marches, Fight to Halt Showing of Film," *Tattler* (Spring 1974 Special): 30.

24. Richard Woods, *The Devil* (Chicago: Thomas More Press, 1974), 9.

25. Ibid., 23.

26. Quoted in "Exorcist Fever," *Time*, February 11, 1974, 53.

27. Robert W. Balch and Margaret Gilliam, "Devil Worship in Western Montana: A Case Study in Rumor Construction," in *The Satanism Scare*, ed. James T. Richardson, Joel Best, and David G. Bromley (New York: Aldine de Gruyter, 1991),, 25.

28. Steve Kissing, "I Thought I Was Possessed By The Devil. The Truth Shook My Deepest Beliefs," *HuffPost*, July 21, 2018, https://www.huffpost.com/entry/possession-devil-hallucination_n_5b4f9df9e4b0de86f489574f.

29. Frank Newport, "Most Americans Say Religion Is Losing Influence in U.S.," *Gallup News*, May 29, 2013, https://news.gallup.com/poll/162803/americans-say-religion-losing-influence.aspx.

30. Greg Kilday, "People are Getting the Hell Scared Out of Them': 'Exorcist'—A View from the Catholic Church," *Los Angeles Times*, January 21, 1974, E11.

31. Bernard Doherty, "The Smoke of Satan on the Silver Screen: The Catholic Horror Film, Vatican II, and the Revival of Demonology," *Journal for the Academic Study of Religion* 33, no. 1 (2020): 66–96.

32. Quoted in Cliff Linedecker, "Pagan, 3 Witches View Possession Differently," *Tattler* (Spring 1974 Special): 20.

33. Peter L. Berger, "The Devil and the Pornography of Modern Consciousness," *Worldview* 17, no. 12 (1974): 37.

34. "The Exorcism Frenzy," *Newsweek*, February 11, 1974, 61.

35. Greenson, "A Psychoanalyst's Indictment of 'The Exorcist,'" 42.

36. "The Exorcism Frenzy," 60.

37. Ibid., 63.

38. Ibid.

39. Edward B. Fiske, "'Exorcist' Adds Problems for Catholic Clergymen," *New York Times*, January 28, 1974, 15.

40. Greenson, "A Psychoanalyst's Indictment of 'The Exorcist,'" 41.

41. "The Exorcist Haunts MDs at Georgetown," *American Medical News* 17, no. 9 (March 4, 1974): 14.

42. Quoted in Brottman, *Hollywood Hex*, 38.

43. Castle, *Step Right Up!*, 187.

44. W. Scott Poole, *Satan in America: The Devil We Know* (New York: Rowman & Littlefield, 2009), 162.

45. Brottman, *Hollywood Hex*, 39.

46. Beverle Houston and Marsha Kinder, "Rosemary's Baby," *Sight and Sound* 38, no. 1 (Winter 1968): 17.

47. Quoted in Brottman, *Hollywood Hex*, 51.

48. "'Rosemary's Baby' Censored in London," *New York Times*, January 14, 1969, 35.

49. Schreck, *The Satanic Screen*, 139.

50. Robert Chapetta, "*Rosemary's Baby* by Roman Polansky [sic] and William Castle," *Film Quarterly* 22, no. 3 (Spring 1969): 38.

51. Bill Ellis, *Raising the Devil: Satanism, New Religions, and the Media* (Lexington: University of Kentucky Press, 2000), 178.

52. Castle, *Step Right Up!*, 229.

53. Quoted in John Brosnan, *The Horror People* (New York: New American Library, 1977), 141–142.

54. Chapetta, "*Rosemary's Baby*," 34.

55. Ellis, *Raising the Devil*, 159.

56. David Frankfurter, "Awakening to Satanic Conspiracy: *Rosemary's Baby* and the Cult Next Door," in *Deliver Us From Evil: Boston University Studies in Philosophy and Religion*, ed. M. David Eckel and Bradley L. Herling (New York: Continuum, 2011), 78.

57. Schreck, *The Satanic Screen*, 137.

58. Arthur Lyons, *The Second Coming: Satanism in America* (New York: Dodd, Mead, & Company, 1970), 162–163.

59. Steve Fishman, "The Devil in David Berkowitz," *New York Magazine*, September 8, 2006, https://nymag.com/news/crimelaw/20327/.

60. Quoted in Schreck, *The Satanic Screen*, 137.

61. Thomas B. Allen, *Possessed: The True Story of an Exorcism* (New York: Doubleday, 1993), 224.

62. Grady Hendrix, "Remembering William Peter Blatty, 1928–2017," *Tor.com*, January 13, 2017, https://www.tor.com/2017/01/13/remembering-william-peter-blatty-1928-2017/.

63. William Baer, *Classic American Films: Conversations with Screen-Writers* (Westport, CT: Praeger, 2008), 181.

64. Nick Freand Jones (dir.), *The Fear of God: 25 Years of "The Exorcist"* (1998).

65. Baer, *Classic American Films*, 182.

66. John McGuire, "70 Years Ago: The St. Louis Exorcism that Inspired the Movie 'The Exorcist,'" *St. Louis Post-Dispatch*, April 18, 2019, https://www.stltoday.com/news/archives/years-ago-the-st-louis-exorcism-that-inspired-the-movie/article_fbdec b6a-9d3c-5903-a12c-effd4f7a7713.html.

67. Hendrix, "Remembering William Peter Blatty."

68. Jones, *The Fear of God*.

69. Charles Champlin, "Critic at Large: Priest Plays Priest in 'The Exorcist,'" *Los Angeles Times*, August 25, 1972, G1.

70. Quoted in George Case, *Here's to My Sweet Satan: How the Occult Haunted Music, Movies and Pop Culture 1966–1980* (Fresno, CA: Quill Driver Books, 2016), 31.

71. William Peter Blatty, "There is Goodness in 'The Exorcist,'" *America Magazine*, April 15, 2019, 39.

72. Kilday, "People are Getting the Hell Scared Out of Them," E1.

73. "The Author Of 'The Exorcist,' William Peter Blatty, Dies At 89," *NPR.com*, January 14, 2017, https://www.npr.org/2017/01/14/509807205/the-author-of-the-exorcist-william-peter-blatty-dies-at-89.

74. Gerald R. Barrett, "William Friedkin Interview," *Literature/Film Quarterly* 3, no. 4 (Fall 1975): 355–356.

75. Hendrix, Interview with the authors.

76. Hendrix, "Remembering William Peter Blatty."

77. Baer, *Classic American Films*, 185.

78. Quoted in Peter Travers and Stephanie A. Reiff, *The Story Behind the Exorcist* (New York: New American Library, 1974), 27.

79. Kilday, "People are Getting the Hell Scared Out of Them," E1.

80. "The Exorcism Frenzy," 66; Allen, *Possessed*, 214.

81. Quoted in Aloi, "Rooted in the Occult Revival," 538.

82. Edward J. Ingebretsen, *Maps of Heaven, Maps of Hell: Religious Terror As Memory from the Puritans to Stephen King* (New York: Taylor and Francis, 2016), 174.

83. Baer, *Classic American Films*, 191–192.

84. Quoted in David Bartholomew, "*The Exorcist*: The Book, the Movie, the Phenomenon," *Cinefantastique* 3, no. 4 (Winter 1974): 13.

85. Barrett, "William Friedkin Interview," 349.

86. "Deliver Us From Evil," *L'Observato Romano*, November 23, 1972, 3.

87. Bartholomew, "The Exorcist," 9.

88. Nick Cull, "The Exorcist," *History Today* 50, no. 5 (May 2000): 46–51.

89. Baer, *Classic American Films*, 189.

90. Joseph P. Laycock, "How the Ouija Board Got Its Sinister Reputation," *The Conversation*, October 18, 2016), https://theconversation.com/how-the-ouija-board-got-its-sinister-reputation-66971.

91. Allen, *Possessed*, 161.

92. McGuire, "70 Years Ago."

93. Joe Nickell and Robert Bartholomew, *American Hauntings: The True Stories behind Hollywood's Scariest Movies from The Exorcist to The Conjuring* (Santa Barbara, CA: Praeger, 2015), 100.

94. Although sources referred to this woman using various pseudonyms, she appears to have been Hulda Emma Schmidt (1882–1964), an immigrant from Switzerland. We thank Michael Kelley of the Kelley Gallery for his genealogical research.

95. Carl Vogl, "Begone Satan! A Soul-Stirring Account of Diabolical Possession in Iowa," trans. Celestine Kapsner, in *Mary Crushes the Serpent and Begone Satan!*, ed. Theodor Gelger (Gilbert, AZ: Caritas Publishing, 2016 [1935]), 65.

96. Blatty, *If There Were Demons*, 22.

97. "Priest Fourth 4 Demons 23 Days to Free Woman," *Tattler* (Spring 1974 Special): 12.

98. Woods, *The Devil*, 31.

99. Baer, *Classic American Films*, 193.

100. Woods, *The Devil*, 29.

101. "World's Greatest Catholic Expert Discusses Possession and the Devil," *Tattler* (Spring 1974 Special): 2.

102. McGuire, "70 Years Ago."

103. Kilday, "People are Getting the Hell Scared Out of Them," E2.

104. McGuire, "70 Years Ago."

105. Marty Gunther and Toni Holt, "Bizarre Accidents, Deaths Plagued 'Exorcist' Set, Staff; Unplanned Images Flashed on Film," *Tattler* (Spring 1974 Special): 16; Bartholomew, "The Exorcist," 9.

106. Baer, *Classic American Films*, 187.

107. Jones (dir.) *The Fear of God.*

108. Charles Derry, *Dark Dreams 2.0: A Psychological History of the Modern Horror Film from the 1950s to the 21st Century* (Jefferson, NC: McFarland and Company), 363.

109. Brottman, *Hollywood Hex*, 104–106.

110. Gunther and Holt, "Bizarre Accidents," 16.

111. "The Exorcism Frenzy," 60.

112. Tom Valentine, "Rite Filmed in 'Exorcist' Is Too Realistic, Says Seer Joe DeLouise," *Tattler* (Spring 1974 Special): 18.

113. Linedecker, "Pagan, 3 Witches View Possession Differently," 20.

114. Roy Meachem, "How Did 'The Exorcist' Escape an X Rating?" *New York Times*, February 3, 1974, 15, 30.

115. King, *Danse Macabre*, 178.

116. Bartholomew, "The Exorcist," 11.

117. Tom Valentine, "Audience Reactions Vary From Laughing to Fainting, *Tattler* (Spring 1974 Special): 6.

118. Meachem, "How Did 'The Exorcist' Escape an X Rating?"
119. Syd Cassyd, "'Exorcist' Has Been One 'Happening' After Another—All Newsworthy," *New York Times*, February 4, 1974, W1.
120. Mike Goodman, "'The Exorcist': Fainting and Fleeing," *Los Angeles Times*, January 6, 1974, 3.
121. "The Exorcism Frenzy," 60.
122. Fiske, "'Exorcist' Adds Problems for Catholic Clergymen," 1.
123. Brigid Cherry, *Horror* (New York: Taylor and Francis, 2008), 58.
124. William Paul, *Laughing, Screaming: Modern Hollywood Horror and Comedy* (New York: Columbia University Press, 1994), 292.
125. Alpert, "In Answer to Dr. Greenson," 43.
126. Eugene C. Kennedy, "A Priest Takes a Look at the Devil and William Blatty: Film," *New York Times*, August 4, 1974, 95.
127. Karen M. Murphy, "The Public Responds to 'The Exorcist,'" *Los Angeles Times*, February 3, 1974, M24.
128. Quoted in Bartholomew, "The Exorcist," 10.
129. "The Exorcism Frenzy," 63.
130. Ibid.
131. "Law Suits, Marches Fight to Halt Showing of Film," 23.
132. Ibid.
133. Rachael Allen, "The Man Who Wants to Free Trump Supporters from 'Mind Control,'" *Slate.com*, June 1, 2021, https://slate.com/human-interest/2021/06/steven-hassan-former-moonie-trumpism-cult-theory.html.
134. Poole, *Satan in America*, 165.
135. Quoted in Woods, *The Devil*, 23–24.
136. "The Exorcism Frenzy," 66.
137. "The Exorcism Frenzy," 60.
138. Ibid.
139. "Most Illness Caused by Demons, Fundamentalist Says," *Tattler* (Spring 1974 Special): 7.
140. "'The Exorcist' Haunts MDs at Georgetown," 14.
141. "The Exorcism Frenzy," 61.
142. James C. Bozzuto, "Cinematic Neurosis Following 'The Exorcist,'" *The Journal of Nervous and Mental Disease* 161, no. 1 (1975): 43.
143. "Exorcist Fever," 53.
144. Bozzuo, "Cinematic Neurosis Following 'The Exorcist,'" 43.
145. J. S. Burkle, "The Devil and Gilles de la Tourrette," *Journal of the American Medical Association* 228, no. 5 (April 29, 1974): 567.
146. "The Exorcism Frenzy," 63.
147. "The Exorcism Frenzy," 60.
148. Woods, *The Devil*, 14–15.
149. Robert Graysmith, *Zodiac Unmasked* (New York: Berkley Books, 2007), 151.
150. "Youth Tells of 'Possession' After Seeing Film," *The Times*, October 30, 1975, 2.
151. "Youth is Found Guilty of 'Satanic' Murder," *The Times*, November 1, 1975, 3.

152. Richard Gallagher, *Demonic Foes: My Twenty-Five Years As a Psychiatrist Investigating Possessions, Diabolic Attacks, and the Paranormal* (New York: HarperOne, 2020), 26.

153. "Church Members Protest Showing of 'The Exorcist,'" *Boxoffice* 104, no. 22 (March 11, 1974): SW2.

154. Darryl Jones, *Horror: A Thematic History of Fiction in Film* (London: Arnold Publishers, 2002), 189.

155. Stephanie Sumell, "Creator of Horror Cult Classic Leaves Behind Lasting Legacy," *The Acorn*, November 8, 2012, https://www.theacorn.com/articles/creator-of-horror-cult-classic-leaves-behind-lasting-legacy/.

156. Kaye, "How *The Omen* Wrote the Bible on Satanic Horror."

157. Hendrix, *Paperback from Hell*, 49.

158. Kaye, "How *The Omen* Wrote the Bible on Satanic Horror."

159. "Curse of The Omen and Other Hollywood Hexes," *The Herald*, October 22, 2005, https://www.heraldscotland.com/news/12474820.curse-of-the-omen-and-other-hollywood-hexes-from-the-omen-to-the-exorcist-and-rosemarys-baby-there-are-tales-of-fatal-accidents-devil-worship-doomed-planes-and-car-crashes-barry-didcock-looks-at-some-of-the-most-cursed-films-of-all-time-and/.

160. Brad Duren, "Reckoning the Number of the Beast: Premillennial Dispensationalism, *The Omen*, and 1970s America," in *Divine Horror: Essays on the Cinematic Battle Between the Sacred and the Diabolical*, ed. Cynthia J. Miller, Cn A. Bowdoin Van Riper, eefferson, N.C.: McFarland,217),: 53–63.

161. Kaye, "How *The Omen* Wrote the Bible on Satanic Horror."

162. Steve A. Wiggins, *Holy Horror: The Bible and Fear in Movies* (New York: McFarland, 2018), 132.

163. Edwin Benson, "Defeating *Good Omens* Shows that Protest Work," *Return to Order*, April 2020, https://www.returntoorder.org/2020/04/defeating-good-omens-shows-that-protest-work/. In 2023, Amazon did announce a second season of *Good Omens*.

164. Philip Jenkins, "*The Omen*, *Good Omens*, and Why Neil Gaiman is Not the Antichrist," *Patheos.com*, June 28, 2019, https://www.patheos.com/blogs/anxiousbench/2019/06/the-omen-good-omens-and-why-neil-gaiman-is-not-the-antichrist-sorry/.

165. "Exorcist Fever," 53.

166. Gunther, "Satanist Calls Film a Boon for Christians and Devil-Worshippers," 21.

167. Drew Beard, "Horror Movies at Home: Supernatural Horror, Delivery Systems and 1980s Satanic Panic," *Horror Studies* 6, no. 2 (2015): 211.

168. Beard, "Horror Movies at Home," 216–217.

169. Philip Jenkins, *Decade of Nightmares: The End of the Sixties and the Making of Eighties America* (New York: Oxford University Press, 2006), 182.

Chapter 4

1. Quoted in Gerald Brittle, *The Demonologist: The Extraordinary Career of Ed and Lorraine Warren* (Los Angeles: Graymalkin Media, 2013), 17.

2. Michael W. Cuneo, *American Exorcism: Expelling Demons in the Land of Plenty* (New York: Doubleday, 2001), 30.

3. On impression management, see Erving Goffman, *The Presentation of Self in Everyday Life* (Garden City, NY: Doubleday Anchor Books, 1959), 238.

4. Ray Garton, Electronic communication with the authors, April 13, 2022.

5. Bill Hayden, "They'll Deliver You From Ghoulies, Ghosties," *Evening Journal*, March 4, 1974, 21.

6. NESPR, "Where It All Began: Ed and Lorraine Warren," https://tonyspera.com/about/.

7. Ed Warren and Lorraine Warren, "Ghosts, Witches, and Demons: Ghost Hunters Ed and Lorraine Warren, T.V. Personalities Show and Tell Of Their 27 Years of Supernatural Experiences." Undated pamphlet. Courtesy of the Archives of St. Bonaventure University.

8. "The Warrens," https://edandlorrainewarren.com/about-3/.

9. Garton, Electronic communication with the authors, April 13, 2022.

10. This trip is referenced in a postcard from Lorraine Warren to Alphonsus Trabold (May 28, 1976). Courtesy of the Archives of St. Bonaventure University.

11. Jerry Solfvin, Interview with the authors, September 14, 2022.

12. "Ghost-hunters Stalk Prey in a College Hall," *Philadelphia Inquirer*, February 26, 1978, 1–2M; Ed Warren et al., *Satan's Harvest* (Los Angeles: Graymalkin Media, 1990), 174.

13. Hayden, "They'll Deliver You."

14. Brittle, *The Demonologist*, 23.

15. Ibid., 24.

16. Ed Warren, Lorraine Warren, and Robert David Chase, *Ghost Hunters: True Stories from the World's Most Famous Demonologists* (Los Angeles: Graymalkin Media, 2014), 41.

17. Cheryl Wicks, Ed Warren, and Lorraine Warren, *Ghost Tracks* (Los Angeles: Graymalkin Media, 2012), 4.

18. Dr. Moss was most well known for her research of Kirlian photography, which was purported to capture the psychic aura of people and objects. Although on school grounds, the lab was unsanctioned by UCLA and was often at odds with the University. After ten years of largely fruitless research, the lab closed in 1978 after failing to produce any papers or results of scientific value. Moss was released from UCLA shortly thereafter. See Sean Green, "UCLA Lab Researched Parapsychology in the '70s," *The Daily Bruin*, October 26, 2010, https://dailybruin.com/2010/10/26/ucla_lab_researched_parapsychology_in_the_70s.

19. Solfvin, Interview with the authors, September 14, 2022.

20. "Episode 25: Dr. Barry Taff," *ParaPeculiar Podcast*, December 2022.

21. Hayden, "They'll Deliver You."

22. John C. Peterson, "In Search of the Supernatural," *Connecticut* 35, no. 3 (April 1972): 54.

23. Peterson, "In Search of the Supernatural," 56.

24. Solfvin, Electronic communication with the authors, September 25, 2022.

25. J. F. Sawyer, *Deliver Us From Evil* (Westfield, MA: Phillips Publishing Company, 1973), 17–18.
26. Warren and Warren, "Ghosts, Witches, and Demons."
27. Brittle, *The Demonologist*, 35–36. Unlike *The New York Times*, this source reports that apparitions started *after* the Warrens were scheduled to speak but before their lecture.
28. Pat Okerson to Douglass Associates (September 28, 1973). Courtesy of the Archives of St. Bonaventure University.
29. Warren and Warren, "Ghosts, Witches, and Demons."
30. Art Thomas, "The Warrens Discuss Ghosts and Haunted Houses," *The Exponent* (n.d.) Courtesy of the Archives of St. Bonaventure University.
31. Hayden, "They'll Deliver You."
32. Garton, Electronic communication with the authors, April 13, 2022.
33. Betty Joan Burr, "The Case of Douglas Dean," *Focus*, October 26, 1973. Reprinted in Sawyer, *Deliver Us From Evil*, 165–173.
34. Philip A. Douglas to Reverend Alfonse Thibault (February 8, 1974). Courtesy of the Archives of St. Bonaventure University.
35. The account in *Focus*, based on Betty Joan Burr's interview with Ed, has serious inconsistencies with internal church documents describing the exorcism that were not publicly available in 1973. For example, Ed described the exorcism as taking place in a monastery rather than a hospital. It also describes impossible quantities of projectile vomit, which was not reported in internal documents. It is possible Ed combined information available in 1973 with details from the book *Begone Satan!* describing a different exorcism that occurred in Iowa in 1928. That text does describe vomiting, and an exorcism performed in a convent.
36. Sawyer, *Deliver Us From Evil*, 20–21.
37. Brittle, *The Demonologist*, 12.
38. Wicks, Warren, and Warren, *Ghost Tracks*, 17.
39. Steve A. Wiggins, *Holy Horror: The Bible and Fear in Movies* (New York: McFarland, 2018), 163.
40. Bernard Doherty, "The Smoke of Satan on the Silver Screen: The Catholic Horror Film, Vatican II, and the Revival of Demonology," *Journal for the Academic Study of Religion* 33, no. 1 (2020): 66–96.
41. "Clergy Scored by Paranormal Expert for Rejecting Demons," *Tattler*, Spring 1974, 6.
42. Brittle, *The Demonologist*, 262.
43. Sean McCloud, *American Possessions: Fighting Demons in the Contemporary United States* (New York: Oxford University Press, 2015), 37.
44. Warren et al., *Satan's Harvest*, 165.
45. (Rev.) Alphonsus Trabold to Mr. Philip A. Douglass (February 28, 1974). Courtesy of the Archives of St. Bonaventure University.
46. Grady Hendrix, Interview with the authors, December 20, 2020.
47. Garton, Electronic communication with the authors, April 13, 2022.
48. Matt Baxter, Interview with the authors, March 16, 2022.
49. Ibid.

50. Jerry Solfvin, Interview with the authors, September 14, 2022.

51. Garton, Electronic communication with the authors, April 13, 2022.

52. Ibid.

53. Baxter, Interview with the authors, March 16, 2022.

54. Ibid.

55. Kim Masters and Ashley Cullens, "War Over 'The Conjuring': The Disturbing Claims Behind a Billion Dollar Franchise," *Hollywood Reporter*, December 13, 2017, https://www.hollywoodreporter.com/tv/tv-features/war-conjuring-disturbing-claims-behind-a-billion-dollar-franchise-1064364/.

56. Brittle, *The Demonologist*, 186.

57. Masters and Cullens, "War Over 'The Conjuring.'"

58. Tony DeRosa-Grund, *IMDB.com*. https://www.imdb.com/name/nm0220533/?ref_=ttfc_fc_cr3.

59. Masters and Cullens, "War over 'The Conjuring.'"

60. Gabrielle Moss, "My Date with 'The Conjuring's' Lorraine Warren," *Medium.com*, June 3, 2021, https://gabriellemoss.medium.com/my-date-with-the-conjuring-s-lorraine-warren-2d5a1a9382af.

61. Brittle, *The Demonologist*, 52–62.

62. The NESPR website tells the same story as *The Demonologist*, but with different names for many of the characters. *The Demonologist and Ghost Tracks* also disagree about where "Annabelle" claimed she died: in a car accident or a field where the apartment would one day be built.

63. Ed Warren and Lorraine Warren, "Case of a Spirit that Couldn't Accept Death," *The Tattler*, August 26, 1973.

64. Susan Roberts, *Witches U.S.A.* (New York: Dell Publishing, 1971), 206.

65. Joseph Laycock, "The Paranormal to Pop Culture Pipeline," *Religion Dispatches*, July 8, 2014, https://religiondispatches.org/the-paranormal-to-pop-culture-pipeline/.

66. Bryan Alexander, "'Annabelle: Creation': The 'True' Story of the Evil Doll Star," *USA Today*, August 7, 2017, https://www.usatoday.com/story/life/movies/2017/08/07/annabelle-creation-true-story-evil-doll-star/543202001/.

67. Ed Susman, "Cabbage Patch Dolls Can Be Possessed By the Devil," *National Enquirer*, September 4, 1984. Courtesy of the Archives of St. Bonaventure University.

68. "Bathsheba Sherman and the Evil Doll Annabelle: The True Story Behind 'The Conjuring,'" *Mysteries Unsolved*, August 9, 2021, https://mysteriesrunsolved.com/2020/10/bathsheba-sherman-annabelle.html#The_True_Story_Of_Bathsheba_Sherman_The_Conjuring_Witch.

69. Joe Nickell and Robert Bartholomew, *American Hauntings: The True Stories behind Hollywood's Scariest Movies—from The Exorcist to The Conjuring* (Santa Barbara, CA: Praeger, 2015), 213.

70. Nickell and Bartholomew, *American Hauntings*, 214.

71. Ibid., 221.

72. J'aime Rubio, "The Real Bathsheba Sherman—True History vs. "Conjured" Fiction," *Dreaming Casually (Investigate Blog)*, July 14, 2015, https://dreamingcasuallypoetry.blogspot.com/2014/07/the-real-bathsheba-sherman-true-history.html.

73. Ed Warren and Lorraine Warren, "How Witch Hunt Victim Found Her Revenge," *The National Tattler*, March 31, 1974, 10.

74. Troy Taylor, "Help Save Bathsheba Sherman's Grave," February 22, 2022, https://www.facebook.com/authortt/posts/4833144030115878.

75. *The Numbers*, https://www.the-numbers.com/.

76. Samuel Z. Arkoff and Richard Trubo, *Flying through Hollywood by the Seat of My Pants: From the Man Who Brought You I Was a Teenage Werewolf and Muscle Beach Party* (Secaucus, NJ: Carol Publishing Group 1992), 227–228.

77. Robert E. Bartholomew and Joe Nickell, "The Amityville Hoax at 40: Why the Myth Endures," *Skeptic Magazine* 21, no. 4 (2016): 8–12.

78. Taffy Sealyham, "The Amityville Horror Pt 1," in *Seekers of the Supernatural Presents Conversations with Ed and Lorraine Warren* (n.p.: OmniMedia Publishing 2011), 1.

79. Jay Anson, *The Amityville Horror* (New York: Pocket Star, 2006 [1977]), 303.

80. Solfvin, Interview with the authors, September 14, 2022.

81. Bartholomew and Nickell, "The Amityville Hoax at 40," 9.

82. Clarence Petersen, "Tempo: Demonologists hellbent on selling 'Amityville II,'" *Chicago Tribune*, September 23, 192, D1.

83. "The Catholic Church and the Hoax," *The Amityville Murders*, https://web.arch ive.org/web/20110707134033/http://www.amityvillemurders.com/catholic.html.

84. Arkov and Trubo, *Flying Through Hollywood by the Seat of My Pants*, 228.

85. Associated Press, "'Amityville Horror' Amplified Over Bottles of Wine,—Lawyer," *Lakeland Ledger*, July 27, 1979, 2A.

86. Associated Press, "'Amityville Horror' Amplified," 2A.

87. Solfvin, Interview with the authors, September 14, 2022.

88. Joseph Egelhof, "New Amityville 'Haunted' House Owners Want Out," *The Chicago Tribune*, December 24, 1978, 4.

89. Gerald Brittle to Rev. Alphonsus Trabold (June 12, 1980). Courtesy of the Archives of St. Bonaventure University.

90. Flyer for "Seeking the Supernatural" lecture at St. Bonaventure University, March 21, 1985.

91. Chris Wood, "Diabolic Obsession," *Maclean's*, November 3, 1986, 10B.

92. Joe Nickell, "Enfield Poltergeist." *Skeptical Inquirer* 36, no. 4 (July/August 2012): 12–14.

93. Ibid., 13.

94. Ibid., 14.

95. Greg Newkirk, "Conjuring the Truth: Enfield Poltergeist Investigator Says Ed and Lorraine Warren Never Investigated Case," *Week in Weird*, January 7, 2016, http://weekinweird.com/2016/01/07/conjuring-truth-original-enfield-poltergeist-inves tigator-says-ed-and-lorraine-warren-never-investigated-the-case/.

96. Quoted in R. L. Smith to Alphonse Trabold (August 26, 1972), 2. Courtesy of the Archives of St. Bonaventure University.

97. Gerald Brittle, *Devil in Connecticut* (New York: Bantam Books, 1983), 70–72.

98. Dudley Clendinen, "Defendant in a Murder Puts the Devil on Trial," *The New York Times*, March 23, 1981, B1.

99. Ibid.

100. Francis Richards, Carl Glatzel Jr., and David Glatzl, "Alone Through the Valley: The True Story Behind The Devil in Connecticut," https://web.archive.org/web/2008122 4191937/http://www.geocities.com/devilbustedinct/news.html.

101. Clendinen, "Defendant in a Murder Puts the Devil on Trial." Another source said that four "minor" exorcisms were performed on David. See "Brothers Sue World Famous Psychic Lorraine Warren for False Accusations in Devil book," *Mass Media Distribution Newswire*, October 8, 2007, https://web.archive.org/web/20080829012 011/http://www.mmdnewswire.com/brors-sue-world-fmous-psychic-lorrine-wrren-for-flse-ccustis-in-devil-book-2347-2.html.

102. "Brothers Sue World Famous Psychic Lorraine Warren."

103. Peter S. Hawes, "Man Who Claimed Demonic Possession Released One Month Early," *Associated Press*, January 23, 1986, https://apnews.com/article/c758c33ba 4756f757e1dfec4f0abd39e.

104. Richard, Glatzel, and Glatzel, "Alone Through the Valley."

105. Clendinen, "Defendant in a Murder Puts the Devil on Trial."

106. Richard, Glatzel, and Glatzel, "Alone Through the Valley."

107. "Brothers Sue World Famous Psychic Lorraine Warren."

108. "Martin J. Minella," *Minella, Tramuta, & Edwards, LLC.*, https://mtelawfirm.com/martin-j-minnella/.

109. "Brothers Sue World Famous Psychic Lorraine Warren."

110. Warren et al., *Satan's Harvest*, 55.

111. "By Demons Possessed? Son Attempts Father's Crime," *Associated Press*, November 8, 1992, http://web.mit.edu/~mkgray/afs/bar/afs/net/user/tytso/usenet/americast/twt/news/620.

112. Warren et al., *Satan's Harvest*, 311.

113. Jeffrey J. Steffon, *Satanism: Is It Real?* (Ann Arbor, MI: Servant Publications, 1992).

114. "By Demons Possessed?"

115. Sheena Delazio, "'Demon in Home' Grabs Our Attention," *The Times Leader*, March 2, 2008, https://web.archive.org/web/20080305004915/http://www.timesleader.com/news/20080303_03lookback_smurls_sd_ART.html.

116. Delazio, "Demon in Home."

117. Taffy Sealyham, "True Haunting of Jack and Janet Smurl," in *Seekers of the Supernatural Presents Conversations with Ed and Lorraine Warren* (n.p.: OmniMedia Publishing 2011), 1.

118. Benjamin Radford, "The Story Behind 'The Haunting in Connecticut,'" *NBC News*, March 26, 2009, https://www.nbcnews.com/id/wbna29895615.

119. Radford, "'The Haunting in Connecticut'"

120. Taffy Sealyham, "Haunted Funeral Home," in *Seekers of the Supernatural Presents Conversations with Ed and Lorraine Warren* (n.p.: OmniMedia Publishing 2011), 2–4.

121. The Warrens' nephew, John Zaffis, reported the stay lasted nine full weeks. Sealyham, "Haunted Funeral Home," 14.

122. Garton, Electronic communication with the authors, April 13, 2022).

123. Garton, Electronic communication with the authors, April 13, 2022). Garton felt that across the Warrens' cases, there seemed to be a preoccupation with reports of anal sex. Anal sex appears repeatedly in Malachi Martin's *Hostage to the Devil* as well.

124. Ibid.

125. John W. Morehead, "Ramsey, Bill," in *Spirit Possession around the World*, ed. Joseph P. Laycock (Santa Barbara, CA: ABC-CLIO, 2015), 299–300.

126. "Mountain Monster Tried to Snatch My Boy, Says Mom," *San Antonio Express*, May 9, 1976, 17. Newspaper reports state Lorraine had read about the story and decided to investigate herself. *Ghost Tracks* reports that locals approached the Warrens for help while they were doing a lecture tour.

127. Warren, Warren, and Chase, *Ghost Hunters*, 35–38.

128. Ibid., 38.

129. Natasha L. Mikles and Joseph P. Laycock, "Tracking the Tulpa: Exploring the 'Tibetan' Origins of a Contemporary Paranormal Idea," *Nova Religio: The Journal of Alternative and Emergent Religions* 19, no. 1 (2015): 87–97.

130. Marc A. Eaton, "'Give Us A Sign of Your Presence': Paranormal Investigation As A Spiritual Practice," *Sociology of Religion* 76, no. 4 (2015): 407.

131. Daniel Wise. "Twenty-First Century American Ghost Hunting: A Late Modern Enchantment" (Dissertation, University of Virginia, Department of Religious Studies, 2020), 96–122.

132. Darryl V. Caterine, *Haunted Ground: Journeys through a Paranormal America* (Santa Barbara, CA: Praeger 2011), ix.

133. Desmond Ryan, "On Movies––They're Advisers on Demons, Evil," *Philadelphia Inquirer*, October 3, 1982, F3.

134. Ryan, "On Movies."

135. Carey Hayes, Chad Hayes, and Diana Walsh Pasulka, "The Catholic Supernatural," *OUPblog*, October 29, 2014, https://blog.oup.com/2014/10/the-conjuring-movie-q-a-pasulka-hayes/.

Chapter 5

1. "An Article on Exorcism," *Father Martin's Website*, https://web.archive.org/web/20120110093829/http://starharbor.com/fr_martin/exorcism.html.

2. Rory Carroll, "Condemned to a Life in Purgatory for Falling Prey to a Sinner in the Vatican," *The Guardian*, March 17, 2002, https://www.theguardian.com/world/2002/mar/17/books.religion.

3. "An Article on Exorcism."

4. Lia Eustachewich, "'Exorcist' Priest Died After 'Possessed' Child Spoke to Him," *New York Post*, January 13, 2017, https://nypost.com/2017/01/13/exorcist-priest-died-after-possessed-child-spoke-to-him/.

5. Michael W. Cuneo, *American Exorcism: Expelling Demons in the Land of Plenty* (New York: Doubleday, 2001), 56.

6. Malachi Martin, *Hostage to the Devil: The Possession and Exorcism of Five Contemporary Americans* (New York: HarperOne, 1992), 11.

7. Robert Blair Kaiser, *Clerical Error: A True Story* (New York: Continuum, 2002), 148.

8. Sarah Colwell, *Disguised as a Man: Malachi Martin and Me: Part II—Hostage to the Devil* (n.p.: Smashwords Edition, 2016), 67.

9. Cuneo, *American Exorcism*, 17.

10. Paul Likoudis, "Interview with Malachi Martin," *Catholic Citizens of Illinois*, May 15, 2004, https://web.archive.org/web/20100417191716/http://www.catholiccitizens.org/press/contentview.asp?c=14897.

11. "Death and Conspiracy," *Hostage to the Devil Podcast*, August 13, 2020.

12. Christopher Lehman-Haupt, "Books of the Times: Why Religion Has Failed," *New York Times*, March 9, 1970, 35.

13. Colman McCarthy, "Declarations of a Jesuit 'War,'" *The Washington Post*, March 27, 1987, D3.

14. Kathleen Hendrix, "Giving the Devil More Than His Due?" *Los Angeles Times*, May 20, 1976, E1.

15. Hendrix, "Giving the Devil More than His Due?" E1.

16. Kaiser, *Clerical Error*, 245.

17. Ralph Sarchie and Lisa Collier Cool, *Deliver Us From Evil: A New York City Cop Investigates the Supernatural* (New York: St. Martin's Press, 2001), 233.

18. Elaine Woo, "Obituaries; Malachi Martin; Author, Former Jesuit Priest," *Los Angeles Times*, July 31, 1999, 20.

19. Edward K. Kaplan, *Spiritual Radical: Abraham Joshua Heschel in America, 1940–1972* (Yale University Press, 2007), 243.

20. Kaplan, *Spiritual Radical*, 254.

21. Kaiser, 147. Sue is described by the pseudonym "Mary" in Kaiser's novel.

22. Kaiser, *Clerical Error*, 154.

23. Sarah Colwell also reported that Martin encouraged her to use birth control, including an intra-uterine device, despite his professed identity as a Catholic priest. Echoing accusations about Ed Warren, Colwell also reported that Martin offered to procure an abortion for her after she missed her period. See Colwell, *Disguised as a Man: Malachi Martin and Me: Part II.*

24. Kaiser, *Clerical Error*, 255.

25. Ibid., 259.

26. Letter from Father William Van Etten Casey to the Most Reverend H. E. Cardinale, D.D., JC.D., November 1, 1965, http://callmejorgebergoglio.blogspot.com/2014/08/apostate-fr-malachi-martin-helps-break.html. This site also features a letter to Robert Kaiser from Father John Courtney Murray S.J., dated July 10, 1964, confirming details of Kaiser's story.

27. Kaiser, *Clerical Error*, 284–285.

28. John F. McManus, "Malachi Martin: The Catholic Church in Crisis," *The New American*, June 9, 1997, 39.

29. Boris Kachka, *Hothouse: The Art of Survival and the Survival of Art at America's Most Celebrated Publishing House, Farrar, Straus & Giroux* (New York: Simon & Schuster, 2014), 119.

30. Memo of the Harry Guggenheim Foundation, The Henry Allen Moe papers, Malachi Martin—correspondence, Folder 1.

31. Kachka, *Hothouse*, 120.
32. Kakia Livanos to Henry Allen Moe, The Henry Allen Moe papers, Malachi Martin—correspondence, Folder 5.
33. William H. Kennedy, "In Defense of Father Malachi Martin," *Seattle Catholic*, July 2002, https://www.oocities.org/whkinfo1/malachi_martinsophia.htm.
34. "Death and Conspiracy." Sarah Colwell reported that Martin was Kakia Livanos's boyfriend and that he lived in her apartment. However, Martin also maintained a smaller apartment nearby where he would have liaisons with Colwell. Colwell expressed certainty that in the 1980s Martin was juggling a number of illicit romantic relationships in addition to his long-term relationship with Livanos. Electronic communication with the authors, September 17, 2022.
35. Hendrix, "Giving the Devil More than His Due?" E1.
36. Kakia Livanos to Mr. Newton Minow, September 30, 1968. The Henry Allen Moe papers, Malachi Martin—correspondence, Folder 5.
37. Malachi Fitzmaurice-Martin to Dr. Henry Allen Moe, November 1, 1968, The Henry Allen Moe papers, Malachi Martin—correspondence, Folder 5.
38. Anna Rubino, *Queen of the Oil Club: The Intrepid Wanda Jablonski and the Power of Information* (Boston, MA: Beacon, 2009), 259.
39. Kachka, *Hothouse*, 378.
40. Rachael Riley, "Bragg to be Subject of Hollywood Exorcism Movie," *The Fayetteville Observer*, October 26, 2019, https://www.fayobserver.com/story/entertainment/movies/2019/10/26/was-fort-bragg-location-of-exorcism-in-1980s/2421246007/.
41. Martin, *Hostage to the Devil*, 17.
42. William Peter Blatty, "'Hostage': Giving Possession a Bad Name," *Los Angeles Times*, February 29, 1976, 13.
43. Martin, *Hostage to the Devil*, 174,
44. Francine Du Plexxix Gray, "Lucrative Possessions," *The New York Times*, March 14, 1976, BR3.
45. Martin, *Hostage to the Devil*, 262.
46. John Nicola, "Sermon of Admonition," *National Review*, May 28, 1976, 567–568.
47. Martin, *Hostage to the Devil*, 24.
48. Norris Merchant, "Hostage to the Devil," *Commonweal*, August 27, 1976, 569.
49. Peter S. Prescott, "The Possessed," *Newsweek*, March 8, 1976, 80.
50. Cuneo, *American Exorcism*, 21.
51. Ibid., 23.
52. Hendrix, "Giving the Devil More than His Due?" E1.
53. Martin, *Hostage to the Devil*, 354.
54. Ibid., 212.
55. Nicola, "Sermon of Admonition," 568.
56. Richard Woods, "The Devil You Know," *National Catholic Reporter*, April 29, 2005, http://www.natcath.org/NCR_Online/archives2/2005b/042905/042905m.htm.
57. Blatty, "Hostage," 13.
58. Ibid.
59. Malachi Martin, "The Scientist as Shaman," *Harper's Magazine*, March 1, 1972, 61.
60. Blatty, "Hostage," 13.

61. Hendrix, "Giving the Devil More than His Due?" E1.

62. Hendrix, "Giving the Devil More than His Due?" E1.

63. Cuneo, *American Exorcism*, 24.

64. Ibid., 56–57.

65. "An Article on Exorcism."

66. Hendrix, "Giving the Devil More than His Due?" E1.

67. M. Scott Peck, *Glimpses of the Devil: A Psychiatrist's Personal Accounts of Possession, Exorcism, and Redemption* (New York: Free Press, 2005), 32.

68. "An Article on Exorcism."

69. John Grasmeier, "Malachi Martin's Exorcism Snake Oil," *Angelqueen.org*, March 2007, https:/www.cathinfo.com/general-discussion/detailed-angelqueen-article-about-malachi-martin-being-a-fraud/.

70. *Coast to Coast AM with Art Bell*, May 4, 1998.

71. "Death and Conspiracy."

72. Stafford Betty, "The Growing Evidence for Demonic Possession": What Should Psychiatry's Response Be?" *Journal of Religion and Health* 44, no. 1 (Spring 2005): 17.

73. Woods, "The Devil You Know."

74. This is the Douay-Rheims translation, the preferred English translation for most traditionalist Catholics.

75. Hendrix, "Giving the Devil More than His Due?" E1.

76. In the exorcism of Emma Schmidt in Iowa in 1928, two of the possessing demons were identified as Lucifer and Beelzebub. Albert Bandini, an Italian-born priest, wrote a pamphlet condemning this claim and arguing that Lucifer and Beelzebub are clearly two names for the same entity. In Bandini's opinion, Schmidt's exorcism was more informed by German folklore than Catholic doctrine. A similar assessment could be made of Martin's demonology. See Albert R. Bandini, *Angels on Horseback: A Critical Review of the Pamphlet "Begone Satan" Which Relates An Alleged Case of Demoniacal Possession Occurred in Earling, Iowa* (Fresno, CA: Academy Press, 1950 [1936]), 50.

77. Martin, *Hostage to the Devil*, 24.

78. Peck, *Glimpses of the Devil*, 111.

79. Nicola, "Sermon of Admonition," 568.

80. Martin, *Hostage to the Devil*.

81. Nicola, "Sermon of Admonition," 568.

82. Brian P. Levack, *The Devil Within: Possession & Exorcism in the Christian West* (New Haven, CT: Yale University Press, 2013), 60.

83. David Toolan, "Establishing God's Kingdom on Earth," *The Washington Post*, September 23, 1990, I6.

84. Levack (*The Devil Within*, 200) notes these lines were also sometimes blurred by early modern witch hunters as well.

85. Elliott Leyton, *Hunting Humans: Inside the Minds of Mass Murderers* (New York: Pocketbooks, 1988), 166. In February 1979, Berkowitz held a press conference admitting that his claims of demons and spirit possession had been an invention. In a letter to his former psychiatrist, David Abrahemsen, he confessed that "the entire demonic story had been a well-planned, carefully coordinated hoax" (Leyton, Hunting Humans, 170).

86. "An Article on Exorcism."

87. "Son of Sam," *Hostage to the Devil Podcast*, September 18, 2020.

88. Jason Bunch, "These Occult Exorcists Say the Catholic Church Makes Demons Worse," *Vice*, June 15, 2018, https://www.vice.com/en_us/article/4354zp/these-occult-exorcists-say-the-catholic-church-makes-demons-worse.

89. Sergeo A. Rueda, *Diabolical Possession and the Case Behind* The Exorcist: *An Overview of Scientific Research with Witnesses and Experts* (Jefferson, NC: McFarland Press, 2018), 157.

90. "MPD," *60 Minutes*, November 30, 1997.

91. Peck, *Glimpses of the Devil*, 239.

92. Cuneo, *American Exorcism*, 47.

93. Peck, *Glimpses of the Devil*, 83.

94. Ibid., 124.

95. Ibid., 252.

96. Ibid., 251.

97. Ibid., 11.

98. Woods, "The Devil You Know."

99. McManus, "The Catholic Church in Crisis," 40.

100. Kennedy, "In Defense of Father Malachi Martin."

101. *Coast to Coast AM with Art Bell*, October 18, 1996.

102. Jon Dougherty, "Catholic Novelist Malachi Martin Dies," *WND.com*, July 29, 1999, https://www.wnd.com/1999/07/1812/.

103. Charles C. Fiore, "'God's Messenger' At Rest: Father Malachi Martin," *Unity Publishing* (n.d.), https://web.archive.org/web/20070525211635/http://www.unitypublishing.com/newswire/fiore1.html.

104. We wrote the CIA to confirm whether Marro was, in fact, a former employee. The CIA responded that they may only divulge this information if permission has been granted by the individual in question.

105. Sean Burns, "The Order; Directed by Brian Hegeland," *Philadelphia Weekly*, September 16, 2003, 39.

106. Sarchie and Cool, *Beware the Night*, 151.

107. Ibid., 43.

108. Ibid., 63.

109. Ibid., 56.

110. Ibid., 195.

111. Martin, *Hostage to the Devil*, xii. This figure also found its way into Matt Baglio's *The Rite* (2010), suggesting that it is now taken seriously among Catholic exorcists. See Matt Baglio, *The Rite: The Making of a Modern Exorcist* (New York: Random House, 1999), 16.

112. Rocco Parascandola and Larry McShane, "Bustin' Makes Him Feel Good: NYPD Vet Chases Gangsters, Ghosts," *Officer.com*, November 26, 2021, https://www.officer.com/training-careers/specialized-training/news/21247931/bustin-makes-him-feel-good-nypd-vet-chases-gangsters-ghosts.

113. Kevin J. Wetmore, Jr. "Colonial Possessions: A Fanonian Reading of *The Exorcist* and its Sequels," *Social Research* 81, no. 4 (Winter 2014): 894.

114. Chris Alexander, "Penchant Picks Up Rights to Exorcism Book Hostage to the Devil," *Comingsoon.net*, April 10, 2017, https://www.comingsoon.net/horror/news/836133-penchant-picks-up-rights-to-exorcism-book-hostage-to-the-devil.

115. Dave McNary, "Osgood Perkins to Write, Helm Exorcism Thriller 'Incident at Fort Bragg,'" *Variety*, September 26, 2019, https://variety.com/2019/film/news/osgood-perkins-incident-at-fort-bragg-director-lionsgate-1203350753/.

116. Pavel Barter, "Hollywood Films Tale of Irish Priest's Exorcism for US Army," *Times of London*, October 6, 2019, https://www.thetimes.co.uk/article/hollywood-films-tale-of-irish-priests-exorcism-for-us-army-lnt5c3ls9.

117. Sarah Colwell, Electronic communication with the authors, September 17, 2022.

118. Sarah Colwell, Electronic communication with the authors, September 26, 2022.

Chapter 6

1. Quoted in Tom Valentine, "Rite Filmed in 'Exorcist' Is Too Realistic, Says Seer Joe DeLouise," *Tattler* (Spring 1974 Special): 18.

2. Francis Young, *A History of Exorcism in Catholic Christianity* (Cambridge: Palgrave MacMillan, 2016), 213–216; Brian P. Levack, *The Devil Within: Possession & Exorcism in the Christian West* (New Haven, CT: Yale University Press, 2013), 242.

3. Gabriele Amorth, *An Exorcist Tells His Story* (San Francisco: Ignatius Press, 1999), 55.

4. Levack, *The Devil Within*, 252.

5. Brian P. Levack, "The Horrors of Witchcraft and Demonic Possession," *Social Research* 81, no. 4 (Winter 2014): 934.

6. Levack, *The Devil Within*, 258.

7. Schreck, *The Satanic Screen*, 17.

8. Fernando Espi Forcen, *Monsters, Demons and Psychopaths: Psychiatry and Horror Film* (New York: CRC Press, 2017), 65.

9. Keith McDonald and Wayne Johnson, *Contemporary Gothic and Horror Film: Transnational Perspectives* (New York: Anthem Press, 2021), 57.

10. Ernesto de Martino, *Magic: A Theory From the South*, trans. Dorothy Louise Zinn (Chicago: Hau Books, 2015).

11. Roberto Curti, *Mavericks of Italian Cinema: Eight Unorthodox Filmmakers 1940s–2000s* (Jefferson, NC: McFarland, 2018), 118.

12. Tim Lucas, "Say 'La Vi!': The Video Watchdog Interview with Daliah Lavi," *Video Watchdog* 170 (September–October 2012), 30.

13. Ibid.

14. Richard Crouse, *Raising Hell: Ken Russell and the Unmaking of The Devils* (Toronto: ECW Press, 2012).

15. Quoted in Marty Gunther, "Satanist Calls Film a Boon for Christians and Devil-Worshippers," *Tattler* (Spring 1974 Special): 21

16. Gerard E. Sherry, "Priest Reports Using Exorcism to Aid Family," *The Advocate* 24, no. 5 (January 24, 1974): 1; Judy Pasternak, "Obituaries: Father Karl Patzelt, 71; Performed Exorcisms," *Los Angeles Times*, May 23, 1988, https://www.latimes.com/archives/la-xpm-1988-05-23-mn-2015-story.html.

17. Andy Lang, "Exorcism Performed in California," *The Hoya* 56, no. 14 (January 18, 1974): 1.
18. Chris Keating, "Exorcist Talks Demons and Devils," *The Ram* 62, no. 18 (September 11, 1980): 5.
19. Pasternak, "Obituaries: Father Karl Patzelt."
20. Keating, "Exorcist Talks Demons and Devils," 5.
21. Lacey Fosburgh, "An Exorcism by Catholic Stirs a Furor," *New York Times*, January 25, 1974, 23; Thomas Hillstrom, "California Exorcism Creates Furor," *The Observer* 8, no. 62 (January 22, 1974): 1.
22. Keating, "Exorcist Talks Demons and Devils," 5.
23. Michael W. Cuneo, *American Exorcism: Expelling Demons in the Land of Plenty* (New York: Doubleday, 2001), 128.
24. Francis Young, *A History of Anglican Exorcism: Deliverance and Demonology in Church Ritual* (New York: I.B. Tauris, 2018), 143.
25. Lynn R. Buzzard, "Introduction," in *Demon Possession: A Medical, Historical, Anthropological, and Theological Symposium: Papers Presented at the University of Notre Dame, January 8–11, 1975, Under the Auspices of the Christian Medical Association*, ed. John Warwick Montgomery (Minneapolis: Bethany Fellowship, 1976), 17.
26. "Catholic Pentecostals Charged with Unauthorized Exorcisms," *New York Times*, August 10, 1975, 38.
27. Joseph Cardinal Ratzinger, "Letter to Ordinaries Regarding Norms on Exorcism (September 29, 1985)," https://www.vatican.va/roman_curia/congregations/cfaith/documents/rc_con_cfaith_doc_19850924_exorcism_en.html.
28. "A Phenomenon of Fear," *Time*, September 6, 1976, 68.
29. Young, *A History of Exorcism in Catholic Christianity*, 219.
30. Jeff Zacks, *Flicker: Your Brain on Movies* (New York: Oxford University Press, 2015), 96.
31. Felicitas D. Goodman, *The Exorcism of Anneliese Michel* (Eugene, OR: Resource Publications, 2005), 41.
32. Ibid., 106–108.
33. Moshe Sluhovsky, *Believe Not Every Spirit: Possession, Mysticism, & Discernment in Early Modern Catholicism* (Chicago: University of Chicago Press, 2007).
34. Caroline Walker Bynum, *Holy Feast and Holy Fast: The Religious Significance of Food to Medieval Women* (Berkeley: University of California Press, 1987); Rudolph M. Bell, *Holy Anorexia* (Chicago: University of Chicago Press, 1985).
35. Goodman, *The Exorcism of Anneliese Michel*, 199.
36. Adolf Rodewyk, *Possessed by Satan: The Church's Teaching on the Devil, Possession, and Exorcism*, trans. Martin Ebon (Garden City, NY: Doubleday, 1975), 199.
37. Goodman, *The Exorcism of Anneliese Michel*, 174.
38. Young, *A History of Exorcism in Catholic Christianity*, 219.
39. Goodman, *The Exorcism of Anneliese Michel*, 92.
40. Ibid., x.
41. Ibid., 181–182.

42. Eric T. Hansen, "What in God's Name?! A New Film Examines a 1976 Exorcism, Asking What Possessed Those Involved," *The Washington Post*, September 4, 2005, N4.
43. Goodman, *The Exorcism of Anneliese Michel*, xiv.
44. Ibid., 178.
45. Ibid., 248.
46. Quoted in Chris Lee, "Want Horror In the Court? 'The Exorcism of Emily Rose' Makes a Case for Mixing Genres in a Bid to Breathe Some Life Into the Box Office," *Los Angeles Times*, September 8, 2005, E6.
47. Goodman, *The Exorcism of Anneliese Michel*, 187. Father Alt added, "Now [Dr. Roth] is afraid that Anneliese will come out of the grave and take revenge on him. He must have seen too many Dracula films." This comment shows both sides of the exorcism debate can accuse each other of having watched too many horror movies.
48. The Gospel of Mark states that Jesus cried out at "the ninth hour" before dying. The ninth hour may have been between two and three pm. Steve A. Wiggins, *Holy Horror: The Bible and Fear in Movies* (Jefferson, NC: McFarland & Co, 2018), 143.
49. Quoted in Lee, "Want Horror in the Court?"
50. Sean Burns, "Rose Dud; The Exorcism is an offensive adaptation of a true story," *Philadelphia Weekly*, September 7, 2005, 44.
51. Angelo Matera, "Interview with an Exorcist: Father James LeBar Talks About 'The Exorcism of Emily Rose,'" *Free Republic*, October 6, 2005, http://www.freerepublic. com/focus/f-religion/1497645/posts.
52. Anthony Spencer, "Here's Why Theories Suggest the Exorcism of Emily Rose Was Cursed," *The Things*, August 2, 2021, https://www.thethings.com/heres-why-theor ies-suggest-the-exorcism-of-emily-rose-was-cursed/.
53. Paul Meehan, *Cinema of the Psychic Realm* (Jefferson, NC: McFarland and Co., 2009), 100.
54. Barry Taff, "The Real Entity Case," *BarryTaff.net*, August 7, 2011, http://barrytaff.net/ 2011/08/the-real-entity-case-2/.
55. Brent L. Smith, "Demystifying the Paranormal: Dr. Barry Taff Unravels the 'Poltergeist' Mystery," *Reality Sandwich*, December 1, 2014, https://realitysandwich. com/demystifying-the-paranormal-dr-barry-taff-unravels-the-poltergeist-mystery/.
56. "Jeffrey Dahmer, Return of the Jedi and Exorcist 3," (archived October 29, 2021), https://ghostarchive.org/varchive/jsj7bXdaPho.
57. Cuneo, *American Exorcism*, 62–63.
58. Thomas H. Stahel, "'Separate but Equal'; The Exorcism," *America*, April 27, 1991, 473.
59. Richard P. McBrien, "Airing of 'Exorcism' Showed Hidden Agenda," *The Catholic Courier*, May 2, 1991, 16.
60. Frank L. Netti, "Belief in the Devil Does Not Preclude Intelligence," *Catholic Reporter*, May 16, 1991, 17.
61. Cuneo, *American Exorcism*; David van Bioma, "If You Liked the Movie . . ." *Time*, October 2, 2000, 74.
62. Archdiocese of New York, "Update on the Sexual Abuse Crisis" (2020), https://arc hny.org/news-events/response-to-abuse/list/. No accusations were leveled against LeBar until after his death. LeBar was never convicted of any wrongdoing; however,

any alleged victims are eligible for financial compensation through the Church's Independent Reconciliation and Compensation Program.

63. Gyles Brandreth, "An Interview with Fr. Gabriele Amorth—The Church's Leading Exorcist," *The Sunday Telegraph*, October 29, 2000, http://web.archive.org/web/20041106024653/http://www.catholic-exorcism.org/pages/suntelegraph/suntelegraph.html.

64. Young, *A History of Exorcism in Catholic Christianity*, 221.

65. Ron Dicker, "Gabriele Amorth, Catholic Priest and Exorcist, Says He's Done More than 160,000 Exorcisms," *The Huffington Post*, Mary 31, 2013, https://www.huffpost.com/entry/gabriele-amorth-catholic-priest-exorcisms_n_3368017.

66. Eric T. Hansen, "What in God's Name?!," *The Washington Post*, September 4, 2005, https://www.washingtonpost.com/archive/lifestyle/style/2005/09/04/what-in-gods-name/948c4a98-aa1b-468a-ad82-4d80035710fd/.

67. John Thavis, *The Vatican Prophecies: Investigating Supernatural Signs, Apparitions, and Miracles in the Modern Age* (New York: Viking, 2015), 150.

68. Young, *A History of Exorcism in Catholic Christianity*, 232.

69. Chris Jackson, "Reports of Demonic Possession Increasing Since 'New Rite' of Exorcism," *The Remnant*, May 19, 2014, https://remnantnewspaper.com/web/index.php/fetzen-fliegen/item/657-reports-of-demonic-possession-increasing-since-new-rite-of-exorcism.

70. Jean Harris, "Like Trash on the Hall Floor," *Los Angeles Review of Books*, September 21, 2013, https://lareviewofbooks.org/article/like-trash-on-the-hall-floor/; Craig S. Smith, "A Casualty of Romania's Road Back from Atheism," *New York Times*, July 3, 2004, https://www.nytimes.com/2005/07/03/world/europe/a-casualty-on-romanias-road-back-from-atheism.html.

71. Quoted in Monica Filimon, "Loneliness, Guilt, and the Sin of Indifference: An Interview with Cristian Mungiu," *Cineaste* 38, no. 1 (Winter 2012): 20–23, 59.

72. Bruce Westbrook, "'Dominion' Director Says He Feels Vindication with the Movie's Release," *Houston Chronicle*, May 21, 2005, 3.

73. David DiCerto, "'Exorcist: The Beginning' A Poorly Crafted Prequel," *The Pilot*, August 27, 2004, 15.

74. Cuneo, *American Exorcism*, 130.

75. Levack, *The Devil Within*, 243.

76. Eric Eisenberg, "Exclusive Interview: The Rite Director Mikael Hafstrom," *Cinemablend*, January 26, 2011, https://www.cinemablend.com/new/Exclusive-Interview-Rite-Director-Mikael-Hafstrom-22846.html.

77. Levack, "The Horrors of Witchcraft and Demonic Possession," 931.

78. Thavis, *The Vatican Prophecies*, 170.

79. Owen Gleiberman, "William Friedkin's 'The Devil and Father Amorth,'" *Variety*, September 21, 2017, https://variety.com/2017/film/reviews/the-devil-and-father-amorth-review-the-exorcist-william-friedkin-1202564009/.

80. Adding to the confusion, Friedkin described this same scene in an article that appeared in *Vanity Fair* October 2016, but the possessed girl was named Rosa, her boyfriend Guiliano, and her mother was present in the church. William Friedkin, "The Devil and Father Amorth: Witnessing 'the Vatican Exorcist' at Work," *Vanity*

Fair, December 2016, https://www.vanityfair.com/hollywood/2016/10/father-amo rth-the-vatican-exorcist.

81. Gleiberman, "William Friedkin's 'The Devil and Father Amorth.'"

82. Tamlin McGee, "'Unreliable splatter': Vatican exorcists denounce Russell Crowe's Pope's Exorcist," *The Guardian* (April 10, 2023), https://www.theguardian.com/film/ 2023/apr/10/exorcists-denounce-the-popes-exorcist-with-russell-crowe.

83. On spirit possession as an idiom of distress, see Erika Bourguignon, "Suffering and Healing, Subordination and Power: Women and Possession Trance," *Ethos* 32, no. 4 (2004): 557–574.

84. "Mother Details Haunted House Horrors," *Inside Edition*, January 30, 2014, https:// www.insideedition.com/7712-mother-details-haunted-house-horrors.

85. Marisa Kwiatkowski, "The Exorcisms of Latoya Ammons," *Indianapolis Star*, January 25, 2014, https://www.indystar.com/story/news/2014/01/25/the-disposession-of-lat oya-ammons/4892553/.

86. Ibid.

87. "Excerpt from Lake County Police Report" (no date), https://www.documentcloud. org/documents/1005559-excerpt-from-lake-county-police-report.html.

88. "Mother Details Haunted House Horrors": Leah, "Beware of the Demon House. It's Coming for You!" *Ripley's.com*, May 15, 2017, https://www.ripleys.com/weird-news/ beware-of-the-demon-house/>.

89. Marisa Kwiatkowski, "Alleged Demon Home Sells for $35,000," *The Indianapolis Star*, January 29, 2014, https://www.indystar.com/story/news/2014/01/29/alleged- demon-home-sells-for-35000/5040079/.

90. Thavis, *The Vatican Prophecies*, 140.

91. Kwiatkowski, "Alleged Demon Home Sells for $35,000."

92. "What Happened to the Spooky Indiana House Known As the "Portal to Hell?," *Inside Edition*, October 21, 2019, https://www.facebook.com/watch/?v=442774339704825.

93. Phil Potempa, "Merrillville Priest Maginot Still Fighting Demons," *The Chicago Tribune*, October 28, 2020, https://www.chicagotribune.com/suburbs/post-tribune/ opinion/ct-ptb-potempa-column-st-1029-20201028-vzisemq3w5cylg475twkkqv b7i-story.html.

94. Frank Webster, "Catholic Priest Believes Satanic Influence Behind Travis Scott Concert Tragedy," *Bizpackreview.com*, November 16, 2021, https://www.bizpacrev iew.com/2021/11/16/catholic-priest-believes-satanic-influence-behind-travis-scott- concert-tragedy-1163789/.

95. "'Empire' Star Joins Netflix's Possession Film Based On The True Story," *Horrorfuel. com*, April 16, 2022, https://horrorfuel.com/2022/04/16/empire-star-joins-possess ion-film-based-on-the-true-story-of-the-demon-house/.

96. James M. Collins, *Exorcism and Deliverance Ministry in the Twentieth Century: An Analysis of the Practice and Theology of Exorcism in Modern Western Christianity* (Milton Keynes: Paternoster, 2009), 151–152.

97. Catholic News Service, "Construction Begins in Philippines on Asia's First Exorcism Center," *Cruxnow.com*, June 12, 2022, https://cruxnow.com/cns/2022/06/construct ion-begins-in-philippines-on-asias-first-exorcism-center.

98. "Autistic Boy's Death at Church Ruled Homicide," *CNN.com*, August 26, 2003, https://www.cnn.com/2003/LAW/08/25/autistic.boy.death/.

99. Clark Collis, "Little Box of Horrors," *Entertainment Weekly*, August 3, 2012, 50–55.

100. Charles Moss, "Finally, the Truth Behind the 'Haunted' Dybbuk Box Can Be Revealed," *Input*, July 8, 2021, https://www.inputmag.com/features/dybbuk-box-dib buk-kevin-mannis-zak-bagans-haunted-hoax-revealed.

101. Hannah Smith, "Exorcist Warns Against 'Possession' Danger of Getting Devil Tattoos," *Unilad*, October 31, 2021, https://www.unilad.co.uk/life/exorcist-warns-against-possession-danger-of-getting-devil-tattoos/.

102. Anugrah Kumar, "COVID-19 Pandemic, Lockdowns Led to Spike in Calls for Exorcisms: Priest," *The Christian Post*, October 31, 2021, https://www.christianp ost.com/news/covid-19-pandemic-lockdowns-led-to-spike-in-calls-for-exorci sms.html.

103. Thavis, *The Vatican Prophecies*, 164.

104. David Crary, "Exorcism: Increasingly Frequent, Including After US Protests," *Fox 5 News*, October 31, 2020, https://fox5sandiego.com/news/california-news/exorcism-increasingly-frequent-including-after-us-protests/.

105. Chris Rickert, "Priest Who Conducted Elections-related Exorcisms Leaves Madison Diocese," *Wisconsin State Journal*, January 26, 2021, https://madison.com/wsj/news/local/priest-who-conducted-elections-related-exorcisms-leaves-madison-diocese/article_edea011a-4415-5863-8b58-bd3513af09bb.html.

Chapter 7

1. Blanche Barton, *The Church of Satan* (New York: Hell's Kitchen Productions, 1990), 157.

2. Quoted in Andrew Boyd, *Blasphemous Rumours: Is Satanic Ritual Abuse Fact or Fantasy?: An Investigation* (London: Fount, 1991), 258.

3. Debbie Nathan and Michael R Snedeker, *Satan's Silence: Ritual Abuse and the Making of a Modern American Witch Hunt* (New York: Basic Books, 1995).

4. David G. Bromley, "Satanism: The New Cult Scare," in *The Satanism Scare*, ed. James T. Richardson, Joel Best, and David G. Bromley (Hawthorne, NY: Aldine De Gruyter, 1991), 68.

5. Gareth J. Medway, *Lure of the Sinister: The Unnatural History of Satanism* (New York: New York University Press, 2001), 349–350.

6. David Frankfurter, *Evil Incarnate: Rumors of Demonic Conspiracy and Ritual Abuse in History* (Princeton, NJ: Princeton University Press, 2006); Nachman Ben-Yehuda, *Deviance and Moral Boundaries: Witchcraft, the Occult, Science Fiction, Deviant Sciences, and Scientists* (Chicago: The University of Chicago Press, 1985).

7. David Emerson Gumaer, "Satanism: A Practical Guide to Witch-Hunting," *American Opinion* 13, no. 8 (September 1970): 51.

8. David Frankfurter, "Ritual As Accusation and Atrocity: Satanic Ritual Abuse Gnostic Libertinism and Primal Murders," *History of Religions* 40 (May 2002): 359.

9. Michael Barkun (*A Culture of Conspiracy: Apocalyptic Visions in Contemporary America* [Berkeley: University of California Press, 2003], 6) defines superconspiracies as "conspiratorial constructs in which multiple conspiracies are believed to be linked together hierarchically."

10. Philip Jenkins, "Weird Tales: The Story of a Delusion," in *The Last Pentacle of the Sun: Writings in Support of the West Memphis Three*, ed. M. W. Anderson and Brett Alexander (Vancouver, BC: Arsenal Pulp, 2004), 35–41.

11. "Home Counties Horror," *A History of Horror with Mark Gatiss*, October 18, 2010, BBC Four.

12. Andy Paciorak et al., editors, *Folk Horror Revival: Field Studies*, 2nd ed., (n.p.: Lulu and Wyrd Harvest Press, 2018), 13–14.

13. Jeff Jensen, "'True Detective' Creator Nic Pizzalatto on Carcosa, Hideous Men, and the Season 1 Endgame," *Entertainment Weekly*, February 27, 2014, http://www.ew.com/article/2014/02/27/true-detective-nic-pizzolatto-season-1.

14. Joseph P. Laycock, "'Time Is a Flat Circle': True Detective and the Specter of Moral Panic in American Pop Culture," *Journal of Religion and Popular Culture* 27, no. 3 (Fall 2015): 220–235.

15. Ruben Van Luijk, *Children of Lucifer: The Origins of Modern Religious Satanism* (New York: Oxford University Press, 2016), 216.

16. James Randall Noblitt and Pamela Perskin Noblitt, *Cult and Ritual Abuse: Narratives Evidence and Healing Approaches*, 3rd ed. (Santa Barbara, CA: Praeger, 2014), 274.

17. John F. McManus, "Malachi Martin: The Catholic Church in Crisis," *The New American*, June 9, 1997, 40.

18. Ronald Hutton, *The Triumph of the Moon: A History of Modern Pagan Witchcraft*, 2nd ed. (New York: Oxford University Press, 2021), 262.

19. Phil Baker, "Dennis Wheatley," in *The Occult World*, ed. Christopher Partridge (New York: Routledge, 2014), 466.

20. Hutton, *The Triumph of the Moon*, 262.

21. Dennis Wheatley, *The Devil Rides Out* (New York: Bloomsbury Reader, [1934] 2013), 1.

22. Quoted in Bill Ellis, *Raising the Devil: Satanism, New Religions, and the Media* (Lexington: University of Kentucky Press, 2000), 158.

23. Nikolas Schreck, *The Satanic Screen: An Illustrated Guide to the Devil in Cinema* (London: Creation, 2001), 55.

24. Quoted in Baker Phil and Timothy Smith, *City of the Beast: The London of Aleister Crowley* (Cambridge: Strange Attractor, 2022), 55.

25. Schreck, *The Satanic Screen*, 52.

26. W. Scott Poole, *Satan in America: The Devil We Know* (New York: Rowman & Littlefield, 2009), 146.

27. Quoted in John Brosnan, *The Horror People* (New York: New American Library, 1977), 80.

28. On brainwashing claims during "the cult wars," see Massimo Introvigne, *Brainwashing: Myth or Reality?* (Cambridge: Cambridge University Press, 2022).

29. Patrick O'Donnell, "Satanic Celluloid: An Unholy Trinity of Terror Picked by the Black Pope of the Church of Satan," in *Monster Rally*, ed. S. Michael Wilson (West Orange, NJ: Idea Men Productions, 2008), 175.

30. Anton LaVey, *The Satanic Bible* (New York: Avon Books, 1969), 189. Spokespeople for the Church of Satan have since clarified that this was a reference to "The Magic Circle" that formed the original group's core membership.

31. Jeb J. Card, *Spooky Archaeology: Myth and the Science of the Past* (Albuquerque: University of New Mexico Press, 2018), 220.

32. Quoted in Hutton, *The Triumph of the Moon*, 266.

33. Ibid.

34. Card, *Spooky Archaeology*, 221.

35. Robert Fabian, *London After Dark; an Intimate Record of Night Life in London and a Selection of Crime Stories from the Case Book of Ex-Superintendent Robert Fabian* (London: Naldrett Press, 1954), 74.

36. Quoted in Simon Read, *The Case That Foiled Fabian: Murder and Witchcraft in Rural England* (Stroud: History Press, 2014), 133.

37. Thomas Hobbs, "The Unsolved 'Witchcraft' Murder That Shocked Britain," *Vice*, February 14, 2022, https://www.vice.com/en/article/3ab7nb/charles-walton-murder-victim.

38. Diane A. Rodgers, "Folk Horror, Ostension, and *Robin Redbreast*," *Revenant* 5 (March 2020): 57–73.

39. Hutton, *Triumph of the Moon*, 210.

40. Schreck, *The Satanic Screen*, 117.

41. James R. Lewis, *Satanism Today: an Encyclopedia of Religion, Folklore, and Popular Culture* (Santa Barbara, CA: ABC-CLIO, 2001), 70.

42. Ellis, *Raising the Devil*, 158.

43. Baker, "Dennis Wheatley," 446.

44. Barton, *The Secret Life of a Satanist*, 77.

45. Schreck, *The Satanic Screen*, 143. Barton (*The Secret Life of a Satanist*, 80) reports that this suggestion came from Jack Webb, a police inspector with whom LaVey was friends.

46. Aquino, *The Church of Satan*, 176.

47. Gavin Baddeley, *Lucifer Rising* (London: Plexus, 1999), 67.

48. Lewis, *Satanism Today*, 280. Shortly after LaVey founded his group, another Satanic religion formed called The Order of the Ram. This name appears to have been taken directly from one of Wheatley's novels.

49. Carl Abrahamsson, *Anton LaVey and the Church of Satan: Infernal Wisdom from the Devil's Den* (Rochester, VT: Inner Traditions, 2022), 237.

50. Anton LaVey, *The Satanic Rituals* (New York: Avon, 1972), 27.

51. O'Donnell, "Satanic Celluloid," 172.

52. LaVey, *The Satanic Rituals*, 107–110.

53. Peter H. Gilmore, "6/6/06 Satanic High Mass Ritual," *ChurchofSatan.com*, https://www.churchofsatan.com/6606-satanic-high-mass/.

54. Bradley, *Lucifer Rising*, 88.

55. James R. Lewis, "Anton LaVey, The Satanic Bible, and the Satanist Tradition," in *Legitimating New Religions*, ed. James R. Lewis (New Brunswick, NJ: Rutgers University Press, 2003), 112. In LaVey's (*Satan Speaks!* [Venice, Ca.: Feral House, 1998], 5) own account, the idea was put forth by Fred Goerner, a writer. Goerner met LaVey though his wife, Merla Zellerbach, who was a student in workshop for witches run by LaVey.

56. Ellis, *Raising the Devil*, 159; Schreck, *The Satanic Screen*, 138.

57. Gumaer, "Satanism," 69.

58. Quoted in Marty Gunther, "Satanist Calls Film a Boon For Christians and Devil-Worshippers," *Tattler* (Spring 1974 Special): 21.

59. Aquino, *The Church of Satan*, 328.

60. Barton, *The Secret Life of a Satanist*, 157.

61. Schreck, *The Satanic Screen*, 177.

62. Carrol L. Fry, *Cinema of the Occult: New Age Satanism Wicca and Spiritualism in Film* (Bethlehem, PA: Lehigh University Press, 2008), 107–108.

63. Schreck, *The Satanic Screen*, 177.

64. Quoted in Abrahamson, *Anton LaVey and the Church of Satan*, 165–166

65. "Satanic Sources—Film List," https://www.churchofsatan.com/sources-film-list/.

66. Abrahamson, *Anton LaVey and the Church of Satan*, 14.

67. See Michael A. Aquino, *The Church of Satan*, 6th ed. (San Francisco: self published, 2009), 17.

68. Van Luijk, *Children of Lucifer*, 377–379.

69. Jackie Strauss, "'American Horror Story's' Antichrist Responds to Church of Satan Criticism: 'He's a Righteous Character,'" *The Hollywood Reporter*, November 2, 2018, https://www.hollywoodreporter.com/tv/tv-news/american-horror-story-apocaly pse-cody-fern-antichrist-interview-1157074/.

70. Quoted in Abrahamson, *Anton LaVey and the Church of Satan*, 220.

71. Arthur Lyons, *The Second Coming: Satanism in America* (New York: Dodd, Mead, & Company, 1970), 131; Arthur Lyons, *Satan Wants You: The Cult of Devil Worship in America* (New York: Mysterious Press, 1988), 98. The bookstore became The Ram Occult Research Center in 1971, then moved and eventually was renamed Pan Pipes. In 1995, Pan Pipes was purchased by actress Fairuza Balk, who used it to research her role in *The Craft* (1996). She has since sold the shop, which still exists. Donald Michael Kraig, *Modern Magick: Twelve Lessons in the High Magical Arts* (Woodbury, MN: Llewellyn, 2010),

72. Lyons, *Satan Wants You*, 148.

73. Nesta Hellen Webster, *Secret Societies and Subversive Movements* (London: Boswell, 1924), 78.

74. Frankfurter, *Evil Incarnate*, 108.

75. Allan Brown, *Inside "The Wicker Man": The Morbid Ingenuities* (London: Sidgwick and Jackson, 2000), 12–13.

76. Ibid., 15.

77. Quoted in David Bartholomew, "The Wicker Man," *Cinefantastique* 6, no. 3 (1977): 12.

78. Douglas E. Cowan, *The Forbidden Body: Sex, Horror, and the Religious Imagination* (New York: New York University Press, 2022), 158.

79. Schreck, *The Satanic Screen*, 211.

80. Order of Nine Angles, "Guidelines for the Testing of Opfers," (1988), https://darkne ssconverges.wordpress.com/2009/07/10/guidelines-for-the-testing-of-opfers/.

81. James R. Lewis, *Satanism Today: An Encyclopedia of Religion, Folklore, and Popular Culture* (Santa Barbara, CA: ABC-CLIO, 2002), 196. On the connection between the Order of Nine Angles and murders committed and attempted by neo-Nazi terror cells, see H. E. Upchurch, "The Iron March Forum and the Evolution of the "Skull Mask" Neo-Fascist Network," *Combating Terrorism Center Sentinel* 14, no. 10 (December 2021), https://ctc.westpoint.edu/the-iron-march-forum-and-the-evolut ion-of-the-skull-mask-neo-fascist-network/.

82. Richard Woods, *The Devil* (Chicago: Thomas More Press, 1974), 11.

83. Gumaer, "Satanism," 41–48.

84. Alejandro Hernandez, "Satanic Panic in Colorado" *Denver Public Library blog*, December 7, 2021, https://history.denverlibrary.org/news/satanic-panic.

85. Joseph P. Laycock, *Dangerous Games: What the Moral Panic Over Role-Playing Games Says About Play Religion and Imagined Worlds* (Berkeley: University of California Press, 2015), 270–271.

86. Woods, *The Devil*, 43.

87. Ed Warren and Lorraine Warren, "Breaking a Satanic Pact," *The Tattler* (March 10, 1974).

88. Kerr Cuhulain, "Michelle Remembers," July 8, 2002, https://web.archive.org/web/20060525161207/http://www.witchvox.com/va/dt_va.html?a=cabc&c=whs&id=4349.

89. Michelle Smith and Lawrence Pazder, *Michelle Remembers* (New York: Pocket Books, 1980), 14.

90. Gareth J. Medway, *Lure of the Sinister: The Unnatural History of Satanism* (New York: New York University Press, 2001), 176–177.

91. Paul Grescoe, "Things that Go Bump in Victoria," *Maclean's*, October 27, 1980, https://archive.macleans.ca/article/1980/10/27/things-that-go-bump-in-victoria.

92. Denna Allen and Janet Midwinter, "Michelle Remembers: The Debunking of a Myth: Why the Original "Ritual Abuse" Victim May Have Suffered Only From her Childhood Fantasies," *The Mail on Sunday*, September 30, 1990, 41.

93. Cuhulain, "Michelle Remembers."

94. Larry Kahaner, *Cults That Kill: Probing the Underworld of Occult Crime* (New York: Warner Books, 1988), 200–201.

95. Robert D. Hicks, *In Pursuit of Satan: The Police and the Occult* (Buffalo, NY: Prometheus Books, 1992), 176–177.

96. Cuhulain, "Michelle Remembers."

97. Nathan and Snedeker, *Satan's Silence*, 141–142.

98. Allen and Midwinter, "Michelle Remembers: The Debunking of a Myth."

99. Jeffrey S. Victor, "Crime, Moral Panic, and the Occult," in *The Occult World*, ed. Christopher Partridge (New York: Routledge, 2014), 694.

100. Ibid.
101. Smith and Padzer, *Michelle Remembers*, 127.
102. Hicks, *In Pursuit of Satan*, 146. The source of this information is Hicks's interview with Zeena LaVey in 1989.
103. Cuhulain, "Michelle Remembers."
104. Smith and Padzer, *Michelle Remembers*, 159.
105. Ibid., 263.
106. Ibid., 264.
107. Cuhulain, "Michelle Remembers."
108. Grady Hendrix, *Paperbacks from Hell: The Twisted History of '70s and '80s Horror Fiction* (Philadelphia: Quirk, 2017), 41.
109. Grescoe, "Things that Go Bump in Victoria."
110. Kahaner, *Cults that Kill*, 220.
111. Allen and Midwinter, "Michelle Remembers: The Debunking of a Myth," 41.
112. Ibid.
113. Quoted in Kahaner, *Cults That Kill*, 217.
114. Boyd, *Blasphemous Rumours*, 262.
115. Lewis, *Satanism Today*, 228.
116. Hicks, In Pursuit of Satan, 59.
117. Quoted in B. A. Robinson, "Geraldo Rivera: Satanic Ritual Abuse and Recovered Memories," *Religioustolerance.org*, November 7, 2007, https://www.religioustolerance.org/geraldo.htm.
118. Jenny Reichert and James T. Richardson, "Decline of a Moral Panic: A Psychological and Socio-Legal Examination of the Current Status of Satanism," *Nova Religio* 16, no. 2 (2012): 47–63.
119. For critical reportage on an ISSTD meeting, see Joseph L. Flatley, *Satan Goes to the Mind Control Convention: Manchurian Candidates, Recovered Memories, and the Dark Side of Conspiracy Culture (and other stories)* (n.p.: Joseph L. Flatley Press, 2018). On ISSTD founder and former president Bennet Braun, see Richard Noll, "When Psychiatry Battled the Devil," *Psychiatric Times*, December 6, 2013, https://www.researchgate.net/publication/262214055_When_psychiatry_battled_the_devil. On lawsuits against former ISSTD president Colin Ross, see Milly Jenkins, "American Therapy That Could Blow Your Minds," *Independent*, February 9, 1997, https://www.independent.co.uk/news/american-therapy-that-could-blow-your-minds-1277672.html.

Chapter 8

1. Quoted in James T. Richardson, "Satanism in the Courts: From Murder to Heavy Metal," in *The Satanism Scare*, ed. James T. Richardson, Joel Best, and David G. Bromley (New York: Aldine de Gruyter, 1991), 213.
2. Jay Sharbutt "Cauldron Boils Over Geraldo's 'Devil Worship': 'Satan' Wins Ratings, Loses Advertisers," *Los Angeles Times*, October 27, 1988, https://www.latimes.com/archives/la-xpm-1988-10-27-ca-449-story.html.

3. Joshua Gunn, *Modern Occult Rhetoric: Mass Media and the Drama of Secrecy in the Twentieth Century* (Tuscaloosa: University Alabama Press, 2005), 199–200.
4. Craig Reinarman, Harry G. Levine, eds, *Crack in America: Demon Drugs and Social Justice* (Berkeley: University of California Press, 1997), 24.
5. Stuart Hall, Chris Critchter, Tony Jefferson, John Clarke, and Brian Roberts, *Policing the Crisis: Mugging, the State, and Law and Order* (London: Macmillan, 1978), 226.
6. Colin A Ross, *Satanic Ritual Abuse: Principles of Treatment* (Toronto: University of Toronto Press, 1995), 61.
7. Peg Aloi, "Rooted in the Occult Revival: Neo-Paganism's Evolving Relationship with Popular Media," in *Handbook of Contemporary Paganism*, ed. Murphy Pizza and James R. Lewis (Boston: Brill, 2009), 560.
8. David Frankfurter, *Evil Incarnate: Rumors of Demonic Conspiracy and Satanic Abuse in History* (Princeton, NJ: Princeton University Press, 2008), 207.
9. Michael Moynihan and Didrik Søderlind, *Lords of Chaos: The Bloody Rise of the Satanic Metal Underground* (Los Angeles: Feral House Press, 2003).
10. Kathleen Taylor, *Brainwashing: The Science of Thought Control* (New York: Oxford University Press, 2004), 4–5.
11. Rev. David A. Noebel, *Communism, Hypnotism and the Beatles* (Tulsa, OK: Christian Crusade Publications, 1965), 15.
12. Carl Birkmeyer, "The Get Smart Page," 2008, http://www.wouldyoubelieve.com/season3.html.
13. Bob Larson, *Rock and Roll: The Devil's Diversion* (McCook, NE: Bob Larson, 1970), 66.
14. Larson, *Rock and Roll*, 134.
15. John Trott, "Bob Larson's Ministry Under Scrutiny," *Cornerstone* 21, no. 100 (1993): 18, 37, 41–42, https://web.archive.org/web/20060610035955/http://cornerstonemag.com/features/iss100/larson.htm.
16. Lowell Hart, *Satan's Music Exposed* (Huntingdon Valley, PA: Salem Kirban, Inc., 1980), 94.
17. Jacob Aranza, *Backward Masking Unmasked: Backward Satanic Messages of Rock and Roll Exposed* (Shreveport, LA: Huntington House Inc., 1983), 21–22.
18. Jack T. Chick, *Spellbound?* (Ontario, CA: Chick Publications, 1978).
19. Arthur Lyons, *The Second Coming: Satanism in America* (New York: Dodd, Mead & Co., 1970), 125.
20. Gavin Baddeley, *Lucifer Rising* (London: Plexus, 1999), 89.
21. Klemen Breznikar, "Coven Interview with Rick Durrett," *It's Psychedelic, Baby!*, January 2013, https://www.psychedelicbabymag.com/2013/01/coven-interview-with-rick-durre.html.
22. Christopher Partridge, *The Re-Enchantment of the West, Vol 2* (London: T&T Clark International, 2005), 253.
23. Lester Bangs, "Black Sabbath: Album Review," *Rolling Stone*, September 17, 1970, https://www.rollingstone.com/music/music-album-reviews/black-sabbath-188300/.
24. Rebecca Woods, "Black Sabbath: 'We Hated Being a Heavy Metal Band,'" *BBC News*, February 4, 2017, https://www.bbc.com/news/uk-england-birmingham-38768573.

25. James Desborough, "Ozzy Osbourne is 'Terrified' of Horrified Films and Admits He's 'S*** Bricks' at The Exorcist," *Daily Star*, December 30, 2020, https://www.dailystar.co.uk/showbiz/ozzy-osbourne-terrified-horror-films-23241470.

26. Tipper Gore, *Raising PG Kids in an X Rated Society* (New York: Bantam Books, 1988), 87.

27. The technique of backmasking is as old as recorded sound. Thomas Edison invented the tinfoil phonograph in 1877, and he found that he could play recorded sound backward while experimenting with his new invention. Edison and his colleagues were said to be especially fond of recording the phrase "mad dog" and playing it backward to sound like "god damn." See Karen Stollznow, *Language Myths, Mysteries and Magic* (New York: Palgrave Macmillan, 2014), 133.

28. Michael Millis, "Hidden and Satanic Messages in Rock Music," 1982, https://blog.wfmu.org/freeform/2007/01/365_days_1_the_.html.

29. "California Probes Rock Music 'Devil,'" *Chicago Tribune*, April 29, 1982, 2.

30. Ibid.

31. Stollznow, *Language Myths, Mysteries and Magic*, 136.

32. Carlo Affatigato, "Jimmy Page: 'Satanic Meanings in Stairway to Heaven? A Fan Theory," *Aural Crave*, January 8, 2019, https://auralcrave.com/en/2019/01/08/jimmy-page-satanic-meanings-in-stairway-to-heaven-a-fan-theory/.

33. *Record Labeling: Hearing before the Committee on Commerce, Science, and Transportation. Ninety-Ninth Congress: First Session on Contents of Music and the Lyrics of Records, September 18, 1985* (Washington DC: US Government Printing Office, 1985), 118.

34. Belknap died instantly. Vance survived but eventually died three years later.

35. Kory Grow, "Judas Priest's Subliminal Message Trial: Rob Halford Looks Back," *Rolling Stone*, August 24, 2015, https://www.rollingstone.com/music/music-features/judas-priests-subliminal-message-trial-rob-halford-looks-back-57552/.

36. Matthew W. Daus, "Subliminal Messages in Music: Free Speech or Invasion of Privacy?" *University of Miami Entertainment & Sports Law Review* 9, no. 2 (1992): 245.

37. Philip Carlo, *The Night Stalker: The Life and Crimes of Richard Ramirez* (New York: Kensington Publishing Company, 1996), 107–108.

38. Los Angeles Times Archives, "Night Stalker Gets Death: You Don't Understand, Killer Says," *Los Angeles Times*, November 7, 1989, https://www.latimes.com/archives/la-xpm-1989-11-07-mn-1184-story.html.

39. Carlo, *The Night Stalker*, 209.

40. Jesse P. Pollack, *The Acid King* (New York: Simon Pulse, 2018), 150.

41. David Breskin, "Cult Killing: Kids in the Dark," *Rolling Stone*, November 22, 1984, https://www.rollingstone.com/culture/culture-features/long-island-devil-cult-murder-ricky-kasso-david-breskin-901069/.

42. Mara Bovsun, "Justice Story: Satan Runs Amok on L.I. as Teen Confesses to Grisly Murder," *New York Daily News*, November 29, 2011, https://www.nydailynews.com/news/crime/justice-story-satan-runs-amok-teen-confesses-grisly-murder-article-1.983918.

43. Bob Larson, *Larson's Book of Spiritual Warfare* (Nashville, TN: Thomas Nelson Publishers, 1999), 158.

44. Sarah Hughes, "American Monsters: Tabloid Media and the Satanic Panic," *Journal of American Studies* 51, no. 3 (2017): 691–719.

45. Gayland W. Hurst, and Robert L. Marsh, *Satanic Cult Awareness* (Washington, DC: US Department of Justice, n.d.), https://www.ncjrs.gov/pdffiles1/Photocopy/140554NCJRS.pdf.

46. Dennis Dunaway, Chris Hodenfield, and Alice Cooper, *Snakes! Guillotines! Electric Chairs!: My Adventures in the Alice Cooper Group* (New York: St. Martin's Griffin, 2018), 256.

47. The Master Cylinder, *Black Roses (1988) Retrospective*, September 15, 2019, https://web.archive.org/web/20200925140053/https://0themastercylinder0.com/2019/09/15/black-roses-1988-retrospective/.

48. Doug Cowan, *Sacred Terror: Religion and Horror on the Silver Screen* (Waco, TX: Baylor University Press, 2016).

49. Massimo Introvigne, *Satanism: A Social History* (Leiden: Brill, 2016), 469.

50. Introvigne, *Satanism*, 480.

51. Ibid., 481.

52. Moynihan and Søderlind, *Lords of Chaos*, 59–60.

53. Introvigne, *Satanism*, 482.

54. Ibid.

55. Moynihan and Søderlind, *Lords of Chaos*, 95–97.

56. Adam Seligman, Robert P. Weller, Michael J. Puett, and Bennett Simon, *Ritual and its Consequences: An Essay on the Limits of Sincerity* (New York: Oxford University Press, 2008), 176.

57. Ikuya Sato, *Kamikaze Biker: Parody and Anomy in Affluent Japan* (Chicago: University of Chicago Press, 1991), 215.

58. Chris Campion, "In the Face of Death," *The Observer*, February 20, 2005, https://www.theguardian.com/music/2005/feb/20/popandrock4.

59. Spencer Kaufman, "Varg Vikernes Slams Lords of Chaos Movie, Questions Why He's Portrayed by 'Fat Jewish Actor,'" *Consequence of Sound*, January 29, 2019, https://consequenceofsound.net/2019/01/varg-vikernes-slams-lords-of-chaos-movie/.

60. Jeffrey S. Victor, "Crime, Moral Panic, and the Occult," in *The Occult World*, ed. Christopher Partridge (New York: Routledge, 2015), 697–698.

61. Howard N. Snyder and Melissa Sickmund, *Juvenile Offenders and Victims: 2006 National Report* (Washington, DC: Office of Juvenile Justice, 2006), 22.

62. Douglas O. Linder, "The West Memphis Three Trials: An Account," *Famous Trials*, University of Missouri-Kansas City School of Law, https://famous-trials.com/westmemphis/2287-home.

63. Victor, "Crime, Moral Panic, and the Occult," 698.

64. Mara Leveritt, *Devil's Knot: The True Story of the West Memphis Three* (New York: Simon and Schuster, 2003), 58.

65. Tim Hackler, "Complete Fabrication," *The Arkansas Times*, October 7, 2004, https://arktimes.com/news/cover-stories/2004/10/07/complete-fabrication?pico_new_user=true&pico_ui=login_link.

66. Hackler, "Complete Fabrication."

67. Dan Stidham, Case synopsis, 1994, http://www.wm3.org/CaseIntroduction/Page/DAN-STIDHAMS-CASE-SYNOPSIS.

68. Douglas O. Linder, "The Damien Echols and Jason Baldwin Trial (February 28–March 18, 1994): Dale Griffis," *Famous Trials*, University of Missouri-Kansas City School of Law, https://famous-trials.com/westmemphis/2272-griffistestbaldwin.

69. Beth Warren, "Jury Foreman in West Memphis Three trial of Damien Echols Accused of Misconduct," *The Commercial Appeal*, October 13, 2010, https://www.upi.com/Top_News/US/2010/10/13/Juror-misconduct-alleged-in-murder-verdict/28341287001195/.

70. Margaret Cho, "Letter," in *The Last Pentacle of the Sun: Writings in Support of the West Memphis Three*, ed. M. W. Anderson and Brett Alexander (Vancouver: Arsenal Pulp Press, 2004), 189.

71. Aloi, "Rooted in the Occult Revival," 559–560.

72. Frankfurter, *Evil Incarnate*, 31–69.

73. Gore, *Raising PG Kids*, 131–133.

74. Joe Berlinger and Bruce Sinofsky, "Introduction," in *The Last Pentacle of the Sun: Writings in Support of the West Memphis Three*, ed. M. W. Anderson and Brett Alexander (Vancouver: Arsenal Pulp Press, 2004), 11.

Chapter 9

1. Quoted in Joseph Maddrey, *Nightmares in Red White and Blue: The Evolution of the American Horror Film* (Jefferson, NC: McFarland, 2004), 129.

2. "The Modern Day Ed and Lorraine Warren," *Paranormal Thoughts Podcast*, October 2021.

3. Brandy Zadrozny, "Satanic Panic is Making a Comeback, Fueled by QAnon Believers and GOP Influencers," *NBCnews.com*, September 14, 2022, https://www.nbcnews.com/tech/internet/satanic-panic-making-comeback-fueled-qanon-believers-gop-influencers-rcna38795.

4. Catherine Wessinger, "'Cult' is an Inaccurate, Unhelpful, and Dangerous Label for Followers of Trump, QAnon, and 1/6," *Religion Dispatches*, July 19, 2021, https://religiondispatches.org/cult-is-an-inaccurate-unhelpful-and-dangerous-label-for-followers-of-trump-qanon-and-1-6/.

5. Lauren Camera, "Trump's Open Embrace of QAnon," *U.S. News and World Report*, September 23, 2022, https://www.usnews.com/news/the-report/articles/2022-09-23/trumps-open-embrace-of-qanon.

6. Quoted in Stephen Wallace, "Exorcism as a Way of Life," A15. Date unavailable. Courtesy of the archives of St. Bonaventure University.

7. Robert Skvarla, "Conspiracy USA: Jeremiah Films, Bill Clinton, and the Satanic Panic," *Diabolique*, May 17, 2021, https://diaboliquemagazine.com/jeremiah-films-bill-clinton-and-the-satanic-panic/.

8. Matthew Gault, "He Made a Horror Movie About Pizzagate, then the Death Threats Started," *Vice*, November 23, 2021, https://www.vice.com/en/article/jgm84k/he-made-a-horror-movie-about-pizzagate-then-the-death-threats-started.

9. Meredith Blake, "Who Is Q? Maker of HBO Docuseries 'Q: Into the Storm' Believes He Has the Answer," *Los Angeles Times*, March 28, 2021, https://www.latimes.com/entertainment-arts/tv/story/2021-03-28/qanon-docuseries-hbo-who-is-q.

10. Reed Berkowitz, "QAnon Resembles the Games I Design. But for Believers, There Is No Winning," *The Washington Post*, May 11, 2021, https://www.washingtonpost.com/outlook/qanon-game-plays-believers/2021/05/10/31d8ea46-928b-11eb-a74e-1f4cf89fd948_story.html.

11. Q Alerts, "Intelligence Drops," posts 179, 182, qalerts.app.

12. Sarah Colwell, Electronic communication with the authors, September 26, 2022.

13. Maggie Haberman, *Confidence Man: The Making of Donald Trump and the Breaking of America* (New York: Penguin, 2022), 19, 258.

14. Matthew Rosenberg, "Pushing QAnon and Stolen Election Lies, Flynn Re-emerges," *New York Times*, June 2, 2021, https://www.nytimes.com/2021/02/06/us/politics/michael-flynn-qanon.html. Michael Flynn was pardoned by Donald Trump for lying to FBI about his dealings with a Russian diplomat. Since being pardoned, Flynn has toured the country promoting Christian nationalism, claimed COVID-19 was manufactured by "globalists," and that the 2020 election was stolen from Trump.

15. "Adrenochrome," *Santa Cruz Biotechnology*, https://www.scbt.com/p/adrenochrome-54-06-8.

16. "Adrenochrome Monosemicarbazole Drug Price and Information," *MedIndia*, https://www.medindia.net/drug-price/adrenochrome-monosemicarbazone/adrenochrome-monosemicarbazole.htm.

17. Aldous Huxley, *The Doors of Perception and Heaven and Hell* (New York: HarperCollins Publishers, 2009), 11.

18. John Smythies, "The Adrenochrome Hypothesis of Schizophrenia Revisited," *Neurotoxicity Research* 4, no. 2 (2002): 147–150. For a firsthand account of someone eating, snorting, and smoking adrenochrome and failing to experience hallucinogenic effects, see Genaro, "Killing the Myth: Adrenochrome," *Erowid.org*, March 28, 2006, https://erowid.org/experiences/exp.php?ID=51847.

19. Eduardo Hidalgo Downing, *Adrenochrome and Other Mythical Drugs* (n.p.: CreateSpace Independent Publishing Platform, 2013), 137.

20. Hunter S. Thompson, *Fear and Loathing in Las Vegas: A Savage Journey to the Heart of the American Dream* (New York: Knopf, 2010), 132.

21. Brian Friedberg, "The Dark Virality of a Hollywood Blood-Harvesting Conspiracy," *Wired*, July 31, 2020, https://www.wired.com/story/opinion-the-dark-virality-of-a-hollywood-blood-harvesting-conspiracy/.

22. Cortney Drakeford, "Dr. Phil Slammed For Promoting Adrenochrome Interview, Accused Of Exploiting Mental Health Issues," *International Business Times*, September 10, 2020, https://www.ibtimes.com/dr-phil-slammed-promoting-adrenochrome-interview-accused-exploiting-mental-health-3043549.

23. David Emery, "Is a Hillary Clinton 'Snuff Film' Circulating on the Dark Web?" *Snopes.com*, April 16, 2018, https://www.snopes.com/fact-check/hillary-clinton-snuff-film/.

24. Erik Hananoki, "Marjorie Taylor Greene Endorsed a Deranged Conspiracy Theory about Democrats and Satanic Child Murder," *Media Matters for America*, January 26,

2021, https://www.mediamatters.org/facebook/marjorie-taylor-greene-endorsed-deranged-conspiracy-theory-about-democrats-and-satanic.

25. Em Steck, Nathan McDermott, and Christopher Hickey, "The Congressional Candidates Who Have Engaged with the QAnon Conspiracy Theory," *CNN.com*, October 30, 2020. https://www.cnn.com/interactive/2020/10/politics/qanon-cong-candidates/.

26. Norman Cohn, *Europe's Inner Demons: The Demonization of Christians in Medieval Christiandom*, revised edition (Chicago: University of Chicago Press, 1993), 7.

27. Robin Wood, "Der Erlkonig: The Ambiguities of Horror," in *American Nightmare: Essays on the Horror Film*, ed. Andrew Britton et al. (Toronto: Festival of Festivals, 1979), 15.

28. "Police Officer Recalls Moment Capitol Mob Yelled: 'Kill Him with His Own Gun!'" *The Guardian*, January 15, 2021, https://www.theguardian.com/us-news/2021/jan/15/police-officer-capitol-mob-kill-him-with-his-own-gun.

29. Jason Bivins, *Religion of Fear: The Politics of Horror in Conservative Evangelicalism* (New York: Oxford University Press, 2008), 17.

30. Michael Wolff, "Ringside With Steve Bannon at Trump Tower as the President-Elect's Strategist Plots "An Entirely New Political Movement" (Exclusive)" *The Hollywood Reporter*, November 18, 2016, https://www.hollywoodreporter.com/news/general-news/steve-bannon-trump-tower-interview-trumps-strategist-plots-new-political-movement-948747/.

31. Michael W. Cuneo, *American Exorcism: Expelling Demons in the Land of Plenty* (New York: Doubleday, 2001), 272.

32. Jeff Zacks, *Flicker: Your Brain on Movies* (New York: Oxford University Press, 2015), 29.

33. Rebecca Moody, "Screen Time Statistics: Average Screen Time in US vs. the Rest of the World," *Comparitech.com*, March 21, 2022, https://www.comparitech.com/tv-streaming/screen-time-statistics/.

34. On the sacralization of popular culture, see Gary Laderman, *Sacred Matters: Celebrity Worship Sexual Ecstasies the Living Dead and Other Signs of Religious Life in the United States* (New York: New Press, 2009).

35. US Department of Health and Human Services, "Preparedness 101: Zombie Pandemic" (2011).

36. David Hufford, *The Terror That Comes in the Night: An Experience-Centered Study of Supernatural Assault Traditions* (Philadelphia: University of Pennsylvania Press, 1982).

37. As discussed in previous chapters, Jeffrey Dahmer was preoccupied with *The Exorcist III*, Adolfo Constanzo based his idiosyncratic brand of Afro-Cuban religion on *The Believers*, and Pazuzu Algarad was obsessed with horror films generally and *The Exorcist* in particular. Each of these individuals was responsible for multiple murders. However, it is not clear horror films inspired them to commit crimes. Dahmer's interest in films was emphasized by his defense attorney, Constanzo's activity was calculated to demonstrate his value to a drug cartel, and Algarad was diagnosed as suffering from severe mental illness.

38. Zacks, *Flicker*, 101.
39. James M. Collins, *Exorcism and Deliverance Ministry in the Twentieth Century: An Analysis of the Practice and Theology of Exorcism in Modern Western Christianity* (Milton Keynes: Paternoster, 2009), 166.
40. Harry G. Frankfurt, *On Bullshit* (Princeton, NJ: Princeton University Press, 2005).
41. "Satanic Panic Is Making a Comeback."
42. American Library Association, Presidential Committee on Information Literacy: Final Report, January 10, 1989, https://www.ala.org/acrl/publications/whitepapers/presidential.
43. Emily Drabinski and Eamon Tewell, "Critical Information Literacy," *Cuny Academic Works*, 2019, https://academicworks.cuny.edu/cgi/viewcontent.cgi?article=1638&context=gc_pubs.
44. Pauline Kael, "The Exorcist," *New York Magazine*, January 7, 1974, https://scrapsfromtheloft.com/movies/the-exorcist-review-by-pauline-kael/.

Filmography

A Thief in the Night	1972	Donald W. Thompson
Adrenochrome	2017	Trevor Simms
Alice in Wonderland	1951	Clyde Geronimi, Wilfred Jackson, Hamilton Luske
Alien	1979	Ridley Scott
Amityville II: The Possession	1982	Damiano Damiani
Annabelle	2014	John R. Leonetti
Annabelle Comes Home	2019	Gary Dauberman
Annabelle Creation	2017	David F. Sandberg
Anneliese: The Exorcist Tapes	2011	Jude Gerard Prest
Apocalypse Now	1979	Francis Ford Coppola
Belief: The Possession of Janet Moses	2015	David Stubbs
Beyond the Hills	2012	Cristian Mungiu
Black Circle Boys	1997	Mathew Carnahan
Black Roses	1988	John Fasano
Blair Witch 2	2000	Joe Berlinger
Bless the Child	2000	Chuck Russell
Blood Tracks	1985	Mats Helge Olsson, Derek Ford
Burnt Offerings	1976	Dan Curtis
Cannibal Holocaust	1980	Ruggero Deodato
Child's Play	1988	Tom Holland
Cinderella Liberty	1973	Mark Rydell
D@bbe Franchise	2006–2017	Various
Dagon	2001	Stuart Gordon
Dark Shadows	1966–1971	Various
Deliver Us from Evil	2014	Scott Derrickson
Demon	2015	Marcin Wrona
Die Hard 2: Die Harder	1990	Renny Harlin
Evil Dead	1987	Sam Raimi
Exorcist II: the Heretic	1977	John Boorman, Rospo Pallenberg
Eye of the Devil	1966	J. Lee Thompson

Faith and Fear: The Conjuring Universe	2020	Produced by Kevin K. Shah, Craig S. Phillips, Harold Hayes Jr., Travis Graalman
Fear and Loathing in Las Vegas	1998	Terry Gilliam
Footloose	1984	Herbert Ross
Hard Rock Nightmare	1988	Dominick Brascia
Hard Rock Zombies	1985	Krishna Shah
Haxan	1922	Benjamin Christensen
Heavy Metal Massacre	1989	Steven DeFalco, Ron Ottaviano
Hereditary	2018	Ari Aster
Hideaway	1995	Brett Leonard
House of a Thousand Corpses	2003	Rob Zombie
Il Demonio	1963	Brunello Rondi
In the Mouth of Madness	1994	John Carpenter
Invasion of the Body Snatchers	1956	Don Siegel
Invocation of My Demon Brother	1969	Kenneth Anger
Iron Eagle	1986	Sidney J. Furie
It	2017	Andy Muschietti
Jaws	1975	Steven Spielberg
King Kong	1933	Merian C. Cooper, Ernest B. Shoedsack
Le Maboir du Diable	1896	George Méliès
Lords of Chaos	2018	Jonas Akerlund
Lost Souls	2000	Janusz Kaminski
Lucifer's Women	1974	Paul Aratow
Marjoe	1972	Sarah Keernochan, Howard Smith
Midsommar	2019	Ari Aster
Mondo Freudo	1966	Lee Frost
Monster Dog	1984	Claudio Fragasso
Monster's Inc	2001	Pete Docter
Murder Rock	1984	Lucio Fulci
My Sweet Satan	1994	Jim Van Bebber
Night of the Demon	1957	Jacques Tourneur
Nightmare Alley	1947	Edmund Goulding
Paradise Lost	1996	Joe Berlinger, Bruce Sinofsky
Poltergeist	1982	Tobe Hooper
Prince of Darkness	1987	John Carpenter

Psycho	1960	Alfred Hitchcock
Q: Into the Storm	2021	Cullen Hoback, Fredrick Brennan, Craig James
Requiem	2006	Hans-Christian Schmid
Ricky 6	2000	Peter Filardi
Ringu	1998	Hideo Nakata
River's Edge	1987	Tim Hunter
Rock and Roll Nightmare	1987	John Fasano
Rocktober Blood	1984	Beverly Sebastian
Rosemary's Baby	1968	Roman Polanski
Satan's Cheerleaders	1977	Greydon Clark
Satanic Cults and Ritual Abuse	1990	Patric Matrisciana
Satanis: The Devil's Mass	1970	Ray Laurent
Shock 'Em Dead	1991	Mark Freed
Snow White	1937	William Cottrell, David Hand, Wilfred Jackson, Larry Morey, Perce Pearce, Ben Sharpsteen
Speed	1994	Jan de Bont
Spellbinder	1988	Janet Greek
Taken	2008	Pierre Morel
Terror on Tour	1980	Don Edmonds
Texas Chainsaw Massacre	1974	Toby Hooper
The Amityville Horror	1979	Stuart Rosenberg
The Believers	1987	John Schesinger
The Black Cat	1934	Edgar G. Ulmer
The Blair Witch Project	1999	Daniel Myrick, Eduardo Sanchez
The Blood on Satan's Claw	1971	Piers Haggard
The Bourne Identity	2002	Doug Liman
The Brotherhood of Satan	1971	Bernard McEveety
The Burbs	1989	Joe Dante
The Car	1977	Elliot Silverstein
The Clinton Chronicles	1994	Patric Matrisciana
The Conjuring	2013	James Wan
The Conjuring 2	2016	James Wan
The Conjuring 3 The Devil Made Me Do It	2021	Michael Chaves
The Craft	1996	Andrew Flemming
The Crucifixion	2017	Xavier Gens

The Curse of the Omen	2005	John MacLaverty
The Demon Murder Case	1983	William Hale
The Devil Rides Out	1968	Terence Fisher
The Devil's Advocate	1997	Taylor Hackford
The Devil's Rain	1975	Robert Fuest
The Devils	1971	Ken Russell
The DaVinci Code	2006	Ron Howard
The Dunwich Horror	1970	Daniel Haller
The Entity	1982	Sidney J. Furie
The Exorcist	1973	William Friedkin
The Exorcism of Emily rose	2005	Scott Derrickson
The First Power	1990	Robert Resnikoff
The French Connection	1971	William Friedkin
The Gate	1987	Tibor Takacs
The Godfather III	1990	Francis Ford Coppola
The Haunted	1991	Robert Mandel
The Haunting in Connecticut	2009	Peter Cornwell
The Last Broadcast	1998	Stefan Avalos, Lance Weller
The Last Exorcism	2010	Daniel Stamm
The Last House on the Left	1972	Wes Craven
The Lego Movie	2014	Phil Lord, Christopher Miller
The Manchurian Candidate	1962	John Frankenheimer
The Matrix	1999	Lana Wachowski, Lilly Wachowski
The Medium	2021	Banjong Pisanthanakun
The Mephisto Waltz	1971	Paul Wendkos
The Muppet Movie	1979	James Frawley
The Ninth Gate	1999	Roman Polanski
The Omen	1976	Richard Donner
The Order	2003	Brian Helgeland
The Passion of the Christ	2004	Mel Gibson
The Pope's Exorcist	2023	Julius Avery
The Possession	2012	Sam Raimi
The Pyx (The Hooker Cult Murders)	1973	Harvey Hart
The Rite	2009	Mikael Hafstrom
The Season of the Witch	1972	George A. Romero
The Sentinel	1977	Michael Winner
The Seventh Victim	1943	Mark Robson

The Tingler	1959	William Castle
The Town that Dreaded Sundown	1976	Charles B. Pierce
The Virgin Spring	1960	Ingmar Bergman
The Wicker Man	2006	Neil LaBute
The Wicker Man	1973	Robin Hardy
The Witch	2015	Robert Eggars
To the Devil a Daughter	1976	Peter Sykes, Don Sharp
Trick or Treat	1986	Charles Martin Smith
True Detective: Season 1	2014	Created by Nic Pizzolatto
Twilight Zone "The Living Doll"	1963	Richard C. Sarafin
UPC Codes and 666	1994	Patric Matrisciana
We Summon the Darkness	2019	Marc Meyers
Werewolves on Wheels	1971	Michel Levesque
White Noise	2005	Geoffrey Sax
White Squall	1996	Ridley Scott
Witchcraft '70	1969	Luigi Scattini, Lee Frost
Witchfinder General	1968	Michael Reeves

Bibliography

Abrahamsson, Carl. *Anton LaVey and the Church of Satan: Infernal Wisdom from the Devil's Den*. Rochester, VT: Inner Traditions, 2022.

Allen, Thomas B. *Possessed: The True Story of an Exorcism*. New York: Doubleday, 1993.

Aloi Peg. "Rooted in the Occult Revival: Neo-Paganism's Evolving Relationship with Popular Media." In *Handbook of Contemporary Paganism*, Vol 2, edited by James R. Lewis and Murphy Pizza, 538–576. Leiden: Brill, 2009.

Amorth, Gabriele. *An Exorcist Tells his Story*. San Francisco: Ignatius Press, 1999.

Anson, Jay. *The Amityville Horror*. New York: Pocket Star, 2006 [1977].

Arkoff, Samuel Z., and Richard Trubo. *Flying through Hollywood by the Seat of My Pants: From the Man Who Brought You I Was a Teenage Werewolf and Muscle Beach Party*. Secaucus, NJ: Carol Publishing Group, 1992.

Baer, William. *Classic American Films: Conversations with Screen-Writers*. Westport, CT: Praeger, 2008.

Baglio, Matt. *The Rite: The Making of a Modern Exorcist*. New York: Random House, 1999.

Baker, Brian. "The Occult and Film." In *The Occult World*, edited by Christopher Partridge, 446–458. New York: Routledge, 2014.

Baker, Phil. "Dennis Wheatley." In *The Occult World*, edited by Christopher Partridge, 464–469. New York: Routledge, 2014.

Baker, Phil, and Timothy Smith. *City of the Beast: The London of Aleister Crowley*. Cambridge: Strange Attractor, 2022.

Bandini, Albert R. *Angels on Horseback: A critical review of the pamphlet Begone Satan which relates an alleged case of demoniacal possession occurred in Earling, Iowa*. Fresno, CA: Academy Press, 1950 [1936].

Barkun, Michael. *A Culture of Conspiracy: Apocalyptic Visions in Contemporary America*. Berkeley: University of California Press, 2003.

Barrett, Gerald R. "William Friedkin Interview." *Literature/Film Quarterly* 3, no. 4 (Fall 1975): 334–362.

Bartholomew, Robert E., and Joe Nickell. "The Amityville Hoax at 40: Why the Myth Endures." *Skeptic Magazine* 21, no. 4 (2016): 8–12.

Barton, Blanche. *The Church of Satan*. New York: Hell's Kitchen Productions, 1990.

Beard, Drew. "Horror Movies at Home: Supernatural Horror, Delivery Systems and 1980s Satanic Panic." *Horror Studies* 6, no. 2 (2015): 211–223.

Bell, Rudolph M. *Holy Anorexia*. Chicago: University of Chicago Press, 1985.

Ben-Yehuda, Nachman. *Deviance and Moral Boundaries: Witchcraft, the Occult, Science Fiction, Deviant Sciences, and Scientists*. Chicago: The University of Chicago Press, 1985.

Berger, Peter L. *The Sacred Canopy: Elements of a Sociological Theory of Religion*. New York: Doubleday, 1969.

Berger, Peter L. "The Devil and the Pornography of Modern Consciousness." *Worldview* 17, no. 12 (1974): 36–37.

Berger, Peter L. "Secularization in Retreat." *National Interest* 46 (Winter 1996–1997): 3–12.

Betty, Stafford. "The Growing Evidence for Demonic Possession": What Should Psychiatry's Response Be?" *Journal of Religion and Health* 44, no. 1 (Spring 2005): 13–30.

Bivins, Jason. *Religion of Fear: The Politics of Horror in Conservative Evangelicalism.* New York: Oxford University Press, 2008.

Blatty, William Peter. *The Exorcist.* New York: HarperTorch, 2004 [1971].

Blatty, William Peter. *If There Were Demons, Then Perhaps There Were Angels: William Peter Blatty's Own Story of the Exorcist.* Southwold: ScreenPress Books, 1999.

Bourguignon, Erika. "Suffering and Healing, Subordination and Power: Women and Possession Trance." *Ethos* 32, no. 4 (2004): 557–574.

Boyd, Andrew. *Blasphemous Rumours: Is Satanic Ritual Abuse Fact or Fantasy? An Investigation.* London: Fount, 1991.

Bozzuto, James C. "Cinematic Neurosis Following 'The Exorcist.'" *The Journal of Nervous and Mental Disease* 161, no. 1 (1975): 43–48.

Brittle, Gerald. *The Demonologist: The Extraordinary Career of Ed and Lorraine Warren.* Los Angeles: Graymalkin Media, 2013.

Bromley, David G. "Satanism: The New Cult Scare." In *The Satanism Scare*, edited by James T. Richardson, Joel Best, and David G. Bromley, 49–74. Hawthorne, NY: Aldine De Gruyter, 1991.

Brosnan, John. *The Horror People.* New York: New American Library, 1977.

Brottman, Mikita. *Hollywood Hex.* London: Creation, 1999.

Brown, Allan. *Inside "The Wicker Man": The Morbid Ingenuities.* London: Sidgwick and Jackson, 2000.

Bynum, Caroline Walker. *Holy Feast and Holy Fast: The Religious Significance of Food to Medieval Women.* Berkeley: University of California Press, 1987.

Clark, Lynn Schofield. *From Angels to Aliens: Teenagers the Media and the Supernatural.* New York: Oxford University Press, 2003.

Card, Jeb J. *Spooky Archaeology: Myth and the Science of the Past.* Albuquerque: University of New Mexico Press, 2018.

Carroll, Noel. "Why Horror?" In *Horror: The Film Reader*, edited by Mark Jancovich, 33–46. New York: Routledge, 2002.

Case, George. *Here's to My Sweet Satan: How the Occult Haunted Music, Movies and Pop Culture 1966–1980.* Fresno, CA: Quill Driver Books, 2016.

Castle, William. *Step Right Up! I'm Gonna Scare the Pants Off America.* New York: G. P. Putnam's Sons, 1976.

Caterine, Darryl. *Haunted Ground: Journeys through a Paranormal America.* Santa Barbara, CA: Praeger, 2011.

Caterine, Darryl. "Introduction." In *The Paranormal and Popular Culture: A Postmodern Religious Landscape*, edited by Darryl Caterine and John W. Morehead. New York: Routledge, 2019: 1-10.

Chapetta, Robert. "Rosemary's Baby by Roman Polansky [sic] and William Castle." *Film Quarterly* 22, no. 3 (Spring 1969): 33–38.

Cherry, Brigid. *Horror.* New York: Taylor and Francis, 2008.

Clarens, Carlos. *An Illustrated History of Horror Films.* New York: Capricorn Books, 1968.

Cohn, Norman. *Europe's Inner Demons: The Demonization of Christians in Medieval Christiandom*, Revised ed. Chicago: University of Chicago Press, 1993.

Collings, Michael. *Stephen King as Richard Bachman.* Mercer Island, WA: Starmont House, Inc., 1985.

Collins, James M. *Exorcism and Deliverance Ministry in the Twentieth Century: An Analysis of the Practice and Theology of Exorcism in Modern Western Christianity*. Milton Keynes: Paternoster, 2009.

Cook, David A. *Lost Illusions American Cinema in the Shadow of Watergate and Vietnam, 1970–1979*. Berkeley: University of California Press, 2005.

Cowan, Douglas E. *Sacred Terror: Religion and Horror on the Silver Screen*. Waco, TX: Baylor University Press, 2016.

Cowan, Douglas E. *The Forbidden Body: Sex, Horror, and the Religious Imagination*. New York: New York University Press, 2022.

Crouse, Richard. *Raising Hell: Ken Russell and the Unmaking of The Devils*. Toronto: ECW Press, 2012.

Cull, Nick. "The Exorcist." *History Today* 50, no. 5 (May 2000): 56–51.

Cuneo, Michael W. *American Exorcism: Expelling Demons in the Land of Plenty*. New York: Doubleday, 2001.

Curti, Roberto. *Mavericks of Italian Cinema: Eight Unorthodox Filmmakers 1940s–2000s*. Jefferson, NC: McFarland, 2018.

De Martino, Ernesto. *Magic: A Theory from the South*. Translated by Dorothy Louise Zinn. Chicago: Hau Books, 2015.

Derry, Charles. *Dark Dreams 2.0: A Psychological History of the Modern Horror Film from the 1950s to the 21st Century*. Jefferson NC: McFarland and Company, 2009.

Doherty, Bernard. "The Smoke of Satan on the Silver Screen: The Catholic Horror Film, Vatican II, and the Revival of Demonology." *Journal for the Academic Study of Religion* 33, no. 1 (2020): 66–96.

Duren, Brad. "Reckoning the Number of the Beast: Premillennial Dispensationalism, The Omen, and 1970s America." In *Divine Horror: Essays on the Cinematic Battle Between the Sacred and the Diabolical*, edited by J. Miller, Cynthia and A. Bowdoin Van Riper, 53–63. Jefferson, NC: McFarland, 2017.

Eaton, Marc A. "'Give Us a Sign of Your Presence': Paranormal Investigation as a Spiritual Practice." *Sociology of Religion* 76, no. 4 (2015): 389–412.

Eliade, Mircea. *Occultism, Witchcraft, and Cultural Fashions: Essays in Comparative Religions*. Chicago: University of Chicago Press, 1976.

Ellis, Bill. *Raising the Devil: Satanism, New Religions, and the Media*. Lexington: University of Kentucky Press, 2000.

Ellis, Bill. *Aliens, Ghosts, and Cults: Legends We Live*. Jackson: University Press of Mississippi, 2003.

Fabian, Robert. *London After Dark; an Intimate Record of Night Life in London and a Selection of Crime Stories from the Case Book of Ex-Superintendent Robert Fabian*. London: Naldrett Press, 1954.

Forcen, Fernando Espi. *Monsters, Demons and Psychopaths: Psychiatry and Horror Film*. New York: CRC Press, 2017.

Frankfurt, Harry G. *On Bullshit*. Princeton, NJ: Princeton University Press, 2005.

Frankfurter, David. "Ritual As Accusation and Atrocity: Satanic Ritual Abuse Gnostic Libertinism and Primal Murders." *History of Religions* 40 (May 2002): 352–380.

Frankfurter, David. *Evil Incarnate: Rumors of Demonic Conspiracy and Satanic Abuse in History*. Princeton, NJ: Princeton University Press, 2006.

Frankfurter, David. "Awakening to Satanic Conspiracy: Rosemary's Baby and the Cult Next Door." In *Deliver Us From Evil: Boston University Studies in Philosophy and Religion*, edited by M. David Eckel and Bradley L. Herling, 75–86. New York: Continuum, 2011.

Freud, Sigmund. *The Uncanny*. New York: Penguin Books, 2003.

Fry, Carrol L. *Cinema of the Occult: New Age Satanism Wicca and Spiritualism in Film*. Bethlehem, PA: Lehigh University Press, 2008.

Gallagher, Richard. *Demonic Foes: My Twenty-Five Years as a Psychiatrist Investigating Possessions, Diabolic Attacks, and the Paranormal*. New York: HarperOne, 2020.

Giordan, Giuseppe, and Adam Possamai, editors. *Sociology of Exorcism in Late Modernity*. New York: Palgrave Macmillan, 2018.

Goffman, Erving. *The Presentation of Self in Everyday Life*. Garden City, NY: Doubleday Anchor Books, 1959.

Goodman, Felicitas D. *The Exorcism of Anneliese Michel*. Eugene, OR: Resource Publications, 2005.

Gopnik, Alison. "Explanation as Orgasm." *Minds and Machines* 8 (1998): 101–118.

Gottlieb, Sidney. *Hitchcock on Hitchcock*. Berkeley: University of California Press, 2014.

Grafius, Brandon. "Horror and Bible (Six Theses)." In *Religion, Culture, and the Monstrous: Of Gods and Monsters*, edited by Joseph P. Laycock and Natasha L. Mikles, 29–40. Lanham, MD: Lexington Books, 2021.

Graham, Billy. *Angels: God's Secret Agents*. Nashville, TN: Thomas Nelson, 2009.

Graysmith, Robert. *Zodiac Unmasked*. New York: Berkley Books, 2007.

Greenwood, Rebecca. *Let Our Children Go: Steps to Free Your Child from Evil Influences and Demonic Harassment*. Lake Mary, FL: Charisma House, 2011.

Haberman, Maggie. *Confidence Man: The Making of Donald Trump and the Breaking of America*. New York: Penguin, 2022.

Hall, David D., editor. *Lived Religion in America: Toward a History of Practice*. Princeton, NJ: Princeton University Press, 1997.

Hayles, N. Katherine. *How We Think: Digital Media and Contemporary Technogenesis*. Chicago: University of Chicago Press, 2012.

Heisler, Gerald H. "The Effects of Vicariously Experiencing Supernatural Violent Events: A Case Study of *The Exorcist*'s Impact." *Journal of Individual Psychology* 31, no. 2 (1975): 158–170.

Hendrix, Grady. *Paperbacks from Hell: The Twisted History of '70s and '80s Horror Fiction*. Philadelphia: Quirk, 2017.

Hicks, Robert D. *In Pursuit of Satan: The Police and the Occult*. Buffalo, NY: Prometheus Books, 1992.

Hill, Annette. *Paranormal Media: Audiences Spirits and Magic in Popular Culture*. New York: Routledge, 2011.

Houston, Beverle, and Marsha Kinder. "Rosemary's Baby." *Sight and Sound* 38, no. 1 (Winter 1968): 17–19.

Hufford, David. *The Terror That Comes in the Night: An Experience-Centered Study of Supernatural Assault Traditions*. Philadelphia: University of Pennsylvania Press, 1982.

Hutchings, Peter. "By the Book: American Horror Cinema and Horror Literature of the Late 1960s and 1970s." In *Merchants of Menace: The Business of Horror Cinema*, edited by Richard Nowell, 45–60. New York: Bloomsbury, 2014.

Hutton, Ronald. *The Triumph of the Moon: A History of Modern Pagan Witchcraft*. 2nd ed. New York: Oxford University Press, 2021.

Huxley, Aldous. *The Doors of Perception and Heaven and Hell*. New York: HarperCollins Publishers, 2009.

Ingebretsen, Edward J. *Maps of Heaven, Maps of Hell: Religious Terror as Memory from the Puritans to Stephen King*. New York: Taylor and Francis, 2016.

Introvigne, Massimo. *Brainwashing: Myth or Reality?* Cambridge: Cambridge University Press, 2022.

Jenkins, Philip. "Weird Tales: The Story of a Delusion." In *The Last Pentacle of the Sun: Writings in Support of the West Memphis Three*, edited by M. W. Anderson and Brett Alexander, 35–41. Vancouver, BC: Arsenal Pulp, 2004.

Jenkins, Philip. *Decade of Nightmares: The End of the Sixties and the Making of Eighties America*. New York: Oxford University Press, 2006.

Jones, Darryl. *Horror: A Thematic History of Fiction in Film*. London: Arnold Publishers, 2002.

Kachka, Boris. *Hothouse: The Art of Survival and the Survival of Art at America's Most Celebrated Publishing House*. New York: Simon & Schuster, 2014.

Kahaner, Larry. *Cults That Kill: Probing the Underworld of Occult Crime*. New York: Warner Books, 1988.

Kaiser, Robert Blair. *Clerical Error: A True Story*. New York: Continuum, 2002.

Kaplan, Edward K. *Spiritual Radical: Abraham Joshua Heschel in America, 1940–1972*. New Haven, CT: Yale University Press, 2007.

Kermode, Mark. *The Exorcist*. London: British Film Institute, 2011.

King, Stephen. *Danse Macabre*. New York: Gallery Books, 2010.

Koven, Mikel J. *Film, Folklore, and Urban Legends*. Lanham, MD: The Scarecrow Press, 2008.

Kraig, Donald Michael. *Modern Magick: Twelve Lessons in the High Magical Arts*. Woodbury, MN: Llewellyn, 2010.

Laderman, Gary. *Sacred Matters: Celebrity Worship Sexual Ecstasies the Living Dead and Other Signs of Religious Life in the United States*. New York: New Press, 2009.

LaVey, Anton. *The Satanic Bible*. New York: Avon Books, 1969.

LaVey, Anton. *Satan Speaks!* Venice, CA: Feral House, 1998.

Laws, Peter. *The Frighteners: A Journey Through Our Cultural Fascination with the Macabre*. New York: Skyhorse Publishing, 2018.

Laycock, Joseph P. *Dangerous Games: What the Moral Panic Over Role-Playing Games Says About Play Religion and Imagined Worlds*. Berkeley: University of California Press, 2015.

Laycock Joseph P., editor. *Spirit Possession around the World*. Santa Barbara, CA: ABC-CLIO, 2015.

Laycock, Joseph P. "'Time Is a Flat Circle': True Detective and the Specter of Moral Panic in American Pop Culture." *Journal of Religion and Popular Culture* 27, no. 3 (Fall 2015): 220–235.

Levack, Brian P. *The Devil Within: Possession & Exorcism in the Christian West*. New Haven, CT: Yale University Press, 2013.

Levack, Brian P. "The Horrors of Witchcraft and Demonic Possession." *Social Research* 81, no. 4 (Winter 2014): 921–939.

Lewis, James R. *Satanism Today: An Encyclopedia of Religion, Folklore, and Popular Culture*. Santa Barbara, CA: ABC-CLIO, 2001.

Lewis, James R. "Anton LaVey, The Satanic Bible, and the Satanist Tradition." In *Legitimating New Religions*, edited by James R. Lewis. New Brunswick, NJ: Rutgers University Press, 2003: 103-22.

Leyton, Elliott. *Hunting Humans: Inside the Minds of Mass Murderers*. New York: Pocketbooks, 1988.

Lovecraft, Howard Phillips. *Selected Letters III: 1934–1937*. Edited by August Derleth and James Turner. Sauk City, WI: Arkham House Publishers, 1976.

Lucas, Tim. "Say 'La Vi!': The Video Watchdog Interview with Daliah Lavi." *Video Watchdog* 170 (September–October 2012): 19–43.

Lyden, John C. *Film as Religion: Myths, Morals, and Rituals.* New York: New York University Press, 2003.

Lyons, Arthur. *The Second Coming: Satanism in America.* New York: Dodd, Mead, & Company, 1970.

Martin, Malachi. *Hostage to the Devil: The Possession and Exorcism of Five Contemporary Americans.* New York: HarperOne, 1992.

Maddrey, Joseph. *Nightmares in Red White and Blue: The Evolution of the American Horror Film.* Jefferson, NC: McFarland, 2004.

McCloud, Sean. *American Possessions: Fighting Demons in the Contemporary United States.* New York: Oxford University Press, 2015.

McDannell, Colleen. *Catholics in the Movies.* New York: Oxford University Press, 2008.

McDonald, Keith, and Wayne Johnson. *Contemporary Gothic and Horror Film: Transnational Perspectives.* New York: Anthem Press, 2021.

McGee, Adam M. "Haitian Vodou and Voodoo: Imagined Religion and Popular Culture." *Studies in Religion/Sciences Religieuses* 41, no. 2 (2012): 231–256.

McGinn, Colin. *The Power of Movies: How Screen and Mind Interact.* New York: Pantheon Books, 2005.

Medved, Harry, and Randy Dreyfuss. *The Fifty Worst Films of All Time (And How They Got That Way).* New York: Popular Library, 1979.

Medway, Gareth J. *Lure of the Sinister: The Unnatural History of Satanism.* New York: New York University Press, 2001.

Meehan, Paul. *Cinema of the Psychic Realm.* Jefferson, NC: McFarland and Co., 2009.

Mencken, Frederick Carl, Joseph O. Baker, and Christopher David Bader. *Paranormal America (second edition): Ghost Encounters, UFO Sightings, Bigfoot Hunts, and Other Curiosities in Religion and Culture.* New York: New York University Press, 2017.

Montgomery, John Warwick, editor. *Demon Possession: A Medical, Historical, Anthropological, and Theological Symposium: Papers Presented at the University of Notre Dame, January 8–11, 1975, Under the Auspices of the Christian Medical Association.* Minneapolis: Bethany Fellowship, 1976.

Munsterberg, Hugo. *The Photoplay: A Psychological Study.* New York: Appleton and Company, 1916.

Nathan, Debbie, and Michael R. Snedeker. *Satan's Silence: Ritual Abuse and the Making of a Modern American Witch Hunt.* New York: Basic Books, 1995.

Newton, Michael. *Rosemary's Baby.* New York: Bloomsbury, 2020.

Nickell, Joe. "Enfield Poltergeist." *Skeptical Inquirer* 36, no. 4 (July/August 2012): 12–14.

Nickell, Joe, and Robert Bartholomew. *American Hauntings: The True Stories behind Hollywood's Scariest Movies—from The Exorcist to The Conjuring.* Santa Barbara, CA: Praeger, 2015.

Noblitt, James Randall, and Pamela Perskin Noblitt. *Cult and Ritual Abuse: Narratives Evidence and Healing Approaches.* 3rd ed. Santa Barbara, CA: Praeger, 2014.

Nunn, Clyde. "The Rising Credibility of the Devil in America." In *Heterodoxy: Mystical Experience, Religious Dissent and the Occult,* edited by Richard Wood, 84–100. River Forest, DE: Listening Press, 1975.

O'Donnell, Patrick. "Satanic Celluloid: An Unholy Trinity of Terror Picked by the Black Pope of the Church of Satan." In *Monster Rally,* edited by S. Michael Wilson, 169–176. West Orange, NJ: Idea Men Productions, 2008.

Olukoya, D. K. *Power Against Marine Spirits*. Lagos, Nigeria: The Battle Cry Christian Ministries, 1999.

Orsi, Robert A. *History and Presence*. Cambridge, MA: Harvard University Press, 2016.

Paciorek, Andy, Grey Malkin, Richard Hing, and Katherine Peach, editors. *Folk Horror Revival: Field Studies*. 2nd ed. Durham, UK: Wyrd Harvest Press, 2018.

Partridge, Christopher. *The Re-Enchantment of the West: Alternative Spiritualities, Sacralization, Popular Culture, and Occulture*. London: T&T Clark International, 2004.

Partridge, Christopher. *The Re-Enchantment of the West: Alternative Spiritualities, Sacralization, Popular Culture, and Occulture, Vol 2*. London: T&T Clark International, 2005.

Pasulka, Diana Walsh. "'The Fairy Tale is True': Social Technologies of the Religious Supernatural in Film and New Media." *Journal of the American Academy of Religion* 84, no. 2 (June 2016): 530–547.

Pasulka, Diana Walsh. *American Cosmic: Ufos, Religion, Technology*. New York: Oxford University Press, 2019.

Paul, William. *Laughing, Screaming: Modern Hollywood Horror and Comedy*. New York: Columbia University Press, 1994.

Peck, M. Scott. *Glimpses of the Devil: A Psychiatrist's Personal Accounts of Possession, Exorcism, and Redemption*. New York: Free Press, 2005.

Plate, S. Brent. *Religion and Film: Cinema and the Re-Creation of the World*. London: Wallflower, 2008.

Plate, S. Brent. *Religion and Film: Cinema and the Re-Creation of the World*, 2nd edition. New York: Columbia University Press, 2017.

Poole, W. Scott. *Satan in America: The Devil We Know*. New York: Rowman & Littlefield, 2009.

Primiano, Leonard. "Vernacular Religion and the Search for Method in Religious Folklife." *Western Folklore* 54, no. 1 (January 1995): 37–56.

Read, Simon. *The Case That Foiled Fabian: Murder and Witchcraft in Rural England*. Stroud: History Press, 2014.

Reichert, Jenny, and James T. Richardson. "Decline of a Moral Panic: A Psychological and Socio-Legal Examination of the Current Status of Satanism." *Nova Religio* 16, no. 2 (2012): 47–63.

Roberts, Susan. *Witches U.S.A.* New York: Dell Publishing, 1971.

Rockoff, Adam. *The Horror of it All: One Moviegoer's Love Affair with Masked Maniacs, Frightened Virgins, and the Living Dead*. New York: Scribner, 2015.

Rodewyk, Adolf. *Possessed by Satan: The Church's Teaching on the Devil, Possession, and Exorcism*. Translated by Martin Ebon. Garden City, NY: Doubleday, 1975.

Rodgers, Diane A. "Folk Horror, Ostension, and Robin Redbreast." *Revenant* 5 (March 2020): 57–73.

Ross, Colin A. *Satanic Ritual Abuse: Principles of Treatment*. Toronto: University of Toronto Press, 1995.

Rubino, Anna. *Queen of the Oil Club: The Intrepid Wanda Jablonski and the Power of Information*. Boston, MA: Beacon, 2009.

Rueda, Sergeo A. *Diabolical Possession and the Case Behind* The Exorcist: *An Overview of Scientific Research with Witnesses and Experts*. Jefferson, NC: McFarland Press, 2018.

Sarchie, Ralph, and Lisa Collier Cool. *Deliver Us From Evil: A New York City Cop Investigates the Supernatural*. New York: St. Martin's Press, 2001.

Sawyer, J. F. *Deliver Us From Evil*. Westfield, MA: Phillips Publishing Company, 1973.

Schreck, Nikolas. *The Satanic Screen: An Illustrated Guide to the Devil in Cinema.* London: Creation, 2001.

Sluhovsky, Moshe. *Believe Not Every Spirit: Possession, Mysticism, & Discernment in Early Modern Catholicism.* Chicago: University of Chicago Press, 2007.

Smith, Michelle, and Lawrence Pazder. *Michelle Remembers.* New York: Pocket Books, 1980.

Smythies, John. "The Adrenochrome Hypothesis of Schizophrenia Revisited." *Neurotoxicity Research* 4, no. 2 (2002): 147–150.

Steffon, Jeffrey J. *Satanism: Is It Real?* Ann Arbor, MI: Servant Publications, 1992.

Steiger, Brad, and Sherry Hansen Steiger. *Demon Deaths.* New York: Berkley Books, 1991.

Thavis, John. *The Vatican Prophecies: Investigating Supernatural Signs, Apparitions, and Miracles in the Modern Age.* New York: Viking, 2015.

Thomas, Paul. "New Religious Movements." In *The Routledge Companion to Religion and Film,* edited by John Lyden, 214–234. New York: Routledge, 2009.

Toulet, Emmanuelle. *Birth of the Motion Picture.* New York: H. N. Abrams, 1995.

Travers, Peter, and Stephanie A. Reiff. *The Story Behind the Exorcist.* New York: New American Library, 1974.

Truzzi, Marcello. "The Occult Revival as Popular Culture: Some Random Observations on the Old and the Nouveau Witch." *Sociology Quarterly* 13, no. 1 (Winter 1972): 16–36.

Twitchell, James B. *Dreadful Pleasures: An Anatomy of Modern Horror.* New York: Oxford University Press, 1985.

Van Luijk, Ruben. *Children of Lucifer: The Origins of Modern Religious Satanism.* New York: Oxford University Press, 2016.

Victor, Jeffrey S. "Crime, Moral Panic, and the Occult." In *The Occult World,* edited by Christopher Partridge, 692–700. New York: Routledge, 2014.

Vogl, Carl. *Begone Satan! A Soul-Stirring Account of Diabolical Possession in Iowa.* (Translated by Celestine Kapsner). In *Mary Crushes the Serpent and Begone Satan!* Gilbert, AZ: Caritas Publishing, 2016 [1935]: 51-94.

Waller, Gregory A. "Introduction." In *American Horrors: Essays on the Modern Horror Film,* Gregory A. Waller, 1–13. Chicago: University of Illinois Press, 1987.

Warren, Ed, Lorraine Warren, and Robert David Chase. *Ghost Hunters: True Stories from the World's Most Famous Demonologists.* Los Angeles: Graymalkin Media, 2014.

Warren, Ed, Lorraine Warren, Michael Lasalandra, Mark Merenda, Maurice Theriault, and Nancy Theriault. *Satan's Harvest.* Los Angeles: Graymalkin Media, 1990.

Webster, Nesta Hellen. *Secret Societies and Subversive Movements.* London: Boswell, 1924.

Wetmore, Kevin, J. Jr. "Colonial Possessions: A Fanonian Reading of The Exorcist and its Sequels." *Social Research* 81, no. 4 (Winter 2014): 883–896.

Wheatley, Dennis. *The Devil Rides Out.* New York: Bloomsbury Reader, [1934] 2013.

Wicks, Cheryl, Ed Warren, and Lorraine Warren, *Ghost Tracks.* Los Angeles: Graymalkin Media, 2012.

Wiggins, Steve A. *Holy Horror: The Bible and Fear in Movies.* New York: McFarland, 2018.

Williams, Peter W. *Popular Religion in America: Symbolic Change and the Modernization Process in Historical Perspective.* Englewood Cliffs, NJ: Prentice-Hall, 1980.

Winogura, Dale. "William Friedkin." *Cinefantastique* 3, no. 4 (Winter 1974): 14–17.

Wise, Daniel. "Twenty-First Century American Ghost Hunting: A Late Modern Enchantment." Dissertation. University of Virginia, Department of Religious Studies, 2020.

Wood, Robin. "Der Erlkonig: The Ambiguities of Horror." In *American Nightmare: Essays on the Horror Film*, edited by Andrew Britton, Richard Lippe, Tony Williams, and Robin Wood, 29–33. Toronto: Festival of Festivals, 1979.

Woods, Richard. *The Devil*. Chicago: Thomas More Press, 1974.

Wright, Lawrence. *Saints & Sinners: Walker Railey, Jimmy Swaggart, Madalyn Murray O'Hair, Anton LaVey, Will Campbell, Matthew Fox*. New York: Knopf, 1996.

Young, Francis. *A History of Exorcism in Catholic Christianity*. Cambridge: Palgrave MacMillan, 2016.

Young, Francis. *A History of Anglican Exorcism: Deliverance and Demonology in Church Ritual*. New York: I.B. Tauris, 2018.

Zacks, Jeff. *Flicker: Your Brain on Movies*. New York: Oxford University Press, 2015.

Index

For the benefit of digital users, indexed terms that span two pages (e.g., 52–53) may, on occasion, appear on only one of those pages.